DEFENDING FORT STANWIX

DEFENDING FORT STANWIX

A STORY OF THE NEW YORK FRONTIER IN THE AMERICAN REVOLUTION

WILLIAM L. KIDDER

AN IMPRINT OF CORNELL UNIVERSITY PRESS
ITHACA AND LONDON

Copyright © 2024 by William L. Kidder

All rights reserved. Except for brief quotations in a review, this book, or parts thereof, must not be reproduced in any form without permission in writing from the publisher. For information, address Cornell University Press, Sage House, 512 East State Street, Ithaca, New York 14850. Visit our website at cornellpress.cornell.edu.

First published 2024 by Cornell University Press
Printed in the United States of America

Library of Congress Cataloging-in-Publication Data

Names: Kidder, Larry, author.
Title: Defending Fort Stanwix : a story of the New York frontier in the American Revolution / William L. Kidder.
Description: Ithaca [New York] : Cornell University Press, 2024. | Includes bibliographical references and index.
Identifiers: LCCN 2024004816 (print) | LCCN 2024004817 (ebook) | ISBN 9781501777530 (hardcover) | ISBN 9781501777554 (epub) | ISBN 9781501777547 (pdf)
Subjects: LCSH: Gansevoort, Peter, 1749-1812—Military leadership. | United States. Continental Army. New York Regiment, 3rd—History. | Mohawk River Valley (N.Y.)—History—Revolution, 1775-1783. | Fort Stanwix (Rome, N.Y.)—History. | Fort Stanwix (Rome, N.Y.)—Siege, 1777.
Classification: LCC E263.N6 K54 2024 (print) | LCC E263.N6 (ebook) | DDC 973.3/33—dc23/eng/20240313
LC record available at https://lccn.loc.gov/2024004816
LC ebook record available at https://lccn.loc.gov/2024004817

Contents

Preface vii

Acknowledgments xi

Introduction   1

Part I: Setting the Stage for a Siege

1. The Increasing Need to Reestablish Fort Stanwix: May–June 1776   15

2. The 3rd New Jersey Regiment Restores Fort Stanwix: June–October 1776   24

3. Elmore's Regiment Relieves the 3rd New Jersey Regiment: October 1776–May 1777   36

4. Creating a Third Establishment 3rd New York Regiment: September–November 1776   45

5. Recruiting and Training the 3rd New York Regiment: December 1776–March 1777   53

6. Preparing to Relieve Elmore's Regiment: March–May 1777   65

Part II: The 3rd New York Regiment Prepares for a Siege

7. First Elements of the 3rd New York Regiment Arrive at Fort Stanwix: April 1777   71

CONTENTS

8. Colonel Gansevoort Takes Command of Fort Stanwix: May 1777 — 78
9. Dealing with Too Many Needs and Dangers: June 1777 — 96
10. Danger Builds for Soldiers and Civilians Alike: July 1777 — 108

PART III: THE SIEGE OF FORT STANWIX

11. St. Leger's Troops Begin Their Siege: August 1–5, 1777 — 129
12. Willett's Sally and the Battle of Oriskany: August 6, 1777 — 142
13. The Siege Settles In: August 7–9, 1777 — 150
14. The Siege Finally Ends: August 10–31, 1777 — 158

PART IV: DEFENSE AFTER THE SIEGE

15. Adjusting to Garrison Life after the Siege: September–December 1777 — 179
16. A Tiresome and Dangerous New Year: January–May 1778 — 198
17. A British Plot Encourages Desertions: June 1778 — 222
18. Still More Desertions and Continuing Unease: July–September 1778 — 232
19. The Exhausted 3rd Regiment Finally Departs Fort Stanwix: October–November 1778 — 243

Epilogue — 251

Notes 259
Bibliography 305
Index 311

Preface

The story of the American Revolution is one of civil war as much as an account of colonies fighting for independence from their mother country. During North America's colonial history, the stage for civil war was set through the migrations of people from various European cultures, the importation of African people, and settlement among and then dispossession of Indigenous people. These groups did not remain completely separated territorially, culturally, or genetically, and they continually interacted in both friendly and confrontational ways. The political and economic events dividing the colonists into opposing groups supporting or protesting British government actions, and then supporting or opposing efforts to gain independence, simply added to the disruptive pressures already complicating people's lives.

This story focuses on the successful defense of Fort Stanwix, located in what is today Rome, New York, which played an important role in the 1777 Saratoga campaign resulting in the capture of British forces led by General John Burgoyne, widely considered to be a major turning point of the Revolution. Burgoyne's surrender raised Patriot morale and contributed to the formation of the alliance with France, which contributed greatly to victory in the War for Independence. Military history writings generally focus on strategy and tactics, command decision-making, and the effects of weapon types, weather, terrain, and other factors contributing to the outcome of battles and campaigns. Any military event, however, also contains many largely forgotten stories revealing the lives of countless people who contributed to history.

To fully appreciate the importance of the successful August 1777 defense, knowing why Fort Stanwix was an important British objective and how the fort's structural layout and physical condition had evolved up to the time of the siege is critical. It is also essential to examine the qualities and conditions of the diverse peoples who occupied, fought, and lived in and around the fort before, during, and after the siege.

Their stories highlight how the War for Independence was also a civil war between American colonists who were Patriots and those who were Loyalists as well as a conflict that demanded the region's Indigenous peoples choose sides. This book explores the stories of Continental Army soldiers, local militiamen, Indians, and civilians, both male and female, for a fuller understanding of the successful defense.

Vocabulary terms used to identify groups of people or a person's heritage can cause problems due to the origin of the term chosen, how the term has been used over time, and other factors. Identity terms can also appear to project the user's attitude toward the person or people being discussed. I have sought to use terms that the person or group would use to self-identify or find acceptable. Being human, I may have erred in some instances, and for this I apologize in advance. For example, persons supporting the cause of the Revolution can be identified as Patriots or Whigs by like-minded people, or as rebels or traitors by those who oppose them. For this work, I have chosen to use "Patriots," outside of direct quotations. For opponents of the Revolution, the term "Loyalist" is used, except in direct quotations, where "Tory" is employed. This was a difficult decision, because the term "Tory" was widely used as a negative term at the time in the geographic area where the story takes place. For Indigenous people, the term "Indian" has been used on occasion rather than "Native American." I have generally used the term "Haudenosaunee" to indicate the Six Nations, but not all the Iroquoian peoples.

I have standardized the spellings of names of individual people, but it is important to note that spellings could, and often do, vary a great deal from one document or source to another. In most cases, I cannot know if the spelling I have chosen would be agreeable with the person in question.

In the telling of this story, a difficult decision had to be made as to which name to use for the fort. Its original 1758 name, Fort Stanwix, was changed in 1776 to Fort Schuyler. This could have caused confusion at the time, since an earlier, and nearby, Fort Schuyler already existed. To avoid the problem, that earlier fort was often referred to as Old Fort Schuyler, while the name Fort Stanwix remained in common usage.[1] Contemporary sources are not uniform in using one or the other of those names. Evidence for the confusion caused by the name change is found in several documentary sources that give the name as Fort Schuyler, "alias Fort Stanwix," or Fort Schuyler, "formerly Fort Stanwix." By 1790, when the fort site was still being used for meetings with Indians about landownership issues, New York State officials had given up calling it Fort Schuyler and used the name Fort Stanwix in documents.² Today the National Park Service operates the Fort Stanwix National Monument, complete with a replica fort based on extensive archaeological and archival research. I therefore use "Fort Stanwix" throughout this work, except when "Fort Schuyler" appears in quotations from period sources.

Several books examining the Saratoga campaign and its significance have outlined the events at Fort Stanwix and its vicinity as part of the overall military campaign rather than looking at events from the perspective of the outpost's defenders, whose bravery earned it the postwar nickname "the fort that never surrendered."³ As the British troop movements unfolded in the Mohawk River Valley, the human stories of the garrison and the local people, colonist and Indian, Loyalist and Patriot, military and civilian, played out.

The first four chapters of part 1 detail the history and physical characteristics of the fort before the arrival of the troops who would defend it in August 1777. The remaining chapters of this part look at the organization and development of the 3rd New York Regiment as part of the evolving Continental Army before it assumed garrison duty. Part 2 recounts the four months during which the garrison prepared itself and the fort for the anticipated siege. In part 3, I examine the August 1777 siege from multiple viewpoints: those of the garrison soldiers, civilians, camp followers, and Indigenous people. The book's final part details the aftermath of the siege and life at the fort during the following year and the many dangers, discomforts, and pressures the garrison and those around the fort experienced. The story concludes with a look at the fate of the 3rd New York Regiment after it was relieved from duty at Fort Stanwix. In the epilogue, I sketch the postwar lives of some of the fort's prominent defenders, outline the fort's decommissioning and fall into ruin, and describe its late twentieth-century reconstruction and designation as a national monument.

Acknowledgments

The development of this book has been long and rewarding. I have had a longtime interest in the story of the siege of Fort Stanwix since learning that an ancestor served in the New York Continental Line regiment that garrisoned the fort at the time of the siege. Several people and historical societies in the Kingston and Rhinebeck area encouraged and contributed to my growing understanding of that ancestor and the world in which he lived. Visits to the Fort Stanwix National Monument over the past twenty-some years also kept that interest alive and developing. I thank all those people who contributed to my growing understanding of the fort and the siege.

As I developed the concept for this book, my friend and literary agent Roger Williams encouraged its development in many ways. Readers of early drafts included Ricardo Herrera, Mark Edward Lender, Brian Mack, James Kirby Martin, Jim Morrison, David Price, John Ruddiman, Bill Sawyer, Eric Schnitzer, Bill Welsch, and Glenn F. Williams. All their support and valuable suggestions for strengthening the content and style have helped me improve the book significantly and bring it to a level I am proud to present. Of course, any remaining errors or problems are my responsibility alone.

The research for this work extended over many years and dovetailed with research on my ancestor, Peter Scriber, who participated in the siege defense. Research at the Ulster County Genealogical Society in Hurley, New York, laid the groundwork for additional investigations. The David Library of the American Revolution in Washington Crossing, Pennsylvania, and librarian Kathy Ludwig provided valuable help, and Kathy also provided sincere encouragement and interest over a number of years. Living close to the library, I visited frequently, and the atmosphere there was very congenial, leading to conversations with other researchers who gave me encouragement and research ideas that proved helpful. After that valuable facility closed, I conducted some of my later research at the David Center for the American Revolution at the American Philosophical Society in Philadelphia, where the collection was relocated. A visit to the research library division of the New York State Library in Albany also provided important help.

I cannot thank enough Mahinder Kingra, editor in chief at Cornell University Press, for his interest and encouragement. His guidance and discussions about the content and presentation of this book, as well as the publishing process, have been truly beneficial. Others at Cornell University Press also contributed greatly to the development of my manuscript and its presentation. I especially and gratefully acknowledge production editor Mary Kate Murphy and copyeditor Amanda Heller for their very detailed check on my work both in content and style.

To my wife, Jane, who put up with me and traveled with me several times during the research and writing, your encouragement and willing discussions are always helpful and valued. Also, our cat, Izzy, once again has helped me get to work each day and been my work companion, curled up in my lap or on a pillow next to my computer, as she is as I write this. Her affectionate and calming presence is important and appreciated.

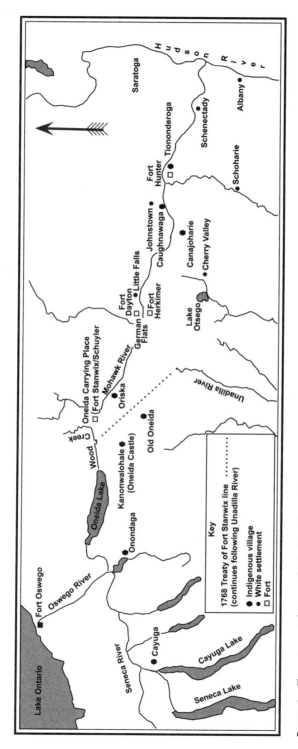

FIGURE 1. The water route between the Hudson River and Lake Ontario with eighteenth-century sites mentioned in this account. Map created by the author.

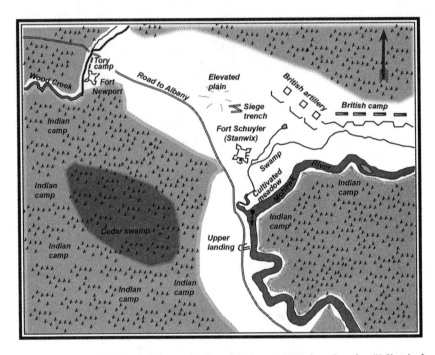

FIGURE 2. The Oneida Carrying Place at the time of the August 1777 siege. Based on "A Sketch of the siege of Fort Schuyler" by François de Fleury, appearing in Luzader, *Fort Stanwix*, 83. Created by the author.

DEFENDING FORT STANWIX

Introduction

On March 26, 1777, Lord George Germain, disappointed that the "rebel" colonists who had been so bold as to declare independence had not been crushed in 1776, wrote to Sir Guy Carleton in Canada that "with a view of quelling the rebellion as soon as possible . . . it is the King's determination to leave about 3000 men under your command, for the defence and duties of that province, and to employ the remainder of your army upon two expeditions, one under the command of Lieutenant General Burgoyne, who is to force his way to Albany, and the other under the command of Lieutenant Colonel St. Leger, who is to make a diversion on the Mohawk River." A third contingent of troops from General William Howe's force in the city of New York area would ascend the Hudson River to meet up with Burgoyne and St. Leger at Albany.[1]

This bold, complex plan for the 1777 campaign aimed to restore momentum toward achieving ultimate victory. Obstructing St. Leger's force at the head of the Mohawk River in western New York would be the British-built French and Indian War–era wood and earth Fort Stanwix, which had been abandoned after that conflict ended. As the War for Independence developed, beginning in 1776 the fort had been substantially rebuilt and garrisoned by Continental Army troops to help relieve the growing fears of both Indigenous and white residents of the Mohawk River Valley. When St. Leger's British troops, Hessian auxiliaries, New York Loyalists, and Indigenous allies reached the headwaters of the Mohawk River early in August 1777, they confidently attacked and laid siege to Fort Stanwix, garrisoned by the 3rd New York Regiment and several smaller units. The successful defense of the ensuing three-week siege delayed St. Leger and ultimately forced his retreat without materially diverting any of the American troops preparing to oppose Burgoyne. The victory by the suffering but gallantly stubborn defenders of Fort Stanwix helped give new hope to the Revolutionary cause and contributed to the momentous surrender of Burgoyne's forces at Saratoga in October.

Fort Stanwix stood at what had become known as the Oneida Carrying Place, or the Carrying Place, or simply the Carry Place, on the vital water route connecting the Hudson River with Lake Ontario. From east to west, boats traversed the region by following the Mohawk River, Wood Creek, Lake Oneida, the Oneida River, and the Oswego River.

Whichever direction one traveled, the journey's first leg was slowed by an opposing river current. That hindrance ceased, however, after one crossed the Carry Place and then traveled aided by the river's flow for the remainder of the journey. The partially fortified town of Schenectady became the route's eastern terminus on account of the Mohawk River's extensive Cohoes Falls, which blocked boat access to and from the Hudson River, known then as the North River. From Schenectady, the route ran west against the Mohawk River's sometimes turbulent eastward current, more than ninety miles to the Oneida Carrying Place near the river's source. At that point, boats required portage—hence the name Carrying Place—to Wood Creek flowing favorably westward for about fourteen miles before emptying into Lake Oneida.[2] After crossing the twenty-mile lake, travel continued aided by westward water flow for about eighteen miles on the Oneida River and then twenty-three miles on the Oswego River to its mouth at Lake Ontario, the route's western terminus.

An eastward journey just reversed these elements. The rivers making up this passage changed frequently in water volume, location and size of sandbars, and number of submerged tree trunks and other obstructions. In the absence of charts and markers, successful navigation required continuous alertness, while forward progress meant switching between rowing, poling, or dragging with ropes, depending on the conditions.

This water route facilitated the important western fur trade of colonists with the Haudenosaunee, whose lands lay along the entire route, as well as other Indians living beyond them. In the seventeenth and eighteenth centuries, control of this water route proved critical during the colonial struggles involving the Dutch, English, and French. As early as 1702, two Indian tribes requested that New York's British governor Lord Cornbury mark the "carrying place" path on trees and remove fallen trees from Wood Creek to facilitate canoe passage.[3] Whoever controlled the Oneida Carry could control the use of this transportation route as its importance expanded with the increasing colonial settlement in the Mohawk River Valley.[4]

The site where Fort Stanwix would be constructed stood on territory long inhabited by the Oneida Nation of the Haudenosaunee. The Mohawk River Valley had some of the richest land in New York and came to support some of the most productive farms in what would become one of the most densely populated areas in the colony. This European contact, initiated long before the fort's construction, produced many upheavals in Oneida life, including severe population losses due to disease and warfare. The Oneidas overcame some of these losses by absorbing colonial settlers and war captives from other Indian nations into their population. Despite the upheavals brought by the white traders and settlers, the Oneidas proudly maintained their strong matrix of customs, beliefs, and practices while also adopting some useful European traditions and technologies.[5]

The eighteenth-century presence of colonial settlers practicing several forms of Christianity—including Palatine Germans, Dutch, French, English, Irish, Scotch, and enslaved people of African descent—living among several Haudenosaunee populations created a complex multicultural landscape in the Mohawk River Valley between the Oneida Carry and Albany. This diverse population experienced economic and political tensions between the Indigenous people and white colonists, as well as internally among both groups.[6]

Against this backdrop, war between Britain and France developed in the mid-1750s, becoming the Seven Years' War in Europe and known as the French and Indian War in Britain's North American colonies. In October 1755, to control the river trade route and passage of supplies from the Hudson River to Oswego, the British diplomatically overcame Oneida resistance and set out to build two small forts at each end of the

Carry Place, which would also help protect the Oneidas from French attacks on their villages. Structures lining the portage road between these forts came to include a brick kiln, a sawpit, a forge, and houses for civilian merchants providing services for the soldiers stationed at the forts. When this trade route became an important military supply line, the French attacked and destroyed one of those forts, Fort Bull, on Wood Creek on March 27, 1756. Learning of a strong French advance into the area from Canada, the British ordered the three remaining Carry Place forts (Williams, Wood Creek, and Newport) destroyed and removed their soldiers thirty miles downriver to German Flats.[7]

In mid-1758, British major general James Abercromby decided it was essential to retake control of the area and ordered General John Stanwix to "take post at the Oneida Carrying Place" with four New York independent companies, 1,400 provincial troops, and a company of rangers. These troops would send out large scouting parties, harass the enemy, and help persuade the Native peoples to support the British cause. Sir William Johnson, superintendent of Indian affairs, who lived seventy-five miles down the Mohawk River at Johnstown, negotiated with the Oneidas to obtain their consent for building a single, much more substantial fort at the Carry Place.[8] He stressed that the fort would also serve as a trading post that would provide "plentiful and cheap trade," and in line with Oneida expectations, he also promised to demolish the fort when the war ended.[9]

On August 23, 1758, soldiers serving under General Stanwix were drawn up around 4:00 p.m. at the Carry Place. After ceremonially firing a twenty-one-gun cannon salute to celebrate the news of their army's recent victory over the French at Fortress Louisbourg on Canada's Cape Breton Island, they gave three loud cheers. Then, resuming their duties, they laid in place the first log to begin construction of the new fort at that vital New York frontier location. The new fort was "crisned" with the name Fort Stanwix about noon on October 20 in honor of the soldiers' commander, who oversaw its construction.[10]

Construction on the fort was optimistically declared to be essentially completed by mid-November. The fort stood half a mile from the Mohawk River's head of navigation, near its upper landing on the eastern edge of the portage, used when the water volume was high enough, and a mile from the lower landing, used when the water level dropped. On the western edge of the Carry Place, the upper landing on Wood Creek was located just below the ruins of Fort Newport.[11] A tributary creek, flowing past the east side of the fort into the Mohawk River and originating at a spring some four hundred yards northeast of the fort, provided a water supply outside the fort in times of peace. Another fork of the creek drained a meadow lying between the river and the bluff where the fort sat. While much of this area on the east side of the fort was somewhat swampy, there was also a meadow that early garrisons and local settlers had cultivated to grow hay. South and west of the fort, the ground sloped off into a great swamp overgrown with cedars. Dense forest closed in just outside the cleared area at the Carry Place. When Continental Army private George Ewing joined the garrison in 1776, he noted in his journal that "the land thereabouts, though very high, is very wet and swampy; the timber, chiefly cypress and white pine, is very large and thick."[12]

During their war against the French, the British used Fort Stanwix as a supply base for expeditions from 1758 through 1760. Although it was never attacked, and its importance decreased as the war continued, improvements were made in spurts. By the war's end in 1763, the fort consisted of massive log and earthen walls, with a bastion at each corner connected by curtain wall ramparts and topped by parapets containing a total of thirty-five cut-out wedge-shaped embrasures to provide protected artillery and musket fire positions. The bastion fighting positions were elevated from the parade level and accessed by an earth ramp known as a gorge or throat. Several buildings stood inside the fort walls, and external defensive structures, ravelins, protected the main gate and sally port.[13]

Both warring nations constructed similar forts based on the designs of the seventeenth-century French military engineer Sébastien de Vauban. These forts were square with four or more protruding structures, the bastions, which allowed the defenders to subject attacking forces to a cross fire. The walls and other defenses were designed to be strong enough to hold out against heavy enemy artillery fire long enough to exhaust the besieging force and compel it to retire. Thick stone outer walls were preferred, but military engineers in North America made do with various available materials and workers within the time constraints of war.

Fort Stanwix was just one of the many Vauban-style forts built during the conflict. French forces had constructed Fort Duquesne in 1754 at the confluence of the Allegheny and Monongahela Rivers, the site of present-day Pittsburgh, but were forced to destroy

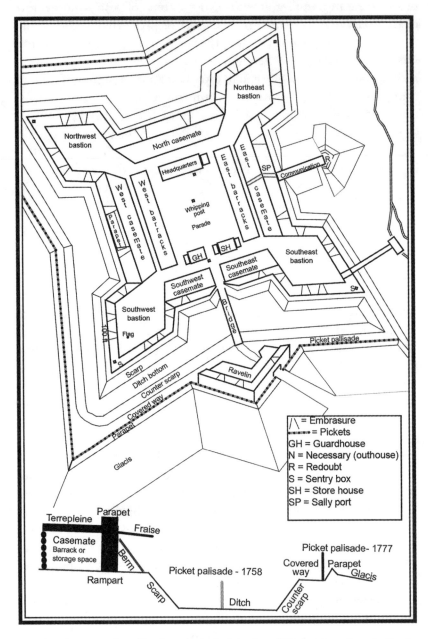

FIGURE 3. Representation of Fort Stanwix physical structure, 1777. Not drawn to scale. Drawing by the author.

it themselves in November 1758 and retreat from the area. The British then built Fort Pitt on the same site. It remained useful during and then after the American Revolution. Other forts involved with French and British troop movements in the Great Lakes and the Hudson River regions included Fort Niagara, Fort Frontenac (in present-day Kingston, Ontario), and Fort Oswego on Lake Ontario. Similar forts along the Hudson River–Lake George–Lake Champlain water corridor included Fort Carillon (Ticonderoga), Fort St. Frederic, and Fort William Henry.

After the war ended, Fort Stanwix's primary purpose switched from guarding the Mohawk River Valley from a French incursion to providing an official British diplomatic presence in Haudenosaunee country, especially among the Oneidas. Yet while the Indians appreciated the trade contacts provided by the fort, maintaining the fort's structure raised their displeasure that it had not been demolished at the war's end, as had been promised. In the immediate aftermath of the war, Indigenous nations in the Ohio Country and the Great Lakes region, angered by the British government's arrogance in their dealings, dishonest traders, and advancing English settlements, plotted to expel the British through military actions, such as Pontiac's Rebellion in 1763.[14] This raised renewed concerns about protecting settlers along the New York frontier and led to renewed efforts, beginning in 1764, to repair Fort Stanwix.

Within a few years, however, the fort was judged obsolete and, abandoned by troops in 1767, quickly began to deteriorate. Without constant maintenance, the fort's earthen ramparts and wooden structures were susceptible to the elements. When the British troops abandoned the site, an "old half pay officer" was permitted to remain "on condition that he shall take care of the buildings for the Kings use and return every thing again to the Crown when required for the use of the Kings Service." He was not expected to maintain the fort's defensive structures. This caretaker was also granted "a small salary" to "take charge of all the stores destined for the Lakes, and to see them forwarded over the portage for Fort Ontario."[15] Two additional former British soldiers, artilleryman John Steeres, sometimes given as Steene or Steeve, and George Reyter of the 4th Battalion of the Royal Americans, also settled near the fort. In June 1774, New York governor William Tryon erroneously stated to Lord Dartmouth that Fort Stanwix had been dismantled. More accurately, the fort had fallen into ruin. That autumn, a major fire destroyed the barracks, leaving only remnants of the main structure still prominent.[16]

Although dilapidated and otherwise abandoned, Fort Stanwix was selected as the site for a council in 1768, where some 3,400 Natives and colonial commissioners from New York, Pennsylvania, Virginia, New Jersey, and Connecticut assembled to adjust the Proclamation of 1763. This proclamation had prohibited white settlement west of the line running north–south through the Appalachian Mountains, connecting the headwaters of rivers flowing west toward the Mississippi and its tributaries. It had become a source of friction between Britain and American colonists encroaching on lands reserved by it for Indians.

In advance of the negotiations, a council house, living quarters for colonial officials, a storage building, and structures for craftsmen were constructed within the remains of the fort.[17] Representatives from the Mohawk, Oneida, Tuscarora, Onondaga, Cayuga, and Seneca Nations began arriving in August, and the negotiations led by Sir William Johnson lasted through October. On November 5, the representatives of the Indigenous nations signed the Treaty of Fort Stanwix, which, amidst intensive lobbying by land speculators and trading agents, expanded the boundaries of the areas permitting white settlement. The treaty line began about eight miles west of Fort Stanwix and continued south and west to the mouth of the Tennessee River in modern-day western Kentucky. The lands west and north of this line were reserved for the Indigenous nations; south and east of the line, which included most of present-day Kentucky, Tennessee, West Virginia, Maryland, and western Pennsylvania, became available to white settlers. The adjustment alienated the Oneidas by allowing white settlement throughout the Mohawk River Valley.[18]

Furthermore, they had wanted to keep control of the Oneida Carry themselves but agreed to "equal use of the carrying Place with the English."[19] The lands around the Oneida Carry would become even more valuable as white settlement increased. Sir William (himself a land speculator) already had plans for a mile-long canal across the Carry Place to further enhance its value. In the wake of the treaty, European settlement continued to expand up the Mohawk River Valley, influencing the Oneidas in numerous ways.[20] They abandoned the wood palisades of their "castles" (as their villages were called), and often replaced their traditional multifamily longhouses with smaller structures. Some individuals began to keep domestic animals for food, to reduce or supplement hunting. Trade increased the number of personal possessions owned by individuals, and new towns emerged. The town of Oriska, today's Oriskany, developed in about the early 1760s several miles east from the fort, where its residents benefited from the commerce associated with the Carry Place.

Shortly after the First Continental Congress adopted the Articles of Association in 1774 and the fighting in the American Revolution began with the events at Lexington and Concord in April 1775, local blacksmith Thomas Spencer, about twenty-eight years old, attended a May 1775 meeting and debate at the colonist-settled village of Cherry Valley, about forty-five miles southeast of Fort Stanwix. Thomas's father was Presbyterian missionary Elihu Spencer, who had served the Oneidas at Onoquaga for a short time in 1748–49. His mother was an Oneida, and because the Haudenosaunee are matrilineal societies, Thomas was considered by all to be Oneida.

Although Thomas's father left the area when he was a small child, Thomas spent equal time living in both cultures while growing up, developed blacksmith skills, learned both languages fluently, and was welcomed and appreciated in both communities, often acting as an interpreter. An influence during his youth was the missionary Gideon Hawley, who had replaced Reverend Spencer. Another tutor may have been the renowned Oneida orator Agwrongdougwas, known to the Americans as Good Peter, who grew up at Onoquaga and converted to Christianity in 1748 under the influence of Reverend Spencer. Thomas Spencer developed some of the same qualities Good Peter was known for, such as honesty, wisdom, prudence, and steadiness.[21]

In 1768, over the course of more than one hundred days, Spencer had helped Sir William Johnson collect Indigenous representatives for the conference at Fort Stanwix that resulted in the Fort Stanwix treaty. He had a solid reputation as a strong Patriot and a good, honest, very skilled man. Like other Oneida men, he developed important skills involved with hunting and traversing the forests, rather than those used in farming. But he also became a blacksmith serving both the Oneida and white settlements. European metal goods, such as pots, pans, axes, hoes, muskets, and farm tools, widely used by everyone, created an increasing need for people with metalworking skills.[22]

The May debate between Loyalist and Patriot settlers at Cherry Valley was held in the town's little church, which filled to overflowing. Spencer made an impassioned, long-remembered speech supporting the American liberties that Patriots were fighting for and their justifiable complaints about British actions. His speech helped strengthen the support of the colonial residents of Cherry Valley for the Patriot cause, and at the end of the meeting most attendees signed the Articles of Association. Spencer would continue to play an important role helping the Patriot cause.[23]

While Cherry Valley residents may have broadly supported the Patriot side, other colonial settlements were more divided in their loyalties, and the members of the Haudenosaunee nations also split over which side to support or whether to remain neutral. The historian Barbara Graymont notes that "for over a century, the Iroquois had been accustomed to thinking of the English as one people—the children of the Great King beyond the sea." The colonists they dealt with in the Mohawk Valley all supported the British against the French. "Now that English unity had been shattered, the Indians had to make a serious adjustment in their own relationships with their white neighbors and carry on diplomacies with two governments, where only one had existed previously." This was an impossible task, and "any attempt on the part of the Iroquois to maintain friendly relations and trade with both sides only aroused the jealousy and suspicion of each side equally."[24]

In general, the Haudenosaunee nations tended toward neutrality in the conflict, though support for the Patriot cause was stronger among the Oneidas and Tuscaroras, while members of the other nations joined with the British. Proximity to white settlements was one factor in these differing loyalties. Religion also played a role. Among Natives who had converted to Christianity, those professing Congregationalism, many of whom had been converted by the missionary and Indian agent for the Continental Congress Samuel Kirkland, often sided with the Patriots. Those who embraced Anglicanism as promoted by William Johnson, the superintendent of Indian affairs for the Northern Department who had organized the 1768 council at Fort Stanwix, often supported the British government and its Loyalist allies. Should white colonial troops be stationed at the Oneida Carry, their actions would influence which way many Indians leaned, toward one side or the other.[25]

The developing eighteenth-century history of the Mohawk River Valley was just one local part of the larger conflict between Britain and its colonists. What to the British and Continentals might have been a sideshow was a critical and very complex civil war among those living in the Mohawk Valley. As the historian Theodore Corbett has stated about the area, "Eighteenth-century battles were not fought in isolation from existing local animosities." British and Continental commanders "had to contend with a civil war of local factions and convictions, doing their best to take advantage of or ignore them." The Patriots demanded and the British asked for loyalty from the countryside, "but existing religious, ethnic, economic, social, and personal alignments were more crucial in deciding which side one supported."[26]

During a June 1775 conference at German Flats, the pro-Patriot Oneidas had advised and urged that "the gate of Fort Stanwix ought to be shut, that nothing might pass and repass to the hurt of our Country." In other words, the abandoned fort should be reconstructed and garrisoned. This would assure any wavering Oneidas that it was worth supporting the Americans. On July 3, at a meeting of the Tryon County Committee, "the associated settlers at Fort Stainwix [sic] represented to this Committee their dangerous Situation of abodes, being few in Number and daily exposed to an Invasion of the Frontiers, desiring a sufficient guard to be posted there at the said Fort." They then reinforced the Oneidas' advice "as their nigh Neighbors, that the gate at Fort Stainwix ought to be shut, to prevent all pernicious passing and repassing of Enemies to the Country." The county committee requested the Committee of Schenectady to send about a hundred men to the fort as "a safeguard to this Country." Nothing came of their request at this time.[27]

By 1776, Johnson Hall, the home of Sir John Johnson, the son of the recently deceased Sir William, who had worked hard to persuade the Haudenosaunee to support the British in the French and Indian War, became the focal point of Loyalist strength in the Mohawk Valley. Major General Philip Schuyler, commander of the Northern Department of the Continental Army and commissioner of Indian affairs, came to believe that to protect the supporters of the Patriot cause in the Mohawk Valley, he must send troops to take Sir John into custody and put down his Loyalist followers. That action would lead to Patriot agreement with the Oneidas about the benefit to be derived from a reestablished and garrisoned Fort Stanwix.

Part I

Setting the Stage for a Siege

CHAPTER 1

The Increasing Need to Reestablish Fort Stanwix

May–June 1776

On June 11, 1776, Major General Philip Schuyler sat down to write to General Washington and alert him to intelligence he had received about the well-known New York Loyalist John Butler arranging a meeting at Oswego to pressure the Six Nations to assist him in "falling on the German Flats," a settlement about thirty miles east of the Oneida Carry Place.[1] Schuyler had recommended "the greatest vigilance to the Committee [of Safety] of that County and to keep parties continually scouring the woods as far as, and even beyond Fort Stanwix to prevent a surprise." He was also trying to arrange a conference with the Indians at German Flats. The Oneidas living in that area supported the American side, and Schuyler felt they should be recognized for that in all dealings. He continued, "I am preparing everything I can with the utmost secrecy for taking post at Fort Stanwix where I propose to be immediately after the conference with the Indians." Having troops at Fort Stanwix, Schuyler would enable the Americans to send a detachment against any of the tribes who "declare against us."[2] But with demands increasing for more troops with the main army, what troops were available to be posted at the frontier fort?

Following the combat at Lexington and Concord in April and Bunker Hill in June 1775, the Continental Congress and General George Washington adopted the New England Army of Observation and raised several battalions in other states to create the Continental Army to besiege the British army in Boston. Initial recruits enlisted for short periods of time since everyone expected a brief conflict. When the Boston siege persisted inconclusively at the end of 1775, that "first establishment" of the Continental Army was restructured into a larger "second establishment" composed of men from throughout the rebelling colonies generally signing on for one-year enlistments, most expiring at the end of 1776. Again, everyone expected that one year would be sufficient to persuade the British government to respond positively to the colonists' determined protests and end the military conflict. Also, the relatively short, clearly defined terms of enlistment reduced fears that the soldiers would become a standing army.

On January 10, 1776, the Continental Congress approved raising, for one year, as part of the Continental Army's second establishment, what would become the 3rd New Jersey Regiment commanded by Colonel Elias Dayton of Elizabethtown, a veteran of the colonial wars with experience in the Mohawk River Valley area.[3] After serving with him for about six months, Lieutenant Ebenezer Elmer praised Dayton in his journal on July 5, 1776, judging that he was a "man of steady, easy, forgiving disposition, who uses both officers and soldiers with the greatest tenderness, by which he has gained the love of the soldiers in general."[4]

By early May, this new regiment was at New York City, where it impressed General Washington, who was preparing that area to repel a major British attempt to make the city its base of operations to destroy Washington's army and end the Revolution. A base at New York would be at one end of the land and water route to Quebec, Canada, where another British army was based. The British would benefit from holding both ends of the route and potentially dividing New England from the rest of the colonies in rebellion. The 3rd New Jersey Regiment must have looked good in their gray coats with dark blue facings and cuffs, new black hats with white binding, buckskin breeches, and relatively new shirts and shoes. Additional high-quality Continental Army units were badly needed for both the defense of New York City and the conquest of Canada. Consequently, Colonel Dayton received orders to take his "Jersey Greys" to Albany and proceed from there to Canada to serve with General John Sullivan's brigade and bolster the campaign to defeat the British stationed there, capture Quebec, and seek to make Canada the fourteenth colony in the rebellion.[5]

At that time, fewer than three thousand inhabitants resided within the Albany stockade, which had early developed as a fur-trading post and now served as a center for the distribution of agricultural products,

THE INCREASING NEED TO REESTABLISH FORT STANWIX   17

lumber, and other goods. The largest manorial grant of the area was the manor of Rensselaerswyck, which surrounded Albany. Workers in the countryside consisted of a combination of white freemen and enslaved Black people.[6]

When the Jersey Greys assembled at Albany on May 8, young private George Ewing described that town impressively as

> situated on the west side of the North or Hudson River, one hundred and ninety miles above New York, and it is one of the oldest towns in the colony; the inhabitants chiefly Hollanders. The city is between two and three miles long on the river and half a mile wide, and is built on the lowland by the side of the river and nearly level with the water, with a very high hill lying back of it, on which is the ruins of an old fort, which overlooks the town.[7]

His full description would help him remember this experience and relate it when he returned home and was among people who had heard of, but never seen, Albany.

Everyone in Dayton's regiment anticipated proceeding on north from Albany to Canada, where they would be introduced to confronting the enemy on the battlefield. Dayton's orders, however, unexpectedly changed radically at Albany. On May 14, General Schuyler told Colonel Dayton to proceed instead, with most of his regiment, to Johnstown on the Mohawk River, where he was to arrest Sir John Johnson and win control of the many Loyalists there with him.[8]

After information kept coming in that Sir John was undertaking efforts to create a power base to oppose the Patriots, General Schuyler led three thousand troops to Johnstown in January to disarm Johnson and his followers. To stay free, Loyalist Sir John had given his parole, pledging not to engage in activities against the cause. By May, however, he was known to be actively stockpiling arms and recruiting men for a New York Loyalist battalion.[9] Two days later, Dayton's inexperienced regiment was drawn up on parade, and forty capable men and two officers from each company, a total of about 340 officers and men, were selected to depart on a secret mission. They were to go to Johnstown, leaving the rest of the regiment at Albany.[10]

Dayton's detachment headed west by way of Schenectady on May 17. Schenectady had developed as a fur-trading post and by 1777 had about five hundred residents surrounded by agricultural landholdings.[11] Captain Joseph Bloomfield described it as "a very neat pleasant & well built town on the west side of the Mohawk River & far preferable (though not so large) as Albany."[12] Ewing described it as "a very pretty little town on the south side of the Mohawk River, sixteen miles above Albany; the inhabitants likewise Hollanders, and very kind and hospitable."[13] Lieutenant Elmer found it "a very fine village, lying on the east side of [the] Mohawk River, with a large number of stately buildings."[14] Everything they saw was new to the officers and their men from New Jersey, who recorded their sometimes conflicting impressions to enrich their memories and provide answers for relatives and friends who would later ask them about what they had observed in New York.

At Schenectady, the detachment picked up the Mohawk River and a roughly parallel land road and set off for Johnstown. Upon arriving there, Private Ewing found Johnstown to be "a very small town, about six miles from the Mohawk River, in a very fertile spot of land."[15]

Shortly after arriving at Johnstown on May 19, Dayton heard that Sir John Johnson, with three hundred or more men, mainly Scottish settlers, had departed for Canada, or possibly Niagara. The skeptical Dayton was not convinced that Sir John and his party had departed and believed they might "still be lurking in the woods." Sir John, however, had indeed left the area and commenced a long and arduous nine-day journey with his followers to Canada.[16] Johnson had received a colonel's commission to raise and command a regular provincial force of Loyalist volunteers, including the men who had left the Johnstown area with him, to be called the King's Royal Regiment of New York. In addition to their desire to aid the British in their war against the "Patriots," Johnson and his followers wanted to regain their land from the rebels and retake control of the Mohawk River Valley for Great Britain.

The Johnsons, originally Catholic settlers from County Meath in Ireland, were one of the primary families in the Albany area, involved in rivalry for power with the Schuylers, Van Rensselaers, and Skenes. Sir John's father, Sir William Johnson, had held county offices, including colonel of militia, in Albany County until 1772, when the new Tryon County was formed, which included Johnstown as its county seat. Sir William had taken away responsibility from the Albany Indian commissioners, who had been led by the Schuylers and other patrician families, to control the fur trade. Shortly after, the Johnsons began bringing in several hundred Scottish Highlander families as settlers and giving them good deals to establish their farms. Their militaristic culture and their Roman Catholic religion intimidated the Protestant Palatine German, Dutch, and English settlers. As in the Albany area, there were also pockets of Black people working the land for their enslavers in the Mohawk River Valley.[17]

Agreeing with advice offered by several local people, Dayton decided to take possession of Johnson Hall "in order to cut off the communication of provisions & intelligence, from that quarter, to Sir John's party." He also suggested that Congress might think it proper to "station a parcel of men here, during the next season," and noted that the public buildings in Johnstown could be made "very defensible" at little expense.[18]

Schuyler told Dayton on May 22 that he had requested that the Albany and Tryon County Committees of Safety, the leaders of the Patriot cause in that area, take all necessary measures to "secure the county against the infernal machinations of the Tories" and remove them. Dayton should do everything he could to assist them with his troops. Schuyler hoped the committees and Dayton would work together with "attention and vigilance," along with "that regard to humanity, which I trust, will always characterize the Friends of Liberty in America."[19] Dayton took possession of Johnson Hall and stationed guards and sentries there. At his request, Lady Johnson surrendered all the estate's keys, along with many of Sir John's papers so Dayton could examine them.[20]

Schuyler informed Colonel Dayton about recent intelligence indicating that Sir John had gone to Niagara and might soon join with an enemy party at Oswego, at the western end of the water route that included the Oneida Carry. Therefore it would be advisable to move Lady Johnson to Albany, along with all the local Loyalists and their families. And if somehow Sir John should fall into his hands, Dayton was to send him to Schuyler under "such a guard as that there may be no danger of a rescue." After doing everything he could to settle things at Johnstown, Dayton should post himself "in the most advantageous place on the Mohawk River to secure that part of the country and awe the enemy and remain there until further orders." To help select the best place to occupy, he should consult with the Tryon and Albany committees of safety.[21] While Schuyler did not say it just yet, Fort Stanwix prominently fit the definition of "most advantageous" place.

Schuyler complimented Dayton on his operations in Tryon County, which had involved interactions with Patriots, Loyalists, and Indians, stressing that he had conducted himself with great prudence that reflected well on himself as an officer and a man of sense.[22] Dayton had performed a very difficult job, given the divisions among both the European settlers and the Indians. Yet Dayton's work at Johnstown had also revealed some disciplinary issues among his officers and men, including some plundering of Johnson Hall.

Concerned that bateaux were traveling on the Mohawk River to trade with the northern enemy troops and Indians, Schuyler wrote the Albany Committee of Safety on May 27, instructing that no bateau should be permitted to pass the unoccupied remains of Fort Stanwix, except any boat specifically designated to trade with friendly elements of the Six Nations.[23] Bateaux were flat-bottomed, double-ended boats constructed of pine planks fastened to oak ribs and used for both trade and military purposes. Typically twenty-five to thirty-five feet long and very heavy compared with the Indigenous people's canoes, bateaux could carry cargoes weighing up to several tons, consisting of some combination of trade goods, provisions, military supplies, construction supplies, and people. Each bateau normally required a crew of two to four oarsmen and a steersman, who steered the boat at the stern with a long sweep oar. The crew usually rowed, but sometimes had to pole or get out and push the craft in shallow water. A sail could be used when conditions allowed, though fallen trees in the water greatly obstructed their progress.[24]

Since no Continentals occupied the deteriorated fort, Schuyler's order would have to be enforced by local militia. Partly because of that, Schuyler wrote to John Hancock on May 31 that both he and the Albany committee believed it was necessary for Colonel Dayton's regiment to remain in the area "at least for the present."[25] Therefore, the seventy-three 3rd New Jersey Regiment men left behind at Albany now set out for Johnstown. The regiment would avoid service in Canada and the defeats and illnesses encountered by the Continental Army units deployed there. Events were unfolding and pressure was building that would soon lead to stationing troops once again at Fort Stanwix.

About this time, an Oneida delegation recommended that to garner Indian support, the Americans must demonstrate greater resolve in their war with the British and provide a focal point for increased trade to strengthen economic ties with the Indians. The Indians were increasingly dependent on European cloth, clothing, tools, and a variety of other items they could not make themselves. A trading post where they could purchase needed items was essential, not just the "gifts" that were distributed as part of diplomatic encounters or given in times of emergency.²⁶

Acting on that message, and recognizing that a garrisoned fort would also provide protection for white colonial settlements, General Schuyler recommended to the Continental Congress in June that it post troops at the former Fort Stanwix, make the fort also a trading post, and be sure to inform the Indians that they were doing both. He felt that this action should please the people of the nearby Oneida town of Oriska, as well as other Oneidas. An American trading post would give local Indians more reason to remain neutral or even support the Americans. The garrison would also help protect Oneida villages from British and Loyalist incursions. Schuyler notified Washington three days later, even before receiving positive feedback from either Congress or the general, that he was preparing to post troops at Fort Stanwix, the key to Patriot diplomacy with the Indians.

General Schuyler found local support for his decision when he learned from Presbyterian missionary and congressional Indian agent Reverend Samuel Kirkland on June 8 that the Indians believed they could no longer remain neutral and had to make their choice of which side to support. For several decades before, during, and after the war for independence, Kirkland served as a missionary, government agent, and interpreter with the Haudenosaunee and frequently as chaplain for Continental troops stationed in the Mohawk Valley. Kirkland recommended that "if a party of 500 men with two or three rifle companies were sent to Fort Stanwix, it would annoy our enemy and strengthen our friends, and protect that part of our frontier." He stressed, however, that it was important to act quickly: "And I must say, from a regard to my fellow men that if this matter should be long delayed tis my real opinion we shall soon hear of hostilities committed upon those defenseless frontiers."²⁷

Schuyler had to act fast but felt he should have permission from higher authority for such a major move. That same day he wrote to Hancock arguing that he fully understood the necessity to station troops "where Fort Stanwix formerly stood," emphasizing that "the least acquaintance with that part of the country points out the importance of the post and that it ought to be occupied by us to prevent its being done by the enemy." Schuyler reinforced with Hancock that if it were left unmanned, the enemy could use Fort Stanwix as a place to "send provision &c by water and form a magazine for the supply of the Indians in their interest." Doing so would help the British win over the support of Indians who might otherwise have been friendly to the American cause. Schuyler noted the only reason the Americans had not already garrisoned the fort was confidence in the Indians who were loyal to them. Divisions among the Haudenosaunee, however, now made things less secure. Therefore, he optimistically promised, "in ten day's time we shall have a fort there, and keep a body of men sufficient to cut off any parties that may attempt to destress our frontiers." While the complex Indian affairs needed straightening out in many ways, Schuyler unequivocally promised, "I shall however make every preparation for taking post at Fort Stanwix, and hope to conduct it in such a manner and with so much celerity as to impress on the Indians . . . that we are capable of acting with vigour, that we do not mean to be trifled with."[28]

Schuyler also wrote to General Israel Putnam at New York on June 8 that he was hastening to Albany to take measures for securing the western New York frontier. Foremost in Schuyler's mind was the belief that he was "obliged to order Col. Dayton to take post at the place where Fort Stanwix was." But fearing that he risked disfavor if he acted without permission from Congress or Washington, he told Putnam, "Before I order Col. Dayton to take post there[,] I wish, if time will permit, to hear from General Washington on the subject, and have therefore enclosed my letter to Congress that if General Washington should happen to be at New York, he will please consider it directed to himself, and give me his order."[29] Time was of the essence, so he would act without permission if need be and hope for the concurrence of Washington and Congress.

Washington wrote to Schuyler on June 13, "It will be necessary to employ Colonel Dayton and his Regiment . . . in securing a Post where Fort Stanwix formerly stood, which I esteem of much Importance." Congress also quickly approved reoccupying Fort Stanwix on Friday, June 14, 1776.[30] But which troops would garrison the fort? Large numbers of troops were still needed in Canada, and having left Boston, the enemy were on the brink of bringing the war to the New York City area with the largest expeditionary force ever assembled by Britain. On June 20, General Schuyler wrote to Major General John Sullivan from Albany that Colonel Dayton was in Tryon County, where Johnstown and Fort Stanwix were located, adding, "We shall[,] I have to believe[,] have our hands full in that Quarter." Therefore "I am preparing every thing to take post at Fort Stanwix & to repel the threatened invasion of the Mohawk River."[31] Because Colonel Dayton had spent time in the Mohawk River Valley area during the French and Indian War, including at Fort Stanwix while it was under construction, as well as during his recent work there, he was a logical choice for this command.[32]

Despite being in such a strategic location, the old fort had not seen much action, and its usefulness seems to have been mostly theoretical. As Colonel Dayton prepared to garrison the fort with his inexperienced regiment, he must have wondered just what obstacles he would face in restoring the fort and preparing to defend it from attack while also helping his men learn the skills of soldiers and adapt to army life on the frontier.

CHAPTER 2

The 3rd New Jersey Regiment Restores Fort Stanwix

June–October 1776

Captain Bloomfield of the 3rd New Jersey Regiment, together with Major Hubbell, whom he described as "with us in character of an engineer," set out to "see the situation & make report of the state of Fort Stanwix." After a difficult journey in "the wilderness following each other through a blind foot path," they arrived at 8:00 a.m. on June 28 and Bloomfield experienced "a view of the ruins of this once strong & beautiful Fort, which is accounted to lie on the highest ground in all America."[1]

After about two weeks at Johnstown, the 3rd New Jersey Regiment marched some forty miles to German Flats, which Private Ewing described as "a large piece of intervale land lying on both sides of the river, inhabited by Germans." Ewing also considered the area to be "the most fertile spot of land that I ever beheld—their produce is chiefly wheat, oats, and peas, with some Indian corn."[2] Several days later, six companies marched on to Fort Stanwix, while Captain Bloomfield's company remained behind to garrison German Flats. The 3rd New Jersey Regiment began garrison duty divided among Fort Stanwix, Johnstown, and the German Flats area.[3] The weather during Ewing's several summer months at the fort was so wet that he recorded in frustration, "We had hardly two clear days together."[4]

Most of Dayton's approximately five hundred troops, accompanied by Continental Army engineer Major Nathaniel Hubbell, began arriving at Fort Stanwix on June 28, 1776.[5] Unknown to the soldiers at that time, this was just days before the adoption by the Continental Congress of the Declaration of Independence, which would dramatically change, or formalize, the objective of the war. It would no longer be a war of protest to restore expected rights but a treasonous war for political independence. Joining the New Jersey troops at the dilapidated fort were 150 troops of the 4th New York Regiment, seventy-five Tryon County militiamen expecting to continue traveling on to Canada, and two hundred additional county militiamen.

Captain Bloomfield described the fort in his journal as "large & well situated having a glacis, breast-work ditch & a picket fort before the walls which are also well guarded with sharp sticks of timber shooting over the walls on which is four bastions." The glacis was the long, easy slope of earth around the fort providing open ground and visibility of the enemy. At Fort Stanwix it extended out about seventy-five feet, although the standard was more like 120 feet.[6] An earthen parapet at the highest point on the glacis provided shelter for the covered way, a broad, flat shelf of ground wrapping around the works bordering on the counterscarp of the ditch and protected by the parapet rise of the glacis and a line of pickets forming a palisade.[7] Across the ditch from the covered way were the rampart walls Bloomfield so casually mentions as forming the square fort. These weathered and eroded ramparts were log cribs filled with earth primarily taken from digging the wide ditch surrounding the fort at the base of the ramparts.

Bloomfield also noted the remains of a sally port on the east side, the covered way, and the bridge and raveling in front of the entrance gate. Inside the fort, he found the ruins of five houses and barracks, built to protect supplies and accommodate the officers and men, which had burned down in the 1774 fire. Clearly, the fort had not been totally dismantled as reported earlier that year. Viewing the ruins of "this once strong & beautiful fort," Bloomfield had to use his imagination to develop "a better idea of the strength & importance of a fort than any thing I ever before saw or read." He observed that five or six families had settled "in this rich and beautiful campaign country."[8] Ewing noted only three or four settler families living near the fort and as many at the nearby small Indian town of Oriska.[9] By about 1760, several settlers, including John Roof, a native of the German state of Baden-Württemberg, a man named Brodock, two retired soldiers, and a French fur trader, among others, were living at the Carry Place near the new fort. In 1759 John Roof had married Mary (Anna Maria) Leonard and then leased his land at the Carry from Oliver Delancey, one of the proprietors of the Oriskany patent. Roof became an innkeeper who also assisted with portaging goods for the Indian trade and became a trader with the Indians himself. On August 28, 1761, the Roofs' son John was born at Fort Stanwix. These people became very well known to the soldiers of the fort garrison and a number became tragically involved in the siege.[10]

Later that day, Bloomfield went to the Oneida Castle for talks with various Indians. He visited the home of a leading Oneida war chief and firm American friend, Skenandoah, "who lives in a good house built in the Dutch fashion. This sachem & Mr. [Thomas] Spencer the Indian interpreter spent the evening with us & were very good company." Bloomfield returned to German Flats on June 30, while most of Dayton's regiment settled in as well as they could in what remained of Fort Stanwix.[11]

On July 11, Bloomfield noted in his journal that he saw an artillery company on its way to Fort Stanwix, "for which fort all our regiment excepting my company are ordered to get in readiness to march tomorrow."[12] That artillery company may have had several pieces of artillery and the equipment required to employ it in the fort. Throughout its history, the fort never mounted the complete number of cannons originally planned for the thirty-five embrasures distributed throughout the four walls and bastions to accommodate them. The garrison at the fort would not have an artillery company until January 1777. Whatever inadequate artillery supplies the fort did acquire during its history came to the fort piecemeal.[13]

Just how Dayton's men found shelter at the fort is not stated, but they undoubtedly quartered in any usable space in the fort casemates or in tents they erected in and around the fort, just as they had at Johnstown. The casemates were areas built into the ramparts to provide shelter from artillery fire. In Fort Stanwix, where they were constructed to be used as quarters for some of the troops, they had plank floors and brick fireplaces with chimneys extending through the ceiling. The north casemate contained six evenly spaced fireplaces and was probably divided into rooms twenty feet square to be used for officers' quarters—especially the staff officers. The other casemates probably housed enlisted men and company-level officers, with perhaps some space used for workshops or other purposes. Just what condition the casemates were in when Dayton's men arrived is not known, but they were no doubt limited in their usefulness.[14]

Dayton's men spent about a month and a half making themselves as comfortable as possible at the fort, establishing guard and other military routines, conducting some training, sending out scouting patrols, and performing some initial restoration work on the ruins. A somewhat surprised Bloomfield noted in his journal on August 6 that one day the previous week Colonel Dayton had ordered his officers and men at Fort Stanwix to "form, by manning the lines, firing cannon & small arms &c. &c." and then had, very prematurely, proclaimed the restoration work on the fort to be "finished." He also declared that the fort was henceforth to be "called Fort Schuyler," in honor of his commander, the commander of the Northern Department of the Continental Army, and New York native, Major General Philip Schuyler.[15] While this was an official name change, Dayton's action did not stop many people from continuing to call the fort by its original name. Mohawk Valley people may have continued to use the original name because there was an older nearby fort from the French and Indian War named Fort Schuyler, so using the name would cause confusion. Others may not have wanted to honor a powerful family from outside the Mohawk Valley, and Philip Schuyler in particular, because of his leadership role in the devastating Patriot defeat in the Canadian campaign. Schuyler, however, had been a strong proponent of restoring and garrisoning the old fort, so the name change was appropriate in that context.

While Colonel Dayton might have wished to report that the fort had been returned to a satisfactory condition, the full restoration had in no way been completed. For only a couple of weeks, Dayton and Hubbell had been struggling to fulfill their orders to either rebuild the old fort or build a completely new one. Finding that the fort had erroneously been reported demolished, they clearly had chosen to rebuild and repair what remnants remained rather than demolish what was left and start over from scratch. Time was of the essence, and restoration could be accomplished much more quickly than clearing ground and building a totally new structure. Because of manpower and supply limitations, however, Dayton and Hubbell had been able to put the fort in adequate condition to accommodate only about two hundred men and restore limited defensive structures to provide protection from small arms fire and very light artillery. On August 2, the 4th New York Regiment troops serving with Dayton received orders to relocate downriver, thus removing some badly needed fort restoration laborers.[16]

That same day, General Schuyler reported from German Flats that Lieutenant Edward McMichael of the 3rd New Jersey Regiment had just brought in a report from a scouting party he had led to Oswego on the shore of Lake Ontario. Schuyler noted, "If the intelligence it contains should be true a reinforcement would be necessary in this quarter." Accordingly, Schuyler ordered Dayton to continually keep scouts from his garrison out toward Oswego while also sending out Indians to scout and keep an eye on things.[17]

McMichael's report stated that he had learned that three British regiments along with a number of Loyalists, and Indians commanded by Colonel Guy Johnson (nephew of Sir William and cousin of Sir John Johnson), all the Indians under the command of Lieutenant Colonel John Butler (another Mohawk Valley friend and associate of the Johnsons), and any British regulars available from Niagara under Lieutenant Colonel John Caldwell, were expected to gather at Oswego. After organizing, they planned to march against Fort Stanwix and German Flats. If McMichael's intelligence was correct, the garrison would soon be defending the fort. Colonel Butler had also sent, as a spy, an Indian named Thomas Davis from Niagara to German Flats to report on the conference with the Oneidas there.

Desertions, sometimes to the enemy, frequently occurred among the military units that garrisoned Fort Stanwix throughout its history. Over the course of the war, about 20 to 25 percent of Continental Army troops deserted, often within three months of enlistment. The heaviest desertion months were December 1 through April 30, which were also the most active months for enlistments—basically the months between campaign seasons. But desertion could happen at any time, often related to specific events and situations. Dayton's regiment had to deal with a desertion plot in mid-August involving Lieutenant McMichael and several enlisted men.[18] Although McMichael was well respected and had led several important scouting patrols, it may be that he and his confederates had been influenced to desert to the enemy when they heard about the Declaration of Independence being read to the regiment in mid-July. Fighting for independence, rather than to protest specific acts of Parliament, may have motivated their decision, as it did for other Patriots who turned Loyalists at that time.[19]

Sending men out on scouting patrols a considerable distance from the fort always created concerns about desertion, but the patrols were essential. In his journal Ewing stated that he frequently went out on command to Oneida Lake, twenty miles from the fort. Seeking information on enemy activity wasn't his only purpose. He enthusiastically noted that the lake "abounds with excellent salmon and other fish in great plenty."[20]

Just a week prior to the discovery of Lieutenant McMichael's desertion plot, Dayton sent a small patrol commanded by Sergeant Major Isaiah Younglove to Fort Ontario at Oswego. After reaching Oswego without incident, the patrol came under attack in wet weather, and Sergeant Major Younglove along with his men demonstrated great courage and resourcefulness in their defense. Only one man was lost, a Sergeant Aitkins, but several were captured, including Younglove. The British governor in Quebec, Major General Guy Carleton, paroled Younglove after about three months, but his pledge not to participate further in the war meant that Younglove had to leave his regiment. He was replaced by another sergeant promoted to sergeant major.[21]

Private Elijah Moore later stated that on one occasion he left the fort "with a small scouting party" that marched to Oswego, where they "had a skirmish with the Indians."[22] This must have been another of the many patrols, since Moore does not appear in the records as part of the Younglove scouting party. Detachments such as these were sent out to prevent surprise attacks on the fort, or on friendly people living near it, and provide information to make the garrison better able to prepare for an already anticipated siege.

While Dayton had declared the fort restoration to be complete on August 2, General Schuyler at Albany optimistically reported to Washington on August 16 only that "the works at Fort Stanwix are going on with great expedition." Since nourishment for the troops to maintain their energy for work on the restoration projects was always a concern, he also reported that the fort had almost an eighty days' supply of pork and flour in store, and more flour was on its way from Schenectady. In addition, the fort had twenty-three head of "fat cattle" and from them "will receive a constant supply of fresh meat." Therefore he had "no apprehensions that the garrison will be under any difficulty in the article of provisions."[23]

Dayton was concerned about having adequate provisions for his men at Fort Stanwix. He wrote to General Schuyler that the garrison was "well supplied with flour but [in] want of salt provisions."[24] The generally supportive Schuyler took exception to this and, in a letter to John Hancock, inserted an aside arguing that "Colonel Dayton cannot be short of salt provisions as he mentions unless the commissary at his post has made a false return. He has had a constant supply of fresh meat since his last return." He enclosed a copy of that report, which stated that on August 13 the fort had 180 barrels of pork, 226 barrels of flour, and twenty-three head of cattle.[25]

Few of Dayton's soldiers had experienced much previous contact with Indians, but now each man had frequent interactions with Haudenosaunee individuals. Initially, both groups were suspicious of each other. To keep the peace and not alienate the Haudenosaunee, officers strictly ordered their soldiers to put aside any negative prejudices and interact with them in a tolerant manner.[26] As with all orders, these were carried out with varying degrees of attention and skill.

Despite many obstacles, by the mid-eighteenth century the Haudenosaunee had one of the highest standards of living among the Indigenous peoples of North America. The Mohawks and Oneidas in particular began adapting to white ways in dress and metals-based technology. Their longhouses were often replaced with European-style cabins with open-hearth fireplaces and chimneys.[27] They had become dependent on their white neighbors for trade goods and other benefits while maintaining many traditional ways. Considering themselves to be independent, they sought to preserve and protect their territory from white settlement.[28] The problems generated by the civil war and War for Independence reduced many Indigenous people in the area to starvation and destitution.[29]

Negative prejudices among the garrison tended to diminish somewhat as individuals got to know the local Oneidas and found them to be kind and intelligent, possessing a humanity equal to their own. The preconception of wild, animal-like, dirty savages gave way in at least some cases to friendship and trust. Captain Bloomfield recorded several positive comments about Oneida attributes in his journal and made frequent reference to singing, dancing, ball games, and other social activities enjoyed by whites with the Oneidas. Overall, however, prejudices persisted, at least partly because the soldiers were continually hearing negative comments supporting actions to take control of Indigenous lands.[30]

These activities would continue to be part of the garrison experience. Bloomfield particularly admired the Oneidas' strength and their tall bodies "adapted to endure much hardship, [rather] than to continue long at any servile works." He described their physical strength as more like that of "a beast of prey than a beast of burden."[31]

Meanwhile, it was Dayton's men who used their strength more like beasts of burden as they worked on restoring the fort. The Oneidas also performed a major, indispensable role by scouting for intelligence to warn the fort of possible enemy attacks, either in force or in smaller raiding parties.

One problem slowing down restoration work at Fort Stanwix was the reduced workforce resulting from stationing several companies at other locations in the area, including at German Flats. Instead of assisting with the Fort Stanwix restoration, between July 22 and August 21, 1776, a detachment of the 3rd New Jersey Regiment working under the direction of twenty-two-year-old Captain Bloomfield constructed a fort at German Flats. Local militiamen assisted them, as did members of Colonel Samuel Elmore's regiment when it was ordered to the area in August to increase Continental troop strength in the Mohawk Valley. Just as Fort Stanwix had originally been named for the officer commanding the troops who constructed it, the New Jersey troops on August 21 ceremoniously named the new fort at German Flats Fort Dayton, in honor of their regimental commander.[32]

There was growing anxiety about enemy intentions and potential threats to the area that only a restored Fort Stanwix with a complete garrison could thwart. The Oneida interpreter and blacksmith Thomas Spencer relayed updated intelligence frequently to Colonel Dayton. In early September, Spencer reported on local Oneida fears that enemy Indians gathering at Oswego would attack them because "we sit still and meddle not in the war." That is, they remained neutral. After a meeting of Onondaga chiefs, Spencer conveyed their desire that the Fort Stanwix garrison be reinforced "with all speed. We think there is occasion for more troops this way." Spencer wrote to Dayton at 6:00 a.m. on September 4 regarding enemy actions from Canada warning, "They will not be stopped, they will strike wherever they see white people, first here, if they [the local white people] fail, your fort is the next place." Spencer reported that the chiefs expressed their great concerns about taking white soldiers along on their scouting missions. The chiefs felt that the white men lacked the necessary skills to scout effectively and avoid capture by the enemy and that those deficiencies put the Indians with them in danger. The Indians, however, were very agreeable to conducting the long-distance scouting missions without any white participation. The whites could do scouts solely on their own if they wished. Some forty Indians came to the fort on September 27 to meet with Dayton, "in order to establish . . . some sure method of speedily conveying intelligence to each other."[33]

After Colonel Elmore's regiment relieved Captain Bloomfield's company at German Flats, Bloomfield marched his men to Fort Stanwix on September 4 to join with the rest of Dayton's regiment. After an overnight stop at the Oneida village at Oriska, they arrived at Fort Stanwix the evening of September 5, where Bloomfield recorded in his journal, "My company were ordered to occupy a barn for want of tents." While the fort lacked suitable accommodations for his soldiers, Bloomfield did better personally and "dined with the Col. & Major. Lodged at the Colonels."[34]

The fort kept receiving frequent intelligence concerning potential attacks from the west by groups of Indians and Loyalists. At 2:00 a.m. on September 3, the Oneida war chief Skenandoah arrived at the fort with another warrior to report "that a numerous army, chiefly of Indians were that Day to arrive at Oswego." That information was backed up by a report from Thomas Spencer that seven hundred Indians and whites under British 8th Regiment of Foot Ensign Walter Butler, brother of John Butler, were headed for Oswego. Local Indians expected that both they and the fort would be attacked. The rumors, full of variations, kept everyone on edge.[35]

Bloomfield created a very personal image of soldier life at Fort Stanwix in his September 8 journal entry. He complained of being "unwell with a pain in all my bones owing to a cold I have caught after the use of too much Mercurial Ointment for the Itch, a troublesome pestilence prevalent throughout the whole camp amongst both officers & soldiers." He also noted that the restoration work continued, and "the fatigue partys are busily engaged at their respective works without any regard to the day [Sunday] which is no ways distinguished from any other day in the week, unless by the hoisting of the Flagg & flaming Sword of Liberty within the Fort." Nevertheless, anyone who was not at work was "doing wht. is right in his own eyes." Many activities went on a usual, for example, "a scout of 100 men was sent out today."[36]

Although intelligence had suggested that enemy forces would soon appear in the fort's vicinity, Dayton informed General Schuyler on September 11, "No parties have as yet been discovered about or near this place so that I begin even to suspect the truth of the report in general." He kept hoping to receive more reliable intelligence and had been trying to dispatch a scouting party of Indians, accompanied by just one man from his regiment, ordered to find out what they could about the situation at Oswego. The Indian leaders objected to even the one white man being part of the scouting party, so Dayton had to settle for sending a party consisting only of Indians, with instructions that if they should spy any enemy between the fort and Oswego, they were to return with all speed to give warning. Since no one had returned, he believed there were no enemy detachments approaching. He also sent out scouting parties consisting only of his soldiers to confirm, double-check, or gain additional information.

In addition to dispatching scouts out toward Oswego, Dayton constantly kept a detachment, commanded by a captain, stationed at the eastern end of Lake Oneida. He supplied them with axes to fell trees into the river to obstruct the passage the enemy would take to the fort. He concluded his letter by interpreting the evidence around him with rose-colored glasses and boasting to Schuyler that he was not concerned, assuring him, "Our fort is now very strong, our men healthy and spirited, so that I will undertake to vouch for the security of Fort Schuyler."[37] On the nights of September 19 and 20, a party of Mississauga Indians who had been sent to the area to try to surprise and capture or kill soldiers of the fort garrison fired on the sentries, raising alarms of imminent attack on the fort.[38] However, no attack came.

Dayton had to deal with more than restoring the fort and gathering intelligence. He served as a government presence for nearby settlers. Toward the end of September, he held a court of inquiry looking into the behavior of an unpopular Loyalist settler named Thomas Mayre. Even the local Oneidas had requested Mayre's removal because he frequently offended them. Dayton decided to "order Mayre from this place" and sent him under guard to Colonel Elmore at German Flats, with a request to forward Mayre to the chairman of the Tryon County Committee for disposition. He also sent down one Armstrong, apparently a trader or sutler, who had repeatedly disobeyed his orders not to sell rum to the Indians or Dayton's soldiers. Dayton reported about Armstrong that "the Indians he has frequently made drunk and from one he took a gun for a gallon of rum."³⁹

On the evening of September 28, two Oneida runners came to the fort "with the war whoop" to report that Sir John Johnson had arrived at Oswego the previous Thursday with a large force. Sughagearat (White Skin), an Oneida sachem, believed that even though several previous reports had proved false, this intelligence was to be trusted. In his opinion, enemy parties would soon arrive along the Mohawk River and disrupt communication to adjacent areas. Dayton asked for Schuyler's orders on maintaining established expectations and providing the two runners with provisions. He noted that messengers and parties of Oneidas frequently came to the fort, who, following Haudenosaunee diplomatic traditions, "undoubtedly expect we should find them provision."⁴⁰

After occupying and working to restore Fort Stanwix for just about three months, Dayton received orders on October 12 to leave the Mohawk Valley and march for Fort Ticonderoga to reinforce the northern army retreating from Canada and pursued by British forces under Sir Guy Carleton. Colonel Samuel Elmore's regiment at German Flats would replace the 3rd New Jersey Regiment at Fort Stanwix over the course of several days, beginning October 13, 1776. That event was so important to Private Samuel Benjamin that he could still remember the exact date in his old age.⁴¹ Elmore's regiment included about 350 privates, and, as with Dayton's, its manpower would be split between Fort Stanwix, Fort Dayton, German Flats, and Johnstown to secure those locations. Also, because Fort Stanwix could not accommodate them all satisfactorily, only about two hundred men would be quartered there.⁴² Colonel Elmore himself arrived on October 16, and Dayton's regiment marched out on October 20 for Schenectady and then on to Fort Ticonderoga.⁴³

Captain Bloomfield turned twenty-three years old on October 18, just two days before the regiment marched from Fort Stanwix. He reminiscently noted in his journal: "This day twelve months [ago] I was engaged in my profession of the law enjoying the calm sunshine of a peaceable quiet & easy life. Now I am 500 miles from my native place amongst strangers & exposed to all the hardships & fatigues of a soldier's life, no ways settled not knowing where I may be destined next week. Being wet & rainy (as it has been these four days past) stayed at my lodgings."[44]

Dayton's regiment had struggled to improve the fort's defenses as much as they could, considering the difficulties encountered in their situation. Now they would move on, and another recently formed regiment would take up the restoration work and defense of Fort Stanwix.

CHAPTER 3

Elmore's Regiment Relieves the 3rd New Jersey Regiment

October 1776–May 1777

On August 16, 1776, General Schuyler reported to Washington that Colonel Samuel Elmore's regiment was at Albany, but the men refused to march from the town until they were paid and provided with other necessities. While he could pay them, the other items were not available.[1] Schuyler reported more positively, although again overoptimistically, that "the works at Fort Stanwix are going on with great expedition."[2]

Captain Bloomfield and the rest of Dayton's troops departed Fort Stanwix and Colonel Samuel Elmore's regiment entered to replace them. Fifty-six-year-old Elmore was born in Norwalk, Connecticut, on January 19, 1720, and was a farmer in Sharon when he entered military service. He had served as a captain and company commander in the 3rd Connecticut Regiment during the French and Indian War. In the current conflict, he was commissioned on May 1, 1775, as major in Colonel Benjamin Hinman's 4th Connecticut Regiment and served at Ticonderoga and Crown Point. During the winter of 1775–76, he served as lieutenant colonel for Colonel David Wooster's short-term provisional regiment.[3]

Elmore was commissioned colonel on April 15, 1776, to command one of the several second establishment one-year regiments that Congress had authorized on January 8 to be raised from troops then serving in Canada, and to be assigned to the Canadian Department. Recruiting for Elmore's regiment did not begin immediately and once underway progressed very slowly. Recruits did not begin to materialize until April 15 at Quebec and other locations for this Continental regiment credited to Connecticut, although containing officers and enlisted men from Connecticut, Massachusetts, and New York. This diversity coincided with Washington's desire to mix officers and men from several states in the same regiment to help develop loyalty to the full confederation of colonies. That desire had been crushed when it was found to be very unpopular except in cases like this one, where scarce recruits came mostly from regiments at the end of their enlistments and then from several contiguous states.[4] This unusual characteristic created confusion, however, and the recruits were often not sure about their regiment's official status. Most of them understood it was a Continental line regiment, but some thought it was a provincial regiment; various soldiers identified themselves as being in a Connecticut regiment, others in a Massachusetts regiment, and still others in a New York one.

As desired, some men did enlist in Canada. Samuel Doty received his discharge from Colonel Goose Van Schaick's 1st New York Regiment at Albany on April 15 and reenlisted in Captain Lathrop Allen's company of Elmore's regiment. After serving in Canada under Colonel Goose Van Schaick and then General David Wooster, James Dole reenlisted in Canada, following his captain, Theodore Woodbridge, into Elmore's regiment. He remained at Quebec until May 6, when the entire army was forced to retreat south.[5]

Outside Canada, men enlisted in Connecticut, since this was regarded as a Connecticut regiment. One man, Abner Cable, enlisted during April in Captain Robert Walker's company for one year, recalling later that his lieutenant, James Hughes, was a British deserter.[6] Enlistment efforts continued into May. Twenty-one-year-old Samuel Benjamin enlisted on May 1, at Hartland, Connecticut, joining up because, he said later, he had heard "it was deemed necessary to defend the northern frontiers of the then colonies, & that a regiment should be raised & organized for that purpose, and to serve one year."[7] His motivation may have been to protect the colonies from British soldiers and their allies rather than to fight for the ideals of the Revolution.

Men who enlisted in New York and Massachusetts included Jabesh Gray, who enlisted at Canaan, New York, on April 15 in Captain Allen's company,[8] and Samuel Couch, who enlisted at Sandisfield, Massachusetts, in Captain Joel Dickinson's company in May or June. Both men enlisted for one year.[9]

From wherever he enlisted, each recruit marched to Albany to join the assembling regiment. Abijah Lewis, who enlisted for one year on April 15, remembered marching to Albany after enlisting and being "mustered before General Schuyler."[10] Austin Wells enlisted on April 15 in Captain Woodbridge's company and joined it at Sheffield, Massachusetts, before marching directly to Albany, where the regiment was stationed at the Barracks on the Hill.[11]

Noting its slow building process, Washington was unimpressed with Elmore's regiment. He wrote to General Schuyler on June 17: "Congress imagined that two regiments could be raised for this campaigns service out of the corps that served last winter in Canada, I very early gave them my opinion that it was impracticable[.] I wish I had been mistaken." The officers in Canada disapproved Washington's suggestions regarding which men to commission as the regimental officers. Therefore Washington left it up to General Wooster and his officers to appoint them, and they chose Elmore to command one of the regiments. Washington was skeptical about the overall quality of the new regiment. He heard that the full regiment had left Canada but had not received any report of how many men it had enlisted. Only about nineteen or twenty men were reported to have recently gone to Fort Ticonderoga under Captain Robert Cochran, and he satirically criticized the enlistment of these few men as being "the Mighty Work of several recruiting officers of Elmore's Regiment who have had large sums advanced them so early as the month of February for the recruiting service." Other officers of the regiment had applied to him for recruiting money too, "but as I neither knew them, nor by whose leave they came from Canada, I did not chuse to risk any more." Washington did plan to order Elmore to New York City, "not that I expect any considerable good will result from it," and suggested it might be better to break up the regiment and reassign "such of the officers as are proper to be employed."[12]

Elmore's Regiment received orders at Albany on August 1 to join Washington's army at the city of New York. The men boarded four sloops that set sail down the North (Hudson) River toward New York, but then received new orders to return to Albany and the barracks.[13] Washington felt that coming from so far away, they would not be able to get to New York in time to help him there.

On August 25, the regiment marched to Schenectady, then Johnstown, and then German Flats, where they found Colonel Dayton's regiment constructing Fort Dayton. They helped complete it and also built barracks for the troops that would occupy the fort.[14] Elmore's regiment replaced Dayton's at Fort Stanwix toward the end of October, but some men remained at Fort Dayton until November engaged in scouts, keeping guard, and constructing a picket fort, along with ordinary camp duty. While stationed at Fort Stanwix, most men simply performed general duties, like Private Austin Wells, who later recalled being engaged in scouts and garrison duties while at Fort Stanwix.[15]

Several men long remembered being assigned to specific duties. Jabesh Gray had enlisted at Canaan, New York, on April 15 for one year in Captain Allen's company. During the winter, Major Cochran ordered him to serve as one of the bodyguards for local militia brigadier general Nicholas Herkimer near Little Falls in the town of Canajoharie.[16] Nathaniel Root served as steward for the hospital and for a time was quite sick himself, receiving a discharge in February 1777.[17]

On November 19, Schuyler wrote to inform Congress, "I shall order to the value of about fifteen hundred pounds, in Indian goods, to Fort Stanwix, to be there disposed of at such a price as to give no umbrage to the Indians."[18] Clearly these goods were not gifts but items to be traded to the Indians, hopefully at prices attractive to them. Perhaps a local fur trader, such as the Frenchman Stephen Delyrod, or a designated garrison officer, would act as the fort's trade agent. Mohawk River Valley leaders William Johnson and Jelles Fonda had established fur trade operations in the early 1770s, including Delyrod's at the Carry.[19]

As the year ended, the Continental Army, very short of recruits, sought veterans to reenlist while it went through the transition from its second establishment to its third. Whereas the second establishment enlistments generally had been for one year, the new third establishment regiments required three-year or duration of the war commitments. Though enlistments in many current regiments expired at the end of December, Elmore's regiment would continue in service for an additional four months as a result of its long delay in starting to organize. In addition, Congress had authorized men in second establishment regiments to reenlist into third establishment units before their enlistment expired. Therefore, while suffering the usual losses to disease, combat, and desertion, in December and January, Elmore's regiment also lost men persuaded by eager recruiting officers to reenlist early into third establishment regiments.

CHAPTER 3

Major Robert Cochran of Elmore's regiment was chosen in November to serve as major in the third establishment 3rd New York Regiment, to be commanded by Colonel Peter Gansevoort, so he too would leave the regiment early. Cochran was born in Colrain, Massachusetts, in March 1738 and at various times lived in Bennington, Rupert, and Rutland, Vermont. A Private Robert Cochran served in 1764 in Captain John Fassett's company of Vermont militia, and a Captain Robert Cochran commanded a Connecticut company under Benedict Arnold at Crown Point. Then a Robert Cochran entered Colonel Elmore's regiment, credited to Connecticut, as a captain on April 15, 1776, and was the captain noted by Washington to be with a few of Elmore's men at Fort Ticonderoga. Cochran was promoted to major in Elmore's regiment on July 25, and several months later was selected as the 3rd New York Regiment's major on November 21, 1776.[20] Assuming, as is likely, that all these men are the same Robert Cochran, he brought a varied and substantial military background to Elmore's regiment.[21]

Accepting his commission in Gansevoort's regiment, the talented and aggressive Cochran became active in its recruiting efforts. Ironically, Colonel Gansevoort informed Cochran in a December letter that he had sent newly commissioned Captain Aaron Aorson to Fort Stanwix to recruit men in that neighborhood.[22] Since Cochran knew Elmore's regiment very well, Gansevoort was sending him to assist Aorson. Cochran had spent time at various places in the area while serving with Elmore in the western Mohawk River Valley, so he knew not only current soldiers who could be encouraged to reenlist in the 3rd New York Regiment but also civilian men in the area who could be recruited. Indicative of the communication problems of that time, Gansevoort had not yet heard whether Cochran had accepted his appointment to the regiment, so he wrote again requesting confirmation from him.[23]

While competing with other regiments seeking recruits or reenlistments for the 1777 Continentals, Aorson and Cochran recruited some men from Elmore's regiment for the 3rd New York. A muster roll of Elmore's nine companies dated April 1776 to January 1777 shows several companies stationed at Fort Dayton and others at Fort Schuyler. Interestingly, Fort Schuyler is further identified on the muster roll as "alias Fort Stanwix." At least a dozen men are marked as reenlisted with Captain Aorson in December and January. Other men on the muster not identified as recruited by Aorson also show up around the same time in his company. One of these men was Henry Bass, who enlisted

December 1, 1776, for the duration of the war. Bass's original name was Henry Curtis. He emigrated to Great Britain from Germany in 1773. The British navy pressed him into service, and when the man-o'-war he had been assigned to lay in Boston Harbor in 1774, Henry found a way to desert and changed his name to Henry Bass. He stated in his later pension application that he enlisted at Fort Stanwix; he did not mention Fort Schuyler.[24]

Another man enlisting in Aorson's company on December 24, for three years, was Jonathan Hunter, about thirty-six years old, who brought one year of experience as a private in Van Schaick's 1st New York Regiment. Colonel Gansevoort described Hunter in his 1780 discharge as being forty years old, five feet, ten inches tall, with a light complexion, light hair, and gray eyes. He was a carpenter by trade, skills that made him especially helpful when working during fatigue duty on the Fort Stanwix restoration.[25]

Other regiments competed with Aorson for signing reenlistment recruits. James Warren of Sharon, Connecticut, about eighteen years old, enlisted for three years in Colonel James Livingston's regiment, called the Canadian Regiment. He had enlisted in Captain Woodbridge's company for nine months in June 1776 and served at Fort Stanwix until January 1777.[26]

An artillery detachment led by Captain Lieutenant Joseph Savage was being raised in January and would be stationed at Fort Stanwix. This detachment consisted of about half of Captain Robert Walker's company of Colonel John Lamb's third establishment 2nd Continental Artillery Regiment, forming that January at multiple locations.[27] Savage held the designation of captain lieutenant while commanding the Walker company detachment. Lieutenant James Furnivall of Massachusetts had originally recruited many of the men, and they were not happy that he left when the less popular Savage took command of the detachment.[28]

As Savage's detachment organized, it obtained recruits from Elmore's Regiment.[29] Several surviving musters show that besides Savage, the detachment consisted of a second lieutenant, three sergeants, three corporals, three bombardiers, three gunners, a drummer, and about thirteen to seventeen matrosses. Bombardiers tended the exploding shells fired by mortars and howitzers. Matrosses ranked just below and assisted the gunners in loading, firing, and sponging the guns. They also were issued muskets to act as guards. This detachment might seem inadequate for a fort expected to mount many heavy artillery pieces for its defense. At the time of the August siege, however, the fort had just four 9-pounders and four 6-pounders mounted on garrison carriages, and two 3-pounder fieldpieces on traveling carriages.[30] Cannons were identified by the weight of the cannonball they fired. For example, a 9-pounder fired a cannonball weighing nine pounds.

Throughout this time, in continuing his efforts to keep the Oneidas either neutral or actively supporting the Revolutionary cause, General Schuyler struggled to maintain the fort as a trading post. Reverend Kirkland, who resided at the fort, reported to General Schuyler in mid-January just how pleased the Oneidas were that the trading post had been opened. As he put it, "They pour in by Shoals." Kirkland also made sure that he enthusiastically reported to the Oneidas about the victories of Washington at Trenton and Princeton, pleasing them so much that they cheered and shouted, in addition to firing off shots in celebration. Kirkland even approved when Schuyler presented them with six barrels of rum, though the clergyman had been doing all he could to persuade the Indians not to drink alcohol.[31]

While losing men reenlisting in other units and sending out scouting parties, Elmore's disintegrating regiment continued the fort's restoration work as best they could, supervised by Major Hubbell. That did not progress rapidly, however, and on December 28, the frustrated Continental Congress resolved to strengthen Fort Stanwix, ordering everyone involved, especially the engineer, quartermaster, and commissary departments, to do whatever was necessary to accomplish the work.[32]

Then, in mid-March 1777, the French engineer Captain Bernard Moissac de Lamarquise, serving with the Continental Army, became very interested in the restoration efforts at Fort Stanwix and submitted to General Schuyler a plan to rebuild the fort. Lamarquise had served with the Continentals in the Canadian campaign and, more recently, at Fort Ticonderoga and Mount Independence, standing across from each other on opposite shores of Lake Champlain. He had developed a plan to construct a Vauban-style square fort on Mount Independence very similar to Fort Schuyler in layout.[33] A higher-ranking and more experienced Continental engineer, Colonel Jeduthan Baldwin, who had arrived at Ticonderoga on February 24, replaced the Frenchman. Grasping for ways to speed things up, General Schuyler accepted Lamarquise's plan and put him in charge of the Fort Stanwix restoration, apparently having lost confidence in Major Hubbell, who remained at the fort to assist him.[34]

Although preferring to remain neutral in the conflict between the Patriots and the British, the Oneidas understood that they could not avoid the conflict and that their territory would experience enemy raids. Helping the Americans could help them defend their villages.[35] Now, in early 1777, word began to spread that the British, under a plan submitted by General John Burgoyne, could be expected to invade New York as part of an effort to split the colonies along the Hudson River–Lake Champlain divide. That three-part plan included sending a force from Oswego on Lake Ontario across the vital New York transportation route, including the Oneida Carry, to bring them to Albany.

In mid-March 1777, friendly Oneidas began a regular watch along the St. Lawrence River to keep an eye on developments that might threaten Fort Stanwix. They also scouted the nearby area on the approach to the fort to detect any small bands of Indians sent out to observe or harass the environs of the fort. That strong, eloquent supporter of the ideals of the American cause, Oneida blacksmith Thomas Spencer, proved to be one of the best scouts. He contributed so effectively that a Mohawk band loyal to Britain tried unsuccessfully to kidnap him, along with the very active and influential Presbyterian missionary Samuel Kirkland.[36]

An immediate obstacle to progress at Fort Stanwix was that the remaining enlistments of Elmore's shrinking regiment would expire in mid-April. Therefore in mid-March, General Schuyler ordered Colonel Peter Gansevoort to bring his still organizing 3rd New York Regiment to the fort and relieve Elmore's troops. As we have seen, each of the first two Continental Army regiments and the artillery company sent to garrison the fort had been recently formed and seen little or no action. The men in Dayton's and Elmore's regiments had occupied the fort for only about three and seven months respectively, suffering the anxiety of a possible imminent attack while serving out brief one-year enlistments.

Next we will examine Colonel Gansevoort's regiment to understand its condition upon arriving to defend the fort. The 3rd New York Regiment was destined to serve at the fort for about eighteen months, constantly threatened by enemy action, including enduring the pivotal three-week siege, while enlisted for a minimum of three years or the remainder of the war. As we have also seen, during its first two months, in December and January, this brand-new regiment had even sought recruits from Colonel Elmore's regiment. To fully understand this new regiment, destined to arrive at the fort in April and May and defend it in August, it is important to understand its origins and early development as well as the background, the skills, and even the personalities of its officers and men. It is one thing to know a regiment by its official title, commander's name, and legislated personnel strength. But a regiment is not a piece on a game board. It consists of several hundred unique and constantly changing individuals working together, more or less willingly and skillfully, in a common cause.

Chapter 4

Creating a Third Establishment 3rd New York Regiment

September–November 1776

Shortly after November 21, 1776, tired thirty-nine-year-old Continental Army lieutenant Henry Tiebout, serving in the 1st New York Regiment and camped at North Castle, near White Plains, New York, proudly learned that he had been offered one of the eight captain's commissions in the recently authorized 3rd New York Regiment being raised for the army's third establishment. While many of his fellow officers would not be selected for service in those regiments and would leave the army, Henry had proved himself qualified through his abilities and actions. His promotion was not just the result of knowing the right people.[1] At the time Henry received word of his commission, the other men selected as officers for the 3rd New York also learned of their assignments. All of them had been involved in the cause for some time and brought a variety of experiences to their new positions. Their joint challenge was now to build their new regiment into a cohesive unit prepared for whatever duty those in authority would order it to serve. They probably expected, however, that they would engage in open field combat as part of a group of regiments fighting together, rather than undertake the isolated defense of the frontier Fort Stanwix.

By the fall of 1776, the War for Independence, recently declared in July, was in serious trouble. The British army had pretty much had its way during the summer and fall campaign around New York City and

Westchester County, while the Continental Army became greatly diminished in numbers due to military action, disease, desertion, and enlistment expiration. To compound matters, most remaining enlistments would expire in about six weeks.

To keep an army in the field, Washington had persuaded Congress in September to raise a third establishment of the Continental Army, this time consisting of men enlisted to serve until the end of the war, however long it should last. The reasonable fear of a professional standing army, available to those in power who could use it to run roughshod over the populace, made obtaining congressional action a difficult task. Yet Washington persisted, and on September 16, 1776, while the army was at Harlem Heights on Manhattan Island, with just over three months left on its enlistments, the Continental Congress resolved that eighty-eight regiments, including four from New York, should be raised "as soon as possible, to serve during the present war."[2] No more short-term enlistments: the new version of the 3rd New York would be one of those long-term regiments.

The Continental Congress resolved that the new regiments would contain eight companies, each consisting of ninety officers and men, making a total of 720 men in the regiment. The regimental field and staff officers brought the total up to 728 officers and men in the full regiment. Each company would contain four commissioned officers (a captain, first lieutenant, second lieutenant, and ensign), six noncommissioned officers (three sergeants and three corporals), two musicians (a drummer and a fifer), and seventy-eight privates. The New York Convention appointed the commissioned officers for the New York regiments, who would then recruit all the noncommissioned officers, musicians, and privates. Each of the eight captains would have to build his company from scratch, not inherit it.

Washington hoped to persuade veterans, who had already endured much suffering, to reenlist in one of the new regiments. One way to motivate these men would be to assure them that they would serve under highly competent and respected officers. Washington, along with many other people, had been very disappointed with the quality of the officers serving in his first and second establishment armies and wanted to make sure that only the best current officers received commissions in the third establishment.

To command the new regiment, Congress appointed the newly promoted twenty-eight-year-old Colonel Peter Gansevoort, presently in command of Fort George at the southern end of Lake George.

Gansevoort belonged to the third generation of an influential Dutch family of prominent Albany brewers and merchants and spoke with the remnants of a Dutch accent. Not much is known about his early life in Albany, but he began his military career when he obtained a commission as a lieutenant in the Albany County militia on May 4, 1775, and though lacking the experience of many older officers, he proved that he possessed good leadership qualities.[3] This, combined with his connections to other influential New York families, helped him obtain a commission on June 30, 1775, as major in the first establishment 2nd New York Regiment, commanded by his future brother-in-law Colonel Goose Van Schaick.

Gansevoort led much of the regiment north with General Richard Montgomery's forces during the invasion of Quebec and commanded it during the taking of Fort St. Jean and then Fort Chambly. This service acquainted him with the problems of the young Continental Army and the complex, frustrating problems faced by officers in their efforts to train and properly equip their men. While participating in the attacks on Montreal, he became quite ill and, during the follow-up advance on Quebec City, was reduced to being carried on a stretcher by the time the force reached Trois-Rivières.

After spending the winter in Montreal recovering from his illness, when the invasion of Canada fell apart in the spring, Gansevoort retreated south in the fighting withdrawal that stopped the British advance at Lake Champlain. At the end of the year, he continued serving in what became the second establishment of the 2nd New York Regiment. Promoted to lieutenant colonel on March 19, 1776, he was assigned in June by General Schuyler to command Fort George, near the site of the French and Indian War massacre at the surrender of Fort William Henry.[4]

His time at Fort George became contentious when his commander, Major General Horatio Gates, questioned his ability to command and satisfactorily comply with the orders of his superiors.[5] Gates, twenty years older than Gansevoort, had served most of his adult life in North America as a British army officer. After the Seven Years' War, in 1772 Gates left England and came to Virginia to settle. When the war broke out, he became a major general and was considered one of the best administrators in the Continental Army.[6] Gates considered himself superior to less experienced Dutch colonials such as Gansevoort and General Philip Schuyler. Unlike them, Horatio Gates was born of working-class parents in Maldon, Essex, England, in 1727. The conflict with Gates was aggravated by Gansevoort's close Albany family association with General Schuyler, whom Gates hoped to supersede as commander of the Northern Department of the army. The interpersonal conflict, however, did not derail Gansevoort's promotion to colonel of the 3rd New York Regiment on November 21, 1776.[7]

So far in his career, Gansevoort had gained valuable experience dealing with many of the same problems that he would encounter at Fort Stanwix, except for defending against a siege. In addition to facing supply problems, desertions, illness, difficulty communicating with higher authority, and negotiations with Indigenous people, he had also dealt with fort construction and repair problems like those he would soon encounter at Fort Stanwix.[8]

Men enlisting in the 3rd New York Regiment came to highly respect and like their commander. Gansevoort's granddaughter Catherine Gansevoort Lansing would later record that with his "somewhat florid complexion," his deep gray eyes highlighting strong and prominent features, and his standing over six feet tall, with a chest measuring forty-six inches and a waist forty-three inches, Gansevoort projected a commanding presence. She also noted his lighter side, pointing out that he "was wont to say jocosely that he 'had not a single tooth in his head,' a statement quite in accordance with the facts as every tooth of his was a double tooth." Another appealing characteristic was his love of both listening to and playing music.[9]

Gansevoort's second-in-command would be the newly promoted thirty-seven-year-old Lieutenant Colonel Marinus Willett, born on Long Island into a family of blended English and Dutch heritage. His father worked as a teacher, then operated a ferry between New York City and Long Island, and then kept a tavern in the city.[10] As a youth, Marinus obtained some schooling while also learning and practicing the trade of cabinetmaking. As a sixteen-year-old youth he was shocked to observe a British press-gang forcing men into service in the Royal Navy against their will. This distressing scene left an indelible mark on him that contributed to his determined opposition to British rule.[11]

Willett began military service during the French and Indian War as an eighteen-year-old lieutenant in the provincial militia. After participating in the disastrous attack on Fort Ticonderoga, he then served in the successful capture of Fort Frontenac in August 1758 (coincident with the beginning of construction on Fort Stanwix). He became very ill at the fort, but recovered enough to return home in December 1758, only to learn that his older brother Isaac had been lost at sea while serving on a British privateer.[12]

Willett resumed working as a cabinetmaker and conducting auctions at his New York store. At the age of twenty, he married Mary Pearsee, the daughter of a fellow cabinetmaker.[13] He placed a newspaper ad in 1772 promoting his shop at "the upper end of Maiden Lane, near the Oswego Market," where he held auctions and also had available for "private Sale, at all Times, on very short Notice, Cabinet and Chair Work of all Sorts, made in the best and neatest Manner."[14] By May 1774, he was serving customers at two locations and advertised that "there is on hand at either of the above places an assortment of choice mahogany furniture."[15]

While doing well as a cabinetmaker and merchant, during the developing Revolutionary movement Willett also proved to be a significant rabble-rouser and street fighter, one given to intimidation rather than philosophical discussion of issues. A large, fearless, articulate, and zealous man, he projected leadership physically. He had a tall, finely proportioned, commanding figure, giving him, like Colonel Gansevoort, the immediate air of a military man. His handsome face with its blue eyes and pleasing countenance combined with kind manners to make him stand out in a group as a gentleman. He hated all forms of dishonesty and sham, and came across as blunt, plain, and outspoken, fearing nothing. Although "only" a mechanic rather than a learned thinker, he could be very persuasive.[16]

Active in protests during the turbulent 1760s and early 1770s, Willett joined the Sons of Liberty in New York City, earning a reputation as a dynamic leader in the mob protests.[17] He served as a lieutenant in a volunteer militia company and on April 23, 1775, shortly after the events at Lexington and Concord, participated in an attack on the city arsenal.[18]

Perhaps his most famous protest action occurred on June 6, 1775. The small British garrison at New York had been given permission to join the troops at Boston. Except for each man's musket and equipment, however, all other arms and military stores were to be left in New York.[19] Willett confronted a detachment of British soldiers attempting to remove five wagonloads of muskets to be hoisted onto HMS *Asia*. He reputedly grabbed the lead British horse, encouraged a crowd to gather, stopped the soldiers from taking the muskets, and even persuaded one soldier to desert to the American cause.[20] Patriot authorities would later use those muskets to arm the first regiment raised by New York State.[21]

CHAPTER 4

On June 28, 1775, Willett received a captain's commission in Colonel Alexander McDougall's first establishment 1st New York Regiment and participated in the invasion of Canada, earning General Schuyler's commendation for acting "with remarkable attention and propriety."[22] Continuing his service in a second establishment regiment, Willett fought in the September and October 1776 battles around New York before receiving his lieutenant colonel's commission in the 3rd New York Regiment in November. A decade older than his new colonel, Willett brought complementary experiences and leadership skills that would inspire his troops.

The third-ranking field officer would be Major Robert Cochran, another highly respected and experienced officer whom we met previously serving as major in Colonel Elmore's regiment at Forts Dayton and Stanwix when he agreed to accept his commission as major in the 3rd New York Regiment. Like Willett, he was not from a powerful family, but from his previous experience and his personality, skills, and energy, he had demonstrated the high-level officer qualities Washington sought for the third establishment of the Continental Army.

To successfully carry out the orders of these three regimental field officers while maintaining a cohesive and motivated group of enlisted men, the individual captains commanding the eight companies in the regiment would be crucial leaders. Washington was especially pushing to raise the quality of company captains as well as the lieutenants and ensigns who would be their subordinates.

To help ensure that only high-quality officers would be commissioned, on October 15 the New York Convention of Representatives, the transitional government operating after the Declaration of Independence until the April 1777 adoption of the New York State Constitution, sent a committee to each second establishment New York regiment. Each committee asked the regimental colonel to rate his subordinate officers. For example, Colonel McDougall did not hesitate to clearly state the good and bad qualities of his individual officers, and unhesitatingly judged Lieutenant Henry Tiebout to be "a good officer; fit to take charge of a company," that is, to be promoted to captain.[23] When Colonel Lewis Du Bois rated his regiment's officers, he judged Captain Elias Van Bunschoten to be "an active, brave" officer.[24] Both of these men would soon be among those selected as captains for the 3rd New York Regiment.

On November 15, 1776, the Committee of Arrangements of the New York Convention, charged with appointing New York's third establishment Continental Army officers, met at Fishkill to review the reports on the character and merits of the officers recommended for commissions and commissioned those they selected on November 21.[25] They assigned each selected captain a number between one and eight to identify his seniority among his regiment's eight captains. Companies would be listed in order of their captain's seniority and known officially by those numbers. Because companies were commonly identified by their captain's name, the captain's reputation was a very important motivator for his men to serve in their company with pride.

The eight captains appointed to the 3rd New York Regiment brought a variety of experiences in the Revolutionary movement. Several had experienced military service during the French and Indian War, while others had participated in the protest events leading up to the War for Independence and served in the colonial militia. Future captain Henry Tiebout had previously served as second lieutenant in a New York volunteer militia company known as the Prussian Blues and enthusiastically signed a petition stating that it was a "matter of the utmost consequence to the Liberties of America, that every member of the community capable of bearing arms should acquaint himself with Military Discipline, in order (if possible) to avert the distresses which are now hanging over them."[26]

Several of the new captains had served in the first establishment 1st or 3rd New York Regiment with General Richard Montgomery on his 1775 Canadian expedition and gained experience attacking enemy fortifications. Several more men had continued service in the second establishment of the 3rd New York Regiment and served in the 1776 Canadian campaign. Several others had served in the second establishment 1st New York Regiment, and on July 9, 1776, future 3rd New York Regiment captains Lieutenants Henry Tiebout, Leonard Bleeker,[27] and Cornelius Jansen[28] stood with their men of the 1st New York Regiment and heard the Declaration of Independence read in New York City. After the reading, the large, emotionally aroused crowd then toppled the gold-plated lead statue of King George III standing nearby, and these lieutenants no doubt got caught up in that high-spirited incident.

The 1st New York Regiment did not see much action in the summer and fall New York campaign until the Battle of White Plains on October 28, in which they found themselves in the thick of things on Chatterton's

Hill. There, according to Brigadier General Rufus Putnam: "The British in their advance were twice repulsed; at length, however, their numbers were increased, so that they were able to turn our right flank. We lost many men, but from information afterwards received there was reason to believe they lost many more than we. The rail and stone fence, behind which our troops were posted, proved as fatal to the British as the rail fence and grass hung on it did [at Bunker Hill]."[29]

Their second establishment commissions had not expired, and fighting continued, but these officers would need to leave their current posts and commence building the third establishment regiment scheduled to become part of Washington's main active force in the new year.

Chapter 5

Recruiting and Training the 3rd New York Regiment

December 1776–March 1777

Who were potential recruits for the 3rd New York Regiment?[1] The first soldiers to confront British troops in 1775 had been New England militiamen, including minutemen responding at Lexington and Concord, who then besieged Boston. These men were true citizen-soldiers, generally middle-class farmers and tradesmen fighting to protest British policies and actions. But they were part-time soldiers and did not expect to become involved in a long war. The highly motivated men who had served in the full-time first and second Continental Army establishments had experienced hardships, illness, defeats, and casualties in battle, and many became confronted by the need to return to, and stay with, their families, farms, and trades to maintain subsistence. Many also felt that the Continental Congress and their provincial, then state, governments had not fulfilled their part of the contract to supply enlistees with adequate food, clothing, equipment, and pay. It was also now clear that Continental Army service required men who did not have other commitments that they would need to abandon to be able to perform full-time military service over a period of years. Many veterans felt that when their enlistment expired, they had done their part for the cause and now it was time for others to step forward. But would they?

Appointing the commissioned officers was only the start to building the regiment. To complete the process, the chosen officers needed to enlist men into their companies and then train them to work together in proper military fashion. We saw earlier that the recruits for Colonel Elmore's second establishment regiment had all marched to Albany, where the full regiment organized over several months before heading west on the Mohawk River. The 3rd New York Regiment would organize at two locations about eighty miles apart, creating a challenge to building a unified, well-trained regiment in which men would feel proud to serve. Colonel Gansevoort took post at Albany to work with Major Cochran and Captain Aorson to recruit men, while Lieutenant Colonel Willett took post at Fishkill to build and train the other companies. Continually sending out company officers to recruit at scattered locations increased the normal difficulties officers experienced in organizing, training, and building cohesive units at both locations.

The captains at Fishkill tried to assemble their subordinate officers as quickly as possible and commence recruiting their companies. To take Captain Tiebout's company as an example, his three newly commissioned subalterns—two lieutenants and one ensign—gradually assembled amid confusion over whether or not some individuals had accepted their commissions and agreed to serve in their assigned companies. Each officer was of course a unique human being with his own personality and life concerns outside his military duties, and each group of officers contained men with a variety of experiences and personalities. Some had previously known one another, while others had not.

Assisting Captain Tiebout was thirty-seven-year-old First Lieutenant Isaac Bogart from Albany, married with two young children, who had previously served as a second lieutenant in the 4th New York Regiment in 1776.[2] Second Lieutenant Thomas McClellan had been commissioned in Captain Thomas De Witt's[3] company on November 21, but then switched to Tiebout's at an unknown date soon after November 26. He had previously served as a second lieutenant beginning in June 1776 in Colonel John Nicholson's Continental regiment.[4] Young twenty-year-old Ensign Christopher Hutton had been recommended for his commission personally by Lieutenant Colonel Willett, his fellow city of New York resident.[5] Hutton had served in Colonel Lasher's New York militia regiment in 1775–76 along with Henry Tiebout and had served in Colonel William Malcolm's New York regiment, "with great credit."[6]

For various reasons, not all the company-level officers arrived rapidly at Fishkill, so company commanders lacked their complete leadership teams needed to recruit and begin training their men. Some officers had not yet even confirmed their acceptance of a commission and willingness to serve, and some were trying to change their assignments. Willett reported from Fishkill on December 10 that First Lieutenant Henry Pawling of Captain De Witt's company and Ensign Samuel English of Captain Jansen's company had unexpectedly joined a different regiment. Willett also noted that it had not yet been possible to contact Second Lieutenant James Blake of Captain James Gregg's[7] company, Lieutenant William Mead of Tiebout's, and Lieutenant Prentice Bowen of Captain Houston's to learn of their plans. Captain Houston himself was a mystery as to his intentions. First Lieutenant Jonathan Persee of Captain Van Bunschoten's company had not responded to inquiries, and Willett believed Persee, who may have been a relative of Willett's wife, did not want to accept his appointment and would not report, although he had not yet formally declined it. A Jonathan Pearsee became a captain in the 4th New York Regiment, so he apparently opted for the higher rank.[8]

Even at the top, the structure of the regiment came together slowly. Colonel Gansevoort wrote to Lieutenant Colonel Willett on December 11, stating that finally he had received official word informing him that Willett had accepted his November 21 appointment as his lieutenant colonel. Along with the letter, Gansevoort sent Willett £1,800 to distribute among his company officers to facilitate recruiting. He asked Willett to inform him by January 1 which officers had accepted or declined any of the money and the number of men recruited by each officer. He also ordered Willett to see that "the officers are kept faithfully to do this business that we may be ready to take the field as early in the spring as may be necessary." As an incentive, Gansevoort ended his letter by noting that the officers recruiting with him "meet with very good Success." They had no idea just where the spring campaign "field" would be or what they would encounter there and certainly did not suspect that they would serve at the isolated frontier Fort Stanwix for a year and a half.[9]

Gansevoort's officers began recruiting during the period of the Revolution proclaimed by Thomas Paine in *The American Crisis* to be "the times that try men's souls," and they often had to deal with the kind of man Paine would label "the summer soldier and the sunshine patriot [who] will, in this crisis, shrink from the service of his country." It was not an easy task for recruiters to find one of the men celebrated by Paine "that stands it now" and "deserves the love and thanks of man and woman" by enlisting.[10] The war appeared to many people on both sides to be nearly over. General Washington was completing his retreat across New Jersey during the final days of November, doggedly pursued by General Lord Cornwallis. That retreating second establishment Continental Army would essentially disintegrate at the end of December when the enlistments of most of its soldiers expired. The second establishment 3rd New York Regiment was part of that retreating army, and it was hoped that men could be recruited from it for the new regiment. Persuading civilians to enlist, or veterans to reenlist, in the regiments being built proved very difficult, given what people had heard about the current army's situation and condition.

When officers went out to recruit, they did not enlist men into the Continental Army, after which the enlistees would go to boot camp and then be assigned to a regiment and company. Instead, men enlisted directly into a company, generally through the efforts of officers from that company or another in the regiment. To build their companies, the captains and their three newly appointed subordinates had to convince men, who frequently had various reasons to hesitate, that serving under them, rather than someone else or not at all, was a good idea. The ultimate reality was that the companies varied in size over time, and none consistently achieved its full complement of privates.

In many ways, companies as well as regiments competed for recruits. In some cases, recruiters might direct a potential recruit to a different company because it offered something more appealing to him, such as containing men he already knew. Recruiting had to be very active, often including drama and drumming, not just setting up a desk where men could fill out paperwork when they came and lined up either drafted or eager to join. Captains who had good acting skills might do much better than more introverted officers. Where interest was lacking, recruiters had to do all they could to stir up a desire to join the army in their company or at least their regiment. Enlisting was an act of faith on the part of the recruit. He had to believe already, or had to have been made to believe, that enlisting would be beneficial either for pursuing his ideals or enriching his life in some way.

While a desire to support the great cause of freedom and independence could motivate enlistment, many men required material incentives, including immediate cash bounties, combined with credible promises of regular pay, decent food, new clothing, and free land after the war. The Continental Congress established that each man enlisting for the duration of the war in third establishment regiments as a noncommissioned officer or private would receive a $20 bounty and qualify for a one-hundred-acre land grant upon the honorable completion of his service. Individual states would be responsible for providing their recruits with arms, clothing (with the cost deducted from the men's pay over several months), and "every necessary."[11] The recruiting officers would soon learn just how effective these incentives to serve the cause were.

Although many officers and certainly some enlisted men were true philosophical "patriots," the reality was that Patriot leaders were hiring an army to fight for them and their ideals. Some economically struggling men enlisted in the hope of a better, more prosperous life after the war.[12] Many recruits considered their enlistment to be an employment contract in which they pledged to serve faithfully for a stated time period in exchange for pay, bonuses, and land, along with the clothing, food, shelter, and equipment necessary to do their job. How would they react when those contracted expectations did not materialize as promised?

Even polished entreaties and material incentives could not always counteract the fears raised when men heard veterans vividly recount extreme horror stories and complain about the hardships, diseases, rigid discipline, defeats, and lack of material support they had suffered. Therefore, recruits entering the third establishment tended to come from poorer groups and to be younger men in their teens or early twenties seeking to prove their manhood, land a paying job, or have an adventure.[13] Unlike somewhat older men who owned land, had a business, or had a growing family, they could afford to make the army their full-time commitment for multiple years.

To help his officers recruit, Willett distributed funds in various amounts, ranging from $160 to $400, based on his confidence in each officer's prospects for successful recruiting. Some money was held back to give to the still absent officers, who, he hoped, would arrive at some point. Captain John Houston was not yet present, even though he had reportedly received £200 from the state treasurer to use for recruiting.[14]

When men could be persuaded to join, some enlisted for the duration of the war, as Congress at first required. When recruiters, however, found men reluctant to enlist for an indefinite length of time, Congress revised the requirement several times in November, first allowing enlistments for a three-year minimum with some of the same bounties as for the entire war. On the one hand, if the war ended in less than three years, soldiers would be paid for the remainder of the three years. On the other hand, if the war stretched beyond that time, the men who had enlisted for three years could leave the army with no repercussions. So the army could still dissolve at some point. Later in the month, orders then stated that a man could enlist for three years, or the entire war. Men enlisting under that combination would have to remain in the army if the war extended beyond three years, but they could be discharged without additional pay if the war ended before three years had expired.[15] These changing and confusing options resulted in many enlistees', and their regimental officers', being unsure about the length of time each man had committed to serve. This would be especially difficult, and contentious, when the war persisted after three years.

Recruiting only initiated the process of building the regiment into a disciplined and cohesive fighting force. The regiment's officers had not yet become a leadership team who knew, understood, and trusted one another. The officers kept running into questions that needed answers. Willett found it necessary to inquire in a late December letter to Gansevoort about the simple matter of what uniform the officers would wear.[16] New enlistees could not be integrated into a fully functioning organization, only into a developing one. Veterans entering the regiment at least had an idea of what they would encounter and what they would need to know, whereas the raw recruits had no idea. Proper facilities to promote unit development were lacking. The recruits assembled for initial training at a rendezvous camp at either Albany or Fishkill. Neither site had an established physical compound designed to house and support them or any accessible warehouse where recruits could draw clothing, muskets, and other equipment. Nor was there a corps of veteran "drill sergeants" organized to train them and help them develop a sense of unit identity—in other words, no basic training or boot camp as we understand it today.

Take Captain Tiebout as an example. Although he did not have his three company subordinates from day one, a nucleus of privates for his company began forming on December 3, when eighteen men enlisted at unrecorded locations. Most were veterans of the second establishment 1st New York Regiment who knew Tiebout and Willett from that service. Several of them had been serving under Lieutenant Tiebout when he received his promotion to captain. One, James Kerr, enlisted for the duration of the war, while others enlisted for one of the other options.[17] In a support deposition for recruit Ichabod Stoddard's 1819 pension application, Tiebout stated that he enlisted Stoddard for three years

RECRUITING AND TRAINING THE 3RD NEW YORK REGIMENT 59

on December 3, 1776, and described him as a twenty-three-year-old blacksmith, standing five feet, seven inches tall with a light complexion, brown hair, and blue eyes.[18] These veterans brought military skills and an understanding of army life and its routines that would be helpful. Nevertheless, they had not all served together in the same company or under the same officers.

To enlist men from outside the army, Willett's recruiting officers circulated to various locations away from Fishkill, but only in New York State. They often signed up men currently serving in local militia companies. Abraham Wright, with one year of militia experience, enlisted in Tiebout's company at Peekskill for three years or the war and was then marched to Fishkill.[19] John Jones, who was possibly a first-time recruit, enlisted for the war. Henry Flinn enlisted for the war but would serve only until January 1781, while Peter Genious enlisted for the war but would desert in June.[20] These men who did not have Continental Army experience would benefit from, or be distracted by, the variety of knowledge, skills, and experiences demonstrated by the veteran nucleus.

Getting men to enlist did not mean they would fulfill their commitment with the regiment. Of the eighteen initial enlistees, five later deserted from the army, and one died of illness just a few months after enlisting. One became a prisoner of war. One advanced to corporal and one to sergeant in Tiebout's company. Three stayed in the army for the war but were transferred to other companies in the regiment before the army disbanded. Just seven of these initial recruits served in Tiebout's company throughout the six and a half years remaining in the war.[21] Almost all the men were from New York, but among the men from other states was recruit Lockard Luce, or Lewis, who came from Somerset County, New Jersey, with no apparent previous service. His widow's deposition in her pension application says that he enlisted in the New York line on December 3, 1776, for three years or the duration of the war in Captain Tiebout's company and spent the entire time under Tiebout.[22]

Turning recruits into a quality fighting force proved a formidable task during that winter. Willett took pains to ensure that the recruits "were drilled and clothed, as well as the situation of things would admit."[23] Recruits entered companies usually just one or two at a time, requiring captains to quickly develop an understanding of each man and help him fit in. Captains needed to determine how much each man knew about soldiering and why he had agreed to enlist. Because of the expected social distance between commissioned officers and enlisted men, much of the work with recruits centered on the noncommissioned officers, although this varied from company to company.

On a cold January 4, 1777, a Tiebout company recruiting party stopping at Rhinebeck, New York, on the Hudson River enlisted Peter Scriber, a local twenty-two-year-old farmhand with some blacksmith training.[24] They marched Scriber the twenty-seven or so miles south to Fishkill, much as Abraham Wright had been marched north the sixteen miles from Peekskill.

Scriber apparently had no previous military experience and had probably not been motivated to join by the very recent military successes at Trenton and Princeton that were renewing and encouraging the Patriot cause. Peter was the grandchild of Palatine German refugees from Europe's religious wars brought by the British to the Hudson River Valley around 1709 to produce naval stores, especially pine tar. When that project failed, many of the Palatine families moved to the Mohawk River Valley, toward the Carrying Place and other locations. Peter's family, however, settled in Rhinebeck, and whether Peter enlisted because he was a confirmed Patriot or was simply a young man seeking adventure or a steady job is unknown.

He had declined to declare himself a strong Patriot when, at age twenty-one, along with other family members, he refused to sign the Continental Association, the protest agreement developed by the Second Continental Congress not to purchase certain British goods.[25] Peter's parents and a brother, uncomfortable with the cause, emigrated to Canada, to the province of Quebec, just over the New York border, where they remained for the rest of their lives. Other extended family members remained in New York and at least tolerated the Patriot cause. This is just one example of how the controversy over how to react to the acts of Parliament split families and communities. Attitudes could also change as a result of new developments or rethinking positions. Allegiances could also switch because of some level of coercion.

Peter had a girlfriend, Clara Van Etten, descended from a Dutch family living in Rhinebeck. Both families belonged to the Reformed Church in Rhinebeck, so Peter and Clara grew up knowing each other. Clara's family also split in their allegiance over the war. Were Peter and Clara of the same mind and supportive of the cause? One thing is certain: Peter was not running away from a disappointing or contentious romantic relationship when he enlisted.[26] History would prove the eternal commitment that young Peter and Clara felt for each other.

The same day Peter signed up, Francis Chambers enlisted in Captain Abraham Swartwout's company,[27] and Abraham Garrison joined what would become Captain Bleeker's company. Chambers would desert two weeks later, while Garrison remained for the duration of the war, just like Peter Scriber.[28]

Scriber was one of the young men and boys totally ignorant of how to conduct themselves as proper soldiers in a professional army. The veterans who had enlisted in Tiebout's company could provide models for him, but those models were very inconsistent, depending on the attitude and experiences of each veteran. While Scriber appears to have been a steady, motivated recruit, this was not true of all the men joining the regiment. For example, some enlisted just for the bounty money and then deserted, often to join another regiment and collect another bounty. Thomas Harrington enlisted for the duration of the war in Tiebout's company on February 3 but deserted the same day, becoming the company's first known deserter. The frequent occurrence of "bounty jumping" caused Gansevoort and Willett to order their recruits to wear a blue or yellow ribbon on their hats until the regiment was fully organized and uniformed.[29] Each of the other seven companies experienced enlistment gains and losses like Tiebout's.

We can picture Peter Scriber and the other recruits for an extended, unspecified term after their enlistments wearing the civilian clothes they had brought from home, but now sporting the pieces of colored cloth in their hats designating them as soldiers. We don't know how soon it was before the recruits were able to dress like soldiers or even how soon each man was issued a musket, since those were also in short supply.

During January, several more recruits joined Tiebout's company,[30] though discouragingly, men were not enlisting in large numbers. Occasionally, recruits would join family members in a company. On January 29, Robert Wilson, about fourteen years old, enlisted as fifer for the company of Captain James Gregg. Wilson had lost his father in 1775, and his mother, along with Robert and his five siblings, had been driven out of New York City when the British landed in July 1776. They relocated to Albany. Robert's mother was Captain Gregg's sister, so it appears that Gregg was taking his nephew under his wing. Throughout his adventurous life, Wilson always "idolized" his uncle.[31]

CHAPTER 5

Willett still did not know by February 7, over two months into the life of the new regiment, whether all his subordinate officers had accepted their appointments. He reported to Colonel Gansevoort that Lieutenant Black of Captain Gregg's company had not reported or communicated in any way. Willett had reported this to the Committee of Arrangement of the New York Convention so that the vacancy could be resolved.[32]

Despite the obstacles he faced, Willett was determined to create a finely tuned professional regiment, ready to take on any difficult assignment. Therefore, Willett made great efforts to fill his men's days with drills and with learning the necessary skills to take care of themselves and whatever muskets and equipment they were given.[33]

Orders repeatedly went out to sergeants and corporals to see that their men appeared in a soldier-like manner in all respects when on parade and to make sure that their men's weapons were in good working order. All of this, of course, assumed the men had been supplied with enough clothing, muskets, and other equipment to be able to present a "soldier-like" appearance. The sergeants and corporals could only do what was possible within the current supply situation. Because it was vital for each soldier to know how to take care of his own musket, these noncommissioned officers had to ensure that their men learned how to clean their muskets and how to disassemble and reassemble them. If any soldier in the company required someone else to clean his weapon for him, his company's noncommissioned officers would be held accountable.[34]

Willett was frustrated by the quantity of necessary items his enlistees lacked. Although there were supplies of clothing, muskets, and other equipment at Fishkill, the actual quantity received by his men, though unclear, was clearly insufficient.[35] When he sent a return, a written report, of the regiment's strength and the state of its equipment to Colonel Gansevoort at Albany on February 7, Willett noted that the regiment lacked a number of pouches, blue and scarlet cloth for the designated regimental blue uniform coats with red facings, white linen, buttons, and belts for holding bayonets and other items. He reported that he would try to purchase blue and scarlet cloth and asked Gansevoort if there was any white lining and buttons at Albany. It was necessary that enough of these items be sent to supply the full regiment, since there was no prospect of getting them at Fishkill, and the old ones were already mostly in very bad shape. Having only one set of clothes that were worn every day resulted in rapid deterioration. At least he did judge whatever muskets he had received to be very good and of the correct caliber for the available musket balls.[36] When Willett requested additional muskets for his regiment from General William MacDougall, the general turned him down on account of insufficient quantities being available.[37]

Frustrated, Willett reached out to General Schuyler for muskets, pointing out not only that it was important to obtain enough arms to train his recruits, but also that having fully armed men and an adequate supply of arms would give him "an even chance with the [other] regiments about here in recruiting."[38] Potential enlistees did not want to join an ill-equipped regiment.

Retaining the men in the army and maintaining proper behavior after their enlistment proved to be a persistent problem. On February 8, John Christy or Christie of Captain Gregg's company deserted and enlisted in Colonel Van Schaick's regiment, a classic case of bounty jumping. When caught, he was court-martialed and received one hundred lashes for desertion and an additional one hundred lashes for then enlisting in another regiment.[39]

A man could be court-martialed for just about any offense and then suffer the penalty designated by the court if found guilty. The court-martial proceeding, either at the general or regimental level, was more like a hearing than a trial. The defendant was tried not by a jury of his peers but rather by a board of usually five officers designated by the officer convening the court-martial, often the regimental colonel for non–death penalty cases. The board of officers acted as both judge and jury. Most verdicts had to be confirmed by the regimental commander. Only death penalty sentences needed to be confirmed by higher authority than the regiment's colonel.[40]

Each captain ordered a sergeant to make a "size roll" for the company and deliver a copy to Adjutant George Sytez, the administrative officer of the regiment, who would combine the information into the regimental size roll. The size roll recorded a variety of information about each man enlisting in the company, including his physical description, and was supposed to be kept up to date and record when men joined or departed the company.[41] Sytez had served as a second lieutenant in the 1st New York Regiment in the Canadian campaign, where Colonel Van Schaick rated him as a "good adjutant, very good."[42]

By February 21, three months into the regiment's life and with the spring campaign approaching, the constant coming and going of officers and men in the still incomplete and ill-equipped regiment had prevented effective training of the recruits in important military skills and behavior. Willett felt it was time to begin exercising—that is, training—the men as a group. The officers organized each company into squads based on performance of the required exercises. The "Grand Squad" consisted of those proving most expert, while the second squad contained those who were merely acceptable. The third, the "Awkward Squad," contained the poorly performing men who required frequent additional drilling by the appointed drill corporal, by "ones, twos, or three at a time either for their uncommon awkwardness or as a punishment for small offences."[43] The winter weather frequently hindered training, just as it did everything else.

Willett wrote to the New York Provincial Congress on March 7 requesting an additional £800 to be used for bounty money. This was probably because by the end of February, frustrated in their recruiting efforts, the regiment's officers had come to believe that potential recruits would enter military service only if offered bounty money.[44]

The regiment was now about four months old and still not completely developed, although it would soon be ordered to depart Fishkill for active duty with other elements of the army. The regiment was still geographically split, too, and neither Gansevoort nor Willett knew what the regiment might be called upon to do in the 1777 campaign. The men who had enlisted in the regiment still wondered just what they had gotten themselves into. They could see that their regiment was still not completely formed and had no definitive duty in prospect. Many must have asked themselves why they had enlisted.

Chapter 6

Preparing to Relieve Elmore's Regiment
March–May 1777

Commenting on the army's incomplete regiments, General Schuyler wrote to Washington on March 25 from Albany that Gansevoort's regiment was "still more deficient." Seven of the eight companies were recruiting at Fishkill. He had ordered the "less than 200 men," probably more like one hundred, raised by Colonel Gansevoort in the Albany area and stationed at Skenesborough and Fort Ann to relieve Colonel Samuel Elmore's regiment at Fort Stanwix. Major Cochran and the recruits taken from Elmore's regiment would soon be returning to familiar territory. Hopefully they had not joined the 3rd New York Regiment to get away from Fort Stanwix. At least they had avoided one winter of duty there. General Schuyler reminded Gansevoort that Elmore's regiment enlistments would expire on April 15, "beyond which not a man of them will remain, even one day" at Fort Stanwix.[1]

Finally, on March 8, Willett received orders to leave the makeshift rendezvous camp at Fishkill on March 12 and march his troops to Fort Constitution, near Peekskill on the Hudson River.[2] The men being raised by Colonel Gansevoort near Albany, however, would not be joining him there.[3] Receiving orders for Fort Constitution duty must have brought conflicting thoughts to Willett as well as his officers and troops. Was this to be a long-term assignment to help garrison the fort?

Would they ever join the main army under General Washington, where the important action would more likely take place?

By March 12 the company commanders had done all that they could to create a core of soldiers that could be expanded and improved through continuous recruiting and training. But none of Willett's companies had yet recruited its full quota of privates, and some were still short of noncommissioned officers and musicians. In an unusual situation, when Tiebout's company departed Fishkill, it contained seven men who would serve together with Tiebout for six and a half years, until the army was dismissed in 1783.[4]

Recruiting continued during the garrisoning of Fort Constitution. At Albany, Colonel Gansevoort received orders to submit a complete regimental return to his superior officer, a virtually impossible task given his geographically divided regiment. To make matters even more difficult, Gansevoort had received orders to take his Albany-based recruits west to Fort Stanwix, increasing their distance from the companies serving with Willett at Fort Constitution. Totally frustrated, Gansevoort wrote to the president of the New York Provincial Congress requesting his regiment be consolidated at one location. In addition to the problems created by recruiting and training issues, Gansevoort knew from Major Cochran that Fort Stanwix needed a great deal of reconstruction work to make it defensible, not to mention habitable for his men, but he did not yet know all the specifics.[5] He might have preferred receiving orders to join Willett at Fort Constitution on the Hudson River, an important waterway, rather than to garrison an isolated frontier outpost on the Mohawk. It would be interesting to know what word picture Cochran painted for him to make the Fort Stanwix prospect seem either attractive or bleak.

Willett's garrison at Fort Constitution continued to change almost daily.[6] William Sears, who had enlisted in Tiebout's company on February 1 for three years, deserted the first day at Peekskill, but three new men enlisted several weeks later on March 16: Warren Roberts, Seth Rowley, and James Steward. Roberts enlisted for three years and would earn a reputation as a good and faithful soldier.[7] Twenty-year-old Rowley, who brought six months of experience with Colonel Heman Swift's Connecticut State Regiment in 1776 at Ticonderoga, also enlisted for three years.[8] Steward enlisted for the war but deserted the next day.[9]

Eighteen-year-old Henry Ritter, with family ties to the Mohawk River Valley, enlisted for the war at Manheim, New York, in Captain Tiebout's company on March 22 but did not join the company immediately. He had previously served in the militia around his home at Manheim and at Fort Ticonderoga, helping to build the floating bridge between the fort and Mount Independence.[10]

Willett's companies got their first taste of combat when the British raided the Continental supply depot at Peekskill just about ten days after they had arrived at Fort Constitution on March 23. Responding to orders from General McDougall, commanding at Peekskill, Willett marched most of his troops out of Fort Constitution to a location outside of town where McDougall had collected his troops. Willett persistently, but unsuccessfully, offered to attack the British picket. McDougall finally, although reluctantly, approved Willett's plan at 4:00 p.m.

As Willett's partially trained men entered their first firefight together, their inexperience glared brightly when they discharged their muskets early at too great a distance. Determinedly Willett pressed them on, ordering his men to fire smartly on the British, and then ordering them to fix bayonets. These actions, combined with the increasing evening darkness that prevented the British from knowing the full size of the attacking force, caused the British to retreat to their main body. The 3rd New York Regiment's first firefight greatly impressed the men who participated in it. Over forty years later, previously inexperienced Jonathan Pinckney of Tiebout's company still recalled being at what he called the "battle of Peekskill."[11]

Willett lost two men killed in the fighting, including David or Daniel Ackerman of Captain Bleeker's company, who had enlisted on January 1, and four or five wounded. For many men, this was the first time they lost a friend or acquaintance to combat wounds. One item captured from the British was a blue camlet cloak, which Captain Swartwout proudly kept as a memento of his first combat action in the 3rd New York Regiment. Or, perhaps thanks to the lack of clothing supplies, he simply needed it. One day that cloak would play an emotionally meaningful role in the life of the regiment.[12]

After this small battle, recruiting continued. Twenty-two-year-old Nicholas Christman enlisted in Tiebout's company for three years on March 30. He knew the Mohawk River area, where the regiment would soon be stationed, and had Palatine refugee ancestry on his father's side, like Peter Scriber and Henry Ritter. His mother was Oneida, so it is likely he was also considered an Oneida, like blacksmith Thomas Spencer. He was a veteran of the Tryon County rangers and had served in the 2nd New York Regiment during the Canadian campaign and the taking of Forts St. John's, Chambly, and Montreal. This was a recruit who brought important attributes and knowledge to the regiment[13]

Manpower changes continued almost daily in the 3rd New York companies. On March 31, Colonel Gansevoort asked the chairman of the Committee of Arrangements of the New York Provincial Congress to promote Ensign William Colbrath and commission him as a lieutenant. Gansevoort described Colbrath as a very capable officer who had previously held the rank of lieutenant in Colonel John Nicholson's regiment, which later became the 5th New York Regiment. Colbrath would keep, or be credited for keeping, an important journal during the August siege.[14] The same day, Gansevoort had to report that he had been unable to gather all the required information to write up a complete return of the number of men in his regiment, as requested several weeks earlier.[15]

By the end of the month, according to surviving records, Tiebout's company had only about thirty-four men, still some forty-four privates short of its authorized company strength. Other companies ranged between nineteen and sixty-six men, with most in the twenties and thirties. In addition, there were still spot shortages of noncommissioned officers and musicians throughout the companies.[16]

Willett and Gansevoort still wondered when they would be able to unite their regiment and whether that union would take place at Fort Stanwix, where the troops with Gansevoort had been ordered. These men, and perhaps those they commanded, wanted to contribute to winning the cause by taking on a main British force while being led by their commander in chief rather than just exist in the army at some backwater outpost conducting drills.

Part II

The 3rd New York Regiment Prepares for a Siege

CHAPTER 7

First Elements of the 3rd New York Regiment Arrive at Fort Stanwix

April 1777

April 15, 1777, proved to be a difficult day for Colonel Elmore and his officers and men at Fort Stanwix. No units from Colonel Gansevoort's 3rd New York Regiment had arrived yet to relieve them, and it was the final day of their enlistments. A dispute arose among Elmore's officers and soldiers as to whether their one-year enlistment allowed them to leave that day or if they had to serve the full day and not leave until April 16. The soldiers insisted that they could leave during the day on April 15. Because their relief force had not yet arrived, however, their officers insisted that they stay at least through the following day and requested that they volunteer to remain several additional days to facilitate the transition. Some men did extend their enlistments, including Samuel Benjamin, who volunteered to stay five or six additional days. Simeon Blin, about twenty-one years old, apparently made the same commitment and was discharged on April 20 at Fort Stanwix. Major Cochran did not show up on April 16 either, but Elmore discharged some men on the morning of the seventeenth. Cochran finally reached the fort later that day, bringing only a modest detachment of 3rd New York Regiment soldiers.[1]

As April began, Lieutenant Colonel Willett had not yet received orders to depart Fort Constitution, so he maintained the never-ending, repetitive cycles of recruiting and training his men. Company officers rotated out on recruiting duty, and the gains and losses among enlistees continued to retard the development of strong unit identity.[2] Disease apparently began to take its toll on April 30, when Private Jacob Saylor, one of Tiebout's December 3 initial enlistees, died.[3] To help reduce, if not eliminate, desertions, captains received orders on April 22 to write up physical descriptions of deserters to be given to recruiting officers, who might spot a deserter and could apprehend him. This measure would especially help address bounty jumping.[4]

Captain John Houston's situation remained unclear to Willett. On April 9, Willett wrote to the New York Provincial Congress stating that Houston had received recruiting money in December but four months later had still not sent a word. Willett reported that the previous night he had "heard from authority that I am obliged to credit that he [Houston] has gone to the enemy." Willett asked the convention to appoint a captain to replace Houston as soon as possible, adding, "*May he be a clever fellow.*"[5] Houston was omitted from regiment musters as of January 1777, and First Lieutenant Leonard Bleeker, who had served with Willett and Tiebout in the 1st New York Regiment, was transferred to the 3rd New York Regiment to replace him. Originally commissioned as a first lieutenant for the third establishment 1st New York Regiment, Bleeker had resigned in protest over his concerns about the manner of officer selection for the 5th New York Regiment. He nevertheless accepted the captain's commission in the 3rd New York, receiving it just a month short of his twenty-second birthday. He ranked eighth in seniority among Gansevoort's captains in terms of both his military experience and his young age.[6]

Men continued to run afoul of orders and face court-martial. The situation was so chaotic that misunderstandings could occur easily, and Willett became upset when General McDougall confined Second Lieutenant Prentice Bowen, accusing him of "plundering some of the inhabitants at Peek's Kill." Willett did not know the details but was quite distressed because he considered Bowen to be "a steady, modest, careful, brave, intelligent officer" who was the most useful subaltern in the regiment. Bowen was about thirty-four years old and had been recommended by his militia colonel "in the strongest manner" for appointment in the third establishment army.[7] Things must have worked out for Bowen, because he was later assigned to be the regiment's quartermaster.

The continual supply inadequacies meant that company commanders again received orders on April 7 to make a return of the arms and accoutrements presently available in their company, listing the quantity of each item currently on hand, accounting for missing items, and reporting the number short of what was needed.[8] Five days earlier the captains had required their men to mark and number all their belongings to make recovery of items lost, stolen, or sold a bit easier. The ongoing supply shortages and lack of adequate pay had created temptations for men to sell whatever they were issued. Officers had to keep a vigilant eye out to prevent soldiers from soliciting potential buyers for their new, or even worn, articles of clothing, when they were fortunate enough to have them.[9]

The Fort Stanwix garrison at the beginning of April consisted primarily of Colonel Elmore's regiment and Captain Lieutenant Savage's artillery detachment. Elmore's men were scheduled to depart on April 15 to be replaced by elements of the 3rd New York Regiment, expected daily to relieve them. Elmore knew Gansevoort's advance troops were on their way to the fort under the command of his former major, Robert Cochran, but he did not know precisely when they would arrive.

While at Schenectady, on his way to Fort Stanwix, the French engineer Lamarquise wrote Colonel Goose Van Schaick on April 9 telling him that General Schuyler had instructed him to "enlarge the fort at Fort Schuyler with a company of carpenters" and as many men as could be spared from the troops stationed there. Whether accurate or not, he had heard that Gansevoort's regiment would be bringing five hundred to six hundred men to the fort. Incorrectly believing that his orders were "to take down part of the fort & make it larger," Lamarquise felt compelled to declare that "unless more troops are sent, I shall not be able to take any part of it down." The engineer apparently had encountered Major Cochran's detachment on their march to the fort and was concerned that he would not be "able to do much to that garrison with what men is gone up with Major Cochran & the small company of carpenters." He would "be glad" to get to work, however, "when the remainder of the regiment will be up."[10]

When Elmore's men began departing the fort on April 15, they left behind several of their former comrades now serving in the artillery detachment, as well as in the soon to arrive 3rd New York Regiment. Additionally, some men, including Samuel Drew, instead of leaving the fort and moving on with their lives, enlisted in other regiments now that their time with Elmore had expired.[11] Joseph Eldridge received his discharge from Elmore's regiment at German Flats in April and then enlisted in Savage's detachment at just about the time Major Cochran arrived.[12] Each man had personal reasons for the decisions made at the end of his enlistment.

Major Cochran, Captain Aorson, and their men finally arrived at some point during the day on April 17 after their long journey from Albany, finishing up on the miserable road connecting Forts Dayton and Stanwix. Cochran immediately met with his former commander, Colonel Elmore, to learn about the current situation at the fort. Cochran's force was small enough that the men could be accommodated in the casemate barracks. The men must have been concerned about the small size of the garrison, well under two hundred soldiers, including both infantry and artillery, in addition to the still incomplete restoration of the fort. Colonel Elmore did not feel comfortable turning over command of the fort to Cochran and his small advance force and was determined to wait for the arrival of Colonel Gansevoort and transfer command directly to him. Three days after Major Cochran arrived, so did Captain Lamarquise, accompanied by twenty carpenters.[13] These two arrivals raised hopes for greater activity in restoring the fort to a defendable condition.

Colonel Elmore was still at the fort on April 22 when he wrote to General Schuyler that he had been visited by about a hundred Indians on April 18. They came because they had heard he would be leaving the fort. Elmore met with them and learned that the influential Loyalist John Butler had advised the local Indians to remain neutral and not get involved in the war. The Indians saw this as clear hypocrisy, given Butler's activities pushing other Indians to actively support the British. The Oneidas planned a meeting at Onondaga and were determined to have nothing to do with the British. Elmore was happy to report that he "was informed by one of the chiefs that the Indians are all very well pleased with their treatment by me & the troops of this post & told me if I wanted any assistance from them, that they would grant all that lay in them to do with all possible dispatch." Elmore caustically noted Cochran's late arrival in a postscript stating, "I expected to have been relieved by the expiration of the time that the regiment was engaged for." While his regiment had mostly dissolved, Elmore still needed to be relieved as fort commander by Gansevoort, not Cochran. He still had some men with him, though lacking sufficient clothing for even those few, and he wanted to be relieved as soon as possible. He was also concerned that "Major Cochran hath arrived at this post with a small detachment, but not so many as have gone from my detachments."[14]

Major General Horatio Gates wrote to Colonel Gansevoort, still at Albany, on April 24, informing him that Congress had appointed Gates to replace General Schuyler as commander of the Northern Department. Gates was very familiar with the original Fort Stanwix thanks to his French and Indian War experience there while it was being built. Gansevoort must have felt sympathetic toward Schuyler and somewhat anxious to be serving again now under Gates, who had previously criticized him for not following orders precisely and in a timely manner. Gates made it a point to order Gansevoort clearly and firmly to be sure to send him complete, up-to-date returns of men, provisions, and military supplies regularly on the first and fifteenth of each month, even though the regiment was not yet united, and officers were still out recruiting. Two days later, Gates wrote to Gansevoort directing him to "proceed directly to Fort Schuyler, and take the command of that post, relieving Colonel Elmore, whose time of service is expired." He also repeated his long list of detailed information on various subjects that he expected Gansevoort to send him on a regular basis.[15]

After Lamarquise's arrival, it did not take long for him to come under criticism for the slow and awkward progress on restoring the fort, and he endeavored to defend himself. In an undated memorandum, apparently to General Gates, he listed the restoration projects that he had completed during his first week or two. First, Lamarquise had made handles for the axes, pickaxes, spades, and other tools. He had then constructed a new guardhouse at the fort's entrance, in addition to sentry boxes "where necessary," whatever that meant. The guardhouse had two sections, one for confining prisoners and one for housing the main guard on duty. That space also served as a location to post garrison orders so every man could read them, at least those who were literate, or have someone read the orders to them. The prisoner section had two rooms separated by a wall, with a central fireplace to heat both rooms. The two rooms together measured sixteen by twenty feet.[16] Then, by order of "the general," he had built a twenty-four-foot by twelve-foot house for "one Stefanny," Stephen Delyrod, the local French fur trader, whose wife was an Oneida.[17]

Lamarquise had constructed a small store to keep provisions under cover and completed a house for Indians to use when they came to the fort for trade. He upgraded the fort's barracks facilities, probably those in the casemates, to accommodate about two hundred men with wooden bunks and had plans to eventually put the fort's barracks "in a state to receive 500 or at least 400" occupants. None of those accomplishments, however, served to upgrade the fort's deteriorated defensive works. He argued that this was because the small garrison had not been able to provide enough laborers to put the log and earth defenses in "proper order." But even given sufficient manpower, "the grass will not be of sufficient strength for 15 days, to cut turf" to emplace on the earthen surfaces to strengthen them and retard erosion. In the meantime, he had used the few workers he did have to "open a road to the westward of the fort where he can get cedar and pine near at hand, whereas before they were obliged to go three miles to fetch a piece of wood as also firewood." There were several species of trees in the area near the fort. In the swampy area to the southwest, the trees were mostly pine and white cedar. There were also white pines in the swampy area on the east side of the fort. The other wooded areas contained elm, beech, rock maple, birch, poplar, and some wild cherry, providing varieties of lumber with many uses for strengthening the fort and sustaining the garrison.[18] Defending his overall accomplishments, Lamarquise argued he had done what he could with the inadequate resources given him, primarily men.

Lamarquise promised that once Gansevoort's entire regiment arrived, he would "set about the fort and trim [?] it up with turf &c from the bottom of the ditch &c." He would also "raise the parapet with cedar (as there is enough about a mile from the fort) by the end of next month," but to do that "it will be necessary to order 200 to 300 militia to assist in that work if no other troops are to be sent but Gansevoort's." Both cedar and pine were useful for construction, but cedar was more resistant to rot and insects. The engineer also planned to build what he believed to be a much-needed hospital so that men could be treated at the fort rather than being sent out, as had been required for Major Cochran, who he noted "is now very ill." To do that, while needing common laborers, he also needed skilled carpenters. After his arrival, Lamarquise had discovered that ten of the twenty civilian "carpenters" he'd brought with him were actually "shoemakers, tailors, & smiths who did not understand their business for which they engaged." Of course he did not blame himself for this but stated that they had probably "imposed on the good faith of the quartermaster general" to get their jobs. He fired them and began looking to hire properly skilled men.[19]

FIRST ELEMENTS OF THE 3RD NEW YORK REGIMENT ARRIVE

No one at the fort knew just how long they had to get things ready to defend it against attack by an enemy of unknown size and composition. The threat was real, however, and everyone in the fort needed to keep busy to complete the restoration as soon as possible while also performing all their other duties. As the 3rd New York Regiment began the process of taking on the major role of fort defense, they saw the effects of the poor thinking of engineer Lamarquise. They also saw the continuing inability to provide enough materials and sufficient appropriate laborers given the speed necessary to complete the required work. Could this situation be turned around and the fort made ready in time?

CHAPTER 8

Colonel Gansevoort Takes Command of Fort Stanwix

May 1777

Colonel Gansevoort finally arrived at Fort Stanwix on May 3 and promptly relieved the overextended Colonel Elmore of command of the fort. Two days later, he wrote to John G. Van Schaick at Albany, brother of his beloved sweetheart Caty: "I have just time to acquaint you with my safe arrival at this post on the 3d instant. I find it extremely pleasant and agreeable."[1] He must have been referring to the scenic frontier setting or else did not want to upset John and Caty. More bluntly, in a letter to General Schuyler, then with the Continental Congress in Philadelphia, he declared that the fort was "untenable" and in no physical condition for defense against a well-equipped and determined enemy.[2] Engineer Lamarquise had focused too much time and effort on extraneous construction projects rather than restoring the fort to a defendable condition as rapidly as possible. Gansevoort knew he had to get things moving in the proper direction—and quickly.

As May broke, Major Cochran's detachment settled in at Fort Stanwix while the frustrated Lieutenant Colonel Willett kept anticipating orders to bring on his men, most of the regiment, to the fort to join with Major Cochran, Captain Aorson, and Colonel Gansevoort. While he waited, Willett continued recruiting, training his recruits, and performing garrison duty. Anticipating imminent departure from Fort Constitution, he ordered his company commanders on April 24 to ensure that their men were properly equipped for action and ready to march at a moment's notice.³ But still no orders.

Recruiting parties continued bringing in new men from various locations who needed to be trained and made a part of the regiment. Sometime in May, John Fink, about twenty-three years old, also known by his Dutch name Hans Finkanover, enlisted at Rhinebeck in Captain De Witt's company for three years. He had previously served in the militia as a minuteman. From Rhinebeck, he was marched to Albany, then a few days later to Schenectady, where he may have joined in with Willett's troops, and "after a short halt, he thinks not over a day, they marched to Fort Stanwix."⁴

An interesting enlistee on or about May 1 was eighteen-year-old farmer William Fink, five feet, nine inches tall with a fair complexion and gray eyes. He had been born in 1759 at Canajoharie in the Mohawk River Valley and as a young teenager had served in the Tryon County militia company of Captain Jacob Klock. At one point he had been "drafted" to go to Fort Stanwix for five months, probably during the command of Colonel Elmore. During those five months he was called out many times on alarms and scouts, and generally guarded against incursions by the "common enemy." In April, his regiment had been called out on an alarm responding to an enemy incursion at "Ball's-Town." On their march, they encountered a recruiting party commanded by Lieutenant William Colbrath. For some unstated reason, even though out with the militia, he signed in to Captain Bleeker's company and immediately marched for Fort Stanwix. While a strong Patriot, Fink may have been taking on more than he should.⁵

Tiebout's company took in several recruits in early May, but a number of them did not join the company until it was on its way to Fort Stanwix.⁶ The confusion of some men over enlisting for the duration of the war or just for three years continued. Seventeen- or eighteen-year-old Albert Acker probably enlisted at Poughkeepsie and marched to Albany, where he then mustered into Tiebout's company during its march to Fort Stanwix later in the month. He thought he had enlisted for three years but was later told it was for the war.⁷

Personnel changes in other companies included the addition of a sergeant, fifer, drummer, and one private in Van Bunschoten's company, and a corporal and two privates in Bleeker's company. Captain Thomas De Witt gained a sergeant and nine privates but had four desertions. Gregg's company gained a corporal and a private, but two privates deserted. Jansen's and Swartwout's companies reported no changes.⁸

Additions and losses to individual companies were not just numbers. Each man represented a special skill, leadership experience, or other personal quality that either enhanced or diminished the company's capabilities. Stability over time allowed a company to develop more cohesion and comradeship—assuming everyone got along.

Back at Fort Stanwix, two days after Gansevoort's arrival on May 3, nineteen-year-old Han Jost Hess, also known as Joseph Hess, another recruit from the Mohawk Valley area and a cousin of Christian Shell in Captain De Witt's company, enlisted at Fort Stanwix for service in Captain Van Bunschoten's company.[9] His enlistment added to the growing number of recruits from families living in Mohawk Valley communities who were familiar with local people, the fort, the transportation route, and the general landscape.

The prospect of changing duty stations did not reduce discipline issues or the need for courts-martial at Fort Constitution. On May 9–10, a court-martial found Sergeant William Maxwell of Captain Bleeker's company guilty of an unspecified offense, sentencing him to be reduced in rank to private and given sixty lashes. Willett reprieved the lashes but not the rank reduction.[10]

Service in the Fort Stanwix garrison included frequent contact with Oneidas and other members of the Haudenosaunee nations. Gansevoort held the common negative prejudices of the colonists toward the Indians. While he did his duty by offering the Indians supplies and treating them respectfully, he avoided forming any personal friendships, believing this would prevent him from being blinded to any developing indications of underlying treachery. Gansevoort felt his priority was getting the fort prepared for defense against the expected enemy threat.[11]

Life at the frontier fort required a variety of important behavioral restrictions by those in the garrison. Although building the fort had been sold to the Oneidas as a benefit to them as a trading post, Gansevoort ordered the entire garrison to parade the evening of May 7 to hear a strict order from General Gates totally prohibiting any person associated with the army, and all local inhabitants, from trading with the Indians. For those able to read, Gansevoort followed up by posting those orders prominently on the Fort Stanwix gate, the fort headquarters building, and the tavern of local resident John Roof. Gansevoort warned of severe punishment for any person disobeying this order.[12]

Three days later, on May 10, the last remnants of Colonel Elmore's regiment marched out from the fort for Albany.[13] This left the small number of men under Major Cochran and Colonel Gansevoort, combined

COLONEL GANSEVOORT TAKES COMMAND OF FORT STANWIX

with Savage's artillery detachment, as the primary garrison. Willett's companies were still at Fort Constitution awaiting orders.

Gansevoort did well in his relations with the Oneidas, and this became known to his brother Leonard, who wrote him on May 17 letting him know that he had heard about those good relations. He also understood that Peter might be less than enthusiastic about his assignment and wanted to "encourage a promising young officer who had been deprived of future military glory by being relegated to a post in the backwoods." He tried to put a good face on things by reminding Peter that "there being no probability of any descent from the Westward you will be oblig'd to cast about in your Mind in what respect you can contribute to the Welfare of your Country." For Leonard, that meant the good relations Peter was building with the Indians, because "it is an object of the greatest moment not to this state in particular but America in general to maintain Peace and amity with them."[14] He hoped this only partially correct observation would help Peter maintain his morale.

Finally, after sprucing up Fort Constitution during a Saturday field day, just two months after arriving, Willett's troops departed the fort on the evening of May 12 and boarded three sloops, which made their way up the Hudson River, arriving at Albany on Saturday, May 17.[15] During the trip, Private Christian Gaines of Captain Van Bunschoten's company deserted on May 15. Willett and his troops marched off from Albany on Monday morning, May 19, trudging the sixteen-mile sandy road cut through scrub pine to Schenectady and stayed there until the following day.[16] The army was still recruiting men: Joseph Purchase enlisted for three years in Tiebout's company on May 20.[17]

Companies of bateau men, often local militiamen attached to the quartermaster department, made regular trips on the Mohawk River between Schenectady and Fort Stanwix. That afternoon, Willett's men loaded the regiment's baggage onto seven bateaux and set them off west on the Mohawk River, against the current, while they marched on the rutted road that varied in distance from the river, heading in the same direction.[18]

As they passed through Caughnawaga on May 22, new recruit Henry Ritter of Manheim joined Tiebout's company.[19] Recruiters continued signing up new enlistees in various locations who would join the regiment in due course.[20] After a five-day, sixty-mile (as the crow flies) trek,

Willett's tired soldiers arrived at Fort Dayton on May 25, and that day, Conrad Friday and John Lansing enlisted for the war.[21]

Lieutenant Colonel Richard Livingston of the 1st Canadian Regiment commanded a detachment stationed at Fort Dayton. Recently that post had developed a reputation for drunkenness and lack of discipline, and Willett had received orders from General Gates, through Colonel Gansevoort, to arrest Livingston and leave a detachment of the 3rd New York to relieve the garrison. Upon arriving, Willett placed Livingston under arrest and formed up a detachment consisting of Captain Thomas De Witt, two lieutenants, two sergeants, two corporals, two drummers, and forty privates to relieve the 1st Canadian garrison. Since De Witt's company was still short of its designated complement of soldiers, men from other companies were detailed to the detachment to fill it out.

Major Cochran arrived at Fort Dayton from Fort Stanwix, sent by Colonel Gansevoort to assist Willett's troops in making the final leg of their journey to the fort. After Willett assigned Captain De Witt and his detachment to garrison Fort Dayton, he left Major Cochran in charge while he, along with regimental surgeon Hunloke Woodruff, organized the rest of the soldiers and camp followers to continue to Fort Stanwix. He expected that Cochran would follow without delay after settling things at Fort Dayton.[22]

Captain De Witt spoke with Captain Robert Wright of the 1st Canadian Regiment, now commanding the garrison after Livingston's arrest, and together they decided that De Witt's detachment should not relieve the 1st Canadian troops until the next day, since De Witt's men were very fatigued. During the afternoon, Captain Timothy Hughes of the 1st Canadian told Lieutenant William Tapp of De Witt's company that Livingston's men, after being informed that their commander had been arrested, were determined to continue serving as the Fort Dayton garrison, against General Gates's orders, until Livingston was released. When Tapp informed Captain De Witt of this, De Witt immediately sent a letter by express rider to Major Cochran, who was then on the opposite side of the Mohawk River. Cochran decided not to leave the area until the following day, and he sent a messenger to Willett requesting forty men to be sent early in the morning as reinforcement to enable him to properly relieve the garrison if there was any trouble.

Then, shortly after the beating of tattoo that evening, Lieutenant Tapp was lying in bed when he heard drums sounding, fifes playing, and men "huzzaing" in an assembly ordered by Livingston. The twenty-seven-year-old Tapp had been born in London in 1750 and came to American about 1767, when he was sixteen years old. When the war began, he was commissioned an ensign on February 24, 1775, in Colonel Alexander McDougall's 1st New York Regiment, promoted to second lieutenant on June 13, and appointed regimental quartermaster on July 5. He then served in the Canadian campaign with Colonel James Nicholson's regiment. He had married Mary Smith of Jamaica, Long Island, at Fishkill on April 19, just a month before arriving at Fort Dayton. Mary was probably pregnant and traveling with him; she would give birth at the fort in December. Later at Fort Stanwix, people commented that Mary, a stalwart and energetic woman, "rendered important service to the garrison."[23]

Tapp dressed, rushed to Lieutenant Colonel Livingston's room, demanded that even though under arrest and no longer in command, he dismiss his men to their quarters, and swore that he would not leave until Livingston had done so. Just as firmly, Livingston informed Tapp that his men would remain out for as long as he pleased and ordered Tapp to leave the room. Tapp then heard a voice rise above the yelling crowd that the 1st Canadian men should be turned out under arms, whereupon Adjutant John Bateman of the 1st Canadian proceeded to order some of the men to turn out, although for no apparent reason. Frustrated that he had been unable to restore peace and quiet, Tapp returned to bed.

Not long afterward, Sergeant John Burns and David Garvy of Captain Hughes's company and Sergeant John Clarke of Captain Wright's company barged into Tapp's room declaring that Lieutenant Colonel Livingston wanted to see him.[24] Tapp inquired for what reason, and after they answered "for Fun," Tapp told them he would not go because he was tired and needed rest. The men then vehemently ordered, "By God you shall go or we will make you." Jumping out of bed, the insulted Tapp demanded to know who the men were who took "so much insolence upon them to an officer." When they responded by blowing out the candle, Tapp immediately suspected they intended to stab him and "withdrew instantly until the candle was lighted again." He then told 1st Canadian Regiment ensign John Gates to order the men out of the room, but Gates retorted that Tapp had no authority over him or his men. When Tapp then asked who commanded the garrison, he was told "the soldiers did and not the officers."

Sergeant Burns shouted at Ensign Josiah Bagley of the 3rd New York, calling him a "damned Rascal," and when Bagley ordered Burns out of the room, he replied that he had as much right to be there as Bagley. Ensign Bagley also heard Burns "swear by God" that the New Yorkers would learn the consequences of their actions by morning, because "he could get as many good fellows to stand by him as anybody." The three men confronting Tapp swore "by their Maker" that Captain De Witt and his detachment could not relieve the garrison until Livingston was freed from arrest.

During this disturbance, Captain De Witt angrily approached Lieutenant Colonel Livingston demanding that the drums cease to beat after tattoo. Livingston told him that he was the regiment's commander and "it was at his own pleasure whether they should or not." De Witt then reminded Livingston that, because he had been arrested, he had no authority to give orders to his men to carry on as they were doing. Livingston thereupon denied being under arrest and insisted he still commanded the garrison until properly relieved. De Witt countered by reminding Livingston that he had earlier acknowledged his arrest. While Adjutant John Bateman was organizing Livingston's regiment under arms, Captain De Witt observed him put on his military accoutrements, and Ensign Bagley heard Bateman say that if De Witt's detachment did not behave themselves, he would fire on them before morning.

With Captain De Witt heavily involved in attempting to put down the apparent mutiny, Lieutenant Tapp, accompanied by Ensign Bagley, departed the fort and crossed the Mohawk to alert Major Cochran to the troubles. Upon hearing their report and returning to the fort, Cochran ordered a court of inquiry to sit immediately and investigate the complaint lodged by Captain De Witt. The bi-regimental court consisted of Captain Van Bunschoten, acting as president, and three members from Livingston's regiment—Captain Wright, Captain Hughes, and Ensign Gates—along with ten officers from the 3rd New York: Captain Bleeker, Captain Gregg, Captain Tiebout, Lieutenant Defendorff, Lieutenant Tapp, Lieutenant Warner, Lieutenant Livingston, Ensign Bagly, Ensign Hutton, and Ensign Lewis. Several members of the court would also be witnesses.

The testimony provided by Lieutenant Tapp, Captain De Witt, and Ensign Bagley spelled out the basic story. In addition, Sergeant Henry Herald of the 1st Canadian Regiment testified that Sergeant John Burns had told him that he had made an offer to Livingston that he would go and kick Tapp out of the garrison, and Livingston had approved with "a nod of his head." Burns then asked Herald to go with him to Lieutenant

Tapp's room, but when they got there, Captain Hughes ordered him away and he obeyed immediately.

Following this, Sergeant Major Welding of Captain Swartwout's company testified to hearing that Sergeant Burns had drunk to the king's and royal family's health in a tavern while among some men of Gansevoort's regiment. Burns, who apparently served in the French and Indian War, defended himself, saying that "having been in his [the king's] service, [he] should always regard him while he was able to carry arms." Tapp further testified that Livingston's quartermaster, James Davidson, had been present and encouraged the mutinous proceedings, but Captain De Witt could not verify that for the court.

After the inquiry's conclusion, Major Cochran sent off Lieutenant Colonel Livingston, Adjutant Bateman, and Quartermaster Davidson, along with three others from the regiment, under guard to General Gates at Albany. Cochran immediately wrote to General Gates telling him about the incident, attached a transcript of the inquiry testimony, and sent it with Livingston's guards.[25] No further record of this case exists. The three officers removed continued their normal duties in the 1st Canadian Regiment, although not at Fort Dayton. Aside from the inquiry transcript, this incident remains mostly a mystery.

The man sent to Albany in charge of the prisoners, First Lieutenant Henry Defendorff of Captain Van Bunschoton's company, had enlisted as a sergeant in the 2nd New York Provincial Battalion on July 20, 1775, was promoted to second lieutenant in November and then to first lieutenant in July 1776. In late May 1776, Defendorff had run into Captain Joseph Bloomfield of the 3rd New Jersey Regiment traveling east on horseback from Johnstown, escorting Lady Johnson to Albany. When about twenty Loyalists surrounded Bloomfield, determined to take his horse, Defendorff helped Bloomfield drive them off.[26]

Despite his several notable accomplishments, Defendorff was initially passed over for commission in the 1777 third establishment. He had apparently offended one of his regiment's field officers. A leading member of the New York Committee of Safety supported and promoted his case for advancement, however, stressing that Defendorff had "done some very extraordinary services" and was "full of spirit and pride." Defendorff's colonel, Goose Van Schaick, also supported him and wrote to the Committee of Arrangements in late December that Defendorff was worthy of promotion and retention. As a result,

CHAPTER 8

Defendorff was commissioned a first lieutenant in Van Schaick's third establishment 1st New York Regiment, but for some reason was soon transferred to Captain Van Bunschoten's company of the 3rd New York Regiment.[27]

In the morning, De Witt's detachment, seemingly without further incident, relieved the 1st Canadian Regiment troops from their garrison duty and prepared to remain at Fort Dayton pending further orders. Christian Shell of German Flats, who had enlisted on April 15 in Captain De Witt's company, later recalled that his company remained at Fort Dayton for "two or three weeks" before completing their journey to Fort Stanwix.[28]

While Willett's men prepared for and made their march to Fort Stanwix, the men already at the fort with Captain Aorson continued their restoration work as other duties allowed, under the direction of Captain Lamarquise. The restoration effort had accomplished little, thanks to the inadequacies of Lamarquise, the small number of laborers provided, and the inability to get necessary supplies to him. On May 14 Assistant Deputy Quartermaster General Henry Glen wrote to Gansevoort from Schenectady that although General Gates had refused to provide Glen with additional bateaux for supply transport, he had ordered Ensign Myndert Wemple of the 2nd Albany County Militia, commanding a company of bateau men, to continue carrying supplies between Little Falls and the fort. He also asked Gansevoort to assign some men on command to operate the four bateaux that Captain Aorson's men were then using to transport boards, limestone, and other supplies. Glen would pay Aorson's men until he received additional troops to be sent from the Hudson River to man those bateaux.[29]

Then, on May 15, senior command of the Northern Department changed again when Congress directed General Schuyler to proceed there and retake command, relieving General Gates. On May 22, Congress defined the Northern Department, resolving "that Albany, Ticonderoga, Fort Stanwix, and their dependencies, be henceforward considered as forming the northern department."[30] It must have been a relief to Gansevoort to again be serving under a commander who supported him, and Schuyler, who had land interests in the area, was another officer who had known Fort Stanwix from its beginnings.

The narrowly focused Lamarquise still did not comprehend the need for speed in making the fort defendable. He could not grasp that he would never be blessed with the time and resources to make a "perfect" fort that would bring honor to him for both its design and its quality of construction. Rather, he desperately needed to optimize all available means to rapidly make the incomplete fort strong enough to withstand an anticipated enemy attack. Defending his lack of progress, Lamarquise argued to General Gates on May 19, at the time when Northern Department command was devolving back to Schuyler, that since the fort was essentially destroyed, it was "absolutely necessary" to make everything completely new, including barracks, ramparts, parapet, and covered way. In other words, he stubbornly continued to believe that he needed to dismantle the remains of the old fort and build a completely new structure. He complained that if his only source of laborers was to be Colonel Gansevoort's regiment, he could not completely repair the fort in the time required. Instead of creating an ingenious plan to achieve as much as possible with what he had, he just stated that it could not be done. And it was not his fault. He continued to plead, "I wish you would send a reinforcement as soon as it is possible and give orders to the Quarter Master General to supply the necessities of the Garrison, by means of which I can in a little time put the place in condition not to fear the enemy."[31]

Fifteen days after leaving Fort Constitution and completing a slow trip along the Mohawk River with heavily laden bateaux, the companies under Willett, minus the men left with De Witt at Fort Dayton, arrived at the Carry Place landing about 1:00 p.m. on Monday, May 28.[32] The soldiers must have been disturbed to see the dilapidated structure and then be told to unload their gear in it. Once they were settled, their labor would be required for repair and construction projects while they were also garrisoning the fort and preparing for its defense by going on scouting parties, conducting military training drills, and performing other regular military activities.

Now about six months old, the regiment was not yet even dressed uniformly. It had been decided to outfit the 3rd New York Regiment in blue uniform coats with white lining and red facings for the turned-back coattails, cuffs, collars, and lapels. Supplies, however, had been insufficient in both quality and amount. As a result, men wore coats and jackets of various lengths, made from a variety of fabrics colored brown, red, blue, and other hues with linings in different colors. Many men still wore at least some of the clothing they had worn when they enlisted. Most men had an infantry cocked hat. Uniformity of muskets, bayonets, and cartridge boxes was even more important than uniform clothing but was also not always possible to achieve.[33]

Nevertheless, De Witt's men united for the first time with the men of their regiment who had arrived several weeks earlier with Major Cochran and, as always, continued absorbing new recruits. That day, May 28, Patrick Mahan enlisted in Tiebout's company, and twenty-one-year-old Conrad Acker enlisted on May 29, both for the duration of the war.[34]

Private Henry Ritter of Tiebout's company was just one of the men who was immediately struck by, and would vividly remember into his old age, the incompletely restored fort. He clearly recalled that because of its condition, after their arrival "he & the soldiers worked there and finished it."[35] Equally unimpressed, Lieutenant Colonel Willett found the fort to be "in a weak and untenable state." He noted that the "fort had fallen into decay; the ditch was filled up, the pickets had rotted and fallen down." He described the fort, much as Captain Bloomfield had over a year earlier, as square, "with four bastions, surrounded by a ditch of considerable width and depth, with a covert [covered] way, and glacis around three of its angles; the other being sufficiently secured by low, marshy ground." Even if only three bastions were complete, probably all four mounted at least one cannon. The larger cannons had stationary carriages mounted on platforms, while the light cannons had traveling carriages.[36]

Willett used the past tense in describing several of the fort's elements, including "in front of the gate there had been a drawbridge, covered by a salient angle, raised in front of it on the glacis." A row of vertical pickets erected in the center of the ditch were now rotted away. More positively, he noted that at least there were still some "rows of horizontal pickets fixed around the ramparts under the embrasures," forming a fraise to break up and slow down enemy forces scaling the rampart walls.[37]

Colonel Gansevoort dutifully promised General Gates that he would provide engineer Lamarquise with "every assistance in my power to promote the speedy completion of the works." Primarily this meant that, virtually daily, he would order the soldiers of his regiment to perform fatigue duty, except when serving as guards or scouts. Gansevoort, however, felt that pushing the men even to that extreme would not be enough to complete the required work, because "the whole fort and barracks is to be new modelled," according to Lamarquise's demand. The engineer just would not give up on his desire to build a completely new fort, and this led to continuing frustration.[38]

Among his many problems, Gansevoort also struggled to accelerate the slow turnaround time for bateaux traveling between the fort and Schenectady. He had been expecting one group of boats for about six days. When bateaux arrived at his end of their journey, Gansevoort always had them unloaded quickly and sent back the same day, or at least the following morning. He wondered why those in charge at the other end of the bateau trips could not do likewise. If he was to speed up the fort restoration work, he needed additional bateaux to bring lumber from a sawmill located between the fort and Caughnawaga. He also could use at least ten bateaux to bring in lime, needed to make the mortar for brick fireplaces, and boards for construction of barracks, bunks, tables, and other projects.

Willett continued to be highly critical of Lamarquise, finding him "wholly incompetent to this task."[39] The very hard work of the garrison's soldiers had proved ineffective under his direction. Willett wanted to get rid of him, but Colonel Gansevoort was hesitant since it was General Schuyler, his superior officer and the fort's namesake, who had assigned Lamarquise to manage the restoration work. So Lamarquise remained in charge of restoration.

Like Dayton's and Elmore's men before them, Gansevoort's soldiers, and the wives and children traveling with them, had to find ways to carve out accommodations for themselves in the fort's incomplete barracks and casemates or pitch tents in or around the fort. At this point the barracks spaces inside the fort had been partially restored but were still unable to accommodate the required number of people. Two buildings facing the eighty-five-by-ninety-foot parade at the center of the fort where troops assembled for mounting guard, exercising, reviewing the guard, inspecting arms, witnessing punishments, and holding parleys with Indians provided quarters for company-level officers and enlisted men. Each building was divided into several rooms, and each room had a fireplace. When completed at an unknown date, the East Barracks was approximately twenty feet wide and 110 feet long with a floor of wooden planks nailed to sleepers resting on the ground. The West Barracks was approximately twenty feet wide and 120 feet long, also with a wooden plank floor.[40]

CHAPTER 8

Blatantly displaying his questionable competence, Lamarquise insisted on construction of a large new building intended to serve as an additional barracks to stand outside the fort, just beyond the foot of the glacis. That location would not only make the structure useless but also clearly be a hindrance during a siege.

Meanwhile, the more important work on the fort's defensive structures lagged.[41] The infuriated Willett kept inspecting and finding the restoration work to be faulty, ineffective, and incompetent. He diligently reported all his findings to Colonel Gansevoort, who took no immediate action. Meanwhile, the soldiers must have resented being ordered to work on useless projects rather than on improvements geared to protect them during a siege.[42]

When they did work on fort restoration, Gansevoort's troops labored to replace rotted timbers and rebuild old structures or build new ones using freshly cut logs. They had to replace all the vertically set pickets of the palisade around most of the fort. For the earth structures, they had to fill in areas that had eroded away and then add slabs of sod to the slopes to diminish the effects of artillery fire as well as erosion. In the barracks and casemates, wooden bunks for the soldiers were being constructed. Brick fireplaces, primarily for cooking, were built or being built in each room with brick chimneys passing through the casemate or barracks roof. Work details went out to chop down trees, bring in the logs, collect sod, and even improve the miserable road to Fort Dayton. To hinder possible enemy troops attacking eastward from Lake Ontario, work parties cut down trees on the banks of Wood Creek, felling them into the creek to obstruct the passage of bateaux.[43]

The lack of vital supplies contributed to everyone's unhappiness. Colonel Gansevoort appealed to General Gates on May 23 to immediately send him a "quantity of rum," noting that his "fatigue and work-men have already been 7 days without it, what little is left being reserved for the Indians who daily come and go from this Place."[44] Gansevoort signed an order on May 26 to purchase rum for the fatigue parties working under the engineer's supervision. The men on those fatigue parties cut down trees, cut back the forest, served as wagoners bringing in supplies, and worked as artificers, such as carpenters and blacksmiths, reconstructing the fort. The fatigue party men always got whatever rum was available before anyone else, but the amount varied.[45]

The perpetual problems involving lack of pay and clothing for the garrison drove twenty-six members of Captain Lieutenant Savage's artillery detachment to desperately petition General Schuyler on May 17 for pay and "cloathing." Graphically emphasizing their needs, they complained, "Some of us is mounting guard barefooted."[46] They also were not very happy serving under Savage. Twenty-three men signed a petition stating that they had been promised they would serve under Captain Lieutenant James Furnival, who had recruited them, but then left the company for unknown reasons, leaving them under Savage, whom they did not want as their commander.[47] This is a clear example demonstrating that officer quality was one important factor in encouraging men to enlist.

The lack of sufficient supplies continued to drive soldiers to make a profit from, rather than carefully use, any items issued to them, and company commanders repeatedly received orders to take care that soldiers did not "sell their clothes, armor, [or] accoutrements." The insufficient supplies also made it difficult to enforce the general order to the soldiers not to trade with the Indians. To prevent such sales to anyone, in accordance with the garrison orders issued May 30, every Saturday at 3:00 p.m. each man had to account to his captain for "such articles as have been delivered to them." The captains would ensure that any man found guilty of selling items would be punished.[48]

The Fort Stanwix garrison knew that British army commanders were planning a strong effort to crush the rebellion that year and that the fort's position at the Oneida Carry on the ancient travel, trade, and war route put it directly on the probable path of British troops, along with their Loyalist and Indian allies. Indeed, Fort Stanwix stood directly on the route of a force to be led by Lieutenant Colonel Barrimore Matthew "Barry" St. Leger in the 1777 campaign.[49] The British believed that the Americans would need to divert some of their troops forming to oppose Burgoyne near Albany to deal with St. Leger, but he would still be able to join with Burgoyne.

St. Leger was about thirty-nine years old, born in Ireland of Huguenot ancestry, and had served as a young officer in the Seven Years' War in Canada, continuing to serve there after the war. Having risen rapidly in rank while theoretically accumulating a store of military knowledge and leadership skills, he might seem a natural choice for appointment to command. Two weaknesses in his appointment, however, were that his previous duties had not included service in the wilderness, and he had no personal experience working with the Indians, who would make up a large part of his force. As the historian John Luzader puts it, "St.

Leger was unfit by training, experience, and temperament for leading these warriors."⁵⁰

In recognition for commanding a force of that size, St. Leger had requested and now held the local rank of brigadier general, or simply brigadier, while continuing to hold the rank of lieutenant colonel in the 34th Regiment of Foot. He was free to command this diversionary force because his regiment had been deemed unfit to accompany General Burgoyne's troops, criticized as a unit in which the men were more attentive to their duties than their officers were.⁵¹ Employing appropriate military protocol, however, Burgoyne chose St. Leger to head the diversionary force because he was the senior lieutenant colonel outside of the troops heading south. When the campaign ended, he would revert to that rank.⁵²

The plan called for St. Leger to lead a force consisting of one hundred men from his 34th Regiment of Foot, one hundred men from the 8th Regiment of Foot, 342 Hessen-Hanau light infantrymen known as Jäger, and forty artillerymen with two 6-pounders, two 3-pounders, and four 4.6-inch coehorn mortars. Some of these numbers, especially the Hessen-Hanau Jäger, may be higher than the number later involved in the campaign. These troops would be supplemented by Loyalist Sir John Johnson's King's Royal Regiment of New York, known as the Royal Greens or Royal Yorkers, Loyalist John Butler's company of rangers, and "a sufficient number of Canadians and Indians." The Indians would include many Mohawks persuaded to fight for the British by Sir John Johnson and led by the Mohawk leader Joseph Brant. Young Brant, brother of Sir William Johnson's Mohawk mistress and housekeeper Mary Brant, also known as Molly, had been a favorite of Johnson, who sent him to Eleazar Wheelock's school in Connecticut. The well-educated Brant became highly respected in both cultures as a political and military leader. In the words of the historian Alan Taylor, at his home "at Canajoharie, Joseph thrived as both a colonial gentleman and a Mohawk chief."⁵³ He became a strong British supporter in the colonial wars and maintained that loyalty during the American Revolution.

We have seen that Johnson had fled to Canada with some followers to avoid arrest by Colonel Dayton's 3rd New Jersey Regiment troops in May 1776. Now, a year later, Sir John and his followers would return to the Mohawk River Valley as part of St. Leger's estimated seven hundred to eight hundred white troops and eight hundred to one thousand Indians.⁵⁴ Exactly how many men St. Leger ultimately led on his diversion is difficult to know. A document captured in

August gave his force as containing about 1,400 men. These included 200 British troops, 80 Hessen-Hanau Jäger, 380 King's Royal Yorkers, 70 Butler's rangers, 50 Canadians, 20 artillerymen, and 600 Indians, though the document may have been drawn up before all the Indian allies had joined.[55]

When Colonel Dayton's 3rd New Jersey Regiment first reoccupied the fort, small bands of Oneidas had worked with him to scout out British and Loyalist activity to the west around Oswego. Then, in mid-March 1777, the Oneidas began a regular watch along the St. Lawrence River to keep an eye on developments that might threaten the fort. Oneida blacksmith Thomas Spencer continued to prove one of the best scouts.[56] Now, in a May 22 letter requesting intelligence about the enemy, Gansevoort informed Spencer that he had provided two gallons of rum to the man who delivered Spencer's recent letter and asked him to immediately send out four Oneidas to Oswego to learn what they could about British, Indian, and Loyalist activities.[57]

Concurrent with Willett's arrival on May 28, some Oneidas entered the fort and told Colonel Gansevoort that they had journeyed to Canada to urge the Mohawks not to "take up the hatchet" in favor of the British. On their way, they met some of the enemy marching from Canada to Oswego, where Sir John Johnson was to have a conference with the Indians and after that "we might hourly expect them."[58] Responding to this intelligence, Gansevoort pushed his men even harder to carry on the work needed to make the fort defendable and also to obstruct boat passage on Wood Creek to hinder the enemy's approach.[59] Enemy Indian scouts frequently appeared in the area, and for their personal safety, Gansevoort issued orders forbidding garrison members to venture too far outside the fort. He also forbade firing guns outside the fort, a practice that had become common because of the tasty passenger pigeons that were plentiful and tempting targets in the nearby woods.[60] Unexpected gunfire near the fort would raise an alarm; also, it was important to conserve gunpowder, and the pigeons were so numerous that could be captured with nets.

Fort restoration work continued daily. On May 30, General Orders instructed one subaltern, one sergeant, and fifteen privates "to hold themselves in readiness to embark tomorrow at ten o'clock on six bateaux to fetch boards for the use of this garrison. The officer who

CHAPTER 8

commands the party is to call tomorrow morning at eight o'clock for orders." Additionally, each day until further notice, one captain, one subaltern, one sergeant, and one hundred privates would be ordered out for fatigue under the direction of Lamarquise. More routinely, to maintain the cleanliness of the garrison to the greatest degree possible, each company was to furnish one man to the quartermaster sergeant to serve as a camp color man. The camp color men worked under the quartermaster to maintain camp cleanliness.[61]

While members of the Haudenosaunee nations preferred neutrality, they were often drawn to one side or the other because of geography and close trading ties. The Oneidas residing nearer to American posts such as Fort Stanwix tended to favor the Whigs or remain neutral, while tribes farther west and closer to British posts tended to favor the British—if they did not stay neutral. The Haudenosaunee lived amid white settlers who were also divided in their loyalties to England and who tried to persuade the Indians to support one side or the other, or at least remain impartial. The influence of the extended Johnson family brought many Mohawks to the British side, while other nations continually tried to remain neutral. In the area near Fort Stanwix, the white settlers favoring the Whigs predominated. Supporting the British would have put the Oneidas in military conflict with their white neighbors.[62]

Men of the 3rd New York who had not previously been acquainted with members of the Haudenosaunee probably agreed with the private, but not publicly expressed, image of them held by General Schuyler, who described them as "a compound of all the vices without a single virtue."[63] Many people held negative stereotypes of the Indians as lazy, unkempt, boorish, and brutal savages. As we have seen, that disrespect could lessen for some whites after meeting them, as it had previously with some of Dayton's and Elmore's men. This did not eliminate all racist feelings and actions, which still strongly prevailed.

Colonel Gansevoort's men must have had very mixed feelings about doing duty at such an isolated and insecure frontier post. The nearest settlement, Fort Dayton, where they had left Captain De Witt and his detachment, was thirty miles down the Mohawk River. Only a few Indian huts and a rough trail through tall trees, cluttered with massive

COLONEL GANSEVOORT TAKES COMMAND OF FORT STANWIX

root systems, lay between the two forts.[64] Several disaffected men soon deserted, and others would follow.[65]

Could Gansevoort and Willett get the fort ready before the arrival of a powerful, diverse enemy? An attack was coming. It was just a matter of when and by how strong a force.

Chapter 9

Dealing with Too Many Needs and Dangers

June 1777

British general Burgoyne's army of about eight thousand men set off south from Canada on June 13, amid much pageantry, to begin its portion of the planned three-part 1777 campaign. Ten days later, the white core of Brigadier St. Leger's force departed Lachine, across the St. Lawrence River from Montreal, commencing the portion of the 1777 campaign that would result in the siege of Fort Stanwix. Recently received intelligence erroneously indicated to St. Leger that only about sixty men occupied a "picketed place" at the Oneida Carry. Another mistaken belief among Mohawk Valley–area Loyalists shared by St. Leger was that backers of the Patriot cause in the valley would return to supporting the king when this British force arrived. They eagerly anticipated taking revenge on the rebels and regaining property that had been seized from them. While St. Leger's force began its journey with great confidence, the Fort Stanwix garrison became increasingly aware of Indian advance parties boldly prowling around the fort to gather information, taking scalps and prisoners when opportunities arose. These periodic harassing raids increased the tension felt by the men at the isolated fort and vividly demonstrated to the garrison just what their fate would be if they stayed to fight and later were captured or surrendered. This assuredly increased their determination to never surrender and to do all they could to strengthen the fort before the full enemy force assaulted them.[1]

As June began, Colonel Gansevoort continued to receive conflicting intelligence from Oneida scouts regarding potential Loyalist and Indian attacks in the area. He especially appreciated the frequent reports from Oneida blacksmith Thomas Spencer, whom he considered "a very intelligent Man and a warm friend to our cause."[2] While food supplies for his men may have been questionable, Gansevoort personally appears to have been eating well. He reported to his fiancée, Caty, "I must inform you that I have exceeding good living here plenty of veal[,] pigeon and fish of different sorts."[3] Just how he obtained these delicacies he does not say, but he must have acquired them locally.

Reports from the numerous scouting expeditions, no matter how conflicting, reinforced Gansevoort's determination to complete work on the fort speedily. Yet, despite constantly placing all men fit for duty, and not on command or guard duty, on restoration fatigue parties, the effort still progressed very slowly. There were just too few men available to accomplish the job. On June 1, Gansevoort had to report in frustration to General Schuyler that "nothing of any importance" had yet been done "towards the strengthening [of] the fortification which at present has little more than the name of a fortification." Regarding defense structures, engineer Lamarquise had "just laid the foundation of a salient angle before the gate," while at the same time, "the carpenters are employed in framing a barracks to be raised just before the glacis opposite the south bastion."[4] This was the barracks that would be a useless hindrance during a siege.

Later in the month, Gansevoort wrote to Schuyler about dealing with the house of settler Thomas Mayre, located quite near the fort. Colonel Dayton had ordered Mayre, a Loyalist, to leave the area the previous September, and upon his departure, his house and barn had been confiscated and his fences destroyed. The tar-floored barn had been dismantled to provide a location for constructing the new barracks that Captain Lamarquise insisted on building. Lamarquise additionally wanted to tear down Mayre's house, which stood on the glacis.[5]

Gansevoort continued to meet with frustration trying to solve his many problems, such as locating and transporting construction materials, and this contributed to the slow progress of restoration. To speed things up, fatigue parties cut a road to allow about two thousand wooden pickets to be "drawn out of the swamp," and by mid-June those pickets were lying around the fort ready to be put in place. Gansevoort needed to send as far as Canajoharie for boards, and although there was a supply of lime as near as Little Falls, he had to request bateaux from Canajoharie to carry it to the fort.[6] Helpfully, several expected bateaux arrived with badly needed boards on June 16. Soldiers and the bateau crews quickly unloaded the cargo and made the boats ready to set out again, along with another four bateaux presently at the fort. To crew each boat, Adjutant Sytez selected three men from the regiment who had proved most skillful in handling bateaux.[7]

While Gansevoort and his officers felt they needed additional resources to transport supplies, General Schuyler came to believe that Gansevoort had been requesting more resources than were required. He wrote to Gansevoort on June 9, "I am advised that all the economy is not made use of that ought to be and that the engineer employs a greater number of carriages [wagons] than are necessary."[8] Gansevoort replied that Lamarquise had only about twelve wagons and really needed about eight more to conduct his work satisfactorily. Moreover, even if he could have twenty more, there would still be important work for all of them.[9] Gansevoort does not mention the teams of horses required to pull the wagons and their extensive needs regarding harness, food, and care, or the human work required to fulfill those needs.

Even though Lamarquise concentrated more on living space than on the fort's defenses, there was never enough to accommodate all the men assigned to the fort. Men occupied whatever shelter could be made available in the casemates and barracks, while probably many continued to live in tents. The poor quality of the barracks and other deficiencies made the fort "insufficient to contain the few men" in the garrison, wrote Gansevoort.[10]

A casemate was like a cave, but with a wall, doors, and windows to the outside world. Accommodations in a casemate were better protected from artillery fire than those in a freestanding barracks. Before wood floors were added and suitable beds and furniture could be constructed, soldiers could simply lie on the dirt floor with their blanket, perhaps padded for comfort with some hay. Over time, flat bunk shelves were constructed along the back wall, where soldiers could sleep side by side in a group. Even after bunks were constructed, some men may still have slept on the floor just because there were too many of them for the wooden bunks to accommodate. Rooms often contained piles of hay for bedding. Tables and chairs were added when available. Brick hearths were constructed for the men to cook their rations and gain some heat in cold weather, so the rooms contained stacks of firewood to burn. Extra clothing, packs and bags, canteens, bayonets, and other items could be hung on pegs in the wall or on the bunk framework. Muskets stood in cone-shaped clusters from which each man could grab his own when needed.

East and west wooden barracks flanked the parade ground with walkways running between them and the casemates they paralleled. The barracks' furnishings were similar to those in the casemates, though with double-decker bunks large enough for two men to share on each level.[11]

Still, to address the full extent of the needed work, Gansevoort required more men than he had, and sickness among the garrison greatly reduced the already insufficient workforce. Gansevoort believed that one of the causes contributing to his men's poor health was a shortage of cooking utensils. He reported that men had to share utensils, and "while waiting, some men used random pans to boil up water to cook their meat while others roasted their beef on sticks."[12]

If obtaining labor and materials for fort reconstruction proved difficult, so did securing sufficient quantities and varieties of food supplies for the garrison. Beef, pork, bread, flour, oatmeal, rice, peas, butter, and salt were among the chief foods needed but not always provided. In addition, cheese, bacon, suet, fish, fowl, raisins, and molasses were also part of the expected diet. Any fresh vegetables such as potatoes, parsnips, carrots, turnips, cabbage, and onions sent to the fort were primarily for the sick.

While rum gets the most attention in documents concerning the fort's liquid needs, other beverages consumed included beer, cider, and wine. In addition to food supplies shipped to the fort by the army, officers and soldiers could purchase food and tobacco from sutlers and local farmers. Some men also tried hunting, although firing weapons outside the fort remained against orders.

Bread for the garrison could be made in the bakehouse located in the bombproof shelter in the southeast bastion. The space was approximately twenty feet square with a floor of hard-packed earth, and it contained a brick fireplace with brick-paved hearth. An egg-shaped arched oven that stood behind the fireplace could accommodate twenty six-pound loaves of bread at one time, large enough to provide full rations for the entire garrison.[13]

The garrison also kept a garden to help supply itself with perishable foods. On June 24, garrison orders assigned one corporal and three privates to attend the garden the following day to prevent any theft from it.[14] Gansevoort had written to his beloved Caty just the day before, "I am confident that the State of New York cannot produce of so elegant a garden as we have here at present, with two fine summer houses, and a stream of water which runs round the whole."[15] The garden stood in a bend of the creek that ran near the southeast bastion and came to be known as the "snowshoe garden." Exactly who in the garrison did the gardening work and who benefited from the produce is not mentioned.[16]

Despite all of this, in June, even General Schuyler at Northern Department headquarters complained about the "very inadequate" quantity of provisions at Fort Stanwix, and Colonel Gansevoort noted that although the fort was undermanned, his garrison was still too large for the quantity of provisions stored at the fort. Especially lacking were salt beef and salt pork, since over twenty thousand pounds of spoiled salt meat had been condemned. Though sensitive to the relationship between adequate supplies and the men's health, Schuyler, perhaps needlessly but out of habit, instructed Gansevoort on June 9 to "let an officer daily inspect into the cooking and see that the utensils be kept clean."[17]

Properly distributing available food supplies was always a concern. For example, it required special attention to make sure that sick men were fed, but that only one ration was drawn for each patient. No provisions were to be issued to men sick in the hospital other than those ordered by the surgeon. Captains were to make sure that men in the hospital were not included "in the provision returns for their respective companies."[18]

An additional drain on garrison provisions involved visiting Indians, who expected to receive "gifts" of food as part of the diplomatic protocol when meeting with other groups. Gansevoort reported that Colonel Elmore had never conveyed to him any official orders about furnishing the Indians with food, but he followed the system he perceived Colonels Dayton and Elmore had adopted.[19] In addition to supplying Indians with food, in accordance with the desire of Congress to ensure friendly interactions with the Six Nations, on June 13, General Schuyler, in his role as commissioner of Indian affairs appointed by Congress, prohibited anyone to make speeches to the Indians except when instructed to do so by the general or the commissioners of Indian affairs. This was in reaction to some self-indulgent officers, such as Captain Lamarquise, specifically mentioned in Schuyler's June 9 letter, who had taken it upon themselves to negotiate with the Indians on their own.[20]

Regarding other needed supplies, Leonard Gansevoort wrote to his brother from Albany on June 13 with the good news that Lieutenant

Thomas McClellan of Tiebout's company had been able to secure various badly needed items from the supplies at Albany. These included sixty "good new French Muskets" and the same number of bayonets, cartridge boxes, and bayonet belts. He also obtained seventy-six blue coats with red facings and white lining, the regulation regimental uniform, and the same number of infantry hats. Ten days later the 3rd New York Regiment received one hundred pairs of shoes.[21] We do not know the exact number of men in Tiebout's company at that time, so we don't know if these items were sufficient for them. If the numbers were close, however, it would indicate that the company was at least somewhere near its expected full strength of some seventy-plus men. How well the coats and hats fit the variously sized men is also unknown, but no doubt men with tailoring skills found themselves modifying garments for fellow soldiers to achieve a better fit. We must wonder whether at least some of the other companies in the regiment received similar supplies at the same time.

In response to its May request, the roughly thirty-three-man artillery detachment also received clothing in late June. Their supply matched the approximate number of men in the detachment and included thirty-two shirts of one kind and thirty-one of a less expensive kind, thirty coats, thirty waistcoats, sixty-three pairs of hose, thirty-two hats, thirty-two stocks, and sixty-three pairs of shoes.[22]

While heavily taxed in time and energy by laboring on the fort's restoration, Gansevoort's regiment settled into garrison duty. Company captains continued to recruit, train, establish routines, and instill discipline in their soldiers while also trying to develop a sense of regimental cohesiveness and pride in the still young and not yet geographically united regiment. On June 2, company commanders received orders to ensure that the men serving as their waiters also participated in training drills, so they would be just as skilled as the other men in their company. Company officers were to attend exercises with their men and not leave everything to the sergeants and corporals, who were especially focused on training their "awkward" men frequently to ensure that they would become competent. Everyone continued to learn his assigned duties and attempted to meet the colonel's expectations. On June 2, orderly sergeants were reminded to report to Adjutant Sytez for orders when the drums beat the sergeants' call. The frequent repetition of such basic orders indicates that the daily instructions were given not to prevent problems but rather to correct observed deficiencies or help develop consistency in routines.

CHAPTER 9

Cleanliness in the overcrowded quarters was difficult to maintain, even with the continuous daily work of the camp color men, leading to repeated orders for all bedding to be kept clean and well aired. Officers or privates on guard duty had orders not to bring their blankets—not a major problem in the warm June weather. The officer of the day was to see that soldiers' quarters were kept "clean and sweet." Adjutant Sytez was to make sure that all men on guard duty had their hair powdered, their person perfectly clean, their clothes in good order, their arms bright and accoutrements in good order.[23] This would help present a professional appearance that would hopefully inspire feelings of pride in the regiment while also impressing the local population and people passing through the fort. Achieving that professional look, however, proved quite difficult, given the short supplies and normal wear and tear on clothing.

Recruiting continued, and eight new faces appeared in Tiebout's company during June.[24] On June 9, Samuel Vader of Rhinebeck, Private Peter Scriber's hometown, about eighteen years old, enlisted in Captain Swartwout's company and was marched by way of Albany to Fort Stanwix.[25] Sometime about June, nineteen-year-old private John Dop, or Dops, recently discharged from eighteen months' service in a Tryon County ranger company, came to Fort Stanwix to join the Continental Army. Finding "no other regiment being on that post at that time" except the 3rd New York, he enlisted in Bleeker's company. Dop would later recall the many scouts he participated in as well as the fatigue work making "improvements" to the fort and keeping it "in repair."[26]

Alexander Lemmon, born in Ireland, was about twenty-seven when he enlisted in Captain Gregg's company in June. He became known as a humorous and eccentric man, called the "left-handed barber" because he was a barber by trade and naturally left-handed. He also stood out because of the gunpowder burns on his face received during his service in the 1775 Canadian campaign, which included the Battle of Quebec.[27]

The endless stream of desertions also continued. In addition to the problems in adapting to army life in general, these men may not have taken well to the frontier conditions at Fort Stanwix. Tiebout's company alone had six desertions in June.[28] Peter Genious, one of the recruits enlisting for the war in the first group on December 3, 1776, deserted on June 24.[29]

Personnel numbers for the 3rd New York Regiment for June show an addition of nineteen privates, one noncommissioned officer, and one officer; while thirteen privates deserted, one private and one officer were wounded, and two privates died, including private Timothy Scott of Van Bunschoten's company, who had enlisted on March 1 and died on June 27, probably from illness.[30] This indicated a total of 457 rank and file for the regiment, still far short of the 728 authorized.[31]

To keep track of the continually changing garrison population, artillery and infantry company commanders received their usual orders to make out exact returns of their men on June 15. It was not enough to know just names and numbers of units because they kept changing in size. Lamarquise would make a return of the skilled civilian men working for him. Additional returns were to continue to be made the first and fifteenth day of each month so Gansevoort could keep the commander of the Northern Department informed.[32]

The daily garrison orders record courts-martial for various disciplinary infractions. On June 5, Captain Bleeker was appointed president of a court-martial to try several cases. Sergeant Dowler of Captain Gregg's company had been confined in the guardhouse by Captain Tiebout for sleeping on his post. The court found Dowler guilty and ordered him reduced to private. William Grimsby of Captain Aorson's company was sentenced to receive 150 lashes on his bare back for being drunk on parade and abusing a sergeant. One of the men recruited from Elmore's regiment, John Baker, found himself accused of robbing an Indian but was released from the guardhouse and not tried. To reinforce the men's understanding of the behavioral expectations they had agreed to meet upon enlisting, Lieutenant Bowen read the Articles of War to the regiment at 6:00 p.m. that evening, a periodic reminder.[33]

That reading had little positive effect, and discipline problems continued throughout the month. A court-martial on June 8 sentenced James Turner of Tiebout's company to receive one hundred lashes for taking a pocketbook with nine dollars and a new pocket almanac from William Grimsby.[34] A June 11 court-martial sentenced Edmund Burke of Swartwout's company to endure 150 lashes for disobeying orders twice, abusing Captain Lieutenant Savage on parade, being drunk on duty, and striking Savage twice. James Dawson of Gregg's company was sentenced to suffer 150 lashes for being drunk on guard duty at night. Three men—James Rogers and Cornelius Swartwout, charged with neglect of duty on fatigue and being drunk, and James McCormick on suspicion of theft—were released.[35] A June 28 court-martial ordered one hundred lashes be applied to James Dobbins of Captain Gregg's company for cursing Congress and his captain and "offering to lay a wager that many more [men] would desert."[36] He would have won that wager.

The men of the regiment witnessed these punishments when drawn up to observe them carried out on the parade at the center of the fort under the direction of the regiment's adjutant. To inflict the sentenced lashes, fellow soldiers tied as many as four convicted men, stripped to the waist, to the white cedar whipping post, sarcastically known as the "adjutant's daughter," and company drummers administered the lashes with a cat-o-nine-tails. This punishment was somewhat darkly and amusingly referred to as "kissing the adjutant's daughter." There was always the hope that witnessing the pain as it increased with each lash would reduce incidents of disobedience. Even the fear of such punishment, however, did not prove to be a real deterrent.[37]

Disobeying orders could lead to consequences even more severe than lashings. Despite the orders not to venture far from the fort and not to discharge firearms outside the fort, even officers on occasion let down their guard and risked punishment. On June 25, just two days after St. Leger's force had marched off to use the Mohawk River Valley route to join with Burgoyne at Albany, Captain James Gregg and his dog Tray, along with Corporal Samuel Madison and Gregg's fifer, his fifteen-year-old nephew Robert Wilson, exited the fort just after breakfast hoping to shoot some of the tasty passenger pigeons in the forest.[38] They wanted to get far enough away that their shots would not be heard at the fort, but before they had gone far, Captain Gregg suffered a twinge of avuncular conscience and ordered his nephew to return to the fort. Perhaps Gregg wanted to avoid getting young Robert into trouble if they were caught, not to mention preventing him from being wounded or killed if they were spotted by enemy scouts. Like any boy his age, young Wilson no doubt strongly objected, but his uncle insisted, so he went back.

About 10:00 a.m., a mile and a half or two miles from the fort, several enemy Indians led by Seneca chief Kay-ing-waur-to, conducting a scouting expedition to the fort, spotted Gregg and Madison and fired at them. Their shots killed Madison, while Gregg took a shot "which entered his side, ran along near the middle of the back, passing near the spinal bone, just beyond which it went out." He fell and "lay still pretending death."³⁹ One of the Indians ran toward him, but Gregg did not move in the slightest. He maintained his ruse even while being scalped and receiving a cut to his head from the Indian's tomahawk.

After he was sure that the Indians had departed, the now very weak Gregg crawled over to Corporal Madison and, finding him dead, laid his head on Madison's body, continuing to play dead himself, and passed out. Tray, who was not injured, woke him up by tenderly licking his wounds, but he passed out again. Several hours later, Gregg awoke and tried to send Tray to find help. Tray ran off and discovered two Continental soldiers of the garrison who were fishing at some distance from the attack. They were unaware of the attack, and the Indians had not seen them. When those men saw the agitated Tray run at them and then turn and run back toward the woods while barking and whining, acting as though he wanted them to follow, they did so. Tray led them to the bloody spectacle of Gregg and Madison. Believing both men to be dead on the basis of what they saw, the men immediately ran to the fort and reported the incident.

The duty officer to whom they reported dispatched a party of men at about 2:00 p.m. to retrieve the bodies. Having a family member involved, young Robert Wilson must have been even more devastated than the comrades of the two fallen men. While gathering up the two victims, the party from the fort confirmed that Madison was dead but discovered weak signs of life in the critically wounded Captain Gregg. Securing a large piece of tree bark to use as a litter, four men carried Gregg to the fort.

When they brought him in a little after 3:00 p.m., young regimental surgeon Hunloke Woodruff immediately began assessing Gregg's wounds and doing what he could to address them. Robert Wilson must have been shocked at his uncle's condition but also grateful to him for making him return to the fort. Although relieved that his uncle was still alive, Robert probably feared, like many others, that his uncle would not long survive. The following day, Colonel Gansevoort informed General Schuyler, "Gregg is perfectly in his senses, and speaks strong and hearty, notwithstanding that his recovery is doubtful."

Woodruff treated Gregg skillfully with intense patience as the days of his recovery continued. It took three weeks before he could pronounce Gregg to be out of danger.⁴⁰ Woodruff was just twenty-three years old, born at Elizabethtown, New Jersey. His wealthy merchant father died while he was in college, forcing Hunloke to leave school in 1772. In New York he studied medicine with a relative and at King's

College (now Columbia University). Woodruff began military service when appointed as a surgeon's mate in the first establishment 1st New York Regiment and served in the Canadian campaign.[41]

Two days after the incident, Lieutenant Philip Conine of Captain Swartwout's company wrote to a friend that a man had been killed by the Indians and a captain shot through the body and scalped. He noted the captain was still alive, and the doctors said he might possibly recover, though from what he had seen, Conine believed Gregg's wounds to be mortal.[42]

Another account of the incident, also written on June 27, appeared as an extract of a letter from Fort Stanwix printed in a New York newspaper on August 4. Before giving a full account of the incident, the writer began by informing the letter's recipient:

> There is not at present any appearance of our being attack'd by the enemy: We are however making all the preparations for a defence, which the state of the garrison admits. The Six Nations are in general friendly, and seem resolved not to take an active part against us. We are not therefore under any apprehensions from the body of Indians, though we have reason to fear some mischief will be done by strolling individuals, who do not govern themselves by the sentiments of the nation to which they belong.

It is interesting that he did not pick up a sense of imminent enemy attack from those he met in the garrison. He then told the story of Captain Gregg as he heard it from the men at the fort and noted positively that Gregg "now lies under the care of Dr. Woodruff, who treats him with the greatest attention and tenderness; his recovery is probable."[43]

As an indication of one of the ways the Gregg incident affected his company, Private Samuel Mott later recalled in his pension application that he served in Captain Gregg's company until Gregg was scalped and was then "attached" to Captain Aorson's company, where he served for the rest of the war. The Gregg incident was so powerful a memory that, while he may have remembered it this way, Mott's transfer actually came when Aorson's light infantry company was formed several months after the incident.[44]

The local Oneida Indians became concerned that the soldiers would blame them for the attack and worked with Gansevoort to prevent trouble and retaliation. Prominent leaders from Oriska and Kanonwalohale came to the fort two days after the incident to express their condolences and assure Gansevoort that it was Loyalist-affiliated Indians who had been responsible. Kanonwalohale, today's Oneida Castle, located about seventeen miles west of the fort, was a town of around sixty houses, some built using traditional materials and others reflecting European design. It was the primary Oneida town and home to about one third of the Oneida population.[45] In 1773-74, the Reverend Samuel Kirkland had overseen the building of a large, two-story, white-painted meetinghouse featuring nine glass windows and a sixty-foot steeple. About the same time, at least eight frame and clapboard colonial-style houses had been built by Oneida families there.[46]

The Oneida leaders promised to send runners to other Haudenosaunee groups to seek help in identifying the murderers.[47] The answer didn't come until much later when a receipt was found, signed by Loyalist lieutenant colonel John Butler of the Indian Department. The receipt read, "This may certify that Kay-ing-waur-to, the Sanake [Seneca] chief, has been on an expedition to Fort Stanwix, and has taken two scalps, one from an officer and corporal that were gunning near the fort, for which I promise to pay at sight ten dollars for each scalp."[48]

Gansevoort had been aware since the May 28 report by friendly Oneida Indians that St. Leger's force, including Sir John Johnson's Royal Yorkers, was on its way to attack the fort. Then, General Schuyler wrote Gansevoort on June 30 that according to a report he had, Sir John intended to attack Fort Stanwix, and Gansevoort should put everything in readiness to defend it. He had also notified local Tryon County militia general Nicholas Herkimer to support Gansevoort with his men in case of attack. Gansevoort was told to keep Herkimer informed of any developments and take the usual necessary steps to avoid a surprise attack, including continuously keeping scouts out toward Oswego and any other location the enemy might approach from. Those scouts should do the best they could to determine the number of the enemy and specifically how many were British, Canadians, Loyalists, or Indians.[49]

Time was growing short to complete the restoration of the fort and strengthen it to withstand whatever combination of infantry and artillery the diverse British-led force might employ when they attacked.

Chapter 10

Danger Builds for Soldiers and Civilians Alike

July 1777

Just about a month before the siege began, Gansevoort was doing everything in his power to assist Captain Lamarquise with the fort's restoration. He reported, "The soldiers are constantly at work—even such of them as come off guard are immediately turned out to fatigue." Without further assistance, however, he could not accomplish everything necessary to prepare for the enemy's arrival. He could not carry out the "internal business of the garrison" while also "sending out sufficient parties of observation[,] felling timber into Wood creek," and "clearing the road from Fort Dayton which is so embarrassed in many parts as to be almost impassable." He needed 150 men "speedily and effectually to obstruct Wood creek" and the same number "to guard the men at work in falling and hauling of timber." If he used his men for those duties and continued to send out scouting parties, it "would scarcely leave a man in the garrison," and they might "be easily surprised by a very contemptible party of the enemy."[1]

The garrison's soldiers observed and probably recognized some of the individuals as a group of Haudenosaunee chiefs and warriors entered the fort on July 2 to talk with Colonel Gansevoort and present him with a wampum belt as a token of their friendship. They requested that Gansevoort inform General Schuyler of their visit and gift. Incidents like the one involving Corporal Madison and Captain Gregg had created great concern among the Indians trying to assist the fort garrison or just stay neutral. They must have been very aware of the prejudices that would cause the white men to automatically suspect them of the atrocities, and they had to reach out, rather than stay in the shadows, to build trust.[2]

The following day, Gansevoort assured General Schuyler that he would keep sending out scouting parties to prevent a surprise attack while also continuing the work required to "put this place in the best posture of defense I can." But also, once again, he had to remind Schuyler that although the number of men in his garrison was small, they still put a strain on the supplies of provisions. At present he had "only barrels of beef and pork which is the total of all the meat (tho the flower and peas are considerable larger in proportion)." In addition, "the demands for the Indian department are considerable." General Schuyler notified the Northern Department commissary on July 10 to provide Fort Stanwix with enough food to raise the supply to a "sufficiency for four hundred men for two months."[3]

Gansevoort was also deeply concerned that the fort lacked a "considerable supply of ammunition," and he hoped that Schuyler would quickly be able to send the required amount of powder, ball, grapeshot, and other munitions that Captain Lieutenant Savage had noted as badly needed on a recent return.[4] He added that a large number of the musket balls they did have on hand did not match the caliber of some of the muskets issued to the men. Because of the ubiquitous supply problems, his men had several types of muskets, each model firing a different caliber of musket ball. He requested that bullet molds of different caliber sizes be sent so the unusable musket balls could be melted down and recast in a usable size. Even if that problem was solved, though, they still did not have sufficient gunpowder.[5]

In the continuing fort restoration work, Ensign John Spoor of Captain De Witt's company led a seventeen-man fatigue party out from the fort on July 3 to cut blankets of sod for use in reinforcing and stabilizing the fort's earthen walls. They headed toward an area near the old Fort Newport about two thirds or three quarters of a mile away. While working, they came under attack by a party of around forty Indians sent out from St. Leger's force by Lieutenant Colonel Daniel Claus, deputy superintendent of the Seven Nations of Canada, who as senior Indian Department officer on the expedition served as its superintendent of

Indians. Claus doubted that St. Leger had accurate information about the present situation at Fort Stanwix and wanted to update it. The men sent by Claus, led by Captain John Hare of the Six Nations Indian Department and Mohawk war captain John Deserontyon were to scout the fort and accurately assess its strength and condition. During their bloody skirmish with the sod cutters that followed, the attackers killed and scalped four men, wounded two others, one mortally, and took several men prisoner, including Ensign Spoor.[6]

One wounded man who survived was Private Nicholas Bovee of Captain Aorson's company. After two musket balls tore through his right arm, a tomahawk strike to his hip left him unable to run. He was scalped and left for dead. Soldiers sent from the fort discovered him barely alive, and Privates James Lighthall and Gershom Vanderhyden of his company carried him back to the fort, where he lay in the hospital under the care of Dr. Woodruff for about three months, followed by several months at Albany. He eventually received an invalid pension from New York and for the rest of his life was known to his friends as "Scalpe Nick," "Scalped Nick," or "Sculpen Nick." He died in 1796 at Schenectady.[7]

Ironically, one man killed and scalped was James Rogers of Captain Gregg's company, who, according to his comrades, was ritualistically and "shockingly butchered." The men of Gregg's company could be forgiven for feeling marked. James Empson of Gregg's company was taken prisoner, along with Aaron King and Adam Shades from Captain Bleeker's company and two men from Tiebout's company, John Jones, one of the first enlistees on December 3, 1776, and James Turner, who had enlisted on February 1.[8] His captors killed Aaron King.[9] Conrad Frantz of Captain Aorson's company escaped capture and was able to get back to the fort. Whether in this attack or another one, Thomas Wilson of Bleeker's company was wounded in the left shoulder and arm sometime that month.[10] Gansevoort sent out two parties to pursue the enemy, but they did not find them.[11]

The officer leading one of those pursuit parties, probably from either Bleeker's or Tiebout's company, wrote a letter the next day noting:

> I took a party of men and went after them [the attackers], but was a little too late. I found one of our men on the road half dead and scalped, another coming in, shot through both arms; and about two miles further I found a third dead and scalped,

with a tomahawk sticking in his head. I still pursued on further, but it being towards evening, and having no provision, I thought best to return, and brought in the wounded and dead men. Four men and the Ensign they took off with them, two of whom were of my company.

He then expressed feelings that must have been like many of his men's, writing: "This is another specimen of the tender mercies of the king of Britain, in his hiring the Savages to murder us. By this also, you may read what unnatural animals the Tories are, who have an immediate hand in promoting these barbarities."[12]

Knowing that word of incidents such as the one with Ensign Spoor were circulating, even in newspapers as far away as Virginia, like the account just quoted, Colonel Gansevoort wrote to his beloved Caty Van Schaick on July 5 and told her: "You will undoubtedly hear of some mischief done again by some Indians to a Party of our Men who whare at Work about three Quarters of a Mile from the Fort—I hope this will not occasion the least uneasiness in you, with respect to my safety, I can assure that I think myself as safe in this Fort, as I would in any post of America."[13] He was as much reassuring himself as he was Caty.

The scouts sent out by Claus brought their prisoners immediately to St. Leger, some fifteen miles distant. There, St. Leger's officers interrogated each prisoner separately to prevent coordination of false information. The prisoners' testimony convinced St. Leger's officers that to defeat the fort garrison they would need additional and more powerful artillery pieces. They would also require more soldiers in addition to the previously assigned Hessen-Hanau Jäger, who had not yet joined St. Leger. Displaying significant disrespect for the qualities of his enemy, however, St. Leger completely rejected the intelligence given by the prisoners and took no action, while he still could, to bolster his forces, especially the artillery.[14]

Shortly after this incident, word of the devastating American evacuation of Fort Ticonderoga on July 6 reached Fort Stanwix. Just how Colonel Gansevoort and the garrison reacted to the news is not known, but it must have given them pause as they contemplated the imminent attack on their fort. Gansevoort received a letter from his brother Leonard, dated July 9, relating what was known of the Ticonderoga surrender and calling it "a most shameful affair indeed." He begged Peter and his "Regiment will not be a disgrace to the New York Arms." Leonard could not help adding, "Your Fellow Citizens put a great Confidence in you and your Father flatters himself that you will Conquer or die."[15]

Gansevoort also received a letter from his Caty and wrote back on July 12 telling her he "was very sorry to hear that you were so much distressed on the Account of our army having Evacuated Tyconderoga." He then told her about how he expected several hundred of General Herkimer's Tryon County militia to reinforce Fort Stanwix. To console her he stated: "I could wish that you and the rest of my Friends ware as secure as I shall then think Myself—We are very Busy in Fortifying this Fort, and doubt not but shall give them a warm Reception if they should pay us a Visit." The families of other members of his regiment, especially those who were illiterate, may have been left to worry without comforting words from their relative at the fort.[16] One can only imagine the pressures coming together in Gansevoort's mind.

Before the month was out, newspapers ran many stories and comments about the Ticonderoga surrender. Some accounts stressed the problems leading up to and now resulting from the incident. One declared that "through too great neglect at home, that fortress, on which immense labour and enormous sums have been bestowed, at present answers no other end than as a magazine for the enemy, and to prevent our arms from penetrating into their country." The piece continued, "It is owing to this cause [the lack of support provided], that so many of our forts have been relinquished, and become places of defence for our enemies."[17] Another account stressed what was considered the natural state of fort defense, wondering, "Pray what are forts and lines constructed for, if not to defend against a superior number?"[18] Another argued that this defeat should arouse the desire to avoid another such episode: "It is an event that alarms and rouzes; that leads us to collect ourselves; to unite in the most spirited exertions for the common safety."[19] At the end of the month, the *Pennsylvania Gazette* published a letter from Boston dated July 14 that read: "The public are not appalled, though extremely uneasy at the news of the evacuation of Ticonderoga and Mount Independence. The States have sufficient resources left, and the success of the enemy there may finally turn out to their disadvantage. This however can be no good reason for a council of general officers to determine to abandon it to the enemy with all its stores, and without resistance. Nothing since the commencement of the war has created so general a dissatisfaction."[20] This event would lead to the removal of Schuyler from command of the Northern Department and the reinstatement of Gates during the time when Gansevoort was leading the defense of Fort Stanwix against St. Leger's siege.[21]

On July 17, Oneida sachem Thomas reported to the Tryon County Committee of Safety that he had overheard a meeting that included Daniel Claus and Sir John Johnson in which it was said that they had seven hundred Indians, four hundred British regulars, and six hundred Loyalists at Oswego and were awaiting others. Thomas strongly encouraged the Americans to do all in their power to defend Fort Stanwix because it would be very hard on the local Indians if the fort fell to the enemy. There was still time to reinforce the garrison, but it was running short.[22] St. Leger's force set out on July 19 with their Indian allies and portions of the 8th and 34th British Regiments hoping to surprise the fort and capture it with only small arms. The other forces were to gather at Oswego. By July 25, St. Leger had returned to Oswego. His expedition finally set off for Fort Stanwix on July 26.[23]

Several of the captives from Spoor's party switched from being prisoners to being deserters by joining the enemy. Adam Shades, a shoemaker from Pennsylvania, enlisted in the King's Royal Yorkers on August 5, but his subsequent military history is quite complicated as to his apparently switching loyalties. James Empson and John Jones appear to have deserted to Butler's rangers soon after their capture.[24]

On a more positive note, in a letter dated July 4, the officer who led the party attempting to recover the men taken prisoner from Spoor's fatigue party reported, "Yesterday our worthy Chaplain, the Rev. Mr. Mason, arrived [at Fort Stanwix] safe."[25] Chaplain John Mason was forty-three years old, born in Linlithgowshire, Scotland, and ordained there in 1761 for the Presbyterian ministry. Assigned to New York as minister of the Cedar Street Presbyterian Church, he had been forced to leave the city when the British occupied it. After submitting a request to Congress to serve as a chaplain, he was appointed on November 21, 1776, to serve the 3rd New York Regiment. Where Mason had been since his appointment is unclear. He is not mentioned previously, so this may be when he first joined the regiment. Just two weeks after his arrival at Fort Stanwix, and eight months after his appointment, he resigned for unknown reasons on July 19, 1777. This was just when his services were most needed, as the siege was approaching. He would later serve as a chaplain beginning in October 1778, but at posts on the Hudson River far from the frontier for the remainder of the war.[26]

Two days after the Gregg incident, Schuyler wrote to Congress commenting that it was just one of his many concerns. He especially noted the continuing food supply problems, including the fact that "twenty-nine thousand odd hundredweight" of salt meat had been condemned at the fort.[27] Gansevoort knew that the successful attacks by the enemy on Captain Gregg and Ensign Spoor would "no doubt encourage them to send out greater numbers and the intelligence they may possibly acquire will probably hasten the main body destinated to act against us in these parts. Our provision is greatly diminished by reason of the spoiling of the beef, and the quantities that must be given from time to time to the Indians—It will not hold out above 6 weeks."[28] More positively, the regiment did get another sixty-two uniform coats of some unspecified color in mid-July.[29]

By July 19, Captain Gregg had made great progress recovering from his wounds. His subordinate officers and men, especially his nephew, were no doubt relieved and encouraged when they saw Gregg, with a party to assist him, set off for Albany to continue his recovery, perhaps accompanied by the Reverend Mason, who had resigned as their chaplain that day.

The same day Gregg departed for Albany, Captain Swartwout, Lieutenants Henry Defendorff and Thomas Ostrander of Van Bunschoten's company, John Ball and John Welch of Captain Aorson's company, Thomas McClellan of Tiebout's company, Prentis Bowen and William Colbrath of Captain Bleeker's, and Ensign George Denniston of Captain Gregg's company arrived back at the fort. They had been out recruiting, and one diary says they brought in "a number of recruits for the regiment," though surviving records, which must be incomplete, show that they brought in only about four men: three for Van Bunschoten's company and one for Aorson's.[30]

The deadly Indian attacks near the fort did not significantly discourage desertions. Following the common pattern of desertion within three months of enlistment, several of the deserters had enlisted within just the past couple of months.[31] George Shall, who had enlisted for the war on May 11, deserted on July 20, the same day Private Samuel Sutter of Captain Aorson's company was tried for desertion and enlisting in the artillery and sentenced to receive two hundred lashes.[32]

In other disciplinary matters, James Van Kleck of Captain Swartwout's company was accused of breaking the cock of his gun's firing mechanism in a malicious manner, but it must have been judged an accident because he was acquitted. Kermot Campbell of Captain Tiebout's company was charged with leaving his guard post without permission and becoming intoxicated with liquor and sentenced to endure one hundred lashes. Solomon Meeker of Captain Swartwout's company was acquitted of the charge of stealing a bayonet. The convicted men were scheduled to receive their lashes at 6:00 p.m. on July 19.[33]

General Schuyler finally had had enough of Captain Lamarquise by July 9 and ordered Gansevoort to send him to headquarters at Albany and turn the fort reconstruction work back over to Major Hubbell. Work on the fort still required the exertions of all the men when not assigned to some other duty, putting more pressure on everyone, and preventing the men from recovering sufficiently after hard work sessions. The last week of July was especially exhausting in the summer heat.[34]

The Oneidas depended on the Americans to successfully hold the fort, fearing what their fellow Haudenosaunee Seneca and Mohawk warriors accompanying St. Leger would do to them when they fully attacked the area. They continued their essential help supplying the garrison almost daily with information on the enemy's current location. Nevertheless, because St. Leger did not maintain his varied forces in a compact group, scouts could not acquire complete information on the numbers of the enemy force, their armaments, or the details of their plans.[35]

The Tryon County Committee held a meeting on July 17 at Fort Stanwix to hear intelligence gained by Thomas Spencer, who had returned from Canada five days previously. Staying undercover, Spencer had been able to hear a speech to the Indians by Colonel Daniel Claus, deputy superintendent of the Seven Nations of Canada, inviting them to join the expedition against Fort Stanwix. After commenting on the seizure of Fort Ticonderoga, Claus stated, "The same is with Fort Schuyler, I am sure, . . . that when I come towards that Fort and the Commanding officer there shall see me, he shall also not fire one Shot, and render the Fort to me." Spencer then gave some information on the composition of St. Leger's troops and declared to the committeemen, "Therefore now is your Time, Brothers, to awake, and not to sleep longer, or on the Contrary it shall go with Fort Schuyler, as It went already with Ticonderoga." He continued at great length encouraging the militia to assist Fort Stanwix. Although the committee recommended that the detachment of Major Ezra Badlam at Fort Dayton should be sent to Fort Stanwix, the major declined on account of the lack of clothing for his troops. Despite Spencer's efforts, and those by other Oneidas, reinforcement of the fort by either Continentals or militiamen seemed remote at this juncture.[36]

At Ramapo, New Jersey, General Washington was growing very concerned about the problems General Schuyler was having in obtaining sufficient militia and Continental troops. He was also quite troubled about the ability of Fort Stanwix to withstand an attack by St. Leger. In a letter to General Schuyler on July 24, Washington suggested that, in addition to upgrading the quantity of forces, "from the view I have of the matter I should think it necessary to send General Arnold or some other sensible & spirited officer to Fort Schuyler to take care of that post[,] keep up the spirits of the inhabitants and cultivate and improve the favourable disposition of the Indians."[37] In other words, do what Gansevoort had been working so hard and capably to do. This was not so much a slap in the face to Gansevoort as a newfound respect for the importance of Fort Stanwix in preventing the success of Burgoyne's campaign.

Washington based this thought on the supposition that something formidable was building in the area that required the oversight of a general, not a mere colonel. The presence of a general would be a symbol of Congress's commitment to the defense of the area. It would galvanize the local Patriots, especially the men in the militia, to help resist St. Leger. Whether Gansevoort felt a lack of confidence in him on the part of Washington is not known, but he understood that until a higher-ranking person was assigned to command the fort, it was all up to him. He was also aware that there was great local fear that residents who had so far supported the Revolution would change sides upon the appearance of British and Loyalist troops, unless they felt confident in a larger number of Continentals being added to defend the fort and their area on the river.

To hinder the approaching enemy, on July 25, Gansevoort, who had to intelligently and forcefully use his limited forces to the fullest extent, ordered a detachment of one captain, two subalterns, three sergeants, and fifty privates to be given three days' provisions and be sent out to guard local militiamen working to obstruct Wood Creek by cutting down trees on both sides of the creek so they would fall into the water and intertwine, blocking passage.[38] This would especially delay or prevent British bateaux carrying artillery pieces from bringing the guns

DANGER BUILDS FOR SOLDIERS AND CIVILIANS ALIKE 117

near the fort. Everyone was aware that the enemy was closing in on them and that any individual or small group venturing outside the fort risked ambush by one of the numerous advance bands of Indians.[39] In a July 26 letter to Schuyler, Gansevoort lamented that a group of local militiamen with him at the fort would be departing in two days, since they had been called out for only fourteen days. Also, while he had received word of the enemy advance, he had not received any of the provisions or ammunition he had repeatedly requested, except for a few barrels of flour.[40]

On July 27, Lieutenant Philip Conine replied to a letter a friend had sent him on July 9, reassuring his friend that although he had lately been ill, he was now much better. He reported, "We have nothing new at this place," although from information received from the Oneidas, everyone had "expected the enemy would have been here before this time." He was currently one of a party of fifty Continentals and sixty militiamen, commanded by Captain Bleeker, sent out to scout Lake Oneida. On their return they would join in the efforts to "stop up the passage of Wood Creek." He expressed his hope that "no bad news shall be heard from this quarter," and, not wanting to worry his friend, claimed, "Our men are in high spirits." Conine expressed no doubt that if the enemy appeared, his friend would hear that they met with "a drubbing." As he wrote, a work party sounded an alarm and "fired on a scout of Indians but did not kill any." The Indians ran off. Upon completing his story, and needing to get back to Captain Bleeker's scout party, Conine had to end his letter. He did add a quick note, though, that he expected to come down to see his friend in about seven weeks, if nothing "extraordinary" happened at Fort Stanwix.[41] Just after he finished that letter, however, something tragic did happen at the fort.

Lieutenant Colonel Willett was resting in his room on the warm and clear afternoon of July 27 when everyone in the garrison heard several guns fired quickly in succession, a warning that Indians were nearby. Gansevoort later described hearing four guns about 4:00 p.m. Willett ran quickly to the fort's gate "and on reaching the parapet of the glacis, saw a sentinel running towards the lower edge of it, and at a short distance from him a girl, also running, holding in her hand a small basket." When the girl got nearer, Willett saw blood running down her breast. She had been shot twice through the shoulder, but fortunately the wounds were not mortal. This sixteen-year-old, the daughter of longtime local resident George Reyter, who had served in the 4th Battalion of the Royal Americans in the French and Indian War, had been out with two other girls picking blackberries and raspberries, "not two hundred yards from the foot of the glacis," when suddenly, they were fired on by an estimated four Indians. Gansevoort quickly dispatched Willett from the fort with a party to investigate the place where the shots had been heard, at the edge of the woods perhaps five hundred yards from the fort. There they found two other girls, both tomahawked and scalped. One girl was dead, and the other appeared close to death. Willett's party brought the girls to the fort, where the wounded girl died after about half an hour. One of the dead girls was Caty, the thirteen-year-old daughter of British artilleryman John Steere, who had been stationed at the fort for several years. After his discharge and the abandonment of the fort, rather than return to England, he had been allowed to make his residence in a small house and cultivate a piece of ground near the fort. The other dead young woman was twenty-year-old Lenea Stephane, a servant girl of John Roof.[42]

Gansevoort was especially angered by this attack on noncombatant young women and commented in a letter to Colonel Van Schaick, "I had four men with arms just passed that place, but these mercenaries of Britain came not to fight, but to lie in wait to murder; and it is equally the same to them, if they can get a scalp, whether it is from a soldier or an innocent babe." The killer, however, was apparently not an Indian. Over a year later, Lieutenant Henry Hare of Colonel Butler's rangers confessed to the killing and scalping of Caty Steere/Steene before he was executed as a spy in 1779.[43] If he confessed to save his own life, he failed. If he was trying to settle his conscience on the verge of his death, this would be an example of how the civil war nature of the conflict had led him to adopt scalping as a tactic to terrify his opponents and shift the blame for an act of violence against civilian women.

In response to the enemy closing in on the fort, the following day Colonel Gansevoort "sent off those women which belonged to the garrison which have children." With them he sent the man from Ensign Spoor's party who had been scalped, the seriously wounded Reyter girl, and the sick soldiers in the hospital.[44] Just how many women and children were sent from the fort is unknown, but they included family members of the garrison soldiers and perhaps sutlers and other civilians. At least one soldier's wife, the wife of Private Dennis McCarty, remained at the fort, even though she was pregnant with their first child. Lieutenant Tapp's wife, also pregnant, may have remained as well.

Carrying Place resident John Roof, who served as a captain in the 1st Regiment Tryon County militia and was a member of the county Committee of Safety, took, or sent, his family to Canajoharie. They were welcomed there into the home of Tryon County militia general Nicholas Herkimer, who would very soon lead local militiamen on a mission to support the fort's garrison against St. Leger. At this point, the Roofs had five children: John, sixteen; Adam, four; Susannah, eleven; Barbara, six; and three-month-old Mary. Fortunately, their female children were younger than the girls who had tragically gone berry picking.[45]

With the enemy approaching, all fort activity had to be modified. Orders on July 29 established a guard mounted outside the fort consisting of a subaltern, one sergeant, one corporal, and "18 privates, all the sentinels to be taken from the out Guards, 6 privates to be taken from the Guard in the Fort, to compleat the out Guards agreeable to the above order 1 corporal and 6 privates to be taken from the guard in the fort to take charge of all the cattle belonging to the garrison. They will be particularly careful not to suffer any of the cattle to get near the edge of the woods." The garrison badly needed those cattle.[46]

Two hundred militiamen sent by General Herkimer to reinforce the fort had been committed for only sixteen days, and they needed to depart about July 29 to harvest their wheat and hay. Herkimer did extend their callout to active duty by several days. He also noted that 160 Continentals had set off on July 29 to reinforce the garrison and that, when required, Colonel James Wesson was ready to march his men to the fort from Fort Dayton, where they were stationed.[47]

An Indian rode up to the fort on July 30 carrying a belt of wampum and a letter from the "Sachems of Caughnawaga and the Six Nations" at the Oneida Castle. The letter expressed their determination to remain at peace with the Americans and reported that the enemy force was then at the Three Rivers and that two detachments were to be sent ahead. One party of eight was tasked with taking prisoners, and the other party of 130 had orders to "cut off the communications on the Mohawk River."[48]

About the same time, Captain De Witt arrived with his detachment from Fort Dayton, completely unifying the 3rd New York Regiment in one location for the first time. Private Christian Shell, who had joined

CHAPTER 10

De Witt's company at Fort Dayton, observed on his arrival that the work to restore and improve the fort defenses, which had been underway for over a year, was still not yet complete, so De Witt's company immediately joined in to help finish the work.[49]

Major Badlam also came up from Fort Dayton with 150 men of Colonel James Wesson's regiment who had been stationed there. Together these two detachments increased the fort's garrison by about two hundred men, worsening the already overcrowded living conditions. Mr. Hanson, the garrison commissary, also arrived with the heartening news that seven bateaux loaded with ammunition and provisions were on their way to the fort.[50]

Major Badlam's Massachusetts men lacked enthusiasm for helping the New Yorkers at Fort Stanwix. Badlam had earlier refused to bring them to the fort, in part because his men suffered from lack of clothing, and many were barefoot. The morale of his men was quite low. General Schuyler had been forced to give Badlam a direct order to join the crowded garrison at the fort, even though their clothing and provisions were insufficient. This led to distrust and ill feelings between troops fighting for the same cause. It also meant that the Continental troops in the area were concentrated at Fort Stanwix, leaving none to support the militia in other nearby areas of the Mohawk Valley.[51]

On July 29, a letter from Thomas Spencer was brought by an Oneida messenger informing Gansevoort that two days earlier St. Leger had left Oswego, where some of his troops were now, and that the leading troops should be at Fort Stanwix in two days.[52] Spencer followed with a letter to Gansevoort dated July 29 in which he told of a meeting with Indian chiefs who warned, "There is but four Days remaining of the Time set for the Kings Troops to come to Fort Schuyler and they think it likely they will be here sooner." Spencer let Gansevoort know that the chiefs were concerned and that they "desire the Commanding Officers of Fort Schuyler to exert themselves in their Defense" and "not make a Ticonderoga of it but they hope you will be courageous." They hoped that additional troops would be sent to the fort by General Schuyler. At present, Indian parties were making travel in the area very dangerous for the inhabitants, and everyone expected "we shall be surrounded as soon as they come." He asked Gansevoort to send the letter to the committees so that the "militia may rise up and come to Fort Schuyler." Some local Oneidas would be going to a meeting at Three

Rivers to "declare we are for Peace," but they expected "to be used with Indifference and sent away." As the troops were now very near the fort, he hoped "all Friends to Liberty and that loves their Families will not be backward but exert themselves," because "one Resolute Blow would secure the Friendship of the Six Nations and almost free this Part of the Country from the Excursions of the Enemy." Spencer signed the letter "Your very humble Servt & Well Wisher."[53]

After over a year of work aimed at getting the fort in condition to withstand a siege, it was now just a matter of hours before the test of both the fort and its garrison would begin. For most of the fort's defenders, this would be their first major combat against a large enemy force. The isolation of the fort must have greatly added to their apprehension. They would very soon know how ready they were.

Part III

The Siege of Fort Stanwix

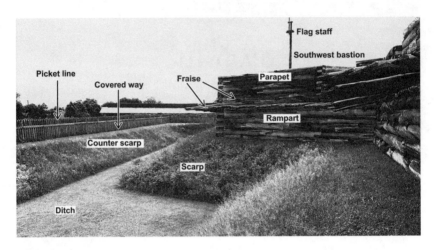

FIGURE 4. Fort Stanwix exterior defense elements. Author photo, Fort Stanwix National Monument, Rome, New York.

FIGURE 5. Fort Stanwix west curtain. This log-and-earth-structured curtain, part of the fort ramparts, connects the northeast and northwest bastions. Photo taken from the gorge leading onto the northwest bastion. The terrepleine is formed by the log roof of the west casemate below it. To the left is the banquette that men could stand on to fire over the rampart's parapet. West barracks on the right edge, sentry box behind it, and headquarters building at back of parade ground. Author photo, Fort Stanwix National Monument, Rome, New York.

FIGURE 6. Fort Stanwix east barracks. Note the piles of firewood and the brick chimneys for the fireplace/stoves. Author photo, Fort Stanwix National Monument, Rome, New York.

FIGURE 7. Fort Stanwix west casemate. The west barracks on the left. Author photo, Fort Stanwix National Monument, Rome, New York.

Figure 8. Fort Stanwix central interior components. Key: A—main gate; B—sentry box; C—guardhouse; D—storehouse; E—light cannon with traveling carriage; F—whipping post; G—senry box; H—headquarters building; I—east barracks; J—east casemate; K—southeast casemate; L—west barracks; M—west casemate and terre-pleine; N—parapet; O—southwest bastion; P—northwest bastion. Author photo of Fort Stanwix model at the Fort Stanwix National Monument, Rome, New York.

Figure 9. Fort Stanwix main entrance. Note the approach from the glacis through the defensive ravelin, across the bridge and drawbridge, and then the main gate. Author photo of Fort Stanwix model at the Fort Stanwix National Monument, Rome, New York.

FIGURE 10. Fort Stanwix southwest bastion. The sentry box at the point and the flag staff. There are six embrasures to accommodate six cannons, but there are only three cannons, two with garrison carriages and one with a traveling carriage. Just how many cannons each bastion had is not known, but none had their full complement. Each cannon had an elevated platform to the rear to absorb the recoil when a cannon was fired. Beneath this bastion in a bombproof shelter was located the fort hospital and also storage space for important papers and other items. Author photo of Fort Stanwix model at the Fort Stanwix National Monument, Rome, New York.

FIGURE 11. Fort Stanwix sally port. Located on the eastern edge of the fort, the port led into an enclosed "communication" passage exiting at a small five-sided redoubt. Author photo of Fort Stanwix model at Fort Stanwix National Monument, Rome, New York.

Chapter 11

St. Leger's Troops Begin Their Siege
August 1–5, 1777

By August 1, Lieutenant Colonel Willett could report that the wall surrounding Fort Stanwix was repaired, although many things could still be improved. He noted: "The parapets were nearly raised; embrasures made on three of the bastions; horizontal pickets fixed around the walls, and perpendicular pickets around the covert way. The gate and the bridge were also made secure, though the time had been too short to make any material alteration in the salient angle, so as to derive any benefit from it."[1] Colonel Gansevoort ordered "a picquet [picket] guard to mount this evening" consisting of one captain, three subalterns, four sergeants, one drummer, and eighty privates.[2] If a gun fired signaling an alarm to turn out and man the bastions, one of the commissioned officers, one sergeant, one corporal, and twenty privates should take position on each bastion.

If the captain commanding the picquet guard believed that the situation required a greater response, he should order "the drum to beat the alarm" signaling the full garrison to turn out to their alarm posts. Major Badlam's Massachusetts detachment would take position on the southeast bastion and the adjacent curtain. Captain Aorson's and Captain Jansen's companies would report to the southwest bastion. Captain Van Bunschoten's and Captain Tiebout's companies would take position on the northwest bastion, while Captain De Witt's, Captain Swartwout's, and Captain Bleeker's companies assembled on the northeast bastion. Captain Gregg's company would assemble on the parade to await further orders. Gansevoort reassured his

CHAPTER 11

soldiers that "it is not doubted but the officers and men at this important crisis will be very alert in turning out in time of an alarm."[3]

Although the enemy's arrival was expected hourly, Gansevoort's morning garrison orders on August 1 routinely instructed "that the officers be careful to inculcate the necessity of cleanliness to their men as much as the preservation of their health depends upon it."[4] This must have amused the men anticipating their health to be much more endangered very soon by objects more immediately deadly than dirt. Maintaining their health, however, would be just as important during the siege as having enough food and military supplies.

Food supplies at the fort included five hundred barrels of flour, sixty barrels of salted meats, "a considerable quantity of peas," and twenty head of fat cattle that had recently arrived. Colonel Gansevoort had obtained an additional fifty cattle from the residents living around the fort.[5] These animals would need to be protected during the enemy attack, most likely by being placed in the fort ditch, which offered at least a bit of shelter. Some may have been placed in the fort itself.

Butchered livestock could replace salt meat when necessary, although by August 8, Gansevoort's superior, General Schuyler, had developed real concerns about the extensive sickness throughout the army, including at Fort Stanwix, due, he believed, to reliance on fresh meat rather than salted.[6] Colonel Gansevoort stated several months after the siege that since taking command of the fort in early May, he had "been only supply'd from hand to mouth and ... from whence this neglect proceeds I cannot tell."[7]

During the day on August 1, three Oneidas rushed into the fort to report sighting three unknown Indians near the Oneida Castle who told them that there were one hundred Indians at "the Royal Block House" on Oneida Lake, near its eastern end, who were headed for Fort Stanwix. Believing that this enemy detachment had been sent to disrupt communications and attack bateaux carrying supplies to the fort, Gansevoort dispatched one hundred men, under the command of Captain Van Bunschoten and three subalterns, to reinforce the guard accompanying four bateaux carrying supplies from Fort Dayton and expected hourly.[8]

Those bateaux arrived at the upper landing the following day, accompanied by a guard of one hundred men commanded by Lieutenant Colonel James Mellon of Colonel Wesson's regiment,[9] reinforced by the one hundred men sent out under Captain Van Bunschoten.

Upon hearing that one hundred strange Indians were in the area, the men acted speedily to transfer the bateau cargo into the fort. Those supplies ensured that the fort had enough provisions and artillery ammunition to last six weeks, but only if the men fired no more than nine cannon shots each day.[10] As soon as the supplies were unloaded and brought into the fort, sentinels stationed on the southwest bastion observed enemy campfires in the woods about two thirds of a mile away near the remains of Fort Newport at the upper landing on Wood Creek.

The two-hundred-man bateau guard entered the fort, and the garrison quickly took up their alarm posts. The fort's defenders now numbered a little fewer than 750, consisting of Continentals and an unknown number of other people, including women, friendly Oneidas, and craftsmen. Very soon some men came running from the landing and breathlessly reported that although the guard troops had marched into the fort, the bateau crewmen had remained with their boats at the landing, where enemy fire wounded two men and the enemy took the master of the bateaux and another man prisoner.[11]

Suddenly, sentries and others looking out from the fort caught sight of a well-known friendly Oneida man from Kanonwalohale running toward the fort, hotly pursued by enemy Indians. This was seventeen-year-old Paul Powless, noted for his great running speed. Powless had been serving with other Oneidas acting as pickets and scouts for the fort when he was spotted by enemy Indians under Mohawk Joseph Brant and Lieutenant Henry Bird, of the 8th "King's" Regiment of Foot, approaching the fort with St. Leger's advance units.

Brant confronted Powless and, while each man held his gun on the other, tried to persuade him to come over to the British side. Powless would have none of it and retreated on the run toward the fort. While running, he alerted other Oneida pickets, who soon came under fire from Bird's British and Brant's Indians. The outnumbered Oneidas escaped their pursuers by using their intimate knowledge of the area terrain to circle around the fort and enter it from the opposite side.[12] Powless's refusal to submit to Brant demonstrated the increasingly strong alliance between the Oneidas and the Continentals. This attack on the fort's Oneida pickets can be considered the opening action of the siege.

Several Oneidas were already in the fort ready to help with its defense, go out to collect information about the enemy force, or deliver messages to spread the word of the enemy approach and seek help to confront it. They could also harass the enemy as opportunities arose.

CHAPTER 11

Chief warrior Han Yerry Tewahangarahken, or Han Yerry Doxtader, and his wife, Tyonajanegen, known to whites as Two Kettles Together, were among the Oneidas at the fort. Han Yerry was in his fifties and very likely the son of a Mohawk mother and a German father. He considered himself to be Oneida, and the Oneidas completely accepted him. He became a highly respected warrior of the Wolf Clan. He and his wife lived at Oriska, where they raised three sons and a daughter. Despite being such an aggressive warrior, Han Yerry was well known for his gentleman's demeanor. Strong supporters of the American cause, Han Yerry and Two Kettles Together would prove quite active and athletic when undertaking their highly valuable contributions, despite the fact that they were no longer young.[13]

Throughout the days leading up to and then during the siege, the fort welcomed many Oneidas seeking refuge there, who then endured the siege alongside the garrison soldiers. Their exact number, age, and gender is not known, but at least some actively helped defend the fort. Among those were Clanis Kahiktoton (Cornelius), Shonoghleoh (Anthony), and Aughneonh (Big Bear), and one of the Oneidas' best warriors, Hanyost T,hanaghghanegeaghu. Clanis Kahiktoton performed extremely valuable service carrying messages between Fort Stanwix and German Flats. Other Oneidas continued harassing the British soldiers and their Indian allies and carried information to the American military and civilian leaders. Helping Gansevoort significantly, Oneidas gathered intelligence on the British forces and traveled to Albany to urge General Schuyler to send troops to assist in defending the fort.[14]

Asked to undertake a mission to spread word that the siege had commenced and to seek reinforcements, Two Kettles Together exited the fort with a horse, avoided capture, and rode express to Fort Dayton. After dark, Paul Powless successfully undertook a similar mission, also avoiding enemy capture. With Burgoyne's force approaching Albany, any spare Continental troops had been ordered there, leaving the Tryon County militia the only military force that could assist the Fort Stanwix garrison.[15]

Now that the long-anticipated siege was a reality, Gansevoort ordered two barns standing near the fort, belonging to residents who had been sent off on July 28, to be burned down to create clear fields of fire and deny their use to the assembling enemy. During the evening of

August 2, members of the artillery detachment loaded two cannons on the southwest bastion with grapeshot and fired at the barns to drive away any enemy Indians who "might have been sculking about them" or looking for food. Then thirty men, accompanied by one of the fort's 3-pounder artillery pieces mounted on a traveling carriage, exited the fort to set the barns on fire and return immediately. They accomplished this task without incident.[16]

Despite the many months of restoration work on the fort, which had been so frequently mismanaged, criticized, and defended with excuses, Private Henry Ritter long remembered that construction still "was not quite done when the enemy under Barry St. Leger came on." Ritter proudly stated that he and the other members of Tiebout's company, and the entire garrison throughout the unfolding three-week siege, "did not retreat 'nor give up the Ship' but kept in the fort, and fought like enraged bull dogs, taking especial care to *Keep within the Pickets*."[17]

The final defensive horizontal pickets protruding from the front rampart walls below the parapet embrasures, the fraise, had been mounted during the night before the British arrived, but none of the parapets had been fully completed. Ritter could have added that even while defending the fort so determinedly during the siege, the garrison soldiers continued their restoration work, much of it at night, and that enemy fire killed several men as they worked. Among other projects, since the French engineer had incompetently neglected to build a secure ammunition magazine, one needed to be constructed. The magazine would be located in a bombproof shelter beneath the northwest bastion.[18]

Bombproofs—areas designed to protect explosives and assorted valuable items from destruction by enemy mortar fire—were built under each bastion. They were essentially caves with walls of vertical wooden boards, or horizontal boards attached to a framework, which supported wood plank ceilings covered over with a substantial depth of soil. Floors were wooden planks on sleepers or just the soil itself. The northwest bombproof contained the magazine for gunpowder and other military supplies. The northeast bombproof was an approximately sixteen-foot square with a six-foot-wide passageway entry. The southeast bombproof contained the bakehouse. The southwest bombproof, which was approximately twenty feet square with a wooden plank floor resting on the soil, served as the fort's hospital. In addition to beds, it would have contained medical instruments and supplies, an operating table, perhaps a water barrel, and other necessary items.[19]

A flag flying over a fort proclaimed the identity of the nation possessing it, and the absence of a flag could indicate a surrendered fort. Fort Stanwix had not been issued a flag to signify its country of ownership. Therefore, as the siege approached, several officers of the 3rd New York Regiment created a large flag they could fly to announce to their enemy that the garrison would not surrender but would stand firm to defend their fort and country.[20] The officers cut pieces of white cloth from ammunition containers and shirts and red cloth provided by "one and another of the garrison." They cut blue pieces from the cloak captured from the British troops at Peekskill, in the initial action fought by elements of the regiment, which Captain Swartwout had proudly kept. From those pieces they stitched together a Grand Union, also known as the Continental, flag. It displayed thirteen red and white stripes with the blue, white, and red British Union flag in the canton.

Then, early on the morning of August 3, the garrison proudly hoisted their flag to the top of the ship's mast-style flagstaff on the southwest bastion and fired a cannon leveled at the enemy's camp.[21] A proud Lieutenant Colonel Willett believed that "the flag was sufficiently large and a general exhilaration of spirits appeared on beholding it wave."[22] Everyone in the garrison felt great pride when they saw the flag raised, even though their fort was still not complete and the siege was just beginning. Some of the officers, including Captain Swartwout, must have felt a special pride knowing they had contributed swatches of cloth for the flag. It is not known just who did the cutting and stitching, but it may have been a soldier with tailoring skills or one or more of the women still at the fort.

Colonel Gansevoort sent a small party to the river landing to check on the condition of the bateaux still tied there. They found the boats undamaged by the British and discovered the missing bateau man. He had been wounded through the brain, stabbed in the right breast, and scalped. Still alive, he was carried to the fort and Dr. Woodruff, but the man soon died. According to the diary of Hessian Jäger First Lieutenant Philipp Jakob Hildebrandt, the bateau man had been "captured by the savages and brought in; two other miscreants who sought to escape were shot dead."[23]

By this point in the campaign, St. Leger understood that he was not adequately prepared and equipped, especially with artillery, to defeat the much stronger than expected fort easily and quickly by assault or even by siege. Hoping to persuade the Fort Stanwix garrison to surrender, St. Leger ordered his troops, not yet complete in total numbers, to march off from their campsites at 4:00 a.m. on August 3. What Hildebrandt estimated to be two hundred Indians led the group toward the fort, followed by his Jäger company, then two companies each of the 8th and 34th Regiments, totaling about 221 men, then a sixty-man detachment of Sir John Johnson's King's Royal Yorkers, and lastly the rear guard of about two hundred Indians. What artillery St. Leger had brought, along with many of his troops, continued to struggle against the obstructions in Wood Creek, and many additional Indians were also still en route.[24]

St. Leger, even though inadequately prepared, had so low an opinion of his opponent that he believed the garrison would surrender simply upon the appearance of his troops. At about 3:00 p.m. he began parading them around the fort. He kept his men out of range, several hundred yards from the fort walls. Nevertheless, the nearly 750 men garrisoning the fort could at least partially analyze St. Leger's force and note that it appeared to be insufficient to take the fort easily.

Some men later recalled in exaggerated terms that St. Leger's force had been very impressive. Private Lawrence Schoolcraft told friends and family that St. Leger's troops landed on the banks of Wood Creek and began their march across the portage to begin the siege. In his later years, desiring to be admired for his bravery in the siege, he described a day of striking scenes and military pageantry that made a great impression on all those present. Schoolcraft recounted that it was a "calm and beautiful morning" when St. Leger's troops began their march from Wood Creek. He and other members of Tiebout's company stood on the northwest bastion and adjoining ramparts looking toward an area indicated to them by "the Oneida sachem" where the enemy would appear.[25]

Soon they heard military music and then saw the red uniforms. The British troops carried their regimental colors, with the British Union flag in the canton and regimental cipher in the center, which they unfurled proudly. This created intense interest among the men on the ramparts, who stood wordless. Indians spread out on the British flanks, adding additional color with their war paint and feathers and generating terror with their loud, piercing cries that could be heard above the British fifes and drums. The fort's occupants gazed at the enemy in silence and not a gun was fired.[26] While no other person present described the appearance of the enemy as such an impressive sight, including Lieutenant Hildebrandt, it is not unlikely that the approaching troops were awe-inspiring to many in the garrison for whom this was to be their initial battle.

Compromising the spectacle was the fact that the British soldiers and Hessian Jäger had marched through water, mud, brush, and other environmental obstacles that had greatly damaged, if not destroyed, the parade ground appearance of the men and their uniforms. One Jäger commented that they were in rags and their green uniform coats had turned brown with dirt, while their leather breeches had become stiff and cracked from excessive exposure to water and sun.[27] This was likely also true of the other units with St. Leger.

The Fort Stanwix garrison troops were also not dressed in parade-quality uniforms. Because clothing had been so difficult to obtain, many men wore hunting shirts, or rifle frocks, combined with variously aged buckskin breeches and waistcoats, and woolen overalls. A German officer at the Battle of Saratoga some weeks after the siege ended said of the Continentals he faced there that "each had on the clothes which he was accustomed to wear in the field, the tavern, the church and in every-day life."[28]

After making their hopefully intimidating appearance, St. Leger's troops collected hay from the local farm fields to use for bedding as they settled in for the siege. Although not all of St. Leger's troops were present yet before the fort on August 3, his force included six hundred to eight hundred Seneca warriors recruited by Butler along the way with promises of plunder and an easy campaign. St. Leger needed the fort garrison to surrender quickly because his Indian warriors would fight only so long as victory was considered certain, and they avoided protracted engagements whenever possible.[29]

Hoping, and perhaps even expecting, Colonel Gansevoort to surrender, St. Leger sent Captain Gilbert Tice with a flag of truce out to the fort with a written, slightly altered copy of a lengthy proclamation generally encouraging surrender written by Burgoyne, but this one carried St. Leger's signature. This was the first time Gansevoort and his men learned that it was Barry St. Leger who was leading the troops attacking them. Captain Tice's walk to the fort, against a backdrop of spread-out troops and Indians, would have been very stirring to impressionable men like Schoolcraft.

As a well-known Loyalist colonial officer with a solid reputation, Captain Tice was a good choice to perform this mission. He had experience gained from service in the French and Indian War, the attack on St. John in September 1775, where he was wounded, and his current service in the Indian Department. Although he came from New Jersey, he and his wife operated a tavern at Johnstown.[30] As Tice approached the fort, even from a distance he could professionally note in some detail the strengths and the not yet restored flaws in the fort's exterior physical fabric. To prevent Tice from studying the fort's interior arrangement and conditions, Gansevoort had him blindfolded before allowing him to enter the fort, a scene long remembered by men of the garrison, including Samuel Veeder of Captain Swartwout's company, who could still describe it in his old age.[31]

Gansevoort received Tice politely and had him ushered across the bridge spanning the fort ditch and its final drawbridge section and through the fort's main gate, where he then crossed over the parade and entered the headquarters building on its north side.[32] This building was divided into four side-by-side rooms with a lean-to on the end. At the time of the siege, one room was Colonel Gansevoort's lodging, one Lieutenant Colonel Willett's, one belonged to Major Cochran and perhaps the adjutant, and one served as a dining room and staff meeting room. The lean-to was either an officers' privy, a woodshed, lodging for an orderly, or a storeroom, or some combination of these.[33]

Once Tice was inside that building and the men had removed his blindfold, several senior officers talked with him. The soldiers at their posts and civilians in the fort must have wondered what the talk was all about while they quietly, but alertly, waited for it to end. They knew their lives might depend on what was being discussed. Speaking with Gansevoort, Tice offered St. Leger's pledge to protect the garrison from any retribution by the Indians or other forces—but only if they surrendered immediately. Gansevoort and his officers, as well as their troops, knew well the story of the siege of Fort William Henry during the Seven Years' War and the massacre of its defenders once they had surrendered after a period of holding out. Gallantly, although still unaware of the precise nature of the enemy force opposing him, Gansevoort rejected the idea of surrender "with disdain," thus setting up a possible future Fort William Henry scenario.[34]

Having made his point clearly, Gansevoort again had Captain Tice blindfolded and led back out of the fort. Tice's observations, and his sense of the qualities of the officers he had spoken to, left him impressed with their resolve. When he got back and filled in St. Leger on his observations and judgments from his discussions, it became even clearer to St. Leger that taking the fort was not going to be the easy task he had been led to, or persuaded himself to, believe it would be.[35] Tice's report must have made St. Leger wish he had taken seriously the information given by the prisoners seized earlier from Ensign Spoor's party. Although the task of restoring the fort had not been completed, Fort Stanwix presented its enemies with a complex, highly organized military defensive work in which all available spaces were actively accommodating the troops and other occupants or were in use for some purpose relating to the defense of the fort. No space was wasted. The fort might not be completely restored, but it was strong enough for a solid defense. By this point, St. Leger knew that a frontal assault on the fort was impossible. His large number of Indian allies preferred hit-and-run attacks, or firing from cover, to making themselves open targets in a massive assault.[36]

St. Leger's very disappointing day appropriately closed with a 10:00 p.m. "severe thunderstorm" producing "streams of rain which left us in a terrible condition," according to Lieutenant Hildebrandt.[37] The earth and timber fort must also have been quite uncomfortable for its occupants.

During the first few nights of August, garrison sentinels continuously scanned the area of cleared land, "looking down the rough trail that disappeared into the endless forest along the Mohawk—looking east, where their families were—whence relief would appear," if in fact it ever came. They frequently saw British and German soldiers in the wood line and smoke from enemy campfires. Tension increased as they watched and listened for any signs of impending attack. The garrison became especially on edge when sentinels occasionally spotted Indians creeping up to the walls in the dark of night to reconnoiter the fort's approaches and defenses.[38]

The siege took another step forward very early on the morning of August 4, when Indians and Jäger advanced to within gunshot of the fort and commenced a brisk fire while concealing themselves behind tree stumps and other natural shelters. The Indians even sought cover among the "bushes, weeds, and potatoes" growing in the fort garden.[39] This greatly distracted the men working to raise the parapets, especially when enemy gunfire wounded several of them. Captains stationed men considered to be marksmen at different parts of the fort to return fire when opportunities arose.[40] Indians also destroyed the settlers' houses and barns still standing near the fort by creating, in the words of Lieutenant Hildebrandt, "an astounding fire." The Indians fired on the fort throughout the day, but with little serious effect. As Hildebrandt noted: "There can be no other explanation other than this: that the Indians do not allow themselves either to be commanded or restrained. Rather they demand as much powder and lead as they intend to shoot up arbitrarily. One can rightly regard this obstinate behavior as wasteful. They fire for a quarter hour—whether they score a hit or not—, and when they do perceive the location of the enemy cannon, not even the devil can produce a result."[41]

Around 11:00 a.m., members of the garrison spotted a party of ten Jäger detached from the main body and fired both cannons and small arms at them. The Jäger took cover behind a thick fallen oak tree and, returning fire with their short rifles, shot down several of the garrison in their defensive positions.[42] Lieutenant Colonel Mellon and his one-hundred-man bateau guard from Fort Dayton were to have returned to German Flats that day, but with Fort Stanwix now besieged, they stayed on as part of the garrison.

During this first day of siege, garrison members observed sights that stayed with them for years. One account records, "A sentinel, posted on the northwest bastion of the fort, was shot with a rifle while walking his stated rounds in the gray of the morning."[43] The easily impressed Private Schoolcraft of Tiebout's company later recalled that members of his company and others at their defense posts observed an enemy Indian marksman in the thick top of a pine tree "standing in the angle." The fort defenders loaded a cannon with grapeshot and aimed it at the tree. Upon being fired, the shot brought the Indian tumbling to the ground along with many pine branches. For Schoolcraft and other members of the company, this relatively small success renewed confidence in their ability to defend the fort.[44]

The firing ceased after darkness set in. One man of the garrison had been killed, Thomas Owens of Captain Aorson's company,[45] and six wounded. A party from the garrison went out at night and returned shortly with twenty-seven stacks of badly needed hay for the cattle being kept in the fort ditch during the siege. That sizable ditch ranged from ten to twelve feet in depth, thirty-five to sixty feet in width at the top, and fifteen to thirty feet at the bottom. Hay was needed in very large quantities for fodder to feed the animals, as well as for use as soldiers' bedding. Haystacks must have been common both outside and inside the fort, perhaps in the ditch if not on the parade. While they were out not far from the southwest bastion, the hay gatherers burned down John Roof's house and barn to clear a field of fire.[46]

About daybreak on August 5, a sentinel on the northwest bastion was killed by an enemy marksman, like the man killed the day before.[47] Frequent exchanges of musketry continued during the day with one defender being shot dead on the northeast bastion. Between 4:00 and 5:00 p.m. the enemy set fire to the barracks that French engineer Lamarquise had uselessly insisted on building outside the fort. The wind blew the heavy smoke toward the fort, which created "considerable inconvenience to the garrison."[48]

During the evening, sentinels and men at alarm posts on the ramparts saw many Indians and some of Sir John Johnson's men moving along the edge of the woods in the direction of Oriska. The reason for these actions was a mystery. Were they going to bypass the fort and attack some settlement down the Mohawk River Valley? Were they trying to draw a detachment out of the fort so they could attack it? When it became dark, the enemy Indians, thought now to number about a thousand, completely encircled the fort and began a terrifying yelling that continued, on and off, most of the night, and succeeded in terrorizing and upsetting the garrison. Combined with the visual images of the burnt-out shells of the various private and military buildings that had been destroyed outside the fort, these auditory enemy psychological assaults presented a very discomfiting image to sentinels and the garrison in general.[49] At some point this day, Platt Sammons of Captain Gregg's company must have decided the British would prevail and deserted to the enemy.[50]

The fort occupants were probably wondering whether the enemy would attack soon in force and try to overpower the fort's defenses and defenders. Or would the enemy firing, at times from fairly safe distances while taking cover using natural defenses, continue for an extended time? Just how many attackers were there? What kind of artillery and how much would they bring up to fire against and into the fort? The garrison would have to wait and see what developed the next day.

Chapter 12

Willett's Sally and the Battle of Oriskany

August 6, 1777

During the morning of August 6, the garrison curiously observed enemy Indians leaving their positions and heading toward the lower landing on the Mohawk River. There was not much early morning gunfire, but a marksman killed another morning sentry on the northwest bastion. Fearing that Loyalists would convey misleading and harmful information concerning the state of the siege to army headquarters, Gansevoort ordered highly regarded Lieutenant Henry Defendorff of Captain Van Bunschoten's company to prepare to leave the fort that evening and make his way through the enemy lines for Albany to inform General Schuyler of the true situation. Defendorff, however, would never be dispatched.

Sometime around midday, three Tryon County militiamen, Adam Hellmer, John Demuth, and John Adam Kember, approached the fort from the woods and were welcomed in. They had traveled all night, avoiding capture by the enemy forces besieging the fort. Once in the fort, they delivered a message from their general, Nicholas Herkimer, to Colonel Gansevoort. The message informed Gansevoort that Herkimer had arrived with "about a thousand" militiamen at Oriska, where he was joined by some of the local Oneida Indians.[1] Furthermore, Herkimer planned a movement against St. Leger's forces designed to relieve the garrison at Fort Stanwix and open the blocked lines of communication in the valley. Finally, Gansevoort was instructed that if he should hear small arms fire indicating a skirmish near the fort that day, he should send out a detachment to reinforce Herkimer's militia and help them break through to the fort. Herkimer also requested that Gansevoort fire three cannon shots as a signal to let him know when his message had been received.[2]

What Gansevoort did not know was that Herkimer's militiamen and Oneida allies had set off toward Fort Stanwix early that morning but were ambushed by those members of St. Leger's forces the garrison had seen leaving the fort area and heading toward Oriska. St. Leger had been informed of Herkimer's plan by Joseph Brant's sister Molly. By the time Gansevoort read the message, Herkimer's men were already heavily engaged in combat. Herkimer probably did not recognize the sound, if he even heard it, when Gansevoort ordered the three cannon shots fired. The garrison followed the signal with three loud cheers to intimidate those enemy troops still besieging the fort.[3]

Even though the garrison heard no sounds of distant combat, Gansevoort and Willett agreed that Willett should lead a sally from the fort to assist Herkimer's force in some manner. Willett's force would consist of 250 men: one hundred from the 3rd New York Regiment, one hundred from Wesson's detachment, and fifty men to service one of the fort's iron 3-pounder fieldpieces mounted on a maneuverable field carriage.[4]

It appears that at least some of the men selected to conduct the sally were volunteers. Conrad Frantz of Aorson's company, who had escaped the ambush of Ensign Spoor's sod-collecting fatigue party a month earlier, later proudly stated that he "was one of the volunteers that turned out of the Fort under Col. Willett." According to Schoolcraft, the men were paraded "in a square" and informed of the plan. Lieutenant Colonel Willett then

> went down into the esplanade and addressed the men to this effect:—Soldiers, you have heard that Gen. Herkimer is on his march to our relief. The commanding officer feels satisfied that the tories and queen's rangers have stolen off in the night with Brant and his Mohawks, to meet him. The camp of Sir John [Johnson] is therefore weakened. As many of you as feel willing to follow me, in an attack upon it, and are not afraid to die for liberty, will shoulder your arms, and *step out one pace* in front.

As Willett finished, at least two hundred men, including Schoolcraft and Frantz, stepped out almost immediately.[5] Matross John Burroughs of Savage's artillery detachment later declared that "he was engaged in the storming of the redoubt [actually the camp] of the British near Fort Stanwix."[6]

Willett selected and organized his force beginning with an advance guard of thirty men to be led by Captain Van Bunschoten and Lieutenant Levi Stockwell of Jansen's company. Van Bunschoten's fifer, David Jones, who volunteered to go, was disappointed not to be chosen to accompany his captain because, he was told, "no music was desired."[7] Another thirty men would form the rear guard under Lieutenant Samuel Allen[8] of Wesson's troops and Lieutenant Henry Defendorff of Van Bunschoten's company. Thirty flank guards would be commanded by a captain and Ensign Joshua Chase of Wesson's regiment. The main body would consist of eight squads commanded by Captain Bleeker, Lieutenants Phillip Conine and Samuel Lewis of Swartwout's company, Lieutenant Benjamin Bogardus and Ensign Josiah Bagley of Bleeker's, Lieutenants Thomas McClellan of Tiebout's and Thomas Ostrander of Van Bunschoten's, and Ensign George Denniston of Gregg's.

Captain Jansen would bring up the rear of the main body. The 3-pounder fieldpiece would accompany them under the direction of Major Badlam and Captain Swartwout. Major Badlam had previously commanded an artillery company when a captain in 1775 for about six months under then Colonel Henry Knox, and Willett must have felt he was better qualified, and higher ranked, than Captain Lieutenant Savage for this mission.[9] Ensigns Peter Magee of De Witt's company and Eldred Ament of Aorson's would lead a fifty-man guard for the fieldpiece.[10]

After two captains had declined to accompany Willett as his aide, First Lieutenant John Ball of Captain Aorson's company, who was about twenty-one years old, volunteered his services and Willett cheerfully accepted him, remarking that he had been just about to ask Ball to take the position.[11]

A severe rainstorm suddenly coming up delayed Willett's sally. But as soon as the storm ended, sometime around 1:00 to 2:00 p.m., Willett led his men out through the sally port and communication and then moved quickly down the old military road about half a mile to a mile, where they discovered Sir John Johnson's undefended camp. Possibly not having heard sounds of the engagement with Herkimer's force, and certainly unaware that it was too late to alter the course of that battle, Willett risked censure for disobeying orders and took a different course of action. He clearly understood the huge benefits to be gained from a surprise attack on Colonel Johnson's depleted Loyalist camp, a nearby Indian camp, and what was possibly British lieutenant Bird's camp at the lower landing, about a half mile distant.[12]

He decided to attack those weakened camps instead of marching on toward Oriska. When they got to Sir John Johnson's camp, according to Private Schoolcraft's later statement, Sir John lay in his tent with his coat off in the warm weather, and when the attack began, he immediately fled with his men through the Mohawk River to get across it.[13] Willett's men took the camp with bayonets, driving Johnson's Loyalists through and across the river, and captured the baggage and supplies the British left behind. The captured items included Johnson's baggage, papers, and correspondence, including letters from St. Leger expressing his contempt for the quality of the American garrison. When these were later read back at the fort, they must have angered the Americans while motivating them to prove their worth to him unquestionably.[14] In addition, Willett's men captured Lieutenant George Singleton of Johnson's regiment, who had been wounded in the battle.[15]

Willett also attacked one of the Indian encampments on the south side of the river about one mile from the fort. Items captured there included more than fifty brass kettles and more than a hundred blankets. These were among the presents Butler had given the warriors who agreed to join the expedition and items that the fort garrison badly needed. Other plunder included a quantity of muskets, tomahawks, spears, ammunition, clothing, deerskins, and a variety of other items. Several flags of uncertain significance were also taken, the first enemy flags to be captured since the Hessian regimental flags taken at General Washington's surprise attack on Trenton the previous December, though probably not as significant.[16] Garrison orders required that all the plunder taken in the sally be delivered to Adjutant Sytez, who would inventory the items so they could be equally divided among the men who sallied forth under Willett.[17]

Several days later, Willett wrote that in his attack, "the Indians took chiefly to the woods, the rest of their troops to the river." He was uncertain about the number of enemy losses, but "six lay dead in their encampment, two of which were Indians, several scattered about in the woods but their greatest loss appeared to be in crossing the river, and no inconsiderable number on the opposite shore."[18]

CHAPTER 12

When made aware of Willett's sally, St. Leger ordered a flanking attack against it. Willett commented, "We were out so long, that a number of British regulars, accompanied by what Indians, &c. could be rallied, had marched down to a thicket on the other side of the river, about fifty yards from the road we were to pass on our return." As Tryon County militiaman Adam Helmer commented, Major Badlam "saluted them with grape shot." That "salute," when augmented by musket fire combined with shots from one of the fort cannons, "soon obliged them to scamper off."[19] Willett found that "the enemy's fire was very wild, and though we were very much exposed, did no execution at all."[20]

Helmer later reported that during the engagement "the enemy were drove off with great loss" and that Willett "then ordered the flanking parties to spread themselves farther out in order to discover whether there were any enemy near them." After hearing there were none, "he ordered his men to take as much of the baggage as they could, and destroy the rest, which they effectually did, each man carrying as much as he could." As they were returning to the fort about 4:00 p.m., "just above the landing, . . . a party of 200 regular troops appeared, preparing to give them battle."[21]

Willett now ordered Captain Jansen to bring forward his rear guard and reinforce the main body. According to Lieutenant Ball, "a close & severe contest ensued in which the little band of Americans stood opposed to not less than seven or eight hundred of the enemy[,] as the prisoners and deserters who entered the fort afterwards acknowledged." According to the American officers who observed the fighting from the fort walls, "the combat lasted for eleven minutes when the enemy ceased to fire and retreated," upon which "the detachment then gave three cheers[,] huzzaed for America[,] and protected by an overarching Providence marched triumphant to the garrison laden with the trophies of victory without the loss of a man or even the receipt of a scratch or wound and bringing with them as prisoners Lieut Singleton & three soldiers of the British Army." One of the prisoners taken that day in Willett's sally died of his wounds that evening at the fort.[22]

From those prisoners they learned of the combat actions that day in the battle with Herkimer at Oriskany, the strength of the enemy, and specifics about their artillery pieces: two 6-pounders, two 3-pounders, and four coehorn mortars. The British were also reported to be in the process of erecting two artillery batteries, one northeast and the other northwest of the fort. Their artillery, however, would prove insufficient to defeat the fort or force its surrender. Gansevoort must have wondered why St. Leger had brought so little artillery to attack a fort.

Among the plunder taken from the British was a scarlet coat trimmed with gold lace, three laced hats, and a good quantity of specie and paper money. The troops had also found a collection of intercepted, but unopened, letters written to their fort commander. Adam Helmer heard several officers comment on their belief that the plunder taken amounted to at least £1,000 in value.[23]

One man noted angrily in his journal that Willett's troops also brought back "four scalps the Indians had lately taken, being entirely fresh and left in their camp. Two of the scalps taken are supposed to be those of the girls [killed picking berries], being neatly dressed and the hair plaited." The men had been so shocked and revolted by the treatment of Captain Gregg, the three girls, and others captured by the Indians that Willett had to take steps to prevent them from scalping enemy casualties and prisoners. Wanting to "teach even the savages humanity," Willett made sure his "men were much better employed, and kept in excellent order." The garrison also saw and cheered the captured British flags "immediately hoisted on our flagstaff under the [homemade] Continental flag, as trophies of victory."[24]

From freed Oneida Indians, Gansevoort learned that Herkimer's relieving force of about eight hundred militiamen, together with some Oneidas, had worked its way toward Fort Stanwix but was headed off at Oriskany by units of Johnson's regiment, Butler's Indian Department rangers, and Brant's Indian forces. Herkimer had been forced to retreat after a daylong battle resulting in heavy casualties on both sides. During the evening, one of General Herkimer's escaped militiamen arrived at the fort and gave a colorful but not entirely believable account of the action, including about his own participation.[25]

As information about Herkimer's battle emerged, young Henry Ritter tragically learned that his Palatine German–born father, Sergeant Johannes Ritter of Colonel Jacob Klock's 2nd "Palatine" Regiment of the Tryon County German Flats militia, had been killed in the fighting. The gruesome story was that Severinus Casleman of Johnson's Royal Yorkers killed him in hand-to-hand combat and then drank his blood.[26] General Herkimer himself and most of his militiamen had Palatine German ancestry.[27]

Young William Fink, who had enlisted while on a militia call-out in May, now found himself fighting and proudly "defending not only the fort itself, but also the rights and liberties of his country." Had he stayed with his militia company rather than joining Bleeker's company, he would have been with the militiamen fighting at Oriskany that day, where his two brothers, Christian and John, had indeed fought. William would sadly learn that Christian received a severe wound and died within a few days after the battle.[28]

At some point, members of the garrison also learned that their Oneida friends, blacksmith and important scout Thomas Spencer and his brother Edward, had been killed in the battle. The two men had gained much respect in the worlds of both their Oneida mother and their white father, and we have seen that Thomas had helped Colonel Gansevoort significantly. Their loss was palpable to the officers and soldiers who had gotten to know them. Just a week before the battle, Thomas Spencer had stated his personal hope that "all friends to liberty and that loves their families will not be backward but exert themselves[,] as one resolute blow would secure the friendship of the Six Nations and almost free this part of the country from the excursions of the enemy." The Oriskany battle would not achieve that goal, however, and securing the friendship of the entire Six Nations would prove impossible.[29] Other Oneida friends of the garrison such as Han Yerry Doxtader and his wife, Two Kettles Together (Tyonajanegen), fought valiantly in the battle and survived. Han Yerry, who received a wrist wound, was said to have killed nine British-supporting Indians. His wife repeatedly reloaded his firearm for him after he was wounded, and some said she herself fought with a brace of pistols. After the battle ended, she rode down through the valley seeking help for the wounded.[30]

One of Herkimer's men captured in the battle, probably known to the garrison men who had formerly served in Elmore's regiment, was Moses Younglove. He had been appointed a surgeon's mate in Elmore's regiment and apparently achieved a great reputation throughout the area. After the regiment disbanded, General Herkimer appointed him on July 12 to be surgeon of his militia brigade. As a prisoner, Younglove would be taken to Canada, though as was usual with doctors, he was able to return on parole.[31]

The battle at Oriskany had destroyed any hope that the local militia could help reinforce the fort garrison and open routes for supplies to reach the fort. While the militia might claim victory because the enemy left the field before they did, Herkimer's force failed in its mission to relieve the siege. Nevertheless, they had briefly drawn away a significant number of St. Leger's forces, enabling Lieutenant Colonel Willett's sally to be highly successful in plundering the British and Indian camps. While it was a disastrous defeat in terms of casualties for both sides, the Oriskany battle was especially damaging to St. Leger, who needed his Indian allies to remain with him despite their anger over losing so many men and leaders. To his benefit, however, the Indians greatly wanted revenge for both the battle losses and Willett's plundering sally. This was also the first major battle in the developing civil war among the Haudenosaunee.[32]

Now, the only hope for Gansevoort's garrison was that General Gates would be able to send a force of Continentals strong enough to drive away St. Leger's force, but that was at best a remote possibility, given Burgoyne's approach toward Albany. Gansevoort had to do all he could to keep St. Leger occupied and prevent him from linking up with Burgoyne. His troop numbers were fewer than St. Leger's, but he did have the fort. On the British side, St. Leger could not just bypass the fort and leave it and its garrison in his rear. He was really in a bind if he could not get the fort to surrender quickly before his Indian forces decided to move on to other actions.

By the end of the day on August 6, the fort garrison had still not yet received any British artillery fire, and it remained unclear just how many enemy troops had arrived to mount a serious attack on the fort. The battle against Herkimer had demonstrated that St. Leger could keep the fort garrison occupied while sending detachments out to attack locations in the Mohawk Valley. With better planning, encouraging additional sallies from the fort might result in greater Patriot casualties, weakening the fort so it could be captured. But St. Leger's Indian losses had been devastating to his Native contingent, and he did not have unlimited time to dally.

Chapter 13

The Siege Settles In
August 7–9, 1777

British officers negotiating with Gansevoort for the fort's surrender on August 8 argued that their Indian allies, after losing many men and several of their chiefs on August 6, now wanted to go down the Mohawk River and vengefully destroy the settlements and tomahawk and knife the men, women, and children they encountered. They were also committed to killing every member of the garrison when they took the fort. General St. Leger had held a two-day council with his Indian allies to try to change their minds, but to no avail, unless the garrison agreed to surrender immediately. The officers also brought Gansevoort a letter purportedly written by two local militiamen captured in the Oriskany battle telling him that his line of communication had been cut off and that the enemy was numerous and had "an excellent park of artillery." They also believed that General Burgoyne was already at Albany, and because the militia had suffered so many casualties at Oriskany, there was no hope of reinforcements for the fort.[1]

After the day of battle on August 6, the military options seemed to have reached a stalemate, though the situation could change quickly. By this point, St. Leger realized that his force was not strong enough to destroy the fort's defenses and that his Indian allies were not going to be part of a frontal assault on the fort. Gansevoort, meanwhile, did not know just how much more artillery and manpower St. Leger had coming. Would it be enough to overcome the fort and its defenders? What direction would the fighting take? How could each side strengthen its position?

An enemy marksman killed another sentinel on the northwest bastion about dawn on August 7, but no one saw where the enemy fire came from. As a result of this regularly recurring tragedy, no one wanted to be the sentinel at that post that night. Then, surprisingly, one man offered to stand guard as a substitute for the man assigned. The volunteer substitute put together a dummy sentinel, complete with musket, and placed it at the sentry post. Then he sat down and peered out through an embrasure. Seemingly right on schedule, a shot was fired that struck the dummy, and at least one man observed that the shot had come from a black oak tree "some 30 or 40 rods distant." Jacob Spicer of Major Badlam's detachment then watched as "a four pounder was quickly loaded with canister and grape," aimed, and fired. The shot was "immediately succeeded by a shout from the garrison, as they beheld one of Britain's red allies tumbling head foremost from the tree top." Curious about the "counterfeit sentinel," several men checked it over thoroughly and found "the holes through the various folds of the knapsack were more than circumstantial evidence that the aim was most sure, and that, had the owner stood in its place, he would have followed to his account those who had preceded him there."[2] After this incident, very little firing occurred during the day, but at one point, enemy troops haughtily approached the fort and called out to the sentinels that they should come out with fixed bayonets so the angry besiegers could pay the garrison back for the attack on their camp during the previous day's sally.[3] The "invitation" was ignored.

Having finally cleared the obstructions from Wood Creek, the British could now bring up their artillery to assist in the siege. The first piece arrived at about 11:00 a.m. on August 7, and by afternoon other pieces were in place. They now had two 6-pounders, three 3-pounders, and four eight-inch mortars. The 6- and 3-pounder cannon fired shot, that is, solid cannonballs, to cause destruction to structures and personnel from their impact. Their fire could be adjusted to exit the cannon barrel either horizontally, point blank, or down to a minus-three-degree depression or up to a twelve-degree elevation to attain more distance. They could also fire grapeshot or cannister, like a giant shotgun, mostly against humans.

CHAPTER 13

The mortars fired exploding shells, also called bombs, that traveled in a high arc over the fort walls and into the fort interior, where they exploded into fragments, injuring structures and personnel. Each shell looked like a large cannonball but was hollow and filled with gunpowder. A fuse inserted through a small hole in the shell and into the powder inside would burn down, causing the shot to explode over or on its target.

Announcing to the garrison that they were now facing artillery, and hoping it would not be recognized as inadequate, the British fired a small cannon at the fort which did no damage. In reply, the probably relieved garrison "laughed at them heartily."[4] The garrison then saw the enemy retire, leaving them to wonder what would come next. Were the British bringing additional and more powerful artillery along with more British, Loyalist, Canadian, and Indian troops to attack the fort? All they could do was keep alert and speculate.

The three militiamen who had brought Herkimer's message the day before departed about midnight, to avoid an enemy encounter, and returned home. Privates Thomas Cavin of Captain Aorson's company and Thomas Benson of Captain Bleeker's also departed that night, deserting to the enemy, perhaps more impressed than others with the capabilities of the British artillery.[5]

The British fired their artillery again the next day. One garrison member noted in his journal for August 8, "The enemy threw some shells at us . . ., but did no damage, and in order to return the compliment, they were saluted with a few balls from our cannon."[6] While the fort may not have suffered any real damage, Jonathan Huggins of Captain Swartwout's company lost his left arm that day.[7] Adam Helmer later said that while returning to General Herkimer's camp overnight, he heard the frequent report of distant cannon.[8]

By this point, St. Leger knew that he would have to find a creative way to overpower the fort relatively quickly or, even better, somehow persuade the defenders that they were doomed to fail and should surrender.[9] After a long day of vigilance and expectations of increased artillery fire, at about 5:00 p.m. the garrison heard the beating of the chamade, or parley, the signal requesting a talk, and saw Lieutenant Colonel John Butler, accompanied by a British officer and a doctor, approach the fort with a flag of truce. After requesting to speak with Colonel Gansevoort, the officers were blindfolded and then led into the fort. Their guards took them directly to Gansevoort's dining room in the headquarters building and removed the blindfolds.

There, according to Willett, "the windows of the room were shut, and candles lighted; a table also was spread, covered with crackers, cheese, and wine." Lieutenant Colonel Butler, Captain William Ancrum of the 34th Regiment of Foot, serving as St. Leger's adjutant general, and the surgeon took seats in three chairs placed at one end of the table. Colonel Gansevoort, Colonel Mellon, and Lieutenant Colonel Willett took seats at the other end of the table. Because Gansevoort wanted as many of his officers as possible to witness this meeting, they nearly filled the room, no doubt arranged by rank with higher-ranking men sitting in whatever chairs were available and the others standing.

After some wine and the usual introductory "compliments," Captain Ancrum, "with a very grave, stiff air, and a countenance full of importance" stated:

> I am directed by Colonel St. Leger, the officer who commands the army now investing the garrison, to inform the commandant, that the colonel has, with much difficulty, prevailed on the Indians to agree, that if the garrison, without further resistance, shall be delivered up, with the public stores belonging to it, to the investing army, the officers and soldiers shall have all their baggage and private property secured to them. And in order that the garrison may have a sufficient pledge to this effect, Colonel Butler accompanies me to assure them, that not a hair of the head of any one of them shall be hurt.

Captain Ancrum then added:

> [St. Leger] hopes these terms will not be refused; as in this case, it will be out of his power to make them again. It was with great difficulty the Indians consented to the present arrangement, as it will deprive them of that plunder which they always calculate upon, on similar occasions. Should, then, the present terms be rejected, it will be out of the power of the colonel to restrain the Indians, who are very numerous, and much exasperated, not only from plundering the property, but destroying the lives of, probably, the greater part of the garrison.[10]

CHAPTER 13

When Ancrum had finished, with Colonel Gansevoort's approval, Willett penetratingly looked Ancrum full in the face and, with firm assurance and confident emphasis, judgmentally responded:

> Do I understand you, Sir! I think you say, that you come from a British colonel, who is commander of the army that invests this fort; and by your uniform, you appear to be an officer in the British service. You have made a long speech on the occasion of your visit, which, stript of all its superfluities, amounts to this, that you come from a British colonel, to the commandant of this garrison, to tell him, that if he does not deliver up the garrison into the hands of your Colonel, he will send his Indians to murder our women and children. You will please to reflect, sir, that their blood will be on your head, not on ours.

Continuing to dominatingly look Ancrum full in the face, Willett proudly proclaimed Gansevoort's and his faith in their position:

> We are doing our duty: this garrison is committed to our charge, and we will take care of it. After you get out of it, you may turn round and look at its outside, but never expect to come in again, unless you come a prisoner. I consider the message you have brought, a degrading one for a British officer to send, and by no means reputable for a British officer to carry. For my own part, I declare, before I would consent to deliver this garrison to such a murdering set as your army, by your own account, consists of, I would suffer my body to be filled with splinters, and set on fire, as you know has at times been practised, by such hordes of women and children killers, as belong to your army.

Reacting to the arrogant British demand and Willett's rock-solid and resolute refusal to even consider it, the aroused and inspired garrison officers present in the room broke into applause. Several of them clearly felt that the only reason the British were trying to scare them into surrendering was the fear that they could not succeed in capturing the fort militarily. Rather than instilling fear in the garrison leadership, St. Leger's demand unintentionally filled them with deeper confidence.[11]

Recognizing that Gansevoort was not going to provide a written surrender for him to take back to St. Leger, Captain Ancrum asked that his surgeon be given permission to visit the wounded British prisoners taken in Willett's sortie. When signaled by Gansevoort, Dr. Woodruff accompanied the British surgeon to go to them. Still hoping for a successful conclusion to their talk, Captain Ancrum then suggested a three-day cease-fire to give the Americans time to think about their ultimate, thoroughly considered response, rather than their initial, quick answer.

When ready to return to St. Leger, Captain Ancrum and those with him were again blindfolded and led back through the fort and outside, where the blindfolds were removed, and they continued on their way.

Late that evening several men were sent out to get water for the garrison, accompanied by guards. One of the guards deserted but left behind his firelock. A sentinel fired at him but missed. The men heard an enemy sentinel challenge the deserter twice and then fire.[12] Jäger lieutenant Hildebrandt recorded that two men "sneaked up" to the picket post of Lieutenant Scheurer, but when challenged, they immediately retreated through the brush and returned to the fort.[13]

The need to counteract recent disturbing setbacks in the war, particularly the abandonment of Fort Ticonderoga, reinforced Gansevoort's already strong personal conviction not to surrender the fort. The words of Thomas Spencer's letter quoting the wishes of the Oneida not to "make a Ticonderoga" of the fort's defense no doubt stuck in his mind along with his brother Leonard's admonition "Your father flatters himself that you will conquer or die."[14]

At 1:00 a.m., Colonel Willett and First Lieutenant Levi Stockwell of Captain Jansen's company departed the fort on a secret mission, avoiding enemy notice.[15]

At 9:00 a.m. on August 9, Gansevoort sent St. Leger a request to submit his surrender demand in writing and indicated he would then respond. St. Leger agreed. As expected, the written demand was essentially identical to what had been conveyed verbally the day before. Shortly after receiving it, Gansevoort sent back his response carried by an officer, accompanied by a white flag and a drummer. The British ordered them to halt about fifty paces from a formation of Jäger, and a senior officer of the 8th Regiment of Foot approached with a white flag to receive Gansevoort's message. When St. Leger read it, that letter removed any doubt about Gansevoort's determination. Gansevoort succinctly and forcefully stated, "I have only to say that it is my determined resolution, with the forces under my command, to defend this fort, at every hazard, to the last extremity, in behalf of the United American States, who have placed me here to defend it against all their enemies."[16]

When hostile British artillery and small arms fire resumed about 1:00 p.m., Gansevoort knew that St. Leger had understood his written surrender rejection and could see the homemade Continental flag still flying over the fort. The Fort Stanwix garrison returned fire. St. Leger's Indian troops, however, were not much involved. According to Lieutenant Hildebrandt, the Indians told St. Leger that if the British could not take the fort with their cannon and mortars, how were they supposed to do it with their small arms.[17]

In response to the exploding mortar shells, Gansevoort ordered all of the fort's provisions brought out to the parade, fearing that blasts from the exploding shells would set fire to the barracks and destroy them. He also ordered all public papers and money to be placed in the bombproof structure that served as the fort hospital in the southwest bastion. While no members of the garrison were killed or wounded during the day, at about 10:30 p.m. the British began a rain of artillery fire that continued until daylight. This fire was very well directed. It killed Benjamin Price of Captain Aorson's company, stationed on the southwest bastion, and wounded another man of the regiment.[18] Recalling these days of siege, Private Henry Ritter commented about the British "firing against & into the fort, & the Americans returned the compliment with cold hearts & determined resolution not to surrender."[19]

Not everyone was as determined as Ritter. At some point that day, Daniel Still of Tiebout's company, who had enlisted for the war on March 1, deserted.[20] Lieutenant Hildebrandt reported that "a captured rebel had escaped from the guard, plus one who claimed to be a deserter. Both were caught in the woods and brought in."[21]

The fort's defenders were individuals with distinct personalities, values, experiences, and hopes for the future. While many got caught up in the heroic desire to resist the British attacks to the death, others leaned more toward survival, even if that meant defecting to the enemy or simply deserting to seek a new direction in life. Bravery and cowardice were part of the mix, but so was calculated reasoning about the value of life and how one wanted to be remembered by future generations. The tension over what to do built up during the long periods of inaction while the men stood ready for whatever the enemy would throw at them next.

Now, several days into the siege, neither side could see a positive outcome developing. Not knowing whether the British had heavier artillery that just had not arrived yet to pummel the fort, Gansevoort's men could only hold their ground and hope the British and their Indian allies would grow weary of the stalemate and leave. St. Leger's officers, meanwhile, could only hope that an increasing number of Gansevoort's men would desert to them to avoid being massacred when the fort eventually surrendered. How much longer could the siege continue?

Chapter 14

The Siege Finally Ends
August 10–31, 1777

About 3:00 p.m. on August 10, sentinels saw three or four enemy soldiers run across a field near the fort, where they set fire to some piles of hay which were then rapidly consumed by the flames. Since the British had been using their blankets for makeshift tents and needed hay for their men to lie on for sleeping, some of the garrison officers hoped this meant the enemy was preparing to leave and cruelly wanted to deny the garrison the use of the hay. Others, though, felt it was only a deception to make the garrison believe the British were preparing to depart, luring Gansevoort to send out small parties that could be attacked to reduce the strength of the garrison, making it easier to defeat the fort quickly.[1]

St. Leger continued to hope that his forces could wear the garrison down by forcing them to stay prepared to shelter from artillery and marksmen while food supplies dwindled and eventually ran out so that surrender became the alternative to starving to death. With luck he could retain at least some of his Indian troops and keep the garrison scared. For the moment at least, things were at a stalemate. How long could it last?

Unknown to Colonel Gansevoort, his officers, and men, information on the fighting at Oriskany and the fort on August 6 had reached

Albany. General Schuyler encouragingly wrote him on August 10 to say that "a body of Troops left this Yesterday and others are following to raise the Siege of Fort Schuyler." Knowing that conditions were tough at the fort, he added, "Every Body here believes you will defend it to the last, and I strictly enjoin you so to do."[2] It would be some time before Gansevoort received that letter, though, and in the interim he had to maintain his resistance to the siege not knowing whether relief was coming or not.

Throughout the day of August 10, the men and women in the fort once again sought protection from musket and artillery fire from the enemy troops, who mostly stayed out of sight. Fortunately, once again the enemy fire did not cause significant damage. The fear of fire damage was high in a fort with so much wood in its structure. Gratefully, and somewhat surprisingly, the fort occupants soon realized that St. Leger had not brought along any of the small incendiary missiles that Jäger lieutenant Hildebrandt called *Bechkräntzse*, consisting of tar-soaked string wrapped around a wood core to create a fireball. This was a strange omission, considering the British were aware that the earthen walls and ramparts had wooden supports, and much of the fort and its buildings were constructed of wood.[3] Yet this omission fits with St. Leger's erroneous understanding that he would not need heavy artillery because the fort was basically in ruins.

Fearing a surprise attack that night, Gansevoort doubled the guard and ordered the garrison troops to sleep with their muskets and ammunition next to them so they could respond to an alarm more quickly. British artillery fire again commenced between midnight and 1:00 a.m. and continued through the night. Most of the early explosive mortar shells passed over the fort, exploding beyond it. The garrison could tell, however, that the British artillerymen were making corrections to the amount of gunpowder being used after watching the performance of each shot. Every series of shots resulted in a few more shells exploding inside the fort.[4]

The only casualty was a young civilian man who took a shot that broke his thigh. This unfortunate man had been brought up in the John Roof family along with Roof's servant girl Lenea Stephane, one of the girls killed and scalped on July 27. Both this young man and Lenea were orphans working for Roof, and he had given his consent for their engagement to marry. When the Roof family departed for Canajoharie after the tragic incident involving Lenea, this young man apparently stayed behind to help defend the fort, no doubt angered by the death of his fiancée.[5]

The garrison continued to receive small arms and artillery fire during the day on August 11 and responded with more small arms and cannon fire of their own.[6] As everyone in the garrison worried and debated over how long the siege would continue, that day they observed a troubling sign that it would not end soon. The British had altered the course of the creek to remove one source of water for the fort. Fortunately, two wells had been opened inside the fort, which, together with an older one, provided sufficient water.[7]

Private John Freeland of Captain De Witt's company must have been one of the recent deserters; he enlisted in the King's Royal Yorkers on August 11. A month later, however, on September 8, 1777, he was recorded as being a prisoner at Fort Stanwix.[8] The reason for his desertion had not been to get away from the fighting, just to change which side to fight on.

Although enemy soldiers generally stayed out of view while shooting to keep the garrison under stress, sentinels did see some men gathering near the boat landing. This led Gansevoort and other officers to hope this movement might be a signal that reinforcements for the fort were approaching. But that hope quickly faded.

When a rain shower broke out at noon, Gansevoort ordered out a fatigue party, accompanied by a subaltern's guard, to bring in some lime barrels, boards, and timber lying at the foot of the fort glacis. Those men accomplished their task without taking any enemy fire. But while they were out, sentinels saw the enemy muster some troops on the road below the boat landing, leading to more speculation about what was developing. At sundown the fort received some British shot and shells fired into the fort. After four shells exploded in the fort at midnight, a thunderstorm broke out and the firing ceased. With the intense darkness and heavy rain during the night, Gansevoort ordered his men to stay at their alarm posts with bayonets fixed and do what they could to keep their gunpowder dry, just in case the enemy attempted a surprise attack on the fort.[9]

As a result of all the military activity and the need for constant vigilance, the living conditions in the fort had been deteriorating. The health of the garrison was equally important to its safety. Rampant sickness could cause the fort to have to surrender. This prompted Gansevoort to order twelve men to be assigned to the quartermaster and remain "constantly" employed as "camp colour men to keep the fort as sweet and clean as our present situation will admit of." He also ordered the quartermaster to fill as many barrels as he could procure with water, and then keep them constantly full.[10]

Camp colour man had been a duty frequently assigned to individuals since the regiment had first formed at Fishkill. The term derived from the British army, where the "camp colour men" assisted the quartermaster to mark out an encampment for a regiment by placing flags, or "colors," to indicate the encampment's borders. In the Continental Army the term mutated to refer to men assigned to keeping an area clean. The colour men dug latrines, called vaults, covered them daily, and every three days dug new vaults after completely covering up the old ones. In addition, they would sweep the camp's, and in this situation the fortress's, streets. They would bury any items of filth or nastiness that might poison or infect the men. A man might be assigned to be a color man because of minor infractions, such as lacking issued equipment or some other problem. He might also just be unlucky: someone had to do it. Their fellow soldiers did not help matters, not always following orders to use the latrine rather than a ditch, wall, or other convenient spot. Sentries were expected to watch for and report any man failing to use a latrine. In addition to human causes of filth, the fort also had to deal with animal waste and areas where slaughtering and burial of the carcasses took place.[11]

Sentinels observed no enemy soldiers during the day on August 12, and the fort received no fire until noon, when some shot and shells came in but caused no damage. The occupants could tell that the British had set up an additional battery to deliver intersecting, although poorly directed, fire against the fort.[12] Sensing that the enemy was increasing in numbers, the garrison suspected that the British and Indians were drawing in their forces between the fort and Oriska for a possible assault. The fort received no fire during the night, however, giving its occupants an opportunity to at least get some brief and uneasy rest.[13]

While all was quiet during the day on August 13, the fort received British fire again at night for two hours. Fragments of one of the artillery shells broke the leg of a man from Colonel Mellon's detachment of Massachusetts soldiers.[14] The garrison orders that day instructed company commanders to have their muster rolls in order and muster their men as soon as possible. Life had to proceed as normally as it could, and Colonel Gansevoort had to prepare to submit his usual bimonthly reports as soon as conditions permitted. Captain Tiebout was appointed officer of the day for August 14.[15] That day the fort took British artillery fire toward evening. This time the only damage occurred when fragments from a bursting shell slightly wounded one of Colonel Mellon's men in the head. One man of Captain Gregg's company posted on the outside picket must have lost confidence that the garrison could continue defending the fort, for he deserted his post, going over to the enemy that night between 10:00 p.m. and 1:00 a.m.[16]

The garrison of about 750 men had been crowded together with the other occupants for two weeks under siege conditions, with no end in sight, in a fort designed for half that number and which even in non-stressful times was not very comfortable. The incoming British artillery and musket fire, especially during the night, while not often deadly, did fray the nerves of the garrison soldiers and civilians. Along with Colonel Gansevoort, the soldiers also worried whether the fort's powder, ammunition, and food supplies would last until reinforcements arrived.

The fort took hits from two British artillery shells at 5:00 a.m. on August 15, but they did no damage. By that time, the curious garrison men trying to keep count of shots fired believed the British had fired 137 rounds at the fort—mostly too small and ineffective to do any harm. That afternoon the British "were very troublesome with their small arms," and one man of the 3rd New York Regiment and one from Colonel Mellon's detachment were slightly wounded. Three shells burst inside the fort that evening, and a woman and an artilleryman of Captain Lieutenant Savage's company were slightly wounded.[17] Garrison orders now required that all troops turn out each day to their alarm posts between 2:00 a.m. and reveille. No one should be absent from the picket from sunrise to sunset.[18]

The men and women of the garrison must have suffered great fatigue from constantly being on alert for a major assault, while not knowing when the next artillery shot might hit near them, and while also carrying out work details. While the fort was besieged, the men still had to care for their everyday needs. There was no mess hall where they could go to eat food prepared by a staff of cooks. The men were divided into groups of six messmates. Each man received his issued rations once a week, and the six men took turns, or one man volunteered, cooking for his messmates on the brick stoves located in the living areas. They also had to take care of their bedding, clothing, and other possessions, as there was no maid service, except when they could get one of the camp women to help them, or janitorial service, except that provided by the members of their company assigned as camp color men.

After experiencing the high-arching fire of St. Leger's mortars, the garrison was surprised on the morning of August 16 to receive what appeared to be direct fire. They did not know that St. Leger was disturbed that his artillery fire was having little or no effect on the sod placed against the fort's defenses and that his coehorn mortars "had only the power of teasing." He sarcastically commented that just "a six-inch plank was a sufficient security for their powder magazine."[19] St. Leger ordered the mortars converted into something like howitzers by mounting them to fire their explosive shells without the high arch typical of a mortar. The mortars, however, did not hold the quantity of powder needed to consistently hit their target when fired in that manner. Most of those shells fell short, but one fell on the parade, killing one of Colonel Mellon's men. The fort continued receiving British fire all day and into the night, but no further damage was done.

Unknown to those soldiers and civilians at the fort who knew him, on August 16, General Herkimer, who had been wounded in the fighting at Oriskany on August 6, died of complications from the amputation of his wounded leg. His death especially affected one of the families living near the fort. Herkimer had served as godfather at the christening of young John Roof, whose family had relocated from near the fort to the Herkimer home as the siege neared. John and another boy had buried Herkimer's amputated leg several days before the general died.[20]

Also unknown to Colonel Gansevoort and the garrison was that General Washington had written to New York governor George Clinton on August 16, noting that he had just read accounts of the battle at Oriskany and Colonel Willett's sally. He acknowledged that although the siege continued, "the Indians, we know, are not a very persevering people, but on the Contrary are apt to be discouraged by the most trifling miscarriages; and two Rebuffs like these, would be no inconsiderable inducements with them to abandon the British Troops, and leave them to prosecute the business alone." He also noted that those engagements with the enemy would "revive the drooping Spirits of our Army."[21] He was obviously convinced that the controversial Oriskany battle had been a victory although it had not succeeded in relieving the besieged fort.

During the evening, a fatigue party exited the fort to bring in much-needed wood but did not remain out long before being called back into the fort. As they arrived back, the garrison heard a "most hideous shout" arising from where the men had just been, coming from Indians who had become aware of the fatigue party. They had banded together and advanced toward the fatigue party at work but did not get close enough to attack before the party was recalled. Upon discovering that their prey had returned to safety, the Indians commenced their shouting. When the garrison fired a cannon at the Indians in response, the soldiers saw them retreat out of sight. They also heard British drums beating to arms. Perhaps the enemy was expecting the garrison to sally out and attack them with a fieldpiece, a repeat of the Willett sally of August 6. No action took place, but at midnight the fort took three British shells, which caused no damage. Unknown to both St. Leger and the fort garrison, Burgoyne's troops had been defeated near Bennington, Vermont, that day.[22] That American success increased the need for a St. Leger victory so he could bring his troops to join with Burgoyne's.

On August 17, the only artillery fire consisted of several shots fired from the fort at its besiegers.[23] Even though they were surrounded and still in great danger, the lack of an enemy assault in force and the relative ineffectiveness of the enemy artillery fire up to this point had diminished any respect the garrison had for their attackers. That development led the garrison on multiple occasions to direct loud taunting and laughter at St. Leger's troops.[24] This was no doubt done to maintain morale in the fort and insult the enemy rather than to intimidate them.

The following day, an enemy musket ball slightly wounded one 3rd New York Regiment man on the cheek, and men on a bastion were disturbed to see a black flag or coat "in the enemy's bomb battery." A black flag was a signal to troops not to take any prisoners and instead kill all of the enemy.²⁵ Garrison orders required that the advance guard keep double sentinels every night until further notice.²⁶

Some days earlier, St. Leger had decided to have his men begin digging a sap, part of a zigzag line of connected trenches, typical in siege warfare, to get their artillery pieces closer to the fort in order to bombard the ramparts with their "howitzers." Having the trenches reach the fort walls could perhaps also help the enemy dig a mine to undermine the northwest bastion.²⁷ This trench digging was going slowly because of the hot August weather and the shortage of available men. Garrison soldiers on guard duty noted on August 19 that the British worked all day on their sap while firing just a few shells at the fort about noon. St. Leger's troops also spent the day constructing a defensive fieldwork protected by an abatis, or obstacle constructed of tree branches, in the unlikely case that Gansevoort should sally out to attack them.²⁸

Lieutenant William Colbrath wrote in his diary for August 19, "At night they struck their trench towards the point of our northwest bastion, and by daylight had got within 150 yards of the ditch."²⁹ Matross Ebenezer Temple of the artillery detachment recalled years later that the British and Indians "approached their lines within 50 rods of the fort."³⁰ Gansevoort must have wondered if digging a siege trench meant that St. Leger was bringing up additional, heavier artillery or additional troops for an assault on the fort. While trying to limit the use of his diminishing powder and ammunition supply, Gansevoort could not allow the men digging the trench to work on it unopposed. He ordered the garrison artillery to fire grapeshot at them periodically throughout that night. The fort took enemy artillery fire in response, but it did no damage.

About midnight, Gansevoort dispatched Ely Pixly of Captain Aorson's company and Ely Stiles of Major Badlam's detachment. They were expected to meet up with Willett, who Gansevoort believed was bringing in reinforcements as part of a secret mission he was on. They were to inform Willett about the enemy activity on the fort's southwest side so that he could attack successfully.³¹ Pixly appears on a muster labeled as recorded at Fort Schuyler, "alias Fort Stanwix," for Captain Albert Chapman's company of Colonel Elmore's regiment on January 11, 1777. He had been one of the men recruited from it when Major Cochran was helping Captain Aorson. So Cochran may have known Pixly well and trusted him, and Pixly must have known the area well because of that previous service.³² Gansevoort gave Pixly and Stiles a message to carry to the first local Patriot committee they could find, assuring the committee that the garrison was "still in high spirits and determined to defend it to the last." He asked that the committee provide his two messengers with "every intelligence you can give us" for them to bring back to the fort.[33]

During the morning of August 20, a musket ball wounded one of Colonel Mellon's men. As the day wore on, seven British shells flew over the fort but only one landed inside it, while the garrison answered every shot the British fired.[34] Sometime during the day, Leonard Maybus of Captain Bleeker's company, who had enlisted on June 10 for the war, deserted.[35] At this point the British sap was approaching near enough that small arms and cannon fire from the garrison troops on the northwest bastion made it too "hot" for the enemy soldiers to work during daylight hours. When evening came, sentinels saw them take up their work and then continue through the night. Even then, although still needing to conserve powder, the garrison put out continual fire that slowed down the work of the British to advance their trench closer to the fort.

By now both commanders were struggling to deal with their limited numbers of men and military firepower. St. Leger knew that his artillery was totally insufficient to reduce the fort, and his troops were not adequate to attempt any assault on it. This was especially true of his Indian forces. Gansevoort did not have a full complement of artillery either and still had to make sure that he used his limited powder supply carefully. His force was not sufficient to exit the fort, take on St. Leger's troops, and drive them away. Abandoning the defensive protection of the fort would have been difficult to justify. For both men, the recent experiences at Oriskany, with its very high casualty rates, affected their decision-making.

At 2:00 a.m. on August 21, another fatigue party exited the fort to collect firewood and brought in a large amount of it without being discovered by the enemy. The garrison continued living with the alternating fire of enemy cannonballs and mortar shells throughout the night. With the morning light, men on duty observed that the enemy sap had approached a bit nearer the fort and that enemy soldiers had begun building a bomb battery. During the day the enemy worked on sections of the sap that were not so close to the fort, and the fort received no artillery fire. The garrison, however, kept up constant firing on the enemy soldiers working in the sap, and everyone stayed at his alarm post all night.[36]

Medical care for the wounded in the fort was very basic and difficult to carry out successfully. Three wounded men died that day. The artilleryman who had been wounded in the knee by a musket ball on August 4, one of Colonel Mellon's men, and the lad living with the Roof family died of their wounds, probably from infection setting in.[37]

That evening twelve garrison marksmen were selected to harass the British sap workers during the night. To distract them, the British sent Indians to approach the fort and draw their attention. This action caused a general alarm, and the fort kept up continuous heavy firing for about two hours while the British countered with brisk cannon and mortar fire. The British fire wounded a garrison artilleryman as well as Nancy McCarty, the pregnant wife of Dennis McCarty of Captain Bleeker's company. Private Adam Happal vividly remembered that an artillery shell explosion took "out of her buttock a piece of flesh as large as a man's fist."[38] Dennis McCarty had served in the earlier 3rd New York Regiment beginning August 26, 1775, and had reenlisted in Captain Van Bunschoten's company in 1776. He would serve until the end of the war.[39]

Several people, perhaps including other women, helped Nancy McCarty and the wounded artilleryman to the hospital in the southwest bastion and put them under the care of Dr. Woodruff and surgeon's mate John Elliott. There they joined other wounded, including Han Yost Hess, also known as Joseph Hess, of Captain Aorson's company, who had been wounded in the arm and the thigh at some point. He would be hospitalized for several months before returning to full duty.[40]

Overnight, Frederick Naugle and Thomas White of Captain Aorson's company deserted and joined the enemy, enlisting in the King's Royal Yorkers on August 22.[41] Cornelius Devan, George Smith, and John O'Neal of Captain Bleeker's company also deserted and enlisted into the Royal Yorkers within days—O'Neal on the day he deserted.[42] These men may have felt that the enemy was about to storm the fort, but they unknowingly deserted on what shortly proved to be the final night of the successful siege defense.

Sergeant Major Welding and two privates received wounds during the morning bombardment of the fort on August 22.[43] Then, at about 3:00 p.m., men watching from the fort saw several British deserters approach seeking asylum, but with no enemy troops pursuing them. Those British soldiers reported that St. Leger's force had been told that Burgoyne's army had been completely routed and the Americans were sending several thousand men to reinforce Fort Stanwix. When the Loyalists and the Indians with St. Leger heard that story, they believed it and panicked. The combination of their personnel losses at Oriskany, the loss of their supplies to Willett's sally, and this new information caused the Indians to depart and leave the British regulars and Loyalists to fight the Continentals alone.[44] Unaware that both items in the story were deliberately false, St. Leger ordered the precipitous retreat of his forces. One of the British deserters now seeking asylum had been retreating with another man, together carrying off an officer's chest, when he made his escape.

Not sure the deserters' account of the enemy retreat was true, Gansevoort ordered all the fort cannon bearing on British positions to fire several rounds. The lack of any return fire seemed to confirm the deserters' report. Then, four more British soldiers came in reporting the British departure and adding that the troops had left behind much of their baggage. Gansevoort immediately ordered Captain Jansen to take sixty men and two wagons out to the British camps. Jansen's detachment killed two Indians and took four prisoners, including one Indian. They discovered that the makeshift shelter huts and the tents that had not been packed up and taken along had been set on fire and left burning. Wine and brandy kegs had been smashed open.[45] They loaded the wagons with as much of the abandoned British baggage as they could and brought it to the fort, where they confirmed to Gansevoort that the British camp was empty. Since night was falling, they did not go back out to collect any remaining baggage that had been left in the camp.

The British deserters also informed Gansevoort that about seventeen Indians were presently at Fort Newport and were quite drunk. Gansevoort ordered Major Cochran to lead a party to attempt to capture them. Cochran returned about an hour later reporting that no one was there, but that he had gone to Wood Creek, where he found the British had left behind eight new bateaux.

While Gansevoort was confirming the enemy's departure, the wounded Nancy McCarty went into labor at the hospital and, most likely assisted by other women at the fort, as well as Dr. Woodruff, gave birth to a healthy baby daughter. Any complications from her wound had not injured the child, and both mother and daughter were reported to the father, and the others in the fort, to be doing well. After three weeks of bloodshed, welcoming a new life at the fort was a great joy.[46]

Two additional men came into the fort around 7:00 p.m. One was local eccentric and Loyalist sympathizer Han Yost Schuyler, known to several local members of the garrison. Han Yost told them that he had been taken prisoner at German Flats and held at Fort Dayton for five days. Then, after being sentenced to death as a spy, he was told by his captors that his death sentence would be commuted and his property would not be confiscated if he agreed to spread false information among the Indians with St. Leger. Schuyler's story would be credible to them because he had a special reputation with the Indians as a prophet, derived from his frequently odd behavior. When he agreed to do as asked, leaving his brother in custody as a guarantee for his faithful performance of the mission, General Benedict Arnold sent him to tell St. Leger the false stories of Burgoyne's defeat and the large number of reinforcements heading to Fort Stanwix.[47]

To back up the story, Arnold also sent out a friendly Indian about an hour later to support what Schuyler said. Thus it had been Schuyler and the Indian who brought in the erroneous information that had caused St. Leger to order his retreat. After he had related that false information to the British and the Indians, Schuyler disappeared to hide in the woods until evening, when he met up with several of the British deserters headed to the fort to give themselves up and came in with them.

Henry Ritter of Tiebout's company, whose father had been killed in the August 6 battle with Herkimer, later recalled "that he saw Hanjost Schuyler, the tory . . ., when he came into the fort, and told Col. Gansevort that St. Leger & his troops were all in confusion & that then was his [Gansevoort's] time to turn out & give him battle; & then they did turn out & the enemy only run; did not pretend to fight back."[48]

Even though the immediate threat to the fort had passed, there were still bands of pro-British Indians operating nearby who posed a lingering threat to the garrison. By this point, Gansevoort knew that troops under General Arnold, though fewer than in Schuyler's false tale, were indeed coming to his relief. He was anxious to receive them, and about midnight sent Arnold a note by messenger giving him an update on the situation at the fort. Having no lingering doubts about their friendship, Gansevoort sent this letter by Oneida allies Anthony and Big Bear, who narrowly avoided capture and delivered the letter to Arnold, still some twenty miles from the fort. The next day General Arnold ordered his troops to the fort by a forced march.[49]

Colonel Gansevoort called the garrison together, probably toward the end of the day on August 22, and proudly spoke to his men, telling them:

> I should be wanting in justice to you if I did not give some testimony of your good conduct during the time you have been in this garrison and especially while we were besieged by the enemy. Believe me that I am impressed with a proper sense of the behavior by which you have done essential service to your country and acquired the immortal honour to yourselves. Nothing can equal the pleasure I have experienced since my absence in hearing and receiving the public appreciation of our country for our service, which is and must be to every soldier a full and ample compensation for the same. Permit me to congratulate you upon the success of the American Army both to the southward and northward. Every day terminates with victory to America, and I make not the least doubt but in this campaign we will effectually establish the Independence of the United States and thereby secure to ourselves the rights and liberties for which we have so nobly stood forth.[50]

The siege had ended almost exactly nineteen years to the day after the installation of that first log on August 23, 1777, and the victory became the high point in the fort's history. By achieving that victory at a time of some worrisome defeats, the fort and its garrison created the foundation for its future nickname, "the fort that never surrendered."

The end of the siege did not bring total relief to the fort's defenders, although Lieutenant Colbrath's journal noted that they were "once more at liberty to walk about and take the free air we had for 21 days been deprived of." Overnight, another British deserter came in and announced that he had just left part of the British force below the Wood Creek bridge.[51] After the sun came up on August 23, Gansevoort sent Major Cochran out with a party to capture them. Cochran returned with three prisoners, four mortars, and some baggage, reporting that he had found seventeen bateaux the retreating British had left there. Private Ritter long remembered that "when St. Leger eased the siege, which was a very sudden movement of his, the Americans went out of the fort & captured their ammunition, cannon, shells, baggage & some prisoners & carried them into the fort."[52]

Gansevoort sent another party to bring in the rest of the supplies left behind the previous night at the enemy's north camp, consisting of ammunition, camp equipment, and entrenching tools. He sent a third party to the enemy's southeast camp, who returned with fifteen wagons and a 3-pounder fieldpiece carriage with all its gear. Most of the wheels on the wagons and carriage had been damaged by the departing enemy soldiers to diminish their usefulness and now needed to be repaired. A fourth party searched out to Canada Creek, where they found a 6-pounder fieldpiece carriage and three boxes of cannon shot that they brought back to the fort. John Dop of Bleeker's company had erroneously believed that Colonel Gansevoort was about to surrender the fort before word of reinforcements caused the enemy to disperse. Now he was pleased to observe that the British had left their "implements, two brass field pieces & some mortars or coehorns." He knew it was the coehorns that had "thrown" shells at the fort and vividly recalled that during the siege, a soldier driving a wagon had lost the top of his head to an exploding shell.[53]

One of the parties took a German Jäger prisoner who reported that after about ten miles of retreating, the Indians fell on the Loyalists, took their weapons, and used the soldiers' own bayonets to stab them. The prisoner had been warned by Butler and Johnson not to go to Fort Stanwix because he would be immediately hanged. He came anyway and instead of being executed found himself welcomed.

Around 5:00 p.m. on August 24, after a fatiguing forced march, General Arnold arrived at the fort with about one thousand men expecting to engage enemy troops. The enemy, however, was already some distance away by the time Arnold's troops reached the area. The garrison saluted Arnold's men with a discharge of powder from the mortars taken from the enemy and all the cannon on the bastions, a total of thirteen pieces. The troops formed up on the bastions and, following the artillery salute, shouted three enthusiastic cheers.[54] Among those cheering were some Oneidas, including Paul Powless and Han Jost.[55] Lieutenant William Scudder of the 1st New York Regiment noted in his journal: "We continued our march, without any molestation, until our arrival at the fort, where we congratulated the old besieged officers and soldiers with joy for their being relieved. The next morning, about five hundred men were sent down Wood Creek after the enemy, but they had gone off."[56]

Neither Colonel Gansevoort nor General Arnold had much desire to pursue the retreating St. Leger. Gansevoort was always concerned about being ambushed outside the fort and suffering an encounter such as Herkimer had on August 6. General Arnold had similar concerns but was also anxious to return to the forces now commanded by General Gates, who had replaced General Schuyler as Northern Department commander in mid-August, to help with the important actions against Burgoyne.

At 10:00 p.m., Arnold wrote a report to General Gates in which he praised Colonel Gansevoort and his officers and men. According to Arnold, they "deserve great applause for their spirited conduct and vigorous defense, their duty having been very severe, and has been performed (I am told) with the greatest cheerfulness." He did not overlook the Oneidas and Tuscaroras, who, he said, had been "exceedingly friendly to us in the present dispute" while the other Haudenosaunee with St. Leger had been "villains." Once Arnold was satisfied that the enemy force had no intention of returning, he reported, "As Colonel Gansevoort has suffered much by the severity of the siege, I have permitted him to go to Albany [on furlough] until you think proper to order him to return." Gansevoort was especially eager to visit his beloved Caty, then at Kingston, New York. Lieutenant Colonel Willett would take command at Fort Stanwix during Gansevoort's leave. After stating his belief that the fort was now out of danger for the remainder of the year, he had to note that, as always, "the works require considerable labor to complete them." To help with that, Arnold would leave six hundred men in the garrison.[57] The question was where they would lodge with the fort already overcrowded.

The soldiers heard the garrison orders on August 24 stating that the plunder taken from the enemy camp, except for any public stores, would be sold at auction outside the fort's gate as soon as the weather permitted. The proceeds of the auction would be divided among the garrison proportionally by rank. Gansevoort appointed the highly trusted Second Lieutenant Prentis Bowen of Captain Bleeker's company to be the vendue master, to receive and pay out money at the auction.[58]

Life returned somewhat to normal. On a rainy August 26, a court-martial acquitted Sergeant Henry Miller of Captain Aorson's company of the charge of allowing an Indian prisoner to escape.[59] When the weather cleared that evening, the 1st Canadian Regiment and Colonel Michael Jackson's regiment, which had arrived with Arnold, departed the fort. The following day, the men from Colonel John Bailey's 2nd Massachusetts Regiment and Colonel James Wesson's regiment, who had endured the siege, also left the fort.[60] Lieutenant William Scudder of the 1st New York Regiment noted that "General Arnold and the New-England troops continued a few days at the garrison and then marched down to join the main army, at Stillwater, leaving our regiment at the Fort, not knowing but the British might again return to the siege."[61]

Then, on August 28, Gansevoort once again had to forbid his soldiers to waste ammunition by firing their muskets without permission.[62]

The three-week siege had ended for the extremely diverse group of people making up the attackers and defenders of the fort. Among the attacking British regulars had been English, Irish, and very likely men from other countries who had enlisted. Those regulars had been accompanied by the Hessen-Hanau Germans; the American Loyalists, who included men of English, Scots, Dutch, and German descent; and some French Canadians. About half of the attackers were warriors from various nations of the Haudenosaunee and other Indigenous people. The defenders of the fort included men of English, Dutch, German, French, and perhaps other European descent, as well as some Oneida men and women. While no Black men have been positively identified among the soldiers, it is very possible that Colonel Wesson's Massachusetts regiment included some, since most Massachusetts regiments included one or more Black enlistees at that time. Occupants of the fort also included white civilians, men and women, and at the very end of the siege a newborn baby girl. The siege was clearly an international event combining a struggle for independence with a bitter civil war among both the Haudenosaunee and the white colonists. Although all actions in the War for Independence exhibited aspects of civil war, the specific human mixture and the memories created in the western Mohawk River Valley and Fort Stanwix make this story unique.

On August 25, General Gates, who had earlier been so critical of Colonel Gansevoort, wrote to Congress: "Great honor is due to Colonel Gansevoort, Lieut. Colonel Willett, and the officers and soldiers of the garrison under their command;—I cannot too warmly recommend them to Congress. The gallant defence of Fort Stanwix, must convince all the western nations of Indians of the superiority of the American arms." Three days later Gates wrote again to Congress to say, "The defeat and disgrace with which the enemy have been obliged to retreat from Fort Schuyler, added to the complete and brilliant victory gained by General Stark and Col. Warner at Bennington, gives the brightest lustre to the American arms, and covers the enemies of the United States, with infamy and shame."[63]

Even after the siege lifted, men continued to desert: Hugh Sommers of Captain Bleeker's company departed on August 31.[64] More positively, other men joined the regiment: on August 28, Henry Witmozer enlisted in Tiebout's company for three years or the duration of the war, though he would not live for even one full year.[65]

We have seen that several Mohawk Valley soldiers served in the garrison at Fort Stanwix. When a drove of beef cattle was sent to the relieved garrison, a number of local women, wishing to visit their husbands, joined the train, many riding horseback. Probably additional women accompanied other supply trains on horseback or walking. A teenage boy recalled that when one cattle drove arrived at a ford on the Mohawk River, "as one of the women was descending the steep bank to the river, a brawny Dutchman, who did not wish to wet his feet, jumped upon the horse's back behind the woman. The horse, offended either on account of this uncerimonious accession to his load or else the reverse order in which his cargo was arranged, sprang forward and, by a well-directed effort, threw the Dutchman into the center of the stream," while the obviously more horse-savvy woman stayed mounted and reached the other side safely.[66]

The soldiers of the fort garrison certainly were aware that the local people, both Indian and white, were suffering. The important supportive actions of individual Oneidas during the siege had greatly impressed leaders such as Gansevoort, Arnold, and others, in addition to many common soldiers. Those friendly actions, however, resulted in other, British-allied Haudenosaunee nations punishing them. Before the Indians with St. Leger had completely evacuated to the north, a war party descended on Oriska while its men were away, causing the women, children, and elderly to flee. That war party destroyed the Oneida town, burning houses, destroying crops, and killing or carrying away cattle. This incident only increased the scope of the Six Nations' civil war. After the siege, both Indian and white residents of the Mohawk Valley area had to pick up the pieces of their lives that had been shattered in the conflict. Those reconstructions of lives had to be undertaken in the shadow of fears felt by many that the fort and valley would soon come under attack again.[67]

After the siege ended, there was still work to be done repairing, constructing, and adding to the fort while that threat of additional action on the frontier persisted. Additions to the fort complex would include a hospital, carpenter shop, blacksmith shop, "Indian House," and a stable standing outside the fort.[68] A "necessary" was a privy or outhouse, equally important as food and ammunition if the health of the garrison was to be kept as strong as possible. The primary necessary was outside the fort's walls, elevated above the creek running near the east side of the fort, and accessed from the southeast bastion by a narrow bridge. At the time of the siege there was at least one other necessary within the fort. Everything considered, the fort seems to have been short on necessaries—surprising given Colonel Gansevoort's concern for cleanliness to prevent disease. Chamber pots were also used, although, like most things, they too were in short supply.[69] Concerns about privies and chamber pots might seem unimportant against an analysis of the siege of a fort, but maintaining the health of the closely packed garrison, especially in the heat of summer, was crucial to its defense.

Sustaining the August siege that prevented St. Leger's troops from joining with Burgoyne proved a major factor in Burgoyne's momentous defeat in October. Burgoyne had to shuffle his plans in reaction to the defeat at Bennington and then St. Leger's retreat from Fort Stanwix. The move to send a relief force under General Arnold, utilizing interior lines in the campaign, succeeded in ending the siege in time for the relief force to rejoin the main force and achieve victory in the battles at Saratoga that resulted in the surrender of Burgoyne's entire army. St. Leger's siege had not proved to be an important diversion allowing for a Burgoyne battlefield victory. Just like the earlier victories at Trenton and Princeton, the successful siege defense at Fort Stanwix lifted morale, especially regarding the Americans' confidence in their troops and their leaders.

The siege might be over, but the war continued. Lieutenant Colbrath's journal entry commenting that the soldiers were "once more at liberty to walk about and take the free air we had for 21 days been deprived of" would prove to be overly optimistic. It would still be several months before Burgoyne surrendered his army to General Gates after the battles at Saratoga. The Continental soldiers of the Fort Stanwix garrison would have to continue serving at an isolated frontier post. While that fort might be secure from concentrated enemy attack, it existed in an area sunk deep in civil war. The morale of the fort garrison would continue to be a major concern even after the victory over St. Leger.

Part IV

Defense after the Siege

CHAPTER 15

Adjusting to Garrison Life after the Siege

September–December 1777

Word of the successful siege defense spread rapidly, recognized and praised in many places, including the Continental Congress. After the loss of virtually every American fort in the New York area in the fall of 1776 and summer of 1777, and noting what seemed to be the unique success at Fort Stanwix, John Adams wrote to Abigail on September 2 that "Gansevoort has proved, that it is possible to hold a Post."[1] Previously, during the siege on August 19, Adams had pessimistically written Abigail, "I think we shall never defend a post until we shoot a General" for abandoning one.[2]

New York congressional delegate James Duane now believed that because of "the bravery & good conduct" of Herkimer, Gansevoort, and Willett, "our Western Hemisphere is changed, the clouds are dispersed, and we can view it without discomposure." He was proud that "Gansevoort & Willett are in the highest Degree of Fame" after the "train of disgrace at all our forts," especially Ticonderoga, which had surrendered. He was not surprised that people were suggesting that Congress should promote Gansevoort to brigadier general and Willett to colonel.[3]

A primary benefit derived from preventing the St. Leger force from overcoming Fort Stanwix and proceeding to join with General Burgoyne's forces approaching Albany was increased confidence in the ability of the American army. Morale among the Patriots rose greatly when the successful siege defense was combined with the August 16 Bennington victory. Wavering individuals became more likely to support the Patriot cause, and Loyalists became subdued. Shortly before the siege was raised, Burgoyne wrote to Lord George Germain that the loss at Bennington had not materially affected the strength or spirit of his troops. Yet Fort Stanwix still held out "obstinately," despite what Burgoyne considered to be the British victory at Oriskany, and the expected rising of Loyalists in the Mohawk Valley had not materialized. He then enumerated several actions taken by his enemy that had been causing him to keep modifying his plans. While expressing his conviction that St. Leger had done everything possible to take Fort Stanwix, he now hoped, and expected, that St. Leger would rapidly bring his forces, unfortunately by a longer and more roundabout route, to join with him at Saratoga.[4]

For the Americans, the nearly simultaneous victories at Bennington and Fort Stanwix, like the similarly close morale-raising victories at Trenton and Princeton eight months previously, were driving expectations in a more positive direction. The recent abandonment of Fort Ticonderoga and the fighting retreat at Hubbardton made the victory at Fort Stanwix even more important for restoring American morale. The subsequent critical American victories at Saratoga in September and October benefited greatly from that morale boost, as well as the inability of St. Leger's troops to join with Burgoyne at Saratoga as planned.

The nature of the continuing war in the Mohawk Valley would now be determined by Loyalists and Indians favoring the British, whose strategy would be to destroy the valley settlements one after another. Since this would be done by avoiding Fort Stanwix, the fort became a lonely, forlorn, and nearly forgotten "sentinel in the forest." The involvement of the Haudenosaunee on both sides in this ongoing struggle was significant in the death of their confederacy and league preserving the Great Peace among the Six Nations. Localism, rather than unity, now prevailed as civil war among and within the Haudenosaunee nations became a reality.[5]

Six weeks after the siege ended, the Continental Congress finally on October 4 extended its thanks to Colonel Gansevoort, his officers, and his troops "for the bravery and perseverance which they have so conspicuously manifested in the defense of Fort Schuyler" and resolved "that Colonel Gansevoort be appointed colonel commandant of the fort he has so gallantly defended." John Hancock was the first to use the title "Colonel Commandant of Fort Schuyler" when addressing a letter to Gansevoort on October 5 transmitting the thanks of Congress and informing him of his appointment. Congress also recognized "the distinguished merit of Lieutenant Colonel Willett, for a repeated instance of his bravery and conduct in his late successful sally on the enemy investing Fort Schuyler." In a letter to Willett, Hancock added his wish "that the commissary general of military stores be directed to procure an elegant sword, and present the same to Lieutenant Colonel Willett, in the name of these United States." Willett, however, endured a long wait before receiving the sword. For economic reasons, it would not be made to present to him until 1785–86, several years after the war ended.[6]

The 1st New York Regiment left the fort for Albany in mid-October. When they reached Schenectady, they learned of Burgoyne's complete surrender, which had occurred on October 17. Lieutenant William Scudder's reaction to the news was no doubt like the response at Fort Stanwix when that garrison received word of the victory. He recorded: "Never were men more thunder-struck at news; for we had not heard a hint of the affair, but lived in daily expectation of hearing of Burgoyne's arrival at Albany, as we had no express for a considerable time. This was news of a most pleasing nature—What a contrast in the countenance and behaviour of every individual! Joy sat on every brow; elevation and cordiality intermingled in all our conversation."[7]

The successful defense against St. Leger's siege of Fort Stanwix had contributed greatly to the victory at Saratoga that would become acknowledged by historians as a major turning point in the war. The lengthy siege had denied St. Leger's force to Burgoyne without requiring large numbers of American reinforcements to be diverted to the fort instead of facing Burgoyne. General Arnold's brief foray to the fort with about a thousand troops just before St. Leger withdrew did not keep him or those troops from participating very famously in the main fighting at Saratoga. The victory at Stanwix contributed materially to the subsequent battlefield victory leading to the surrender of Burgoyne's army. Lacking St. Leger's troops, and those of General Clinton from New York, Burgoyne did not have an army the size he had planned for, while his enemy was stronger, and more capable, than he had anticipated.[8]

CHAPTER 15

Word of the congratulatory Continental Congress resolutions also reached Fort Stanwix about this time, and the 3rd New York Regiment officers wrote to Colonel Gansevoort on October 12 expressing their gratitude for everything he had done to enable the regiment to achieve honor in action.[9]

Nevertheless, while expressing their joy at the news of Gansevoort's "promotion," his officers worried that he would therefore have to leave the regiment. They did not completely understand that his "promotion" was honorary, symbolic, and valid only while the regiment remained at the fort. In some ways it was like Lieutenant Colonel St. Leger's designation as acting, or local, brigadier only while he was leading his detached force. Those officers who did not sign the letter to Gansevoort, such as Captain Tiebout, were away from the fort on furlough or on recruiting assignments. Gansevoort thanked his officers for their kind words and praised their determination and skills as being the primary reason for his success. He also extended his warmest wishes to all the men of his regiment.[10]

The compliments from Congress must have been encouraging, but so was the fact that six men enlisted in Tiebout's company on October 15.[11]

The gains in morale, however, could be fleeting for the men who still had to occupy the fort and stay alert and prepared for renewed enemy action. The heat of summer was turning to fall, with winter on the horizon along with the various problems and discomforts it would inflict on the garrison. The need to maintain vigilance continued, along with the ubiquitous fatigue parties called out to repair and strengthen the fort's defenses. After everyone had been kept on edge with a heightened sensitivity to their surroundings throughout the months spent preparing for the siege, and then during the three-week siege itself, it would now be very difficult to sustain the soldiers' spirits amidst mundane fort activities of seemingly questionable value to the men involved. Complicating the problems of work completion and morale was the coming and going of officers and soldiers on furlough, scouting parties, working parties, recruiting parties, and other activities temporarily taking them away from the daily work of the fort.

The never-ending story of fort repair and restoration continued in October, when Gansevoort sent General Gates a return of the garrison's forces and artillery, including yet another list of supplies needed to complete the fort's fortifications. To justify the items requested, Gansevoort stressed that even he, a non-engineer, could see that the works were "altogether irregular & will ultimately require attention." Engineer Major Nathaniel Hubble was still at the fort, currently in the process of redesigning the bombproof barracks. In Gansevoort's opinion, however, the lumber that Hubble had secured would not protect it from a thirteen-inch shell. Indicating his continuing lack of complete confidence in Hubble, Gansevoort requested that an experienced and able engineer be sent to the fort as soon as possible to complete the work on the fortifications. The season was getting late, and Gansevoort's various requests were motivated by his previous actions that, he said, had demonstrated "zeal for this service of my country & the defense of the Post entrusted to my care." Gansevoort also recommended always keeping a three-month supply of salt provisions at the fort, not to be used unless the fort was besieged again.[12] The October 16 garrison orders also noted the concern that barracks still needed to be completed before winter.[13]

Defending the fort continued to focus on the restoration work that had been a daily part of life for over a year before the siege. Willett reinforced once again the expectation that all men fit for duty, except those on guard, must be "on continual fatigue, renewing & repairing the fortifications." Just as it had before the siege, though, this work cut deeply into military training time and proved a considerable "disadvantage to the men's becoming perfect in discipline."[14] Even though the regiment had now been tested in several forms of combat, the men still needed to maintain and improve military skills already developed while learning new ones. They had not yet fought in a large land battle with multi-regiment formations and movements. The officers particularly believed they needed to have those skills in addition to knowing the single-regiment drills. The garrison orders on September 21 gave detailed instructions for parading the guard, respecting company seniority and men's size, assuming there would be sufficient opportunities for the soldiers, when not on fatigue or other duties, to master those movements.[15] Gansevoort and Willett and their officers knew that their regiment was not developing like those with the main army, where officers and men learned and demonstrated the military skills that they associated with regular army operations, and officers earned advancement in rank. This awareness increased their sense of being isolated at a frontier fort.

Because the war had not ended even if the siege had, the fort defenders continued to face danger from a variety of enemy scouting and attack parties. Any letdown in security measures, or heightened concerns from intelligence gathering, resulted in orders tightening things up. For example, garrison orders on September 2 instructed that the outer gates of the fort were to be closed and locked at dusk, on the long roll of the drums. All men quartered within the fort, as opposed to those occupying tents outside the fort walls, were to be inside at dusk or face punishment. The gate keys were to be delivered to the captain of the day as soon as tattoo beating ended, and he would check to make sure that the gates were securely locked.[16] Orders following on September 10 reinforced the orders that a picket guard consisting of a captain, four subalterns, four sergeants, four corporals, a drummer, and eighty privates would be distributed each evening among the four bastions. Further efforts at security required the troops encamped outside the fort to move to the interior and the mounting of quarter guards in the covered way to prevent desertions, as well as to provide safety for the fort.[17]

The continually modified orders relating to fort security just exemplified the unique situation of Fort Stanwix and the lack of standardized protocols. More orders on September 20 modified earlier instructions and stated that the picket gates were to be shut at dusk and opened at the beating of the troop at sunrise. The inner gates were to be shut immediately after tattoo sounded and opened at reveille. Sergeants were to take roll immediately after tattoo beating, ensure that all the men were in their quarters, and then see that all lights were extinguished. Afterward, any soldier found out of his quarters was to be challenged by the sentinels, and if he did not answer the challenge with the proper password, the sentinel was to fire at him. One order, repeated so frequently that it must habitually have been ignored, was that no officer or soldier was to discharge his weapon in or around the fort without orders.[18]

Scouting parties sent out to discover any enemy movements near the fort continued regularly. On September 11, with Gansevoort away on furlough, Willett received intelligence from one of those parties that some boats had been discovered on Oneida Lake. He sent out another party to gain additional information, but it found no traces of the enemy. Despite this false alarm, he noted that he would be sending out scouts continually to be sure to gain the earliest intelligence "if anything important should arise."[19]

Maintaining peaceful and supportive Indian relations remained vital. Willett informed General Gates on September 2 about a visit from an Onondaga leader and noted that "the Indians have sent me word that they will be at this place on the 7th instant on their way to meet with you at Albany."[20] At that Albany conference, the Oneidas' continuing fear of further military attacks on their villages and the fort was clearly on everyone's mind. They asked the Americans to fortify Kanonwalohale, and perhaps other villages. By this point, the garrison's soldiers must have been aware that any attack on the Oneidas would be considered an attack on the Americans. The Oneidas also pleaded strongly that trade be reopened permanently at the fort so they did not have to rely solely upon "gifts" from the Americans and they could be part of the local economy. Independent traders, not garrison soldiers, could offer a greater supply of items than the American government. Availability of supplies was so important to the Haudenosaunee that the Oneidas could remind the Americans that the British had gained strong influence over the nations through their ability to offer the goods the Indians needed.[21]

The retreat of St. Leger's forces from the area made the confrontation with Burgoyne at Saratoga the primary focus for anyone in the Mohawk River Valley who wanted to assist the cause. Some local Oneidas joined with the Continental Army in the developing Saratoga campaign, and on September 26, General Gates sent Colonel Gansevoort a letter by way of "the Wife of Honyas, a principal Warrior of the Oneida Nation." This phrase referred to Han Yerry and Two Kettles Together. In recognition of Han Yerry's valuable service as leading warrior, assisted by Two Kettles Together, who carried messages on horseback, Gates instructed Gansevoort to deliver three gallons of rum to her for her family's winter supply. In recognition of the overall Oneida contributions, Gates also instructed Gansevoort to provide small amounts of provisions to any Indians who were faithful to the Americans and in want.[22]

Measures to guard against a surprise attack included a December 11 scout composed of a sergeant and six privates that went out to Oneida Lake. Gansevoort also enacted revised alarm post assignments at the fort reflecting current company sizes and the desire to post a similar number of men at each bastion. Captain Aorson's company was to take post on the southwest bastion, Captain Tiebout's the northwest, Captain Bleeker and Captain De Witt's the northeast, and Captain Jansen's, Gregg's, and Van Bunschoten's the southeast. Captain Swartwout's company would assemble on the parade as a reserve awaiting further

CHAPTER 15

orders. While Gansevoort trusted everyone to turn out on an alarm, he ordered "the Officer of the Guard frequently to go the rounds in the night, see that the sentinels are vigilant and alert on their different posts, by which means to guard against the disgrace of a surprise."[23]

Nothing could reduce the routine, mundane fatigue parties that continued in October. On October 22, a sergeant, a corporal, and sixteen privates formed a party to load some wagons as soon as they had had breakfast. To make the work somewhat palatable, each man received half a gill of rum, two ounces, both before and after performing this duty.[24] A week later, a captain, a subaltern, two sergeants, two corporals, and fifty privates cut wood for the garrison.[25]

Company personnel kept changing as a result of enlistments, discharges, and desertions, and these changes led to a variety of disruptions. As men enlisted, they had to learn the "exercises" that the men of the regiment had been learning and mastering since their own enlistments. John Hill, who enlisted in Captain Gregg's company on November 29, must have had no prior military experience. Almost a month later, on December 21, garrison orders proclaimed to everyone in the fort that Private Hill was to attend parade every day at 11:00 a.m. and again at 2:00 p.m., weather permitting, to learn the exercises. Additionally, the designated "awkward" men from each company not on duty were to do the same.[26]

The December 7 muster roll clearly shows that the regiment was still incomplete in the number of men authorized for a full complement. Several recruits did join.[27] Even though recruits were badly needed, however, not all volunteers were welcome. Gansevoort read a letter dated December 16 from regimental paymaster Jeremiah Van Rensselaer, away on command at Albany, alerting Gansevoort that General Gates was concerned because he had heard that a British deserter had been allowed to enlist in the regiment.[28] Enemy deserters were not considered to be reliable additions to Continental regiments. But because finding enough recruits proved impossible, certain restrictions were sometimes overlooked.

Men could receive an early discharge for various reasons. Isaac Seamans of Captain Jansen's company was discharged on November 28 after completing just one year of his three-year enlistment, perhaps for medical reasons.[29] Sometimes men might provide a substitute for their remaining term of service when discharged early for an accepted reason.

ADJUSTING TO GARRISON LIFE AFTER THE SIEGE 187

Eighteen-year-old William Fink, a five-foot, nine-inch-tall farmer with a fair complexion and gray eyes, had enlisted while out on militia duty. He was discharged, perhaps for family reasons, from Captain Bleeker's company in September after supplying a substitute.[30]

Gansevoort's concerns matched just a few of the many felt by his subordinate officers and the men they commanded. Requests for furloughs from both officers and enlisted men continued, although most could not be granted. Such requests often arose from family responsibilities. Prior to his discharge, William Fink, who had lost a brother at Oriskany, was granted a furlough to visit his parents and family.[31] Henry Ritter of Captain Tiebout's company had lost his father at Oriskany. When he received notice that his mother had died, as her oldest child he was granted a furlough to visit his now orphaned siblings. Upon arriving home, Henry found his aged grandfather taking care of his seven younger siblings, including his brother Frederick, about thirteen years old, who would join the army himself in a few years. Henry was single and would not marry until 1786, so he and his grandfather appealed to the Palatine Committee of Safety for relief in November 1777. Creatively, the committee "told one John Cramer [Cremer], a tory who had been arrested & whom the committee were going to hang, that, he might take his choice, to be hung, or take the place of" Ritter in the 3rd New York Regiment. Cremer chose to serve for Ritter "and save his neck from the halter, which was ready in the hands of one of the committeemen to be used without delay if he should choose to be hanged." Ritter and his grandfather took custody of Cremer and "made a representation of his case to Colonel Gansevoort, who was reluctant to discharge the applicant and take a tory in his place, but, on the representation of the distress & helpless condition of his father's family, the Colonel consented." He discharged Ritter and enlisted Cremer, allowing Ritter to return home.[32] He left behind his cousin Christian Shell, who had also been his messmate though serving in a different company, Captain De Witt's.

Ritter remained at home for about a year after leaving the regiment. He worked to support his seven brothers and sisters despite continuing enemy Indian incursions into his neighborhood. Those attacks often resulted in the killing and plundering of his neighbors. He retreated to Palatine, New York, and beginning in the spring of 1779 served in the militia, keeping in readiness to go out at a moment's notice on scouts or to repel approaching enemy Indians and Loyalists. In the summer of 1779, an enemy force commanded by Sir John Johnson came through the area and there was a skirmish. In 1780, Ritter went out on active service in the militia for nine months, serving in the Schenectady and Albany area. Still badly needed at home by his family, Henry returned and his younger brother substituted for him.[33]

The regiment also continued losing men to desertion while punishing others attempting it.[34] Not all deserters left permanently. Hugh Sommers of Captain Bleeker's company who had deserted in August was captured on September 12.[35] On December 1, a court-martial sentenced Sommers and Private John Moore to receive one hundred lashes each for desertion.[36]

Many officers and men strongly desired at least a temporary change of scenery and a break from their grueling garrison routines. Some succeeded in securing a furlough permitting their absence from the garrison for a stated length of time.

We have seen that after the siege Gansevoort almost immediately took a furlough to visit his fiancée, Caty Van Schaick, leaving Willett in command at the fort until his return in late September. Then, granted a furlough to visit his wife, Mary, Willett arrived in Albany on the night of September 29 and sat down to write Gansevoort, informing him that he expected to visit the army units engaged near Saratoga before going on to see Mary.[37] Just hours before the final victory at Saratoga, Willett informed Gansevoort on October 6 that although he had been away from the fort for eleven days, he had not yet been to see his Mary. Willett included a side note that must have brought a chuckle to Gansevoort while demonstrating that the regiment's field officers had a very friendly relationship. Willett advised him to tell young Dr. Woodruff not to lie in bed too long or he would grow "too bulkey."[38]

Gansevoort received a letter dated November 16 from the still absent Willett written at army headquarters near Philadelphia. Willett told him that the British were occupying Philadelphia and he would like to remain with Washington's troops a few days longer to see the army in action. He then indicated that he was also thinking about making a trip to Boston once he left the Philadelphia area, unless Gansevoort needed him immediately at the fort. By this point, if the regiment was going to remain at the isolated Fort Stanwix, Willett desperately wanted to be transferred to the main army.[39] Willett seems to have used his furlough more for professional than for family purposes.

ADJUSTING TO GARRISON LIFE AFTER THE SIEGE 189

Each officer and private had a personal reason for requesting a furlough, beyond just wanting to get away from the fort for a while. It appears that Private Peter Scriber obtained a furlough in September so he could marry Clara Van Etten back at Rhinebeck that month.[40] Their first child would be born just seven months later, raising the question whether Clara had been with Peter at the fort during the siege. Did Peter ask for leave because Clara had become pregnant, and they wanted to get married quickly at their home church at Rhinebeck before the pregnancy became obvious?

The significant number of officers away from duty at the fort was reflected in the December 8 return of staff, field, and other commissioned officers. The colonel, major, adjutant, quartermaster, and surgeon were present, while the lieutenant colonel, paymaster, and surgeon's mate were absent. Willett was on furlough from September 26 to December 20, and Pay Master Van Rensselaer for eight weeks beginning October 16. Four captains were present and four absent. Captain Gregg remained absent on account of his wound of June 25, and Captain Tiebout was on furlough from October 4 to December 18. Five first lieutenants were present and three absent, while four second lieutenants were present and three absent. Lieutenant Thomas McClellan of Tiebout's company was out recruiting from October 4 until ordered to rejoin. Second Lieutenant Gilbert Livingston had deserted. Five ensigns were present and three absent. Several of the missing officers, ranging in rank from captains to ensigns, were out recruiting. Only Swartwout's company was not missing an officer away on that duty.[41]

Just as a soldier might wish for an early discharge from his enlistment, officers might want to leave the army early in good standing. Several days after the December 7 muster, on December 12, Gansevoort wrote a letter to General Schuyler, to be carried by Captain Elias Van Bunschoten, stating that Van Bunschoten was the senior captain in his regiment, by date of rank, not his age, and would like to retire and return to his family in Dutchess County, New York. Gansevoort praised Van Bunschoten's contributions to the cause and noted that he had agreed to return if an emergency arose.[42]

Illness also continued to be a major problem. On September 10, surgeon Woodruff signed a note certifying that Lawrence Schoolcraft of

Tiebout's company "is in such state of health as to be unfit for duty." Below that statement, Lieutenant Colonel Willett wrote that Schoolcraft was permitted "to go to his relations, near Schenectady until his health is reestablished after which he is to join his regiment." Company records show Schoolcraft still absent from the roster in December 1777 because of his illness.[43]

Smallpox became a concern, and on December 23, Gansevoort ordered that a return be made listing soldiers in the garrison who had not had that illness. Men on that list should not ask for a furlough, since smallpox was rampant at Schenectady and Albany and along the Mohawk River.[44]

The successful August defense did not remove, or even reduce, the need for attention to proper behavior, so Willett continued to exhort his troops on morals and cleanliness. In early September he denounced the pervasive swearing and cursing constantly heard among the garrison, reminding his men that such language was against the laws of God as well as the country. A week later he had to remind the troops that, to prevent filth in the fort, everyone must use the "necessaries" to relieve themselves. Two days later he ordered an additional necessary built. Then, on September 20, he reminded the soldiers not to use the necessary house during the day but to use the ditch designated for that purpose.[45]

Discipline continued to be a daily concern. On November 2, to prevent the arguments and personal animosities that often developed from them, orders were given forbidding card games.[46] Gansevoort received orders on November 21 to send thirty-eight-year-old Matross Seth Stow of Captain Lieutenant Savage's artillery detachment to Albany. Described as a stout five-foot, eight-inch man with light hair and blue eyes, Stow was to be tried by court-martial in response to a complaint lodged against him by a sergeant of Colonel Seth Warner's regiment. No record of the court-martial has been found, but Stow continued to serve until deserting to the enemy in April 1779.[47]

Disciplinary infractions related to living conditions and supply problems also continued. Sabins Burch of Captain Swartwout's company was court-martialed on September 21 for stealing a shirt.[48] On November 27, Lieutenant Bogart served on a court-martial for Barnard

ADJUSTING TO GARRISON LIFE AFTER THE SIEGE 191

Wade of Swartwout's company, who was accused of selling his regimental clothes and was sentenced to receive one hundred lashes.[49]

Military drill and duties had to be constantly reinforced. Garrison orders on September 18 stated that all men not on fort restoration fatigue duty, including men coming off guard duty, were to be exercised in basic military skills every afternoon at 3:00 p.m.[50] The routines of army life had not been completely standardized in the regiment, a problem found throughout the army. In an attempt to move things in the right direction, the September 19 garrison orders instructed the company orderly sergeants "to adopt one uniform mode in all the business of their office and especially to be careful that they each follow the same method in exercising the soldiers and relieving the guards." If any disagreement arose about the proper procedures, they must "apply to the Commandant who will determine which to follow." In addition, to avoid confusion, officers should always use the same wording when giving commands.[51]

While one might logically expect such actions to have been standardized much earlier, this was just another indication that this regiment, like the army in general, was still developing consistent standard procedures. This army-wide problem would begin to be addressed in several months when the main army wintered at Valley Forge and General von Steuben created his *Regulations for the Order and Discipline of the Troops of the United States*, which included standard formations, drill, and unit evolutions for use throughout the army. This work would eventually replace the collection of similar, but not uniform, manuals currently in use among the regiments.

The post-siege conditions led to increased tensions among the fort's officers that could not be ignored. A court of inquiry investigated a December complaint that Adjutant George Sytez had improperly assigned an officer to duty. Ensign Christopher Hutton served on that court on December 17. Sytez must have been in the wrong, because Hutton subsequently assumed the duties of adjutant. Sytez continued in the regiment as a company officer but would be omitted from the roster the following May, about the time Ensign Hutton officially became adjutant on May 28, 1778.[52] Several months earlier, in late December,

CHAPTER 15

another court of inquiry had investigated the behavior of Captain Bleeker, accused of ordering Second Lieutenant Ostrander to appear on parade while he was ill. On December 27 the court found that the young captain had indeed acted improperly but did not punish him severely. The incident had no negative effect on Bleeker's military career.[53]

Maintaining adequate supplies at the frontier fort remained a constant concern. Garrison orders on October 12 mentioned an inventory of hides said to be on their way in public boats and carriages to Albany. There, the officer with them would obtain badly needed shoes for the 3rd New York Regiment. Despite this welcome news, word of the October 7 victory at Bemis Heights (Second Battle of Saratoga) that reached the fort that day may have aroused more interest.[54]

Men did the best they could to stay warm with whatever clothing they had. On December 7, garrison orders had to admonish Captain Lieutenant Savage's detachment for appearing on parade improperly uniformed even though they had been provided with uniforms "drawn out of the public stores." They must have been modifying their clothing in any way they could to keep warm. The orders required them to "not again appear on the parade without being dressed in the uniform which is sent for the use of said company."[55]

An official inventory recording provisions available at the fort "a very few days after the siege" listed 460 barrels of flour, twenty-seven barrels of pork, one barrel of salt beef, four casks of Indian meal, ten barrels of salt, 453 pounds of candles, two boxes of hard soap, forty-two head of cattle, two and a half barrels of rendered tallow, twenty-seven gallons of rum, and 382 bushels of peas.[56] Those numbers do not tell the full story. How did those amounts compare with what was needed? How long would they last?

In answer, on September 22 a very frustrated Lieutenant Colonel Willett informed General Gates: "This garrison is in a dismal situation for want of provisions. This day we are compelled to begin upon our salt pork of which we have a sufficiency for only eight days. I have sent a . . . . letter by express to the Commissary of Purchases at Albany some days ago and used every other method in my power to supply this place with provision[,] without effect."[57] The constant repetition of his concerns must have weakened their effectiveness with those officers he inundated with them, who might have helped fix the problem. This, however, was just one of the issues that fueled the desire of

Willett and others to be assigned to the main army, where, correctly or incorrectly, they expected that all types of supplies were more consistently available.

The garrison could do only so much to obtain needed items locally. On September 28, Lieutenant Benjamin Bogardus of Captain Bleeker's company received orders to march the following day with one sergeant, one corporal, and twenty privates, along with horses and wagons, to the destroyed Oneida village of Oriska, where they were to collect all the hay in the fields and stack it for the use of the garrison.[58]

Civilians with the army acting as sutlers had to accept licensing, inspection, and regulation by the military. In response to the excessively high prices they charged for their goods, orders went out on October 30 stating that no one was to sell spiritous liquors or other items to soldiers without the permission of the commanding officer. Also, until lower prices could be guaranteed, no soldier was to buy any liquor or other goods at the present exorbitant prices. Such purchases would result in punishment for disobeying orders.[59]

With winter coming on, concerns increased about having enough food for the fort's human and equine occupants. Garrison orders on November 8 forbade taking forage for horses, or straw for soldiers' bedding, except by direction of the quartermaster.[60] On November 28, Gansevoort received word from the deputy commissary of purchases, Colonel Jacob Cuyler, that forty head of cattle were on their way to the fort. Although Cuyler had very few barrels of salt provisions, as soon as sleds were able to travel on snow, he would be able to send one hundred barrels. He had also ordered John Post, the commissary of issues for the New York Brigade, to send to the fort all that he had. Cuyler also complained that lacking money for two months, he had been forced to purchase items on credit.[61]

In reflecting on his experience with obtaining food supplies since taking command of the fort in May, Gansevoort complained that he had continually been forced to struggle with shortages. During the siege in August, it had been necessary to butcher all the milk cows and swine belonging to local civilians which had been confined within the fort's ditch. Now, with winter commencing, provisions were in such short supply that he feared everything would be gone by December 19.[62] He also felt that his men were still being overcharged by civilians taking advantage of them. On December 14, garrison orders stated that bakers must in no case charge more than one shilling for a six-pound loaf of bread.[63]

CHAPTER 15

When filling in for Gansevoort, still absent on furlough, Willett reminded Gates not only about the "importance of having a larger quantity of salt provisions" but also about the constant need for ammunition.[64] The fort needed to be made ready to withstand any subsequent attack, not only through repairs and improvements to its physical structure but also by increasing its combat resources. Regarding munitions, Captain Lieutenant Savage put together a detailed return on September 1 listing 27,700 musket cartridges, 4,500 flints, five thirty-two-pound barrels of powder, ten and a half sixteen-gallon barrels of powder, and four small six-gallon bags. The fort had four 9-pounder cannon, one of them damaged, four 6-pounders, and two 3-pounders. The 9- and 6-pounders were mounted on garrison carriages and the 3-pounders on traveling carriages. Savage also listed all the various types of ammunition and the tools and implements used in various ways with each type of cannon. There were 120 solid shot cannonballs for the 9-pounders, 183 for the 6-pounders, and twelve for the 3-pounders. Gunpowder-filled paper cartridges numbered ten for 9-pounders, eighty-seven for 6-pounders, and twelve for 3-pounders.[65]

Interpreting Savage's numbers, Willett expressed great concern "that the quantity of ammunition is small" and "there is especially a great deficiency of cannon shot." He noted that the small mortars, known as coehorns, listed in his return had been captured from the enemy along with a few shells for them, "to which there are no fuzzes [fuses]." It would obviously be helpful if fuses could be obtained to make the mortar shells explode a short time after being fired. He also noted that "a parcel of hand grenades would perhaps be serviceable." Three days previously, scouts from the fort had discovered a 3-pounder brass fieldpiece "which the enemy had buried near one of their works."[66]

A December 16 letter to Gansevoort from Van Rensselaer highlights how transportation issues were a large part of the supply problems. Gansevoort learned that the arms he had requested for the regiment would be sent by sled just as soon as there was snow. Enclosed inside the letter Gansevoort was pleased to find a stick of sealing wax which he had requested from Van Rensselaer. The wax came from Van Rensselaer's personal stock.[67]

As winter developed, the men of the garrison were well aware of the supply problems their Oneida neighbors had to endure. The fifty or so residents of the destroyed town of Oriska had remained near their old homes, and Gansevoort received orders to help supply their needs as much as possible until the Continental Congress could put a plan in place to help them. Because he was now very much the friend of the Oneidas, Gansevoort was glad to do what he could for them, even while still having problems supplying his own troops. The other nearby Oneida towns of Kanonwalohale and Old Oneida were in somewhat better condition but not out of danger.[68]

Because an Indian who came inside the fort the day before Christmas had acted suspiciously, some of the men believed he was a spy. The garrison received several orders putting it on heightened alert. Company commanders were to ensure that their men's arms and accoutrements were ready for an emergency. Additionally, as was often the case, orders reminded everyone to take great care when strolling out from the fort. To minimize any possibility of surprise attack, no Indians were to be admitted to the fort before 8:00 a.m. and none admitted who carried ammunition. Information on any Indians who might be staying in the fort overnight was to be reported to the commanding officer each evening. A protective guard consisting of a sergeant and twelve privates must always accompany woodcutting parties.[69] In addition to illustrating security concerns, this provides an example of extra duties taking men away from other important jobs such as fort repair and reconstruction.

Frustrated and angry that reconstruction work on the fort never seemed to achieve the required results, and that Major Hubble was not consulting him or keeping him informed of what he was accomplishing, Gansevoort publicly ordered Hubble on December 28 not to "pull down or erect any kind of works about this fort" without his orders permitting such actions.[70]

Just like everyone else in the garrison, even though General Arnold had granted him a short furlough immediately after the siege ended, Gansevoort still needed a break, a chance to get away from the fort for a time. He departed again on December 31 and achieved what may have been his primary objective for this furlough when he married his beloved Caty Van Schaick on January 12. While expecting Willett to command the fort in his absence, he knew that Willett might not always be present. Therefore he left detailed orders for the most senior officer present, whoever would be in command during his extended absence depending on which other officers were also absent.

Those orders covered a wide range of issues and reveal the many ongoing concerns demanding the attention of the fort commander. To prevent any trouble with the Indians arising from trade disputes, he reinforced the already well-known orders dating back to May 7 that no one at the fort could trade with the Indians. A quantity of logs fit for sawing should be brought to the fort as soon as possible to provide Major Hubble with sufficient timber to bomb-proof the barracks and provide pickets for the fort ditch. Cordwood should be collected as soon as possible but protected and saved for use in the spring; additional wood should be cut to satisfy current daily needs for firewood. A scouting party should be sent out at least once a week to Oneida Lake, and if snowshoes were needed, the officer in command could apply to Fort Stanwix commissary John Hansen for them. The commanding officer in Gansevoort's stead could fix prices on items sold by sutlers to prevent them from overcharging the soldiers. The large quantity of hay at Oriska should be brought to the fort as soon as possible but used only by the "horsilors & slaymen" for feeding the horses. To preserve the hay and cordwood supplies, a corporal and six privates should constantly be assigned to guard them. Major Cochran should send prisoner Sergeant James McCormick of Captain Bleeker's company, guarded by two or three men, in the first sleds returning to Albany and deliver him to the officer of the guard there. McCormick wound up in jail in Albany and was discharged in May 1778.[71]

Amid all these troubles of life at the fort, Mary Tapp, wife of Lieutenant Tapp, gave birth to a baby boy at the fort on December 26, 1777. He was their first child, and they named him William Horatio Tapp, no doubt to honor both his father and General Horatio Gates.[72]

The morale boost among members of the garrison resulting from their successful defense of the fort had not lasted long, even in the seasonable summer and fall weather. Now, the prospect of a long winter at the fort produced an even stronger desire to escape. The men must have wondered whether winter quarters at the fort would provide them rest and recuperation in preparation for the spring campaign. Or would it continue to envelop them in seemingly endless work details carried out amid a threatening existence that would keep them on high alert with little rest?

Table 1 Muster summary, 3rd New York Regiment at Fort Stanwix, December 7, 1777

COMPANY	PRESENT	TOTAL	SICK	FURLOUGH OFFICERS/ ENLISTED	ON COMMAND	DESERTED*	DEAD*
Capt. Van Bunschoten	28	36	3	0/3	1	0	0
Capt. De Witt	28	31	1	0/2	0	0	0
Capt. Jansen	27	31	0	1/3	0	0	0
Capt. Swartwout	46	58	5	1/2	4	1 (Lieut.)	0
Capt. Aorson	73	82	5	0/0	0	0	0
Capt. Gregg	33	39	2	1/3	0	1	0
Capt. Tiebout	74	80	1	1/2	0	4	1
Capt. Bleeker	45	57	5	1/1	2	0	1
Total	354	414	22	5/16	7	6	1

* Deserted and dead refer to those since last muster.

Source: Abstract of the muster rolls of the companies in the 3rd Battalion of New York Forces commanded by Peter Gansevoort, signed by Richard Lusk, December 7, 1777, Fort Schuyler, Horatio Gates Papers.

Chapter 16

A Tiresome and Dangerous New Year

January–May 1778

Lieutenant Colonel Willett and many of the regiment's officers collectively signed a midwinter letter to Colonel Gansevoort on February 21, asking for his help in arranging for the regiment to be relieved from duty at Fort Stanwix and transferred to the main army, where they could serve during the upcoming 1778 campaign. Without reference to their noteworthy successful defense of the fort, they explained that they were making their request "inasmuch, as we have already been one year in this garrison, secluded from those opportunities which are reaped by those corps, who have the honor to serve with the Grand Army, and in a manner condemned to perpetual fatigue, which may be conceiv'd rather a disgrace than honor to a soldier especially whilst the fields of America give so frequent opportunities, for him to display his patriotism and valour." The officers described their regiment, completing its first year of existence, as "young and inexperienced in the manouvres of a Grand Army, where alone we may expect to learn, that Art of War, so essential for the accomplishment of every good officer."[1]

As the year 1778 began, the regiment could have celebrated the successful completion of its first year of existence. For earlier regiments of the first and second establishments of the Continental Army, completing one year of service had essentially been the end of their story, except for men who chose to reenlist in the subsequent establishment.

For regiments in the third establishment, however, one year was just the beginning. During its first year, the regiment had struggled to build itself as fully as possible before playing its major role in defending Fort Stanwix from St. Leger's attack. Each man must have wondered what action, if any, the regiment would encounter in its second year.

On a personal level, Gansevoort inquired in late January whether his new, "higher" rank as colonel commandant carried with it a pay increase. He facetiously complained that his pay as a mere colonel was not enough to allow him to purchase table liquor. Like all officers, he was always concerned about his seniority among the other officers carrying the same rank, since the less senior had to defer to and obey orders given by the more senior. So, on a very practical note, he also asked if he must submit to those colonels senior to him, or whether he now outranked them. He felt his new rank had no value if he still had to defer to them.[2] In reality, only a more senior colonel who came to the fort had to defer to him, and only while there. It was a very local rank and did not carry over to other locations.

For the entire garrison, the new year did not alter the need to occupy, strengthen, and stand ready to defend the fort again. At any time the enemy could renew attacks on the fort and both Oneida and white settler villages in the western Mohawk River Valley. Maintaining morale and discipline among the garrison's soldiers during the first five months of the new year would prove to be an ever-increasing challenge. While examples can certainly be found of a strong esprit de corps among the enlisted men in Continental Army units, several factors made it very difficult to achieve for this garrison. The 3rd New York Regiment was, like many units containing men from diverse ethnic backgrounds, recruited from a wide geographic area, and with different terms of enlistment—three years or the duration of the war. At Fort Stanwix, individuals felt remote from the main army and its operations. They could feel abandoned by the public, too, because of the consistent supply shortages and a lack of recognition for their personal merit. After the capture of Burgoyne's army at Saratoga, which seemed to end the threat of major military forces descending from Canada, and with the British occupying Philadelphia and New York City, the focus of the Continental Army in 1778 appeared to be turning toward areas some distance away from the New York State frontier.[3] But that did not end the more local civil war and frontier aspects of the conflict.

CHAPTER 16

Among the many alerts about potential enemy incursions during the first four months of the year, Gansevoort received a letter from the Marquis de Lafayette dated March 5, ordering him to send out as many scouts as possible to find and capture British officer Christopher Carleton, the nephew of Sir Guy Carleton, who had known Sir William Johnson and lived among the Mohawks, greatly admiring them. Lafayette must have heard that the younger Carleton was back in the area and might be organizing raids. In fact, Carleton would lead raids, but not until the fall of 1778 and then in 1780 in the Lake Champlain region.[4]

To prevent false alarms and conserve ammunition, Gansevoort had to remind his soldiers continually not to carry their muskets out of the fort and fire them in the woods. They were to carry guns only if going on command. A soldier "on command" had been assigned a duty away from the fort. The sergeant of the guard patrolled the woods with his men to detect any firing.[5]

Suspicions arose in mid-April that a scouting party of enemy Indians was "skulking about this place." Accordingly, orders to the soldiers were reinforced not to "straggle into the woods or to go any distance from the fort except they are on command." Work parties were to have proper guards, and scouting parties were to make special efforts to discover any suspicious tracks in the woods. Gansevoort guaranteed a twenty-dollar reward to anyone who captured or killed an enemy in the neighborhood of the fort.[6] Disappointingly, the garrison's orders after the close of the successful siege defense were the same as those during the months leading up to the siege. Life at the frontier fort was unchangingly dangerous and threatening.

May brought evidence of impending Indian raids in the Mohawk Valley, and raids by Indians and Loyalists led by Joseph Brant did occur over several weeks, some quite near Fort Stanwix, keeping everyone in the area on edge, including at the fort.[7] May also brought the very encouraging news that after the military successes in the summer and fall of 1777, including the successful defense of the fort, the French had signed a crucial treaty of friendship, trade, and mutual defense with the Continental Congress. In addition to celebratory statements about this in the daily garrison orders, the troops formed into line and fired a *feu de joie* at 1:00 p.m. Soldiers joyfully fired their muskets into the air in rapid succession one at a time down the line and then back to the beginning.[8] Although they couldn't know this at the time in the midst of the daily grind, their successful defense of the fort had been an integral part of the series of events later considered by many historians to be the major turning point in the Revolution.

The new year did not alleviate Gansevoort's concerns about getting the fort into condition to enable it to withstand another siege. While still on furlough, Gansevoort instructed Willett on March 29 to obtain from French engineer Colonel Jean Baptiste Gouvion, presently with him at the fort, "every necessary instruction to compleat the fort" and to keep him informed of "every necessary wanting at the fort, that I may procure them."[9] Several weeks later, Gouvion was ordered by the Marquis de Lafayette to return to the Southern Army. The frustrated Gansevoort asked General Gates to send him another engineer.[10]

After Gouvion's departure, First Lieutenant and new father William Tapp of Captain De Witt's company was appointed to fill in as "Superintendent of the Engineers Department." He received orders on May 9 to deliver all the quartermaster general's stores to "Mr. [Daniel] Tucker," assistant deputy quartermaster general, who had been appointed quartermaster general of the garrison. Tapp also received orders to see that the damaged guardhouse was properly repaired.[11] Several days later, Tapp inspected all the sentry boxes to make sure they were in good condition and "fixed so as not to be blown down with every trifling wind." While complete information on the number and location of sentry boxes is not available, it appears that, at a minimum, each bastion had one, there was one just inside the main gate, and there was one in front of the headquarters building on the parade ground. In addition, Tapp was to make sure that all gates and fencing outside the fort were in proper condition "to prevent horses and cattle from getting into the meadows and gardens."[12] The live animals were both a necessity for life at the fort and defense of it while also presenting several challenges, in many ways just as the soldiers did.

Gansevoort fully realized that he and the garrison had been fortunate that St. Leger had neglectfully brought along only very light artillery pieces to besiege the fort. Anticipating a possible future repeat of the St. Leger-style attack, throughout January Gansevoort told anyone who might be able to help him about the urgent need for heavy artillery to be emplaced at the fort. He emphasized that if the enemy should attack again, they would surely employ greater force, which would require stronger defenses. Gansevoort made a list for General Gates of the additional artillery needed to enable the fort to withstand another siege and urged getting it there before the rutted path passing for a road from Fort Dayton deteriorated badly with the spring thaw.[13]

In early April, a frustrated Gansevoort was still holding out hope of receiving a response to his critical requests for heavier artillery. He had sent a return of needed artillery supplies to Continental Army artillery major Ebeneezer Stevens but had received only a few items in response. Should his requests continue to go unheeded, Gansevoort absolved himself of any responsibility for the very likely negative consequences to Fort Stanwix.[14]

By April 19, Gansevoort learned that the Board of War had ordered eight heavy cannon to Fort Stanwix, but that for some reason Major Stevens was refusing to send them without further orders. The distraught Gansevoort shot back that if St. Leger had brought some 12- and/or 18-pounder cannon with his troops during their August siege, Fort Stanwix would have been lost.[15]

Governor Clinton still had not received permission from the Congress by May 17 to forward some large guns to Fort Stanwix, but he did express his hope that the lost big guns of Ticonderoga could possibly be retrieved.[16]

Fatigue parties continued to be the bane of the soldiers' existence. In addition to parties addressing the garrison's normal daily needs, a fatigue party was formed on January 7 to cut pickets for fort repair and restoration.[17]

Wood was an essential item for heating and cooking in addition to the large amounts needed for restoration and repair projects at the fort. In order to deal with the snowy weather at the beginning of the year, all military sleds arriving at the fort were ordered to be detained for two days to be used for drawing wood to the fort.[18] A typical fatigue party in February consisted of "six good axe men" supervised by a sergeant to "cut two cords of wood per day." Each man on this duty was to get a half pint of rum a day.[19] Collecting firewood could simultaneously serve other important purposes. Orders went out on March 10 that to further clear the area around the fort, firewood was to be obtained from the woods contiguous to the cleared ground.[20]

In midwinter, since there was not enough hay and straw bedding to keep the men warm, the orders to put out fires in the barracks and casemate rooms each night were rescinded, thus increasing the amount of firewood needed every twenty-four hours.[21]

Orders for the March 13 fatigue parties stated that one captain, two subalterns, six sergeants, and sixty rank and file were to parade at 1:00 p.m. without arms, and the captain was to "call upon the commanding officer for instructions." Lieutenant Tapp was to select six men to cut cedar to make pails and other items for the use of the garrison. He was also to procure some good wood for burning brick at the kiln and have it piled to season. That wood was not to be used for any other purpose. Fort cleanliness had suffered during the winter, and six additional men were to be designated to work with the camp color men for three days to properly clean the fort of every kind of filth. The officers of the day checked that the quartermaster had ensured that the color men did their duty, since clean living spaces led to better health.[22]

To keep the restoration and repair work moving along, the officer of the day walked around all work areas carefully observing the fatigue parties and "artificers" and reported in writing to the commanding officer any problems he observed. Soldiers possessing special skills that made them potential artificers could be temporarily detailed to work with the civilian craftsmen to help with restoration projects. Gansevoort ordered on January 9, however, that no sergeant or corporal could be so employed except on special order from the fort commander.[23] While privates were interchangeable on group assignments, noncommissioned officers were not. Modifications to the general instructions for the makeup of fatigue parties appeared in the garrison orders for April 17. By those orders, any number of men up to seventeen would be commanded by a sergeant, from eighteen to forty by a subaltern, from forty to sixty by two subalterns, from sixty to eighty by a captain and two subalterns, and from eighty to one hundred or 120 by a captain and three subalterns. One sergeant should always be appointed to assist each commissioned officer supervising the party.

A drink of rum was an expected compensation for fatigue duty. Officers commanding a party made a rum return listing all the men on fatigue and sent it to the quartermaster, who would draw rum to be given only to the men included in that return, unless the commanding officer directed otherwise. The superintendent of the engineer's department made up a rum return for the camp color men, wagoners, and artificers and their attendants and sent it to the quartermaster, who would make one composite return.[24]

Modified fatigue party orders on May 19 required all fatigue parties to commence work at 5:00 a.m. until further orders. The superintendent of the engineer's department made sure that none of the artificers overstayed the time allowed for meals, and he deducted a quarter of a day's pay each time a man arrived one quarter of an hour late to work.[25]

Some of the men were fortunate enough to share life at the fort with members of their family. Just how many women and children were living at the fort is not documented. At this time, however, in addition to Nancy McCarty, it is very likely that Mary Tapp was present and perhaps Clara Scriber. Clara gave birth to a daughter, Leah, on April 5 and, along with Peter, may have been back home in Rhinebeck when Leah was christened on April 12. Whatever the number, there were enough women and children at the fort in early February, when concerns about smallpox arose, for Gansevoort to order that any woman or child who came down with that disease was to immediately report to Dr. Woodruff.[26]

In April, Gansevoort ordered a return to be made of all the women with the garrison.[27] This indicates there were more than a few, though the number may have fluctuated. A certain number of wives received rations and quarters, while usually doing some work for the company, such as helping in the hospital. Other women could earn money doing washing, for which soldiers paid them. Orders went out in May that women were not to wash clothes within the fort or the ditch. If there had been only a few women, such a prohibition would not have had to appear in the garrison orders.[28]

Proper food storage was necessary for the "life of the garrison." As with many other needs, the fort's facilities were not yet adequate for that task. The orders for March 15 stated that Lieutenant Tapp was to see that a quantity of spars were gathered and "laid along the parade in order to roll the beef and pork upon, which were to be covered with boards in the best manner possible until proper stores are provided for that purpose." The acting adjutant, Ensign Christopher Hutton, supplied him with a fatigue party to accomplish this.[29] Ensign Hutton officially became adjutant on March 28. The former adjutant, Lieutenant George Sytez, stayed with the regiment as a company officer.[30]

A month later, Colonel Gansevoort ordered "the Bomb Proofs under the SW and NW Bastions fitted up in the best manner possible for the reception of the beef and pork that is in this garrison." Before storing the meat, the commissary had to properly examine it and have it packed in good-quality barrels before stowing, to prevent spoilage from the loss of its pickling. As much meat as possible was then stored in the bomb-proof area under the southwest bastion, because it was "the most airy and agreeable and consequently the most likely to preserve the provisions sweetest and longest."[31]

In mid-March, with the onset of spring, Gansevoort instructed Willett to restore the truck garden for the benefit of the garrison. Although there was too much other important work to justify making fences for the garden as had been done previously, Gansevoort told Willett to run a fence from the place where the Frenchman Stephen Delyrod's house had formerly stood to the river, and another from the "Crippel bush," an area of tangled trees and shrubs at the lower end of Brodock's field, to the river. Each fence should have a swinging gate. The enclosed area should contain the garden and space for grass and hay. Planting should begin as soon as the weather permitted so that "the garrison may not be without vegetables in their season."[32] In mid-April, Willett requested that Gansevoort send seeds for the garden. He also allowed any officer so desiring to fence off a small garden for himself, as long as it was outside the area fenced in for the fort garden.[33]

In addition to concerns over providing food and required items for his troops, Colonel Gansevoort remained obligated to supply local Indians with food and other goods at times. Gansevoort received orders on March 11 from the commissioners of Indian affairs to supply provisions to members of the Six Nations aligned with the Americans whenever they were at Fort Stanwix on public business, or stopping en route to meet with the commissioners of Indian affairs.[34] Gansevoort proudly reported to General Gates on March 12 that the local Indians had been very friendly lately and he expected to be able to complete the fort without difficulty.[35]

In late April, the Board of Commissioners for Indian Affairs at Albany sent a quantity of goods to Fort Stanwix to be distributed as presents to the Indians for their use, not to be treated as trade items. In anticipation of potential problems, orders went out to the garrison not to purchase any of those items from the Indians for any reason.

Anyone becoming involved in any trade with the Indians would face severe punishment. Copies of that order were posted in conspicuous places throughout the fort.[36]

Interactions with friendly local Oneidas continued during this period. Information about the activities at Valley Forge that winter and spring were known to people at the fort, and some local Oneidas traveled there to join with Washington, at least for a time. Action closer to home included the arrival of several French officers serving the Continental Army and working on fortifying the Oneida village at Kanonwalohale. These officers were the twenty-year-old General Marquis de Lafayette and engineers Lieutenant Colonel Jean Baptiste Gouvion, Captain Louis Celeron, and A. Louis de Tousard. Greatly fearing that Kanonwalohale would be attacked, the Oneidas had requested a fort to be built there and garrisoned by Continentals. Meetings were held, plans were made, and construction was begun, but that fort was never completed. The 3rd New York Regiment officers had been willing to supply tools for the work, but because of personnel attrition, they could not supply soldiers for the construction work when they did not have even half the number of troops they needed to keep on guard at Fort Stanwix.[37]

Two Oneida chiefs, William Kayendalongwea and Skenandoah, came to Fort Stanwix on April 22 with news about a recent council at Johnstown, and the next day many Oneidas and some Tuscaroras arrived at the fort to receive presents the officials at Johnstown had been unable to bestow on them and to say farewell to a group of Oneidas setting off to join Washington's army in Pennsylvania.[38]

The garrison especially required adequate clothing during the winter months, but the supply system continued to fail them. In late January, Gansevoort angrily sent Governor Clinton a list of the clothing needed by his regiment, plainly declaring that because of their poor clothing, his troops were "half naked" and in distress. Combining that failure to provide sufficient clothing with the fact that the men had not been paid, Gansevoort questioned just how much could be expected from them and whether they would even continue to serve.[39]

Table 2 Clothing needed for the 3rd New York Regiment, January 22, 1778

COMPANY	HATS	COATS	VESTS	BREECHES	SHIRTS	STOCKINGS	SHOES	BLANKETS	KNAPSACKS	CANTEENS
Capt. Van Bunschoten	26	7	36	14	52	40	50	24	10	10
Capt. De Witt	27	1	26	7	29	29	29	10	6	23
Capt. Jansen	26	5	34	10	70	34	34	25	10	30
Capt. Swartwout	54	3	54	16	88	61	72	31	20	20
Capt. Aorson	85	6	85	31	143	101	123	69	85	44
Capt. Gregg	33	1	33	10	51	33	43	25	33	33
Capt. Bleeker	59	12	58	19	96	68	79	47	29	24
Capt. Tiebout	87	18	87	27	148	87	87	64	81	81
Total	397	53	413	134	677	453	516	295	274	265

Source: Report from Colonel Peter Gansevoort, "Return of Clothing Wanted to Compleat the Third Battalion of New York Forces, Fort Schuyler 22nd January 1778," in Clinton, *Public Papers of George Clinton* (no. 1027), 2: 687.

Doing everything he could to secure a proper clothing supply for his troops, and making the critical situation very clear to his superiors, in early March, Gansevoort ordered a return of the men in each company which also clearly listed the articles of clothing each man lacked.[40] When that return was completed, Gansevoort ordered Captain Bleeker to go to York, Pennsylvania, where Congress was meeting, and present the return to the Board of War. He should personally stress to the delegates the necessity of providing the Fort Stanwix garrison with adequate clothing.[41] In a letter to General Gates, then president of the Board of War, alerting him to Bleeker's mission, Gansevoort pointed out that only half his men had shirts.[42] At the fort, he also reminded his soldiers that it was essential to take whatever measures they could to keep what clothing they did have, both old and new, in good condition so as to promote their health as well as appear professionally military.[43] Gansevoort, who was in Albany at the time, did not know then that on March 10, Lieutenant Thomas McClellan of Tiebout's company had received 233 white, 215 checked, and fifty-two coarse white shirts, seventy-five vests, and twenty-five pairs of shoes.[44] This would help the situation, but only partially.

Gansevoort had to alert Governor Clinton once again in early April to the continuing lack of clothing at the fort.[45] At last Willett rejoiced in a letter to Gansevoort on April 15 at the news that clothing was finally on its way to the garrison.[46] When the shirts, shoes, and other clothing arrived, however, the frustrated Willett informed him that there would not be enough to supply each man with two shirts.[47] Still, they received enough for him to order the men to conduct themselves as though they had sufficient clothing. Garrison orders for April 21 optimistically stated:

> As the men have received such a supply of clothing as will enable each man to take his proper tour of duty for the time to come, it is expected that there will be no deficiencies for the future. Any person that is found wasting or in any way disposing of his clothing will be punished in the most exemplary manner. The sergeants of the respective squadrons are to be very attentive in seeing that all the men keep their clothes whole, clean, and in good order and whenever the mens clothes are exhibited for examination the sergeants are first to view them and after that an officer who is to bring the sergeant to account if he has not been faithful in reporting the state of the men's clothing. This order is of vast importance and too much attention cannot be paid to it.[48]

As the spring campaign season approached, still hoping the regiment would receive orders to join the main army, Willett wryly suggested to Colonel Gansevoort on April 20 that in addition to sufficient clothing, every man should also have a knapsack and a canteen "in case anything should turn up to require us to march."[49] Not only would these items be required in the event of orders to change location, but also if the regiment joined with the main army, it should look fully equipped and ready for action. The men should look like professional Continentals and not like ragged militia.

Governor Clinton bluntly stated on May 17 that the only hope of obtaining clothing for the 3rd New York Regiment was at the state store, which in the first week of March reportedly had 2,428 shirts and ninety-three pairs of stockings. Clinton noted that he had ordered one fourth of that supply forwarded to Fort Stanwix and the remainder divided among the 3rd New York and the other four New York regiments.[50] The same day, an officer of the 3rd New York Regiment arrived at Poughkeepsie carrying a return of the clothing his regiment badly needed. Afterward, the officer he reported to at Poughkeepsie, Robert Benson, informed Gansevoort that in the future, a return of the amount of clothing the regiment had on hand, as well as one listing the clothing needed, would be required to obtain additional clothing.[51] Everyone was asking for clothing from the inadequate supplies, so it had to go to the most needy. Captain Swartwout received another batch of clothing on May 23 which again only partially satisfied the needs of the regiment. This lot consisted of 102 coarse brown-and-white shirts, fifty checked shirts, and 248 white shirts of finer quality, along with twenty-four vests.[52]

Taking care of personal needs and hygiene continued to prove very difficult. In mid-March, the master carpenter received orders to build a good necessary at a place to be pointed out to him by the superintendent of the engineers, presumably Lieutenant Tapp.[53] Then, on May 21, the quartermaster sergeant received orders to have tubs placed in the corners of each barracks for the men to "make water" in. Those tubs were to be emptied and washed every morning.[54] There was a constant struggle at the fort to make facilities as convenient as possible to reduce the random disposal of bodily wastes.

Despite all the measures taken to keep things clean, many members of the garrison did become ill. On April 2, surgeon Woodruff wrote to Gansevoort telling him that he had ordered a supply of medicine and hospital stores. To protect those items, he requested that a trusted soldier or sergeant be appointed to keep watch over them and prevent the bateau men from pilfering any items from the shipment. Woodruff also kept an eye on the weather and its effects on garrison health. He gave Gansevoort, still in Albany, a weather report on April 2, noting that they had been having some fine weather interspersed with periods of rain. He also reported that most of the winter snow around the fort had melted.[55] With the arrival of better weather and the prospects for growing needed crops, orders came out that no one was to engage in sports or other activity among the troops, or with the local Indians, on any part of the meadows scheduled to be enclosed by fences and preserved for mowing hay.[56]

In addition to desertions, companies lost men to incapacitating illness and death by disease. Three men were discharged in May, and for at least one man the reason was an illness that had kept him hospitalized for several months. Two men died in March, one in April, and one in May. Three of them had been very early enlistees, in November and December 1776, but one had enlisted just a month earlier, in April.[57]

By late March, with the prospect of better weather, among the usual concerns about keeping everything as clean as possible to prevent disease, orders went out to air bedding, primarily blankets and any bags containing hay or straw for mattresses or cushions.[58]

A rare surviving glimpse of the regiment's physical condition is found in a "Return of the sick in the Garrison of Fort Schuyler, March 1st, 1778." The return includes both men with some kind of illness and men with physical injuries. The return, which is only for the 3rd New York Regiment, records that each of the eight companies had at least one man sick, and there were ten men in the hospital and twenty-two sick in their quarters, for a total of thirty-two. The number of ill men in each company ranged from nine in Bleeker's and eight in Aorson's to one to four in each of the other companies. Eleven men were lame or had an ulcerous leg, while three others simply had a "debility." Four men had the ubiquitous "itch" badly enough to be kept in their quarters. Men with the itch had red pustules on their bodies caused by the bites of very small insects. Internal medical problems included two men with asthma and four with fevers, while two other men suffered from some form of venereal disease.[59]

Desertions from the regiment could be motivated by any of a variety of reasons, including low morale resulting from the repetitious labor, constant alerts, and inadequate supplies of food and clothing. Three deserters escaped capture in January, one in February, three in March, and three in April, then eight in May.[60]

Not all deserters left permanently or avoided capture. On January 31, Nicholas Christman of Captain Tiebout's company was sentenced to four hundred lashes for desertion on November 28, 1777, and helping another deserter, John P. Everhite of Van Bunschoten's company. Christman had returned to the regiment on his own sometime in January but was still severely punished. John Cremer of Tiebout's company was sentenced to three hundred lashes for desertion.[61] Each case was punished differently depending on its individual factors.

Although he knew that he had to be a strict disciplinarian, Gansevoort was a complex personality. He also needed to clear his mind and relax when he could. He enjoyed music very much. His granddaughter Catherine later owned a music book he had carried during his military service in which he transcribed musical exercises. While in the army he sought out men in his regiment who could help him with his music. A very personal note relating to a desertion is found in his music notebook. It reads, "Colonel Gansevoort's [music] instructor, who belonged to his regiment, and who was an able instructor and made an excellent performer, deserted in 1778." That must have been a particularly painful desertion for Gansevoort. This instructor/performer may well have been Sergeant John Kertel of Captain Aorson's company, who had served as drum major before his promotion to sergeant. Kertel, who had helped prevent desertions, then deserted himself on July 1.[62]

In an attempt to prevent deserters from making their escape, the April 10 garrison orders declared that any soldier not on command and without written permission signed by an officer who was found two miles from the fort would be considered a deserter. No officer was to give any soldier such permission without notifying the commanding officer.[63]

For those officers and men who could not get away on command or furlough, or by deserting, life at the fort continued in less than comfortable and enjoyable ways, and the new year did not see any reductions in discipline issues. The unpleasant winter living conditions and the uncertain future of the regiment resulted in deteriorating interpersonal relationships, leading to grievances both actual and merely perceived. At the beginning of the new year, drummer Robert Moore of Captain Swartwout's company broke down a door and threatened to break Swartwout's head, resulting in his court-martial on January 3.[64] Something must have badly disturbed Moore for him to physically challenge the very popular Swartwout.

It is frequently difficult to say just what the issue was that caused a dispute. Many minor disagreements resolved themselves peacefully with the help of friends or noncommissioned officers, while others ended up in courts-martial. In early March 1778, a heated dispute broke out between Sergeant John Dean of the artillery detachment and camp woman Nancy Weedon, who was probably a soldier's wife. Dean had confined Weedon in the guardhouse for "impeaching his Character." Then he was confined himself, accused of "defrauding Mrs. Weedon of her provision." The two had gotten to the point where they could not reconcile their differences without the help of the court, which investigated their charges, found both not guilty, and released them from the guardhouse.[65] Some serious counseling with their friends must have followed to settle things down.

After Bishop Hadley of Captain Swartwout's company had been confined in the guardhouse for mutiny and disobeying orders, a court-martial found him guilty of the latter, lesser charge and sentenced him to receive one hundred lashes upon his bare back by the drummers of the garrison. Colonel Gansevoort approved the sentence and ordered it carried out the evening of April 19.[66] One is led to wonder just what disobedient actions could be judged mutinous or whether there was interpersonal anger involved that escalated the charge.

Some charges were simply made up to get someone in trouble for some reason. John Willis of Captain Bleeker's company accused Seth Rowley and Jonathan Pinckney of Tiebout's company of abusing him. When they were tried in late February, however, the charges did not hold up.[67] In mid-May, Ensign Peter Magee of Van Bunschoten's company lodged a complaint that he had been ill-used by Captain Bleeker and Lieutenant Tapp, although the court of enquiry held the next day reported that Magee could not support his complaint.[68] Thefts, or perceived thefts, among the soldiers brought occasional charges. On April 13, a court-martial sat to try three prisoners confined in the guardhouse by artillery second lieutenant Isiah Thompson for stealing; the results are unknown.[69]

Rum, and its consumption, was a factor in many offenses. In mid-January, Lieutenant Bogart served on the board for the trials of William McCord of Captain Gregg's company, whom Bogart had confined in the guardhouse for drawing rum without permission, and John Honeywell of Captain Bleeker's company, accused of helping him. McCord was sentenced to one hundred lashes.[70] John Closs of Captain De Witt's company was court-martialed in late January for allowing rum to be drawn from a hogshead under his care as sentinel.[71] The April 8 garrison orders noted that soldiers had been seen coming out of the carpenter shop drunk. These orders warned the carpenters that their rum allowance would be cut off if the problem continued and they would run the risk of being court-martialed.[72] Soon after, John Duncan, working as a carpenter at the fort, was found guilty on April 26 for disobeying the April 8 order by not only selling rum but also receiving a soldier's blanket to pay for it. He was sentenced to have his rum ration cut off.[73]

Ironically, even milk could get a man involved in a court-martial. Individual soldiers could own one or more cows and make some money by selling their milk. But because soldiers received fodder from the fort's supply to feed their cows, the price of milk had been regulated by Gansevoort since the previous September at sixpence per quart.[74] A May 1 court-martial, with Captain Jansen as president, found James Patterson of Captain Tiebout's company guilty of selling milk for ninepence per quart, and the court ordered him to deliver up his cows for the use of the hospital located in the bombproof of the southwest bastion. The commanding officer approved the sentence and ordered acting adjutant Ensign Hutton to deliver Patterson's cows to the hospital steward that evening. After several days, however, Colonel Gansevoort relented "in consequence of the contrition of James Patterson for his offence, and promise of particular circumspection for the future," and ordered "his cows to be restored to him." But he assured Patterson, and all others who owned cows, "that this is not to be a precedent for any future offences of this kind."[75]

Soldiers also owned other animals that could cause difficulties at the fort. A problem developed from hogs running around loose and injuring the fortification works, so the April 5 garrison orders required that the owner of any loose-running hog must have it fitted with a nose ring, so it could be controlled, or it would be killed.[76] Standing orders went out on February 6 that all horses and cows were to be turned out of the fort before the gates were shut at night, "as they are a great nuisance to the garrison." The officer of the day would enforce this and see that the sleds pulled by horses were also removed so they would not clutter up the fort.[77] Even though all these animals were important to life at the fort, the scarcity of appropriate areas to keep them in and the crowded fort conditions made them a problem too.

Cattle were necessary because they provided not only milk and meat but also hides for leather. In April, many valuable animal hides lying about the fort were found to be ruined due to lack of proper care. Such hides were a valuable resource, contributing to the large amount of leather needed for clothing, shoes, harness, and other important items. The butchering process had been designed to produce usable hides as well as meat. To ensure that butchered hides were cured properly to be tanned into leather, Gansevoort ordered the commissary to appoint someone, other than a butcher, to take charge of hides and prevent damage to them. If he found any hides had been damaged during the butchering process, the butchers were to be held accountable for that damage.[78]

The need to obtain recruits for the regiment remained an important job that took officers away from the fort for much of the year. When Gansevoort forwarded his usual first-of-the-month regimental returns to General Gates on April 4, he argued that they revealed the need for an additional one thousand men to fully and effectively utilize Fort Stanwix's defensive works, though adding just four hundred men would allow the garrison to defend against an enemy force three times its size. When Colonel James Livingston's regiment was ordered downriver, it became necessary for Gansevoort to replace them by detaching some of his troops to take quarters at Fort Dayton and Johnstown to protect the Tryon County residents, further diminishing the garrison's size. He also requested that the partial artillery company with him be completed and put under the command of a good and active officer. This was clearly a criticism of Captain Lieutenant Savage's capabilities, supported by the negative feelings of the artillerymen in the detachment toward Savage.[79]

Recruiting continued throughout the winter and spring.[80] Sometime in March, Godfrey Byerd, about twenty-five years old, enlisted at Schoharie. Born in one of the German states of the Holy Roman

Empire, Byerd had enlisted in the British army, probably one of the several thousand men recruited by Hanoverian lieutenant colonel Georg Heinrich Albrecht von Scheither to augment the undermanned British regiments.[81] He was a British "regular" and should not be confused with the "Hessians," sent in regiments by the several German princes under treaty with the government of King George III. Many British regulars were men born in other countries who enlisted in the British army. Byerd had been taken prisoner at Saratoga and become part of the prisoner of war Convention Army, from which he deserted to join the Continentals. Shortly before his successful enlistment, the Continental Congress had resolved on February 26 that "whereas, experience hath proved that no confidence can be placed in prisoners of war or deserters from the enemy, who inlist into the continental army; but many losses and great mischiefs have frequently happened by them; therefore, Resolved, That no prisoners of war or deserters from the enemy be inlisted, drafted, or returned to serve in the continental army."[82] Recruits were very hard to find, however, and Colonel Gansevoort accepted Byerd to substitute for the still disabled Lawrence Schoolcraft of Tiebout's company, who could then be discharged. Byerd was literate, signed his name gracefully, and apparently convinced Gansevoort that he would be a help to the regiment. Despite Congress's suspicions of enemy prisoners and deserters, Byerd would serve faithfully and skillfully through the remaining war years, being promoted to sergeant in 1782. His familiarity with the British army and its actions around Saratoga must have provided hours of interesting conversation with his fellow soldiers in Tiebout's company and others.[83]

With the coming of spring, April saw twenty-four men enlist, spread over five companies, mostly Swartwout's and Bleeker's. May proved even better, with thirty men enlisting, at least one in each company and eleven in Captain Gregg's.[84] Lieutenant Colbrath and Sergeant Lewis Bogardus went out in mid-April to recruit men for Captain De Witt's company, but the company gained only three men in May, all of them on May 30.[85]

On May 4, Captain Swartwout, then at Poughkeepsie, sent a return to Gansevoort in Albany listing the names of men who had been recruited and offered a bounty by Sergeant Bogardus of his company. While recruits Thomas Taylor, Samuel Geake, Moses Dent, and Jeremiah Weldon had already received their bounties, Swartwout requested that the paymaster withhold additional bounty money until he could be present, and that Sergeant Bogardus return to the regiment as soon as possible to assist with further recruiting.[86]

Because Gansevoort and Willett wanted their regiment to present a highly trained image to anyone encountering them at the remote fort, veterans as well as men new to the regiment required constant training, but they could not always get it. To make the regiment's men as skilled in their exercises as possible, a new plan, a modification of the drill plan dating back to February, was laid out on May 3 for that purpose.

All the men belonging to the regiment were divided into three squads. Those most perfect in their exercises were put in one class and were known as the "Grand Squad." Those who did not qualify formed the "Awkward Squad." The extremely unskilled, who did not even qualify for the Awkward Squad, were kept in the basic drill squad of new recruits until they qualified for a higher group. This shows how the constant personnel changes, as well as the many conflicting demands on the men's time, had prevented the full professionalization of the regiment.

Except on field days and special occasions, as soon as morning roll call was finished, weather permitting, those men assigned to the basic drill unit and not out on some assigned duty were drilled for two hours. At 10:00 a.m. all the men not on duty, except for the just relieved guard, would turn out for exercise upon the beating of the long roll. The adjutant then exercised the Grand Squad for one hour, while the Sergeant Major exercised the Awkward Squad for an hour and a half. Those in the basic drill squad were drilled for two hours. At 4:00 p.m. every soldier not on duty was to parade for exercise, the Grand Squad for an hour and a half, the Awkward Squad for two hours, and those in basic drill until the fatigue parties were called in. Company commanders provided sergeants and corporals to lead the drills, and the adjutant made sure all the groups drilled in the same manner. All the officers not on duty were to attend the afternoon exercises and make sure that their drill sergeants and corporals did their duty properly.

The key phrase was "not on duty." The training involved just those men free from other tasks, and those other tasks often required a large percentage of the men. This meant that daily life in the army at the fort involved either some repetitive guard or fatigue party duty or boring drill. Neither activity contributed to high morale and a desire to continue serving.

A break in routine occurred on April 23. Congress had designated that date to be observed as a day of fasting, humiliation, and prayer, during which people were to abstain from all worldly work and recreation. Gansevoort was concerned that because the regiment no longer had a chaplain, there could be no "publick acts of devotion," although he believed that "if we are sincere in our humiliation and prayers however secret they may be performed the Omniscient Jehovah will be well pleased with our services." As it turned out, an unexpected visit from the well-known missionary and sometime chaplain Reverend Samuel Kirkland enabled the garrison to hold formal church services.[87]

Officers received furloughs for a variety of reasons during the winter. Major Cochran, commanding the fort in the absence of Gansevoort and Willett, wrote to Gansevoort by way of Captain Swartwout on February 21 stating that he had allowed Swartwout and Lieutenant Levi Stockwell to go on furlough until the end of March to care for their families. Cochran then requested a furlough for himself and asked Gansevoort to obtain enough cloth to have a badly needed coat tailored for his son.[88] Second Lieutenant Thomas Ostrander was listed as lame and in his quarters on the March 1 muster and then put on furlough beginning March 12 for forty-two days until May 1. Ostrander was omitted from the muster roll in May 1778 and disappears from further records.[89]

Absences noted on the January 19, 1778, officer muster roll include both Colonel Gansevoort, who had gone to Albany on January 1 on another furlough, and Lieutenant Colonel Willett, who had been on leave from September 26 to December 20. Several officers were able to get away on command to conduct work at other locations. Paymaster Ensign Jeremiah Van Rensselaer was on command at Albany from October and surgeon Woodruff went on furlough January 1 for four weeks. Captain Tiebout had gone on furlough on October 4, required to be back on December 15.[90]

One of the last men to secure a furlough was fifer David Jones of Van Benschoten's company. Upon receiving his furlough on March 1, he returned to his home at Fishkill, where, after having survived about a year and a half of military service and the siege, he was thrown from a horse and badly injured. Unable to return to his unit, he appears on company musters as absent sick, first at Fishkill and then at Poughkeepsie, until he was given a discharge on December 7, after the regiment had left

Fort Stanwix. He believed that his brother Thomas, who was the company orderly sergeant, helped with securing his discharge.[91]

Men who had not yet been granted a furlough lost out on March 29, when Gansevoort instructed Willett to allow no additional furloughs, since the spring campaign season was approaching. All men currently on furlough were recalled.[92]

Gansevoort's officers acted collectively on their desire to depart the fort permanently when they wrote to him on February 26 requesting the regiment be reassigned to the main army. Gansevoort replied on March 6, stating that, within the scope of his power, there was nothing he would overlook for the honor and service of his regiment. Probably to no avail, though, he reminded them that Fort Stanwix was of great importance to the American cause, and the defense of the western frontiers depended on it. Things were not going well in meetings with the Senecas and Cayugas, who threatened retribution for their losses in the last campaign. Therefore Gansevoort felt it "would be altogether repugnant to military orders for my regiment in the time of war & more particularly at the opening of a campaign to solicit an exchange of the station which it is assigned."

Recognizing that his officers were separated from the main army that was professionalizing itself under the tutelage of General von Steuben at Valley Forge, he expressed admiration for his officers' desire to learn the ways of the main army.[93]

Despite Gansevoort's efforts to forge his regiment into a highly capable unit, the Continental Congress continued to complicate his task by periodically altering the army's structure. Evidence that another change was coming surfaced when New York governor George Clinton received a request from Congress in February asking for a return of the officers in Gansevoort's and two other New York regiments. This was not to be a seniority list but rather a merit list. The return should rate each officer on his merits by placing the best captain of the regiment at the top of the list, followed by the other captains in descending order of their perceived worth. Additionally, officers "who are worse than indifferent" should be marked with an asterisk, while "those very good with a star." Gansevoort should also send Gouverneur Morris at the Continental Congress a copy of the list of his officers appointed by the New York Congress and note any vacancies that had occurred. The congressional committee members needed these documents to inform their decisions when creating the "new arrangement of the Army," that is, a condensing of the third establishment regiments and redistribution of the soldiers.[94]

At the end of April, Gansevoort received a copy of the new regimental model from Governor Clinton along with orders to determine which of his officers would be "deranged," that is, dismissed because of the elimination of their billet, and send their names to the committee.

Under this reorganization plan, each regiment would consist of nine companies rather than eight but would keep the same overall number of enlisted men. The new ninth company would be designated a light infantry company, with its associated elite unit connotations, and consist of men deemed qualified and drafted from the regiment's regular companies. The light infantry companies from several regiments could be formed into a light infantry battalion, or corps, during a campaign. While the number of companies would increase, the number of officers in each regiment would be reduced, resulting in modifications to the remaining officers' duties. Each of the three field officers—colonel, lieutenant colonel, and major—would now also command a company, with the number of captains cut from eight to six. There would be nine lieutenants, with one designated as captain lieutenant of the colonel's company. Each company would have one lieutenant rather than two, and one ensign. The three commissioned officers of each company would now do the work previously done by four. Staff officers would consist of the paymaster, adjutant, quartermaster, surgeon, and surgeon's mate. This would make a total of twenty-nine commissioned officers, a 25 percent reduction from the previous forty.[95]

After examining and contemplating the governor's instructions on reorganizing his regiment, Gansevoort complained to Clinton that he would be losing some very fine officers, in addition to putting a greater workload on those remaining. To no avail, Gansevoort even offered to forgo his pay and rations if he were allowed to retain those officers being deranged. While complaining about the new arrangement, Gansevoort also appealed once again for a response to his requests to General Gates, the governor, and the Congress for additional, heavier artillery at Fort Stanwix. To his mind, strengthening the fort was much more important than addressing money-saving structure changes that would remove valued people from the regiment.[96]

Gansevoort wrote to his dismissed officers on May 30, telling them that it was by the order of Governor Clinton and the Congress, not by his decision, that they had been left out of the new arrangement. He assured the deranged officers that their dismissal had occurred through no fault of their own and that they had displayed brave and spirited conduct while stationed at Fort Stanwix. He extended the thanks of their country to them for that service.[97] The dismissed officers included Captains Van Bunschoten and Swartwout; Lieutenants Levi Stockwell, Henry Defendorff, Moses Yeomans, Thomas Ostrander, Isaac Bogart, Thomas Warner, John Ball, and Nanning Vanderhayden; and Quartermaster Thomas Williams.[98]

While some of these officers may have felt unappreciated for all their hard work, many ordinary soldiers might have wished that they were the ones being let go by the army. The reorganization, however, reflected the incomplete current enlisted strength of the army, not an effort to reduce it. Those who found army life less than meaningful and rewarding might have been envious of the officers being deranged. They could get back to a "normal" life. Very quickly, concern over men leaving, or planning to leave, without being discharged would become rampant. The problem of desertions had been present since the regiment had first formed. Now, British efforts to increase the number of Continental desertions was going to directly affect Fort Stanwix. Colonel Gansevoort was going to have his sense of duty and leadership challenged to a new degree. It had been one thing to defend the fort against enemy siege; now he would have to defend his regiment from internal collapse.

Table 3 May 1778 changes to 3rd New York company structure

OLD STRUCTURE	NEW STRUCTURE
1st Company Capt. Elias Van Bunschoten* 1st Lt. Henry Defendorff* 2nd Lt. Thomas Ostrander* Ens. Peter Magee	**1st Company** Col. Peter Gansevoort Capt. Lt. George Sytez** Ens. Peter Magee* (2nd Ens.)
2nd Company Capt. Thomas De Witt 1st Lt. William Tapp 2nd Lt. Benjamin Bogardus Ens. John Spoor	**2nd Company** Lt. Col. Marinus Willett Lt. John Welch* (1st Lt.) Ens. Samuel Lewis* (5th Ens.)
3rd Company Capt. Cornelius T. Jansen 1st Lt. Nanning Vanderhayden* 2nd Lt. Moses Yeomans* Ens. Josiah Bagley	**3rd Company** Maj. Robert Cochran Lt. Phillip Conine* (2nd Lt.) Ens. Josiah Bagley* (4th Ens.)
4th Company Capt. Abraham Swartwout* 1st Lt. Philip Conine 2nd Lt. William Colbrath Ens. Samuel Lewis	**4th Company (Light Infantry)** Capt. Aaron Aorson (1st Capt.) Lt. Garrit Staats (6th Lt.) Ens. Eldert Ament (6th Ens.)
5th Company Capt. Aaron Aorson 1st Lt. John Ball* 2nd Lt. Garret Staats Ens. Aldert Ament	**5th Company** Capt. Thomas De Witt (2nd Capt.) Lt. William Tapp (3rd Lt.) Ens. Jeremiah Van Rensselear* (8th Ens.)
6th Company Capt. James Gregg 1st Lt. Levi Stockwell* 2nd Lt. Thomas Warner* Ens. George Denniston	**6th Company** Capt. Cornelius T. Jansen (3rd Capt.) Lt. Benjamin Bogardus* (7th Lt.) Ens. John Spoor* (3rd Ens).
7th Company Capt. Henry Tiebout 1st Lt. Isaac Bogart* 2nd Lt. Thomas McClellan Ens. Christopher Hutton	**7th Company** Capt. Leonard Bleeker (4th Capt). Lt. Prentice Bowen (5th Lt.) Ens. Benjamin Herring* (promoted from sergeant in Bleeker's company) (9th Ens.)
8th Company Capt. Leonard Bleeker 1st Lt. John Welch 2nd Lt. Prentice Bowen Ens. Matthew Potan*	**8th Company** Capt. James Gregg (5th Capt.) Lt. William Colbrath* (8th Lt.) Ens. George Denniston (7th Ens.)
	9th Company Capt. Henry Tiebout (6th Capt.) Lt. Thomas McClellan (4th Lt.) Ens. Christopher Hutton (4th Ens.)
* = officers deranged in new structure	* = officers now serving under a different captain ** = formerly adjutant parentheses = rank seniority within regiment

Source: Revolutionary War Rolls, 1775-1783, 1776-1777, NARA M246, folder 40, May 29, 1778, 14-15, May 30, 1778, 17-18.

Chapter 17

A British Plot Encourages Desertions
June 1778

Colonel Gansevoort received a very disturbing letter from Lieutenant Colonel Willett on June 3 alerting him that a man of questionable loyalty to the cause had been recruited by Captain Swartwout for Captain Lieutenant Savage's artillery detachment. When the new recruits arrived at the fort, Ensign Samuel Lewis of Swartwout's company would be able to point out this man, known by the name Samuel Geake. A second letter received that day, this one from Captain Richard Varick of General Gates's staff, provided additional information on the man and why he could be dangerous. Varick had detained an officer, Major Daniel Hamill, connected in suspicious ways with Geake. Both men had supposedly been captured by the British and held in New York, and both claimed to have escaped and set out to rejoin the American forces. Information had reached Varick, however, that Hamill and Geake had been allowed significant and very unusual liberties while in "captivity."[1]

June was destined to be a severely stressful month for Colonel Gansevoort, much as the previous August with its siege had been. This month, though, the main dangers came from within the garrison. The British had been unable to seize the fort, but as part of an effort throughout the Continental Army, they would now try to diminish the size of the still incomplete 3rd New York Regiment by other means.

As June began, Gansevoort met in council at the fort's headquarters building with Lieutenant Colonel Willett and Major Cochran to make the adjustments necessitated by Congress's regimental restructuring. Making every effort to deal fairly with their officers being deranged, Gansevoort, Willett, and Cochran favorably recommended to Governor Clinton that Lieutenants Thomas Warner, Levi Stockwell, and Moses Yeomans would be very useful commanding any vessels put into use to defend the Hudson River and that Stockwell might justly and usefully be given a captaincy in the ranger service. They also recommended Lieutenant Isaac Bogart and Quartermaster Thomas Williams for service in either the quartermaster or forage master department. Lieutenant Henry Defendorff, Lieutenant John Ball, and Ensign Matthew Potan were known to wish to retire from the service. Although Gansevoort, Willett, and Cochran believed Lieutenants Thomas Ostrander and Van Der Heyden had little to offer, those officers were willing to remain in the Continental line if needed. They praised Captain Swartwout as being very qualified for any office that might be found for him to fill. Regarding the other officers left out by the new arrangement, Gansevoort regretted that he was at a loss as to what to recommend for them.[2]

Probably to the surprise of many, while some officers were preparing to leave, at least one officer returned to the regiment. After being severely wounded when ambushed by Indians while hunting passenger pigeons the previous June, Captain James Gregg had been put under the care of surgeon's mate James Thacher of Massachusetts at the Northern Department Hospital at Albany. Thacher found Gregg to be "a most frightful spectacle, the whole of his scalp was removed; in two places on the fore part of his head, the tomahawk had penetrated through the skull; there was a wound on his back with the same instrument, besides a wound in his side and another through his arm by a musket ball." Thacher had supervised Gregg's long recovery and found that, after a skin transplant, he "appeared to be well satisfied in having his scalp restored to him, though uncovered with hair."[3] After returning to his company, Gregg was prone to proudly show off his wound. According to a pension application deposition from Sarah Osborn, later the camp-following wife of Aaron Osborn of Gregg's company after the regiment left Fort Stanwix, "Captain Gregg had turns of being shattered in his mind and at such times would frequently say to deponent 'Sarah did you ever see where I was scalped,' showing his head at the same time."[4] Despite demonstrating "being shattered in his mind" on occasion, he continued to lead his company through the remainder of the war.

News of the outside world often came to the fort in letters from fellow officers, relatives, and friends. Letters from his brother Leonard, Henry Glen, John Hanson, and Richard Varick inundated Gansevoort with random news, some accurate, some partly accurate, and some totally inaccurate. Leonard accurately noted on June 3 that the Senecas had delivered up their prisoners to the commissioners for Indian affairs on June 2 and that the British were evacuating Philadelphia. They were loading their artillery and baggage onboard their ships, while General Washington remained at Valley Forge with about seven thousand Continentals and four thousand militia.[5]

On June 15, John Hanson sent Gansevoort the latest newspaper and requested it be forwarded to Ensign Ament of Captain Aorson's company. In it Gansevoort read about several skirmishes that had occurred in New York northeast of the fort and that the Tryon County militia had entirely left Johnstown and gathered at a church, "crying for assistance." A portion of the Tryon County militia was garrisoning Cherry Valley, the paper reported, and Colonel Abraham Van Alstyne and Major Henry Van Rensselaer had left Schenectady that morning with 214 militiamen to relieve Tryon County.[6]

Henry Glen reported the killing of Mathias Warmout near Cherry Valley and stated that Sir William Howe had sailed for England in May, "on which occasion the City of Philadelphia was illuminated." Several letters noted the British army's evacuation of Philadelphia, with its possible destination being New York, and that Philadelphia's leading Loyalists were said to have boarded fourteen ships with General Henry Clinton's permission. Clinton was reported to have demanded £60,000 to spare Philadelphia from being torched as the troops departed.[7]

Gansevoort soon after received news in a letter that the British were on the march from Philadelphia into New Jersey and were at Mount Holly on June 20 with General Charles Lee on their right flank and another general officer on their left; George Washington was stated to be fifteen miles in their rear and in pursuit.[8] This was followed by another letter, dated June 29, informing him of the Battle of Monmouth.[9] All this "news" must have caused Gansevoort to sympathize with his officers and men who felt they were on the insignificant fringes of the war and well away from the important developments.

In letters from Valley Forge, Gansevoort learned about his Oneida allies who had joined with the army there in April. On June 13, Lafayette wrote that some of the Oneidas with him were departing while others intended to remain. He encouraged Gansevoort to ensure that the wives and children of those Oneida men received attentive care because, "as their husbands are fighting for us, and cannot provide for them they must be furnish'd with provisions—we owe to be grateful of they'r friendship, and entertain it by all means in our power." There were also the family members of one "Nicolas and two other Frenchmen who have been very useful" to the young French engineer Lieutenant Jean-Baptiste de Gouvion and who should receive any needed attention.[10] By mid-June, most of the Oneidas with Washington had commenced their long journey home, and the remainder set off the following month. While serving with the army and conducting themselves in ways that very positively impressed Washington, several Oneidas had died in combat or been taken prisoners of war.[11]

On a more local and very practical level, Gansevoort must have welcomed a mid-June letter from deputy commissary Cuyler stating that he intended to send his first drove of cattle to Fort Stanwix by the middle of July. He also hoped to forward some flour and other provisions, and asked Gansevoort to send a guard to German Flats to escort them to the fort.[12] It was still not safe to use the road to Fort Stanwix without a guard of armed men. This was further confirmation of the fort's long distance from the main army.

June was often the time of year when eighteenth-century military campaigns got underway, and this year was no exception. On June 3, Richard Varick wrote a newsy letter to Gansevoort in which he reported that one of the soldiers enlisted by Captain Swartwout, the previously mentioned Samuel Geake, who claimed to have been captured twice by the British, was a suspicious character. The man was associated with Major Hamill, who was said to have deserted to the British on the day Fort Montgomery had been lost the previous October 6. Hamill, however, claimed that he had in fact been captured, despite the questions raised by the extraordinary liberties he was allowed while being held in New York City. Varick ordered Gansevoort to take measures to isolate the suspicious recruit to prevent him from observing the artillery stores and anything else of consequence that he might inform the British about if he was spying for them.[13] Willett followed up with a June 5 letter to Gansevoort suggesting that he examine the man and make a written record of the questions and his answers.[14]

Willett also wrote to Gansevoort on June 3 from Schenectady, where he had arrived at 2:00 p.m. and found the militia had turned out to quell a British and Indian attack. Willett reported that Captain Swartwout was in Schenectady on his way to Fort Stanwix with a few recruits. Once there, Swartwout would pack up and depart, having been dismissed in the regimental restructuring. Willett also alerted Gansevoort that Ensign Samuel Lewis could point out the suspicious recruit.[15] The garrison had defended the fort from being overpowered by an enemy force but now faced an internal threat as the British sought to subvert individual members of the garrison to weaken the fort from within through desertion. Gansevoort had to determine how, isolated as he was, he would defend against this threat and try to understand just what authority he had as colonel commandant to punish those who became involved in the plot.

Throughout the first year of the regiment's existence, desertions occurred in patterns like those in other regiments. Spikes in desertions for simple survival, as well as other personal needs, occurred in most units during times of extreme deprivation and feelings of hopelessness. The summer and fall of 1778 would see one of those spikes occur at Fort Stanwix.[16]

Even after the successful and highly praised defense of the fort, the harsh, regimented, and boring living and work conditions no doubt contributed to a desire developing in many men to desert. The "suspicious" man recruited by Captain Swartwout was one player in the British plan who could take advantage of that situation.

With the recruiting of Samuel Geake, the garrison became immersed in the British scheme to insert agents among American troops to encourage men to desert or mutiny, in addition to doing some spying. British general Henry Clinton felt that, contrary to common belief, men who had departed Ireland and sought a better life in the colonies still had "latent seeds of national attachment" to Great Britain. To take advantage of this sentiment while weakening his opponent, Clinton developed a plan to raise a Loyalist regiment whose officers and men would all, or at least mostly, be Irish. Francis, Lord Rawdon, of Ireland had proved himself a capable British officer and rose in rank during the first few years of the conflict. Believing him to be the one person from Ireland in the army "whose situation pointed him out the most strongly for the command" of such a regiment, Clinton put him in charge. In addition to publicly advertising for Loyalist recruits, Rawdon also sought to persuade men in the Continental Army to desert and join his Irish regiment. The project proved very successful. Clinton would be able to report on October 23, 1778, that "above 380 deserters from the rebel army have been collected; and are now in arms in that regiment, contented with their situation, and attached to their officers."[17]

During their imprisonment in New York City, Major Hamill and Samuel Geake had become agents in Rawdon's surreptitious recruiting force. Major Hamill became friendly with his captors and brought Geake before Lord Rawdon. Geake later said that "Lord Rawdon advised him to enlist in the artillery and endeavor to engage as many men as he could (particularly Irishmen) to desert."[18]

Hamill and Geake created the story of their escape from British imprisonment and upon being released traveled up the Hudson River Valley to Poughkeepsie, encouraging any American troops they encountered to desert and join Rawdon's "Irish Brigade." Geake encountered Captain Swartwout at Poughkeepsie and enlisted, expecting to join the Fort Stanwix artillery detachment. About the same time, though, a recently freed soldier who had been imprisoned with them reported Hamill to authorities as being on friendly terms with his British captors. This also implicated Geake.

Geake arrived at Fort Stanwix with Captain Swartwout's recruits in early June, but Colonel Gansevoort, who had by now been warned about the British plot, did not assign him to the artillery. Instead, he placed Geake in Captain Aorson's company.

On June 10 Gansevoort called in First Sergeant Jonathan Kertel of Aorson's company, the man who may have been his music teacher, to enlist his aid in exposing Geake. Kertel agreed to pose as a potential deserter to win Geake's trust. While interacting with Geake, he would report to Gansevoort any plots of desertion or mutiny he saw developing. Kertel then recruited fellow sergeant Francis Jackson to assist him, and both men began meeting with Geake and bemoaning their dissatisfactions with garrison life. This would not have been an unusual topic among the troops.

As the conversation developed, Geake mentioned that Lord Rawdon had sent for him while he was being held in Livingston's Sugar House, an infamous British prison in New York. Rawdon gave him some money and ordered him to go with Major Hamill to enlist as many Irishmen as possible for Rawdon's regiment. Specifically, he had been told to find a way to enlist in Fort Stanwix's artillery, where he would then encourage men to desert and enlist in Rawdon's regiment. Geake had also been instructed to obtain as much information as possible about the conditions at Fort Stanwix, including its ammunition supply, provisions, number of troops, and anything else that would help. Then, after enlisting as many men as he could, Geake was to spike the Fort Stanwix cannon so they could not be fired and proceed with his recruits to Philadelphia, where Rawdon would reward him with a lieutenant's commission.

Geake planned to leave Fort Stanwix on the next weekly "provision day" along with Matross John Henry of the artillery and Thomas Taylor of Captain Swartwout's company, who had recently enlisted. That day was chosen because it would enable the deserters to take a week's worth of provisions with them.

After tattoo was beaten that night, Sergeant Kertel and Quartermaster Sergeant Jackson met together with John Henry and Geake in a small room behind the barracks. They discussed deserting and the information they would take to the British about the fort's artillery. Upon making their final decision, they wrote up and signed an oath stating, "We the undernamed promise to be true to each other and never to divulge to any person whatever unless with each other's consent in Deserting the American Army until we join the British Forces at Philadelphia, as Witness our Hands this 17th Day of June 1778." When all four men had signed, or in Henry's case made his mark, Geake then asked Jackson for a Bible to swear their oaths upon. Jackson departed, but instead of obtaining a Bible, he returned with several guards to arrest Henry and Geake and take them back to the guardhouse for confinement. The guards locked each prisoner in one of the two small prisoner rooms and then returned to duty in the attached lean-to with the other men on guard duty.[19]

In addition to trying to prevent desertions that would weaken the garrison, life at the fort also involved remaining alert to possible Indian attacks. Having returned from his captivity the previous July, Ensign John Spoor had been on furlough until the end of March. While the situation with Samuel Geake was developing, on June 11, Ensign Spoor commanded twenty-six men accompanying two wagons headed out toward the old Fort Bull, about three miles from Fort Stanwix, to bring in timber that had been cut to use for the fort's restoration. They arrived at that timber collection point about 10:00 a.m.

After fully loading one wagon, Spoor sent it back to the fort accompanied by Jeremiah Smith of Lieutenant Colonel Willett's company, guarding the wagoner, a man who resided at German Flats with his wife and five or six children, and his son, about fourteen years old, who had come with him.[20] The wagon had not gone far when a party of Indians fired on the three men. Smith took a fatal shot through his body, and the attackers quickly tomahawked and scalped him. They also tomahawked and scalped the wagoner, who had been shot through the shoulder. When found soon after, the man was still alive and in command of his senses but was not expected to survive. His son escaped unhurt from the ambush. Upon seeing the wounded and scalped men, Captain Gregg and Ensign Spoor could be forgiven if they had flashbacks to the previous year's attacks on June 25 and July 3.[21]

Intelligence reports continued to come in regularly about enemy activity and potential attacks. Toward the end of June, Gansevoort received news that Oneida scouts had reported two birch bark canoes full of men near the eastern end of Oneida Lake and two canoes heading for Oswego. The Oneidas had sent out several scouts on different routes to check on these reports.[22]

Just about a week after the wagon incident with Ensign Spoor, a court-martial was held on June 17 that tried John Henry for attempted desertion. The recently returned Captain James Gregg served as president of the court. Other members of the court were Captain Lieutenant Savage of the artillery, Lieutenant Thomas McClellan of Tiebout's company, Ensign Spoor, and Ensign Josiah Bagley of Jansen's company.[23] During the court proceedings, Sergeant Jackson asked John Henry to reveal who had first asked him to desert, to which Henry replied it was Samuel Geake. Sergeant Kertel then asked Geake if, as alleged, he had intended to go off with thirty men on the next provision day, to which Geake answered that only he, Corporal William Stephens, who lived in the same hut with him, and Thomas Taylor planned to depart.[24] In his attempt at a defense, Henry told the court he had not intended to desert and claimed he had been intoxicated at the time of his signing the oath. Unconvinced, the court found Henry guilty of the charge of planning to desert and sentenced him to receive five hundred lashes on his bare back and be drummed out of the fort with a rope around his neck.

Samuel Geake's court-martial resulted in a death sentence, but that sentence required approval from General Washington. Since Geake's testimony as a witness would help prove the similar charges against

Major Hamill, Washington asked Gansevoort to confine Geake at the fort instead of executing him. Governor Clinton wrote to Washington in September that Hamill had been put in close confinement on the basis of Geake's testimony as recorded at his trial.

On June 18, 1778, Corporal Stevens, who had been confined in the guardhouse on suspicion of intending to desert, also on the basis of Geake's testimony, appeared before the same court and was found not guilty. Thomas Taylor then appeared before the same court and was likewise found not guilty. Even these very public trials, a severe flogging, and a sentence of death did not stop desertions. Sometime between June 22 and July 1, a sergeant of Captain Aorson's company deserted by walking into a British fort while out on a scouting party to Oswegatchie. During the same period, on June 27, Sergeant John Howell from Captain Gregg's company deserted.[25]

At the end of June, Gansevoort learned that deserter John Pearson of Captain Tiebout's company, had been captured while in the company of some Loyalists at Schoharie. Pearson had been granted a twenty-day furlough by Lieutenant Colonel Willett on March 21 and been declared a deserter on April 17 when he did not return.[26]

Regular fort business continued throughout all these incidents. On June 23, Gansevoort wrote to Colonel Cuyler stating that he and Major Cochran had inventoried their provisions and those of the Indian Department and found them to be sufficient for only two months. He pointed out that the families of the Oneidas who were away and serving under General Washington had been consuming a great deal of provisions. Gansevoort requested a quantity of cattle and salt, as he had only two barrels of salt beef left at the fort. Cuyler told him that a drove of fat cattle leaving Albany by July 2 should be at Fort Dayton by July 7. Gansevoort agreed to send a party to accept the drove at Fort Dayton and accompany it as a guard to the fort.[27]

June ended with the news from Henry Glen at Schenectady that "a drove of oxen" was "destined for the relief" of Fort Stanwix. Also being sent were supplies of tar, nails, and iron that had been detained there due to alarms of enemy activity. A convoy of bateaux heading for Fort Stanwix would accompany the cattle drove. Gansevoort was told to send an officer with a squad of guards sufficient for both the bateaux and the cattle. The same squad could not guard both parties because in some places the road for the cattle was at a distance from the river.

The guard troops were considered so essential that Captain Peters of the bateau service had been forbidden to depart Fort Dayton until Gansevoort's troops arrived to escort them.[28]

Close to a year after the siege had ended, the western Mohawk River Valley was still not secure from enemy ambushes, largely because of the civil war nature of the conflict in that area. Defending the fort and the Carry Place was still essential, but it was very difficult to measure any positive changes in that dangerous environment. Many officers and men of the 3rd New York Regiment just wanted to get out of the area and join with the main army, though soldiers from local families might have preferred to stay, because this was the important part of the war to them—the civil war. Only time would tell how many more men would desert before another regiment relieved them from garrison duty defending the isolated fort and allowed them to join the main army, or at least another post.

Chapter 18

Still More Desertions and Continuing Unease

July–September 1778

After leaving the 3rd New York Regiment as a result of the army reorganization, and returning to his wife and four children, Captain Abraham Swartwout wrote Colonel Gansevoort on August 29, by way of paymaster Jeremiah Van Rensselaer. He reminded the colonel of his promise to obtain eight yards of broadcloth for him from the State Commissary of Clothing to replace the blue cloak he had donated for use in making the flag that proudly flew over Fort Stanwix during the siege. Swartwout requested that Gansevoort send him an order for the cloth which he could then present to Van Rensselaer or to Henry Van Veghten for action on it.[1] When Gansevoort bid farewell to Captain Swartwout, he lost an officer whose 1799 obituary would note that "as a soldier he was brave—as an officer humane and intelligent—as a citizen honest—and as a companion pleasing. His wit was genuine and all his own; so poignant that all were delighted; yet so innocent that it never called a blush into the cheek of modesty, or drew a sigh from the bosom of virtue."[2]

Ten months after the siege ended, life for the defenders of Fort Stanwix at the beginning of July in the increasing heat of summer continued to be dominated by the monotonous and unpleasant pattern of alerts and preparations for another attack. The soldiers continued to endure boring work carried out under the very real fear of further enemy attacks on the fort or fatigue parties in its vicinity. While concerns about

STILL MORE DESERTIONS AND CONTINUING UNEASE 233

enemy activity increased that summer, Gansevoort also had to deal with problems brought on by his own soldiers interacting with the civilian population. Sarah Culbertson wrote to Gansevoort from Schenectady on July 1 concerning money owed to her by Dennis McCarty, the man in Bleeker's company whose wife had given birth toward the end of the siege after being wounded the previous night by a British artillery shell. Culbertson's letter attacked McCarty, whom she accused of incurring multiple financial obligations he then refused to pay.[3]

In another case, Henry Starring of German Flats wrote to Gansevoort on July 29 concerning one of his oxen and two hogs killed by soldiers of the 3rd New York Regiment and several bateau men when they came to obtain some lime. Frederick Harter witnessed the ox killing, and the bateau company soldiers had admitted consuming some of the pork. Starring asserted that he had found the hides of both hogs and the head of one.[4] Just how Gansevoort dealt with these complaints is not known, but they were among the many complicating factors to his job that he wished he could avoid.

Military activity conducted by Indians loyal to Great Britain erupted on the Pennsylvania–New York frontier, including a widely reported action, misrepresented as a massacre, at Wyoming, Pennsylvania, on July 3. Then General John Stark informed Gansevoort on July 7 that an intercepted letter addressed to Joseph Brant suggested an attack on Fort Stanwix might occur in the near future.[5] Two days later, Gansevoort learned that, because of the increasing threats, about two hundred men under Lieutenant Colonel William Stacy from Colonel Ichabod Alden's 7th Massachusetts Regiment had left Albany and were on their way to reinforce Fort Stanwix.[6] From a conversation with paymaster Van Rensselaer, Stacy understood that it was unlikely that all his men could be accommodated in the fort's barracks; he had only seven tents with him, however. Fortunately it was summer, in case his men needed to sleep out in the open. Stacy asked Gansevoort to send a guide to him at Fort Dayton because he was not familiar with the road from there to Fort Stanwix. Lastly, Stacy reported that 3rd New York Regiment deserter John Pearson had been brought to him under guard for Stacy to take back to the fort, but unfortunately Pearson had escaped.[7]

While the fort itself remained free from attack, small parties from the garrison participated in retaliatory actions for the British-supported Indian attacks on settlements. The first week of July, Lieutenant Thomas McClellan of Captain Tiebout's company took a party to Oswego, where they destroyed buildings, some public provisions, ammunition, and other stores. McClellan had taken care to relocate to an outbuilding a resident's wife along with her children, bedding, clothes, provisions, and necessary furniture before destroying their house. Gansevoort had also sent out an Oneida Indian scout to learn about the enemy's intentions by infiltrating their camps, and he was expected to return by the middle of the following week.[8]

Gansevoort learned from Colonel Peter Bellinger of the 4th Regiment of the Tryon County militia that he had received news on July 18 of the enemy destruction of Andrew's Town, about eight miles to the south of German Flats. Bellinger reported that four men had been killed and the rest taken prisoner; no women or children were harmed. After complaining that he had repeatedly requested assistance from Albany without result, Bellinger reported that the Indians had been destroying structures in the back settlements and that without proper reinforcement, he would have to abandon German Flats.[9]

On July 19, General Schuyler noted that Good Peter, Skenandoah, and two other Oneidas had requested provisions from Fort Stanwix. Schuyler recommended that Gansevoort supply them to maintain their support in the likelihood of another siege at the fort.[10]

General Stark notified Gansevoort on July 19 that Colonel Alden's 7th Massachusetts Regiment had been ordered to return to Cherry Valley if there was no immediate danger to Fort Stanwix.[11] The fort itself might not be in immediate danger, but the area it protected was another matter. On July 24, Gansevoort was reminded that because the possibility of Indian attack was so strong, unless he provided guards for them, bateaux carrying supplies would not be sent from Fort Dayton to Fort Stanwix. Currently a bateau company led by Captain William Peterson was en route to Fort Stanwix with nine bateaux, collectively carrying eleven barrels of rum, five barrels of salt, some flour, clothing for Captain Lieutenant Savage's detachment, and other stores. Those boats should reach Fort Dayton the following Thursday and had instructions to deposit the supplies there and return immediately to Schenectady—unless an escort guard from Fort Stanwix joined them there.[12] Being assigned to this escort duty made it impossible for men of the 3rd New York Regiment to carry out important duties at the fort while also reminding them that they were stationed on the frontier, which remained very dangerous.

Simply exiting the fort could be perilous. On September 8, Major Cochran, commanding the fort in Gansevoort's and Willett's absences, wrote to Gansevoort that Benjamin Ackerson of Captain De Witt's company had been killed and scalped after departing the fort to fetch a horse in a meadow near the house of John Roof's neighbor, a Mr. Brodock. Working in his room, Cochran heard the firing and ran to the officer of the guard to find out what was happening. Upon being told, he immediately sent out Captain Bleeker with the men of the guard, who had just reported for duty, to rescue Ackerson, but they were too late to save him. Lying near his body they found a wooden war club about two and a half feet long, curved at the end and bearing a steel spike, described as being shaped like a lance, which would be pounded into an enemy while an attacker was striking him. Ackerson had received several severe wounded from it. The rescuers thought the attackers had left it behind as a threat, seeing marks on it which they believed recorded the number of prisoners and scalps taken in previous actions. Whatever the meaning of the marks, it was not unusual for warriors to leave a war club behind as a warning to enemies. Cochran also noted that Jacob Reed, an Oneida warrior, schoolmaster, and interpreter, had returned from Oswego reporting that no enemy were there, but that he had found many fresh tracks in the sand. Reed stated that he had seen some members of the American-supporting Tuscarora Nation at Oneida on September 7 who told him that the Onondagas were coming to persuade the Americans that the Oneidas and the entire Six Nations supported the king. Reed also reported that he had been informed by an Onondaga Indian that an enemy scout of five Indians was near the fort watching for opportunities to take scalps and prisoners.[13]

Major Cochran wrote to Gansevoort on September 18 stating that the sachems and warriors of the Oneida and Tuscarora Nations had arrived at Fort Stanwix to express their uneasiness with any assumption that they had been involved with the recent scalping incidents near Fort Stanwix. The Indians reminded Cochran that they had supported the actions of the rebels from the beginning. While continuing to feel that Colonels Dayton and Elmore had treated them well, they felt that Colonel Gansevoort, who had initially courted them when times were really bad, rather neglected them now. Cochran stated that he had informed the Indians that he appreciated their support and reassured them by commenting that all peoples, his soldiers included, have some bad ones among them. Cochran provided the Indians with a meal and drink and told them of his strong desire to have Indian Department interpreter James Deane at Fort Schuyler.[14] Deane was a white man raised among the Indians and known as an orator among them. He was comfortable in both cultures, completely bilingual. The Oneidas considered him the only white man who spoke their language without an accent.[15]

On July 28 the commissary of clothing, Major George Measam, requested a return of the clothing that would be needed by the troops at Fort Stanwix through the following year. Supplies at Fishkill, recently received from France, should finally allow each man to have a complete uniform.[16] Van Rensselaer wrote to Gansevoort on August 8 reporting that his letters to the clothing department had not yet been answered, though he had been able to find leather for shoes and expected to have enough for the making of fifty or sixty dozen, but none for hats.[17]

Defending the fort now consisted primarily of protecting the supply shipments supporting the garrison. Any supplies coming to the fort by way of Fort Dayton, the normal route, always required a protective escort. Gansevoort learned from deputy commissary Cuyler on July 10 that he would be sending Fort Stanwix "forty head of fat cattle" the following Monday. The cattle would remain at Fort Dayton, however, until Gansevoort sent a party to bring them to the fort.[18] One month later, Gansevoort learned that several bateaux would be leaving Schenectady for Fort Stanwix the morning of August 11 with a load of flour and should reach Fort Dayton by August 15, requiring an escort to Fort Stanwix.[19]

On August 22, Cuyler wrote to Gansevoort noting his surprise at the letter that had reached him in which Gansevoort stated it was no longer necessary to send guards to Fort Dayton to escort cattle and bateaux to Fort Stanwix. Cuyler could not have disagreed more passionately. He argued that he could not find even a single person to hire for driving cattle from German Flats to Fort Stanwix without a guard, and he understood why. Everyone knew it was dangerous work and subject to potential enemy attack. Fort Stanwix would be cut off from supplies unless guards were provided for both cattle and bateaux. In addition to that issue, Cuyler could provide Fort Stanwix only with fresh provisions, because salt provisions would not be available until the fall. And to provide the fresh meat, Cuyler would need an escort at Fort Dayton on September 1 to drive thirty head of cattle to Fort Stanwix.[20] The demand for so many soldiers once again reminded everyone in the fort that a year after the siege ended, everyday life remained dangerous and stressful.

The following day, Henry Glen wrote to Gansevoort stating that the bateau company commanded by Captain Peters, or Peterson, had departed Schenectady with a load of flour, ten barrels of salt, one hundred pounds of tobacco, and other items. As always, Glen warned Gansevoort that he had ordered Captain Peters to unload his bateaux at Fort Dayton and leave the supplies there unless there was an escort awaiting him. The boats should arrive on August 27, wrote Glen, and they must be sent back immediately despite being needed to transport lime to the fort. After explaining other bateau problems he was dealing with, Glen noted that Gansevoort's request for shoes had been given to Jeremiah Van Rensselaer.[21]

In a clear demonstration that the area was still in danger of attacks, German Flats was attacked by three hundred Tories and 152 Indians under Joseph Brant in late September 1778, resulting in the loss of one hundred head of cattle being held there on their way to Fort Stanwix. Altogether, the town lost sixty-three houses, fifty-seven barns, three gristmills, and a sawmill, all burned down, and over seven hundred cattle, horses, and sheep driven off. Most of the residents found refuge at Forts Herkimer and Dayton. Additional raids in the area continued into the fall.[22] In general, the problems encountered in keeping the militia out on active duty made it difficult to get supplies of all kinds to the insecure Fort Stanwix.[23]

Regarding clothing, Gansevoort received a return dated August 20 from Van Rensselaer listing the clothing due the 3rd New York Regiment. Van Rensselaer asked Gansevoort to send to brother Leonard a return of the items that were still needed. This would help Van Rensselaer when he went to Fishkill the following week to procure more clothing. Van Rensselaer also noted that he had drawn three months' pay for the 3rd New York Regiment.[24]

Willett was still away in July, and en route to Fishkill to collect baggage he had left there, when he wrote to Gansevoort about the pride he had felt watching Washington display his leadership at the Battle of Monmouth. As one of the officers still desperately seeking a new assignment, Willett indicated his intention to seek service with the main army so that "he might learn the science of *camp duty*."[25] Similarly, Van Rensselaer relayed war news to Gansevoort on July 23 while expressing his hope to be in New York City within eight weeks and his desire to join the 4th New York Regiment in the field.[26]

Although the plot involving Geake had been crushed, the steadily mounting number of desertions distressed Colonel Gansevoort. Fearing that there might still be undiscovered mutineers in the garrison, he dealt quickly and harshly with all deserters captured in July and August. Nevertheless, completely understanding how the lengthening term of isolated and dangerous garrison duty increased his troops' susceptibility to thoughts of desertion and mutiny, throughout the summer Gansevoort submitted several requests for his regiment to be reassigned.

Frustratingly, severely punishing deserters did not stop other men from deserting.[27] A very significant multiple desertion occurred on August 10, when five men stole a bateau on Lake Oneida. While rowing to Canada, they were captured on August 12 by Tuscarora Indians fishing at Fort Brewerton, about fifty miles away. The Indians returned the deserters to Fort Stanwix on August 13, presenting Gansevoort with a now familiar conundrum. As colonel commandant of the fort, did he have the authority to create a court-martial to try these men for this serious offense that could lead to a death penalty? Gansevoort was still struggling to define just what the rank of colonel commandant meant in terms of his authority. Feeling that he needed to act rapidly, even if not entirely appropriately, he ordered a court-martial to be held on August 15.

The court consisted of Major Cochran as president; Lieutenant Tapp as judge advocate; Captains Aorson, De Witt, Gregg, Jansen, and Tiebout; Captain Lieutenant George Sytez; Lieutenants John Welch, Philip Conine, Gerrit Staats, and William Colbrath; and Ensigns Peter Magee and Benjamin Herring. The five defendants on trial were Nicholas Hansen of Captain De Witt's company, John Calf of Colonel Gansevoort's company, Christopher Tice and Nicholas Hartman of Captain Tiebout's company, and Henry Witmozer, originally of Tiebout's but now of Major Cochran's company. The court found all five men guilty and sentenced them to death by firing squad. Punishments related to desertion could vary greatly. The full situation at the time of the incident and the situation of the individual were considered as well as the danger each case presented to the regiment.

Immediately after completing the court proceedings that day, the 3rd New York Regiment officers wrote to Colonel Gansevoort requesting that the death sentences be carried out without delay. They offered three justifications for doing so, even though army regulations required higher-level authority to approve the sentences. First, desertions had been occurring very frequently, resulting in manpower shortages as well as morale problems. Second, apparently forgetting that a few previous sentences had been set aside or modified by the colonel, they noted that sentences approved by court-martial had always been carried out. Third, they knew that there were many men in the regiment who had become disaffected with regard to the American cause and were contemplating deserting. Those men needed to be very strongly discouraged from doing so. In addition to every officer who had sat on the court, Lieutenants Benjamin Bogardus and Prentice Bowen and Ensigns Christopher Hutton, Josiah Bagley, Samuel Lewis, and Eldert Ament also signed the letter.[28]

The following day, Gansevoort wrote to General Washington to make sure he understood that since March 26, three sergeants, two corporals, and twenty privates had deserted from his regiment, in addition to one bombardier, one gunner, and one matross from the artillery detachment. Gansevoort complained that many of these men had been tried and sentenced but had not yet received their punishment because the commanding general of the Northern Department had not yet approved the sentences. He mentioned the Geake incident and reminded Washington that he still had Geake confined in irons in the fort guardhouse because his death sentence had not yet been approved. The lack of punishment increased the likelihood of additional desertions. Gansevoort's officers frequently overheard garrison soldiers declare that they would rather die than remain at the fort over the coming winter. He firmly believed that he needed to make an example of deserters, or he would not be able to check the growing evil. He then recounted for Washington the full story of the five convicted deserters sentenced to be executed.[29]

Underscoring the seriousness of the desertion problem, just after the court-martial concluded, four men from Captain Aorson's company, one from Bleeker's, and one from Tiebout's deserted from a party out on command under Captain Bleeker while returning to the fort from German Flats. They had been in one of the escort squads required for guarding and driving cattle to the fort. Gansevoort had also heard rumors from his officers that eighty-seven men in the garrison were ready to mutiny at the first appearance of a British force before the fort. In light of these incidents and rumors, although the death sentences had not yet been approved by Washington, Gansevoort responded positively to the appeal from his officers. The entire garrison witnessed the gruesome executions of the five men by firing squad on August 17. Gansevoort must have felt great anxiety and pressure to act decisively in order keep his regiment together and working effectively.

John Fink of Captain De Witt's company would remember for the rest of his life that "there was some dissatisfaction with Col. Gansevoort for causing five men shot for desertion." Apparently, many men believed that the executions were illegal. Fink recalled in old age that three of the

CHAPTER 18

men executed were Germans and the other two were "John Kalp" (John Calf) and "Wit Mosher" (Henry Witmozer).[30] This must have been a very troublesome time for Gansevoort, isolated at Fort Stanwix and unable to communicate rapidly with his superiors, especially Washington. Whether an urgently important action was within his authority or not, he felt he had to act decisively and accept the risks involved.

The day after the executions, Gansevoort had to read and digest a letter from Washington stating that Samuel Geake's court-martial had been illegal because Gansevoort did not rank high enough to have ordered it. To Gansevoort's relief, though, Washington saw no benefit in ordering a second trial for Geake and simply ordered Gansevoort to keep Geake confined because his testimony contained information useful for the prosecution of Major Hamill. Washington also told him not to let Geake know that he might be useful in that way.[31] While supportive of Gansevoort, this letter left open the question of how Washington would respond to the executions.

Gansevoort had written Washington that same day expressing his hope that the general would approve his decision to execute the five deserters. He explained his reasoning: "Although, I could not find the articles of War gave me the fullest authority, yet as Commanding officer I hope your Excellency will approve of it. Nothing but the highest regard for my Country or Extreme Love for the Service would have forced me to an action heretofore unprecedented to me, of a frontier Post, & far distant from the Commander in Chief, & having a separate Commission from Congress as Commandant of this Post, I conceived, myself fully impowered in a case of such great necessity."[32] He hoped that Washington would understand what a terrible bind he had been in when making his decision. He had not acted irrationally out of anger.

Gansevoort received unofficial backing for the executions from General Stark, who assured him, "I think you were very right in your proceedings, considering your circumstances."[33] Gansevoort's brother Leonard also reassured him, "You did well to shoot those deserters[,] everyone says it."[34] It was a real relief to Gansevoort when he received and read Washington's letter dated August 29 expressing his hope that the executions would prove "successful in their intent."[35] Gansevoort had now twice exceeded his authority in legal matters and realized he could have been severely reprimanded or even removed from his position. Washington, however, had essentially decided to overlook Gansevoort's actions, or approve them in retrospect, trusting Gansevoort

STILL MORE DESERTIONS AND CONTINUING UNEASE   241

to deal appropriately with a truly dangerous situation when higher authority was not available. Gansevoort would face additional cases testing his ability to deal with them appropriately.[36]

Just four days later, Francis Cramberry of Jansen's company and Francis Cole of Willett's company, who left the fort to draw water from a spring, were taken prisoner by about twenty enemy Indians, who took them west to an island near the outlet of Lake Ontario. They would remain there until about October 8, when the Indians sold Cole to a French fur trader, with whom he remained until 1783. What happened to Cramberry is not known. Just a few days before their capture, Cole had been involved in a brief exchange of gunfire with Indians at Fort Stanwix.[37]

Although only a couple of Gansevoort's officers deserted from the regiment, after the siege the entire group of officers repeatedly communicated their desire that either the full regiment or the individual officers be reassigned to the main army. They were all very tired of defending the isolated frontier fort. On August 12, Gansevoort forwarded their request for a transfer to the Grand Army to Governor Clinton, who sent it on to General Washington. Gansevoort also emphasized the belief among his officers that the regiment's high desertion rate reflected the problem of keeping the men assigned for too long at one post, especially one where they did little more than the work of common laborers while constantly under threat of attack.[38]

Willett, who remained absent on furlough, wrote to Gansevoort on August 29, expressing his gratitude for being allowed to help his family in their hour of need after the death of one of his children. Willett also stated that the previous Tuesday he had put the officers' request for transfer before General Washington, who told Willett to come see him early the following week to discuss it.[39] That same day, however, Washington wrote to Gansevoort to say that he had spoken with Willett concerning the transfer request but was unable to honor it at the present time. He did promise, though, to transfer the regiment by winter.[40] Gansevoort must have desperately hoped he would be able to keep that promise.

Meanwhile, his men continued to leave by other means. Like Henry Ritter before him, young William Fink was needed at home. Having lost a son at Oriskany, Fink's father came to Fort Stanwix with a substitute for William by the name of Henry Belyer sometime in the spring of 1778. Lieutenant Prentice Bowen, commanding Bleeker's company in his absence, and Colonel Willett in Colonel Gansevoort's absence accepted Belyer as a legal, able-bodied soldier, and signed a discharge for Fink allowing him to return home with his father to Palatine.[41]

Winter was approaching, and Washington would keep his word about transferring Gansevoort's regiment. The order could not come quickly enough.

CHAPTER 19

The Exhausted 3rd Regiment Finally Departs Fort Stanwix

October–November 1778

By early October, the now veteran regiment was still short its authorized number of privates. For example, Lieutenant Colonel Willett's company had a full complement of commissioned officers, noncommissioned officers, and musicians but just thirty-four privates, and Jansen's company had only thirty-six.[1] Mid-October brought far more welcome news. True to his promise, as early as October 17, 1778, Washington notified Governor George Clinton that the 1st New York Regiment commanded by Colonel Goose Van Schaick, Colonel Gansevoort's brother-in-law, would relieve the 3rd New York Regiment at Fort Stanwix.[2]

After eighteen months as the primary garrison defending Fort Stanwix, the men of the 3rd New York Regiment were mentally and physically exhausted. To their credit, most of them had resisted the temptation to desert and had done their best to keep the regiment ready for whatever assignments would come its way. To their relief, Colonel Van Schaick of the 1st New York Regiment received orders on November 4, 1778, that immediately after receiving a clothing supply for his men, he was to march them immediately to Fort Stanwix. The regiment must arrive there as quickly as possible to relieve the 3rd New York Regiment and prepare to defend the fort should it again come under attack.[3] Finally ordered to depart the area, the 3rd New York Regiment wasted no time in leaving.

Generals James Clinton and Edward Hand reported their troop dispositions to Washington on November 28. They noted that Gansevoort's regiment was expected at Schenectady that day and would be stationed there and at Albany to guard stores and stay ready to march if the need arose.[4] Several weeks later, General Clinton informed Washington that he had 388 men of the 3rd New York Regiment with him at Albany. He was dealing with an outbreak of smallpox, and four of Gansevoort's men had caught it. Consequently, he had ordered one hundred men to proceed under an officer to Schenectady for inoculation.[5] The one negative to leaving Fort Stanwix was that the orders did not include a morale-boosting assignment to an important duty with the main army. Nevertheless, spending winter quarters away from the fort might allow the regiment to prepare to serve in some way with the main army in the 1779 campaign.

Leaving behind his difficult and uncomfortable yet familiar situation, as well as many friends and acquaintances, each man of the regiment struggled with his own memories and thoughts about his experiences during the preceding eighteen months. Each man who had been in the regiment during August 1776 also reflected on his contributions to the successful defense of the fort and to what degree he felt pride in them. Conversely, each may have wrestled with his feelings about how the seemingly unending and unpleasant conditions of military life he had endured had caused him to ponder desertion, at least fleetingly. The strongest emotion most officers and men felt was no doubt that of relief, if not pure joy, to be gone from the place.

Most of the men must have been suffering some degree of embedded anxiety following the long months of constantly being on alert for enemy attacks and more than once witnessing the mutilated bodies of comrades, and both male and female civilians, who had fallen victim to apparently random enemy attacks near the fort. Those attacks had created an image in their minds of an inhuman, savage Indian enemy. By contrast, associations with friendly Oneidas who often assisted them had helped at least some of the men develop a better understanding of Indigenous people possessing a humanity equal to theirs. They had also seen white men act in "savage" ways toward their perceived opponents. As in any wartime situation, the fort's defenders experienced and observed the full range of human behavior. While they would no longer be involved, the local and often deadly struggles among the diverse population of supporters and opponents of the long-term conflicts in the Mohawk Valley would continue. Primarily because of the white man's desire for Indian land, the negative racial images of savagery were employed by many whites to justify their mistreatment of and lack of fairness in their encounters with Indians.

Not only had the 3rd New York Regiment garrison suffered from want of clothing and sufficient food at Fort Stanwix, but so had the area's friendly Oneidas. While authorities did distribute clothing to the Oneidas toward the end of April 1778 at Fort Stanwix, the historians Joseph T. Glatthaar and James Kirby Martin note that "during the spring and summer months, many Oneidas dressed in tatters, and sometimes with almost no covering whatsoever." In October 1778, during the final weeks of the regiment's garrison duty, an influx of Oneida refugees came to the area after Patriot forces attacked the towns of Oquaga and Unadilla, which had served as bases for Loyalist and Indian attacks. These refugees put a strain on the local Oneidas' food and other supplies. Clothing shortages were especially hurtful, and the British exacerbated the problem by obstructing the movement of clothing and blankets, thus driving up prices so much that essential items became too expensive for many Oneidas. According to Glatthaar and Martin, "As autumn descended on them and inevitable frigid winter temperatures eventually froze the landscape, the Oneidas struggled to keep themselves and their refugee kin from Oquaga minimally outfitted and warm." General Schuyler again called for a trading post to open at Fort Stanwix where Indians could trade furs for clothing and blankets.[6]

After the 3rd New York Regiment defenders departed the fort, the area around the Oneida Carrying Place continued to experience long periods of inaction interspersed with highly stressful and emotional situations. The victory at Saratoga, which the successful defense of Fort Stanwix contributed to greatly, has often been identified as the "turning point" in the War for Independence. This assessment is defended primarily by the argument that after the Saratoga victory, the French formally joined in the conflict and contributed in many ways to the ultimate victory. Yet just as the defenders of Fort Stanwix remained caught up in the civil war aspects of the conflict in New York for fourteen months after the siege, the Mohawk River Valley residents continued to suffer from the civil war without any letup for the remainder of the War for Independence. Therefore, the siege and the Saratoga victories might have been a turning point for the larger war and the Continental forces in general, but they did not materially change the nature of the war in the Saratoga/Mohawk Valley area.[7]

As the war persisted, Sir John Johnson's Royal Yorkers continued to serve and were treated as part of the regular Canadian army, favored among the various Loyalist units working with the British in that area. Colonel Gansevoort had earlier been warned about raids to be led by Christopher Carleton, one of which took place in October 1778 in the Lake Champlain area. Carleton led a force of 324–390 British regulars, including some Jäger, thirty men of Johnson's Royal Yorkers, and eighty to one hundred Indians. While smaller, this force had a composition very similar to St. Leger's at the time of the siege. In May 1780, Sir John led a force of Indians and regulars, his King's Royal Yorkers, to Crown Point, where he launched forays to attack Johnstown and Caughnawaga in the Mohawk Valley.[8]

The men of the 3rd New York Regiment remained in the Albany area during the winter of 1778–79 and then joined the forces assembling under General John Sullivan for a campaign against the British-allied members of the Haudenosaunee, designed to destroy the Haudenosaunee infrastructure, which devastated much of their homeland. Officers such as Gansevoort and Willett finally had their chance to operate with other regiments in an offensive campaign, the major one of 1779, when they joined other New York regiments in a brigade led by General James Clinton.

This was as much a military campaign to destroy Indian settlements and food crops as it was an effort to defeat enemy fighting forces. During the campaign, Gansevoort noted, "It is remarked that the Indians live much better than most of the Mohawk River farmers, their Houses [being] very well furnished with all [the] necessary Household utensils, great plenty of Grain, several Horses, cows and wagons." He and his men who had been at Fort Stanwix had witnessed this prosperous lifestyle to some extent before but now saw even more of it in locations where the Haudenosaunee had not yet been inundated with colonial settlers.[9] The effects of this campaign proved devastating to the Haudenosaunee for an extended time, resulting in widespread hunger and deaths among women, children, and the aged as well as warriors, along with other consequences.

For the defenders of Fort Stanwix who took part in this campaign, it must have struck some that they and their fellow white soldiers were acting similarly to the enemy Indians and Loyalists who had so savagely attacked them when they were at the fort. Some must have been buoyed by feelings of retribution while others were appalled. Despite the devastation to the Haudenosaunee, the campaign failed to achieve its overall objective of bringing peace to the frontier and helping to bring the war to a favorable conclusion.[10]

After participating in the 1779 Sullivan expedition, Marinus Willett was promoted in 1780 to colonel of the 5th New York Regiment and served until that regiment disbanded on January 1, 1781. He then returned to familiar territory in the Mohawk River Valley and was appointed colonel of the Tryon County militia. In that position he led a force to victory over a combined British and Indian force on October 25, 1781, at Johnstown. Willett also led a force sent to capture Fort Oswego in February 1783, but it proved to be inadequate and retreated. This was the final endeavor of his military career.[11]

Following the Sullivan campaign, the soldiers of the 3rd New York Regiment spent the third winter of their enlistments at the main army's winter encampment at Morristown, New Jersey. This was the winter that featured the worst weather and suffering of the Revolution, though not the highest death toll. Several officers left the regiment that winter. Lieutenant William Tapp, whose wife had been at Fort Stanwix with him and whose first child had been born at the fort a few months after the siege, resigned his commission.[12] Captain De Witt resigned his Continental Army commission on January 7, 1780, but continued to serve as a major in the Ulster County militia levies throughout the war.[13] Major Cochran left the regiment when promoted to lieutenant colonel of the 2nd New York Regiment on March 30, 1780.[14]

In July 1780, Joseph Brant led a retaliatory raid against Kanonwalohale and encouraged the Oneidas to surrender. While a few did, over four hundred took refuge at Fort Stanwix, where Reverend Samuel Kirkland served the garrison as its chaplain. The town lost about seventy-three houses plus crops, horses, personal possessions, and the prominent meetinghouse. This was just one of the many raids by the British, Loyalists, and Indians that damaged local Patriot settlements, both white and Indian.[15]

CHAPTER 19

The Continental Army once again restructured at the very end of 1780, when the five New York regiments were condensed down to just two, partly because of the poor rate of enlistment. Many officers and men of the 3rd New York Regiment transferred into the 1st New York Regiment, including Captains Aorson, Bleeker, Gregg, Jansen, and Tiebout.[16]

At the dissolution of the 3rd New York Regiment, Colonel Gansevoort retired January 1, 1781, and was made a brigadier general of the New York State militia on March 26. In that capacity he became involved in the local civil war activity of the New York and Vermont land disputes and served as a commissioner of Indian affairs and building of frontier forts. Dr. Woodruff, who had married Maria Lansing in May 1779, retired from the army in 1781 to continue his medical practice in Albany.[17]

Most 3rd New York Regiment privates continued to serve in the 1st or 2nd New York Regiments. Peter Scriber remained with Captain Tiebout's company after it transferred to the 1st New York. He served a total of six and half years with Tiebout and was discharged in June 1783. Just how much time, if any, Clara spent with him as a camp follower is not documented, though they had a second child, Jacobus, apparently conceived around November 1781 and born in August 1782. Since Peter was with the army at Yorktown in October 1781, it is possible Clara was with him on that campaign.

Continental Army soldiers continued to garrison Fort Stanwix through May 22, 1781. Lieutenant Colonel Robert Cochran, then serving in Colonel Philip Van Cortlandt's 2nd New York Regiment, found himself commanding his longtime post at Fort Stanwix in May 1781, dealing with the perennial problems of lack of food and clothing for the garrison, when a natural disaster caused much greater damage to its structure than the siege had.[18] When Cochran called a council of Fort Stanwix officers to inspect the damaged works on May 12, they found "more than two thirds of the works broken down occasioned by the late heavy rains" and predicted that the remaining works would be in the same condition within a few days.[19] Cochran alerted General James Clinton on May 13 that "heavy rains have almost ruined the works of this garrison" and the only remaining "strength is the outside Picquets on the Glacis." To restore the fort, Cochran explained that they would have "to begin at the foundation" and "open the remaining part of the works," making the fort vulnerable if attacked. At least five to six hundred men, an engineer, and "a sufficient number of artificers, wagons, tools, etc." would be required to make all necessary repairs over the summer.

Additional damage to the fort may have been human initiated. After explaining the natural disaster damage, in a postscript note the devastated Cochran added: "I am sorry to inform you that this day between the Hours of Eleven and Twelve, this Garrison took fire and consumed every Barrack, notwithstanding every exertion was made to extinguish the flames. I still remain in possession of the works, and have saved the magazine, with a small part of the provisions, tho' at the risque of our lives; in my next shall give you every particular."

A very suspicious General Clinton replied to Cochran:

I cannot find words to express my surprise at the unexpected accident, or how a fire should break out in the middle of noon day, in a Garrison where the Troops could not possibly be absent, after a most violent and incessant rain of several days and be permited to do so much damage. I am sorry to say that the several Circumstances which accompanied this melancholy affair, affords plausible ground for suspicion that it was not the effect of meer accident. I hope when it comes to be examined in a Clearer point of view such lights may be thrown upon it as will remove the suspicion for which there appears too much reason.

After noting that he had requested guidance from higher authority, General Clinton told Cochran: "I would request that you keep possession of the Garrison and endeavour to shelter the Troops in the best manner possible; that you collect all the nails. Hinges &c. &c. of the ruins, and suffer nothing to be lost that is in your power to save. Colo. Cortlandt has my orders to afford you all the assistance which time and circumstances will admit." Clinton also instructed Cochran to send the women and children downriver in boats. By May 17, all in power agreed to remove the entire garrison to German Flats near Fort Herkimer, across the Mohawk River from Fort Dayton, where they would erect defenses.

Several days of further discussion among various officers, including the retired Colonel Gansevoort and General Schuyler, examined the advantages and disadvantages of either rebuilding or abandoning Fort Stanwix and creating something new at German Flats. As had been true throughout its history, the fort could not be adequately supplied with all its necessities, and restoring the physical fort did not seem possible. Compounded by a demoralized garrison, prospects looked bad for the outpost that had suffered so much defending the Carry Place and the Mohawk River Valley. On May 22, Governor Clinton ordered the fort's evacuation and the removal of the garrison to Fort Herkimer, adding, "Colonel Cortlandt's regiment with part of the new Levies will be for a considerable time employed to assist in the Evacuation of Fort Schuyler."[20]

The fort remained abandoned for the rest of the war, further exposing Patriot settlements to British, Loyalist, and Indian raids. Already many settlers' houses had been fortified and neighborhood blockhouses built to serve as rally points and refuges during raids. Yet these defensive measures did not stop the destruction of villages and countryside resulting from the raids.[21]

Several months after the fort's abandonment in 1781, many of the Fort Stanwix siege defenders participated in the very successful siege of Yorktown, Virginia, and witnessed the surrender of General Cornwallis on October 19. With that victory, those men had taken part in both defending a besieged fort and attacking a fortified town under siege. Captain Gregg's young nephew, fifer Robert Wilson, had received a commission as an ensign on June 9, 1781, becoming the youngest commissioned officer in the Continental Army. At the surrender of General Cornwallis at Yorktown, by Gregg family tradition Colonel Alexander Hamilton assigned the eighteen-year-old ensign to take charge of receiving the British colors at the surrender ceremony.[22]

Many of the men who had defended Fort Stanwix were still in the army when it disbanded in 1783, almost six years after the siege. Although now in the 1st New York Regiment, a few men still served under the same captain, such as the eleven men serving under Captain Tiebout who had been with him since the first month of regiment building at Fishkill: Sergeant James Van Blarcum, Sergeant James Patterson, Corporal John Edgerley, Corporal Robert Glen, Corporal Mark Karr, and Privates John Peters, John Frederick, Duncan Campbell, Lockard Lewis, Jonathan Pinckney, and Peter Scriber. Whatever their initial motives for enlisting had been, those men fulfilled their contracts faithfully and survived six and half tough years together. There were also men in other companies who had served together for the same six and a half years.

Epilogue

Peter and Caty Gansevoort lived in Albany next door to Peter's father. They had six children born between 1779 and 1791. When his uncle Johannes died in 1781, Peter took charge of the family brewery and, after the war, concentrated on his businesses in Albany, including lumbering, sawing, and grinding at the Snook Kill Falls in Saratoga County, where he had purchased confiscated Loyalist property. He built a mill town, today's hamlet appropriately called Gansevoort in the town of Northumberland. He served as Albany County sheriff from 1790 to 1792 and as a regent of the University of the State of New York from 1808 until his death on July 2, 1812, just a few days before his sixty-third birthday.[1]

Marinus Willett returned to New York City to resume his work as a merchant. In 1783 he became a founding member of the Society of the Cincinnati and in December was elected to the New York State Assembly. He served twice as sheriff of New York County and worked as a diplomatic envoy to the Muscogee Indians for President George Washington, attempting to ensure that the Indians received fair treatment. When offered a commission as a brigadier general, he turned it down in order not to have to lead military actions against the Indians. After joining the Democratic-Republican Party, Willett served as the mayor of New York City from 1807 to 1808 before retiring from politics after his defeat in a special election for lieutenant governor. His third wife died in 1819. After his August 22, 1830, death, a lavish funeral drew some ten thousand mourners.[2]

Like so many men who had served throughout the war, Major Robert Cochran found himself deeply in debt when the war ended. He recovered his prosperity, however, and lived well at Ticonderoga and Sandy Hook, New York, with his wife and daughters. He had spent more time than any other individual officer serving at Fort Stanwix, beginning with Colonel Elmore's regiment in 1776, continuing with the 3rd New York Regiment, and ending with the fort's destruction in 1781 while serving as the fort commander for the 2nd New York Regiment. Cochran died at Sandy Hook on July 3, 1812, aged seventy-three.[3]

Dr. Hunloke Woodruff lived in Albany with his wife, Maria, and their eight children. He supported both the Albany Dutch Church and the Albany Presbyterian Church, where he served as an elder. He became a prominent physician and teacher, serving in 1806 as president of the Albany Medical Society, while involved in local politics and community organizations. In poor health, Woodruff made out his will in November 1810 and died on July 4, 1811, at the age of fifty-six, highly esteemed and known for his charity and hospitality.[4]

Paymaster Jeremiah Van Rensselaer became a leader of Albany's opposition to the proposed federal Constitution but then served in the first federal Congress, 1789–91, corresponding with Republican notables including Thomas Jefferson. He served as one of the first directors of the Bank of Albany in 1792 and later as president of the bank. Van Rensselaer belonged to several civic organizations, including the Albany Mechanics Society, and was elected lieutenant governor of New York State in 1801, serving during Governor George Clinton's last term, ending in 1804. He died on February 19, 1810, in Albany.[5]

After leaving the regiment in its 1778 reorganization, Captain Elias Van Bunschoten became a captain of associated exempts in the militia. These were men who had previously held commissions or were between the ages of fifty and sixty and were required to turn out only in cases of enemy incursions. In 1779 he was promoted to major, serving with militia levies recruited to defend the frontier and continued in this duty for the remainder of the war. He lived at Specken Kill with his wife, Catalyntje, and their eight children. He served as a lieutenant colonel in the Dutchess County militia until 1797, in addition to holding several political offices. Running into financial difficulties, he was declared insolvent in 1805, whereupon he went to live with his son at Cooperstown, New York, until his death that year.[6]

Captain Thomas De Witt married Elsie Hasbrouck in February 1782, and after the war they lived in Kingston, New York, with their five children. He died at Kingston on September 7, 1809, aged about sixty-eight.[7]

Captain Cornelius Jansen lived in the town of Shawangunk, where he married the widow Christina Low on October 29, 1787. They had four children. An original member of the Society of the Cincinnati, he died at Shawangunk on August 22, 1796, at the age of forty-eight.[8]

After leaving the 3rd New York Regiment in 1778, beginning October 19, 1779, Captain Abraham Swartwout served as captain of a company of Dutchess County militia-associated exempts. Swartwout lived in Poughkeepsie with his wife, Maria, and their seven children. In 1790, he was granted New York State bounty land for his service. He died October 15, 1799, at age fifty-six in Poughkeepsie.[9]

Captain Aaron Aorson was made a brevet major on September 30, 1783. He returned to New York City, where he lived at 28 Nassau Street and kept a tavern on the corner of George Street. In 1786 he served as a deputy under Sheriff Marinus Willett. He appears in newspaper notices about happenings at his tavern through 1800.[10]

Captain James Gregg married Mary Brewster in 1782 and became one of the original members of the Society of the Cincinnati in 1783. Because of the disabilities he sustained in the war, he retired on a disability pension, dying September 22, 1785, in Albany. After his death, the Society of the Cincinnati paid an allowance from time to time to his widow for her support.[11] After the war, his nephew Robert Wilson became a member of the Society of the Cincinnati and a prominent citizen of Manlius, New York. He married Amelia Dunham in 1803, and the couple had four children. They named one son Gregg Wilson in honor of his uncle. Robert died of a fever at Manlius in 1811 when he was about forty-eight years old.[12]

Captain Henry Tiebout was brevetted a major on September 30, 1783, and became a member of the New York State Society of the Cincinnati when it formed. He relocated to Monmouth County, New Jersey, and in 1806 was representing that county in the state assembly.[13] On July 8, 1818, he participated as one of the honored pallbearers, along with Marinus Willett, for the transfer of the remains of their former commander in the Canadian campaign, General Richard Montgomery, from Quebec for burial, amidst great fanfare, at the monument to him that Congress had authorized to be built at St. Paul's Chapel in

New York City.[14] Tiebout continued to support the men who served in his company and in December 1819 made a supporting deposition for the pension application of Private Ichabod Stoddard.[15] At that time, Tiebout was serving as a judge in Monmouth County.[16] Tiebout died in Shrewsbury, New Jersey, on February 23, 1826, at the age of eighty-eight, his death notice reporting that "he died as he had lived, beloved and respected by all that knew him."[17]

Just after the war ended, in November 1783, Captain Leonard Bleeker married Johanna Abeel and took up residence in New York City at 70 Nassau Street. Whether from the effects of the war or some other development in his life, in 1785, at age thirty, he made his profession of faith and joined the Baptist Church. He became well known for his religious beliefs and "was a man of much prayer, and highly gifted in that heavenly exercise." He became involved in many charitable causes; his obituary stated, "It is thought he has been connected with more of the benevolent institutions of the day, than any other individual in the city." While a number of those civic organizations were church related, Bleeker was also a member of the New York Chamber of Commerce for nearly fifty years and treasurer of the New York State Society of the Cincinnati for eighteen years. When General Lafayette visited New York in September 1824, Bleeker, as vice president of the trustees of the New York Free School Society, addressed him about the work of the society in helping to educate children. Bleeker was involved with schools for both boys and girls, including Black children, and supported the New York Manumission Society, which sought to end enslavement.[18] Leonard and Johanna had six children before Johanna died in 1810. Leonard married his second wife, Grace Berrian, in 1818. He died on March 9, 1844, at the age of eighty-eight.[19]

Lieutenant William Tapp settled in New York City, where he became an original member of the Society of the Cincinnati when it formed. He worked as a bookkeeper at the Bank of New York, which was organized by Alexander Hamilton and others in 1784. He died suddenly in New York on March 12, 1795, at the age of forty-five. His wife, Mary, who had given birth to their son William Horatio Tapp at Fort Stanwix, lived until 1827, when she died at age seventy-nine.[20]

After the war, Private Peter Scriber lived at Clinton Corners in Dutchess County, moving to Greene County about 1814. Peter and Clara, whose first daughter was born when Peter was stationed at Fort Stanwix, had six additional daughters born between 1785 and 1800. He was a blacksmith and a farmer, and as early as 1820 he kept a hotel for a time along the turnpike at Gayhead in Greene County. At some point Peter purchased a small farm at Round Top Mountain, where he lived until his death at age ninety-seven on May 22, 1851. He never applied for a military pension. In about 1840, local Catskill artist Alburtis Dell Orient Browere painted Peter's portrait.[21]

After the war, Henry Ritter lived at his home in Manheim. In 1786 he married Anna Maria Margaretha Petrie, known as Mary, at German Flats. He successfully applied for a military pension in April 1832 and lived at Manheim until his death on June 17, 1847, aged about eighty-eight years.[22]

After his many contributions at the time of the siege, Han Yerry Tewahangarahken (Doxtater) continued his leadership role among the Oneidas until his death sometime around 1794. He visited Congress in New York City in 1787 to deal with a boundary dispute and to lobby Congress to appoint a superintendent of Indian affairs. He also dealt with the continuing land disputes among the Oneidas. Two Kettles Together outlived Han Yerry by about thirty years, losing her eyesight in old age. These two energetic and seemingly ageless people deserve to be more widely known among citizens of the United States.[23]

Settlers returning to the Mohawk Valley when the war ended in 1783 carried deep anger over all the raids that had decimated livestock and created a "ravaged landscape" of burned houses, barns, and mills amid bullet-damaged stockades and blockhouses.[24] That anger led to "an indiscriminate hatred of Indians." Even the peaceful and friendly Oneidas who had helped the Patriot cause so much were seen no differently from other Indians. Reverend Samuel Kirkland described the effects of the war on the Oneidas:

> Previous to the revolutionary war, the Oneidas were in a peaceable & flourish[ing] state & many among them had approximated to the first stages of civil society. They had attained some degree of regularity & industry. Their Chiefs had great influence, especially those who sustained a good moral Character & [were] professedly friends to Christianity. The late war proved almost fatal to the nation. A great majority took part with the Americans & lost many of their warriors. . . . In the year 1780 the hostile Indians & [Loyalist] refugees drove them from their villages, burning their church, spreading waste & desolation on every side. . . . When

they returned to their desolated villages after the peace, they were wretchedly poor, their land much overgrown, & their reluctance to labour doubled.[25]

After the war, New York needed to strengthen itself as a state and develop its economy. Land for new settlers was greatly needed, and this would mean continued suffering for the Oneidas and other nations in the Mohawk Valley and adjoining areas as both governmental actions and commercial endeavors continually removed land from Indian ownership and use.[26]

Continuing Fort Stanwix's role in Indian relations, in 1784, amid the struggle to determine the authority of states and Congress, the representatives of the new United States met with representatives of the Six Nations at what remained of Fort Stanwix, at that time a mostly grass- and brush-covered earth shell containing just two bark-roofed earthen-floored huts. The conference concluded with a treaty that failed to end white settler expansion into Indian territories, and additional meetings occurred at the fort until 1790 in continuing attempts to resolve land issues in New York.

The story of the Oneidas' loss of their lands and their subordination to the new United States is one of the tragic episodes in our history. Their struggle for ownership and control of land, as well as basic human respect, reveals the experiences of the Oneidas who had supported the Patriot cause at the Fort Stanwix siege as well as other actions contributing to the Patriot success. Oneida friendship and loyalty were not returned in kind. In the words of the historian Barbara Graymont, "The friendly Tuscaroras and Oneidas were just as ruthlessly imposed upon for their lands as were the former British Indian allies."[27]

By 1787 Reverend Kirkland reported that many Oneidas "mourn and sigh and weep like children in the view of their present miserable state, compared with the white people.... While blessings of every kind flowed down like a river upon the white people as though God begrudged them nothing, calamity, wretchedness and poverty were the lot of the Indians." In June 1789, when Oneidas assembled at Fort Stanwix to receive their first annuity payment from New York for land taken from them, Good Peter told the state agent, "We are so faint that we cannot speak to you, and our Women and Children are come likewise to see you and are very hungry and have no Provisions at Home." An Oneida father of five children seeking relief said, "My family have not tasted any bread, or meat for many days; nothing but herbs and sometimes small fish. I am so weak I can't hoe any corn."[28]

Today the remnants of Oneida land form the Oneida Indian Reservation, bordering Lake Oneida and along Wood Creek west of today's Rome, New York, the site of Fort Stanwix.

Memories of the "the fort that never surrendered" and the people and events associated with it lived on after the Revolution. A settlement started developing in the late 1780s and 1790s in the area including the abandoned fort then sarcastically called the Expense Lot, on account of the high cost of surveying the rough, unsettled territory. Irish-born entrepreneur Dominick Lynch bought the Expense Lot planning to build a town there, to be called Lynchville after himself. He was very ambitious and established businesses including a gristmill, a cotton mill, a sawmill, and a woolen mill. Many residents did not like Lynch, however, because he would only lease them land rather than selling lots to them. The town also became known as Rome when the surrounding township took that name in 1796. Classical names for locations were commonly chosen at that time, and the fact that imperial Rome was renowned for its military history may have been the reason why that name was selected for the township and village developing on this well-known militarily historic site.

The 1797 completion of the Rome Canal connecting Wood Creek and the Mohawk River at the Carry Place stimulated the early growth of the town. Then, construction of the Erie Canal began in 1817 at Lynchville/Rome, greatly facilitating trade between the Hudson River and Lake Ontario. The canal would be continuous, without the need for a Carrying Place. During the canal construction, Lynchville was officially incorporated as the Village of Rome in 1819. Completion of the canal in 1825 brought great prosperity to Rome as new buildings rose on the site of the abandoned fort. The growing town was incorporated as the City of Rome in 1870, and it continued to prosper and expand.

By 1935, interest had developed in constructing a replica of the fort at the time of the Revolution. President Franklin D. Roosevelt signed legislation on August 21, 1935, establishing the Fort Stanwix site as a national monument to be operated by the National Park Service. To benefit their city, the citizens of Rome became defenders of the fort. They supported an urban renewal plan that included clearing the site, conducting archaeology work, and building a reconstruction of the fort on its original footprint.

After extensive documentary and archaeological research, the National Park Service began a reconstruction of the fort in 1974. Mirroring the fort's history in the eighteenth century, when it always seemed to require further work to be complete, the only partially completed fort was opened to the public for the 1976 bicentennial celebrations. It was finished in 1978, and a visitor center, the Marinus Willett Collections Management and Education Center, opened in 2005.

Today, the National Park Service operates the Fort Stanwix National Monument on about sixteen acres in downtown Rome, New York, welcoming visitors year-round and providing numerous opportunities for both historians and the public to deepen their understanding of the siege and other aspects of life over the course of history at the Oneida Carry and the extended Mohawk River Valley. The never-ending trail of research continues to add substance to the story.[29]

Notes

Preface

1. For an example of the name "Fort Stanwix" in common usage, see the *New York Gazette, and the Weekly Mercury,* August 4, 1777.

2. Taylor, *The Divided Ground,* 193.

3. See, for example, Luzader, *Saratoga*; Corbett, *No Turning Point*; Schnitzer and Troiani, *Don Troiani's Campaign to Saratoga–1777*; and Weddle, *The Compleat Victory.*

While the fort's nickname is commonly used and prominently featured on the website for Fort Stanwix maintained by the National Park Service, its origins remain obscure. The earliest use of the phrase I could find was in a short article in the *New-York Daily Tribune,* August 22, 1900.

Introduction

1. Quoted in Luzader, *Saratoga,* 23–24.

2. The portage at the Oneida Carrying Place varied in length from about a mile up to about five miles, depending on the varying water depths in the rivers, which determined how close to the Carrying Place a boat could travel.

3. Broadhead, Fernow, and O'Callaghan, *Documents Relative to the Colonial History of New York,* 4:979.

4. Jacobson, *Battlefield Delineation,* 20.

5. Glatthaar and Martin, *Forgotten Allies,* 24–25; Graymont, *The Iroquois in the American Revolution,* 3. After captives successfully survived a "requickening" process to instill Oneida language and values, they were considered full members of the tribe. Interracial marriages between Oneida women and men from the settler population or other Indian nations produced children accepted as Oneidas because lineage descended through the mother's line. As a result, by the time of our eighteenth-century story, only about 15 to 20 percent of the Oneida population was genetically pure Oneida. Glatthaar and Martin, *Forgotten Allies,* 22, 24.

6. Jacobson, *Battlefield Delineation,* 24–25; Berleth, *Bloody Mohawk,* 31.

7. Luzader, *Fort Stanwix,* 3–5; Jacobson, *Battlefield Delineation,* 21–22.

8. Sir William founded Johnstown and named it after his son, John Johnson, who, we will see, became heavily involved in the actions at Fort Stanwix. In contemporary documents the town is called John's-Town.

9. Luzader, *Fort Stanwix,* 7–8.

10. This account is based on an entry in the journal of Ensign Moses Dorr of Captain Parker's company published in "Documents: Fort Frontenac and Fort Stanwix," *New York History* 16, no. 4 (October 1935): 457, 464. Luzader, *Fort Stanwix*, 11, gives the date as August 26.

11. Scott, *Fort Stanwix and Oriskany*, 158–61.

12. Ewing, "Journal of George Ewing," 471–73.

13. Luzader, *Fort Stanwix*, 11–19; Hanson and Hsu, *Casemates and Cannonballs*, 27; Luzader, Torres, and Carroll, *Fort Stanwix*, 94.

14. Luzader, *Fort Stanwix*, 19.

15. Broadhead, Fernow, and O'Callaghan, *Documents Relative to the Colonial History of New York*, 7:985.

16. Luzader, Torres, and Carroll, *Fort Stanwix*, 126, citing a letter dated April 23, 1775, from Robert Duncan to William Livingston, taken from the *Rome (NY) Sentinel*, March 3, 1969, copied from Fort Stanwix Museum files by Lee Hanson.

17. "1768 Boundary Line Treaty of Fort Stanwix," National Park Service, last updated February 23, 2023, https://www.nps.gov/articles/000/1768-boundary-line-treaty-of-fort-stanwix.htm.

18. Taylor, *The Divided Ground*, 41–44; Broadhead, Fernow, and O'Callaghan, *Documents Relative to the Colonial History of New York*, 8:451; Glatthaar and Martin, *Forgotten Allies*, 69, 180; Jacobson, *Battlefield Delineation*, 25; Hanson and Hsu, *Casemates and Cannonballs*, 9; Berleth, *Bloody Mohawk*, 151.

19. Broadhead, Fernow, and O'Callaghan, *Documents Relative to the Colonial History of New York*, 8:125.

20. Graymont, *The Iroquois in the American Revolution*, 61.

21. To deal productively with both disruptive changes and new opportunities resulting from white colonist contact, some Oneida individuals mastered European languages and the skills associated with European products and processes, such as blacksmithing, while steadfastly maintaining important elements of their Oneida culture. Glatthaar and Martin, *Forgotten Allies*, 29.

22. Glatthaar and Martin, *Forgotten Allies* 70, 89–90, 130, 144. A short biography of Spencer can be found at: Kandice Watson, "Key Figures in Oneida History: Pre-American Revolution," Oneida Indian Nation, accessed January 23. 2024, https://www.oneidaindiannation.com/key-figures-in-oneida-history-pre-american-revolution/. He is mentioned several times in the journals of missionary Gideon Hawley, which can be viewed at: "Gideon Hawley Missionary Journals, 1753-1806," Congregational Library and Archives, accessed January 23, 2024, https://congregationallibrary.quartexcollections.com/manuscript-collections/browse-the-gideon-hawley-missionary-journals. For information on his work for Johnson, see Hamilton et al., *Papers of Sir William Johnson*, 4:324, 10:897–98, 12:343, 516, 543, 625–25, 667–68; Taylor, *The Divided Ground*, 150.

23. Glatthaar and Martin, *Forgotten Allies*, 89–90; Campbell, *Annals of Tryon County*, 33–34.

24. Graymont, *The Iroquois in the American Revolution*, 1, 48.

25. Taylor, *The Divided Ground*, 81–82.

26. Corbet, *No Turning Point*, 371.

27. Graymont, *The Iroquois in the American Revolution*, 69; *Mohawk Valley in the Revolution*, documents 13 and 14, 19–21.

1. The Increasing Need to Reestablish Fort Stanwix

1. Philip Schuyler was one of the four major generals appointed by the Continental Congress on June 19, 1775, the same day Washington was appointed commander in chief. Schuyler was a member of a wealthy Albany, New York, family with experience in the French and Indian War. He and Washington would have a close relationship throughout their lives. See Bollen, *George Washington and the Mohawk Frontier*, 18.

2. General Schuyler, Albany, to General Washington, June 11, 1776, Papers of the Continental Congress, Letters from General Schuyler, June 1775–December 1776, 2:208–9, NARA M247.

3. *Journals of the Continental Congress*, 4:47.

4. Elmer, "Journal of an Expedition," 137.

5. George Washington to John Hancock, April 25–26, 1776, Founders Online, National Archives, https://founders.archives.gov/documents/Washington/03-04-02-0106; originally published in *The Papers of George Washington*, Revolutionary War Series, vol. 4, *1 April 1776–15 June 1776*, ed. Philander D. Chase (Charlottesville: University Press of Virginia, 1991), 125–31.

6. Corbett, *No Turning Point*, 14–15. A manor was a large tract of land granted by the colonial governor to a man, who then leased sections to resident tenants over whom he also often exercised civil and criminal jurisdiction.

7. Ewing, "Journal of George Ewing," 471.

8. General Schuyler, Saratoga, to Colonel Dayton, May 14, 1776, Papers of the Continental Congress, Letters from General Schuyler, 2:149–50.

9. Watt and Morrison, *The British Campaign of 1777*, 33; Taylor, *The Divided Ground*, 78; Graymont, *The Iroquois in the American Revolution*, 81–85. To prevent confiscation of their land or imprisonment, suspected Loyalists might be allowed to give their word of honor, their parole, that they would not engage in military activities.

10. Weaver, *3rd New Jersey*, 14; Elmer, "Journal of Expedition," 108.

11. Corbett, *No Turning Point*, 14.

12. Lender and Martin, *Citizen Soldier*, 58, journal of Captain Joseph Bloomfield, entry for June 4, 1776.

13. Ewing, "Journal of George Ewing," 471.

14. Elmer, "Journal of Expedition," 118. The three different relationships to the river given by these visitors are perfect examples of eyewitness accounts, as primary sources, not always agreeing.

15. Ewing, "Journal of George Ewing," 471.

16. Graymont, *The Iroquois in the American Revolution*, 94.

17. Corbett, *No Turning Point*, 20–21, 25; for more on the diversity of the population, see 9–35; Berleth, *Bloody Mohawk*, 142.

18. Colonel Dayton, Johnstown, to General Schuyler, May 2, 1776, Papers of the Continental Congress, Letters from General Schuyler, 2:157–59.

19. General Schuyler, Fort George, to Colonel Dayton, May 22, 1776, Papers of the Continental Congress, Letters from General Schuyler, 2:161.

20. Colonel Dayton, Johnstown, to General Schuyler, May 23, 1776, Papers of the Continental Congress, Letters from General Schuyler, 2:169–70. See also Graymont, *The Iroquois in the American Revolution*, 92–93.

21. General Schuyler, Fort George, to Colonel Dayton, May 25, 1776, Papers of the Continental Congress, Letters from General Schuyler, 2:171.

22. General Schuyler, Fort George, to Colonel Dayton, May 27, 1776, Papers of the Continental Congress, Letters from General Schuyler, 2:173–74.

23. General Schuyler, Fort George, to Committee of Albany, May 27, 1776, Papers of the Continental Congress, Letters from General Schuyler, 2:177.

24. Rees, *"The uses and conveniences of different kinds of Water Craft"*; Hanson and Hsu, *Casemates and Cannonballs*, 6–7.

25. General Schuyler, Fort George, to John Hancock, May 31, 1776, Papers of the Continental Congress, Letters from General Schuyler, 2:179.

26. Graymont, *The Iroquois in the American Revolution*, 88–89.

27. Reverend Kirkland, Lake George, to General Schuyler, June 8, 1776, Papers of the Continental Congress, Letters from General Schuyler, 2:202; Glatthaar and Martin, *Forgotten Allies*, 118–19; Taylor, *The Divided Ground*, 82–83; Graymont, *The Iroquois in the American Revolution*, 101.

28. General Schuyler, Fort George, to John Hancock, June 8, 1776, Papers of the Continental Congress, Letters from General Schuyler, 2:192–96. See also Graymont, *The Iroquois in the American Revolution*, 101.

29. General Schuyler, Fort George, to General Israel Putnam at New York, June 8, 1776, Papers of the Continental Congress, Letters from General Schuyler, 2:190.

30. Luzader, *Fort Stanwix*, 26–27; Glatthaar and Martin, *Forgotten Allies*, 118–19, 125, 129, 132; George Washington to Major General Philip Schuyler, June 13, 1776, Founders Online, National Archives, https://founders.archives.gov/documents/Washington/03-04-02-0405; originally published in *The Papers of George Washington*, 4:515–18. See also *Journals of the Continental Congress*, June 14, 1776, 5:442.

31. General Schuyler, Albany, to General John Sullivan, Papers of the Continental Congress, Letters from General Schuyler, 2:226.

32. Lender and Martin, *Citizen Soldier*, 11.

2. The 3rd New Jersey Regiment Restores Fort Stanwix

1. Lender and Martin, *Citizen Soldier*, 65.

2. Ewing, "Journal of George Ewing," 472.

3. For a short history of the 3rd New Jersey Regiment see "History," 3rd New Jersey Regiment: Jersey Greys, accessed January 23, 2024, http://www.jerseygreys.org/history.html; Weaver, *3rd New Jersey*, chap. 1; Elmer, "Journal of an Expedition," 108; Ewing, "Journal of George Ewing," 471–72.

4. Ewing, "Journal of George Ewing," 472.

5. Nathaniel Hubbell is something of a mystery with very little documentary evidence about him.

6. Lender and Martin, *Citizen Soldier*, 65; Hanson and Hsu, *Casemates and Cannonballs*, 41.

7. Hanson and Hsu, *Casemates and Cannonballs*, 38.

8. Lender and Martin, *Citizen Soldier*, 65; Elmer, "Journal of an Expedition," 134, entry for June 30.

9. Ewing, "Journal of George Ewing," 472.

10. Jones, *Annals and Recollections of Oneida County*, 326–27, cites and transcribes the *Rome Sentinel* obituary of the son, John, in October 1847, which also gives information about the father and his settlement in 1760. See also pension file of the younger John Roof PF S14,371, National Archives, NARA M804, Revolutionary War Pension and Bounty Land Warrant Application Files.

11. Lender and Martin, *Citizen Soldier*, 66; Graymont, *The Iroquois in the American Revolution*, 225. In various sources Skenandoah is often spelled Skenandon.

12. Lender and Martin, *Citizen Soldier*, 68.

13. Luzader, Torres, and Carroll, *Fort Stanwix*, 82, 94.

14. Hanson and Hsu, *Casemates and Cannonballs*, 33–38: Luzader, Torres, and Carroll, *Fort Stanwix*, 99, 107.

15. Lender and Martin, *Citizen Soldier*, 97; Luzader, *Fort Stanwix*, 27–28; Lowenthal, *Days of Siege*, 11.

16. Luzader, *Fort Stanwix*, 27–28.

17. Major General Philip Schuyler, German Flats, to George Washington, August 2, 1776, Founders Online, National Archives, https://founders.archives.gov/documents/Washington/03-05-02-0414. Lieutenant McMichael's name is sometimes given as William as in Heitman's *Historical Register*, 374.

18. For this story, see Weaver, *3rd New Jersey*, chap. 5.

19. Weaver, *3rd New Jersey*, 66–72. For a discussion of reasons why men might desert, see Ruddiman, *Becoming Men of Some Consequence*, chap. 4; Ward, *George Washington's Enforcers*, 25.

20. Ewing, "Journal of George Ewing," 471–73, quotation at 472. Soldiers were on command when detached temporarily from their company to perform a special task. Examples include scouting parties, work details at the "laboratory" casting bullets or making up cartridges, being part of a guard detail for bateaux or cattle coming upriver or overland to the fort from Fort Dayton, and so on.

21. Weaver, *3rd New Jersey*, chap. 6.

22. Elijah Moore PF S 38,244.

23. Major General Philip Schuyler, Albany, to George Washington, August 16, 1776, Founders Online, National Archives, https://founders.archives.gov/documents/Washington/03-06-02-0037.

24. Elias Dayton, Fort Schuyler, to General Philip Schuyler, September 4, 1776, Papers of the Continental Congress, Letters from Philip Schuyler, 1775–76, 1:450.

25. General Philip Schuyler to Continental Congress (John Hancock), September 8, 1776, Papers of the Continental Congress, Letters from Philip Schuyler, 1:452–54.

26. Glatthaar and Martin, *Forgotten Allies*, 124–26.

27. Berleth, *Bloody Mohawk*, 29.

28. Graymont, *The Iroquois in the American Revolution*, 1–2.

29. For more on the very complex story of white-Indigenous relations and prejudices in New York, see especially Graymont, *The Iroquois in the American Revolution*; Taylor, *The Divided Ground*; and Glatthaar and Martin, *Forgotten Allies*.

30. Competition over landownership between the Oneidas and the colonists was already well underway in the area by the time the fort was built. The somewhat mysterious Sarah Ainse, with both Oneida and settler connections, set up as a trader at Fort Stanwix when it was built in 1758. Seeing the developing economic potential of the area, she struggled to persuade the Oneidas to grant her six square miles of land near the fort. Sir William Johnson, however, got title to the land in 1772 for a group of his friends. The story of Sarah Ainse is quite interesting. Alan Taylor devotes a chapter of *The Divided Ground* to her life, including her involvement in Indian land affairs after the Revolution (396–98).

31. Taylor, *The Divided Ground*, 126–28; Lender and Martin, *Citizen Soldier*, 65–66, 82, 84–85, 109, and passim. See also Scott, *Fort Stanwix and Oriskany*, chap. 4, "Some of King George's Indian Allies Were Far from Being Savages."

32. Lender and Martin, *Citizen Soldier*, 80, 101. Elmore's regiment is the subject of the following chapter.

33. Thomas Spencer, Oneida, to Colonel Dayton, September 4, 1776, Papers of the Continental Congress, Letters from General Schuyler, June 1775–December 1776, 2:355–56.

34. Lender and Martin, *Citizen Soldier*, 104–5.

35. Graymont, *The Iroquois in the American Revolution*, 111–13.

36. Lender and Martin, *Citizen Soldier*, 105.

37. Elias Dayton, Fort Schuyler, to Philip Schuyler, September 11, 1776, Papers of the Continental Congress, Letters from General Schuyler, 2:377.

38. Lender and Martin, *Citizen Soldier*, 107. The Mississaugas are part of the Ojibwa Nation in the Algonquian language family. They established themselves on the north shore of Lake Ontario between 1700 and 1720.

39. Elias Dayton, Fort Schuyler, to General Philip Schuyler, September 22, 1776, in Force, *American Archives*, ser. 5, 2:859.

40. Elias Dayton, Fort Schuyler, to General Philip Schuyler, September 28, 1776, Papers of the Continental Congress, Letters from General Schuyler, 2:380.

41. Lender and Martin, *Citizen Soldier*, 104, 110; Samuel Benjamin PF S 31,546.

42. Revolutionary War Rolls, 1775–1783, 1776–1777, Elmore's Battalion, folder 206, NARA M246.

43. Lender and Martin, *Citizen-Soldier*, 110–11; Ewing, "Journal of George Ewing," 472.

44. Lender and Martin, *Citizen Soldier*, 111.

3. Elmore's Regiment Relieves the 3rd New Jersey Regiment

1. George Washington to Philip Schuyler, August 16, 1776, Founders Online, National Archives, https://founders.archives.gov/documents/Washington/03-06-02-0110; originally published in *The Papers of George Washington*, Revolutionary War Series, vol. 6, *13 August 1776–20 October 1776*, ed. Philander D. Chase and Frank E. Grizzard Jr. (Charlottesville: University Press of Virginia, 1994), 121–23.

2. Schuyler to Washington, August 16, 1776, Founders Online, National Archives, https://founders.archives.gov/documents/Washington/03-06-02-0110; originally published in *The Papers of George Washington*, 6:121–23.

3. See "Connecticut Regiments in the Continental Army," accessed January 23, 2024, https://revolutionarywar.us/continental-army/connecticut; Heitman, *Historical Register*, 215.

4. Wright, *Continental Army*, 50, 58, 242.

5. Samuel Doty PF S 45,326; James Dole PF S 43,518.

6. Abner Cable PF S 10,438. Others included Clark Hyde, who enlisted at Shatford into Captain Walker's company (Clark Hyde PF S 45,407), and James Warren of Sharon, Connecticut, about eighteen years old, enlisted in Captain Woodbridge's (James Warren PF S45,452). Both enlisted in June and for only nine months since the regiment would disband the following April. The much older thirty-one-year-old Nathaniel Root enlisted June 1 in Connecticut (Nathaniel H. Root PF S 18,573).

7. Samuel Benjamin PF S 31, 546.

8. Jabesh Gray PF S 43,643.

9. Samuel Couch PF S 29,717.

10. Abijah Lewis PF S 37,161.

11. Austin Wells PF S 32,054.

12. George Washington to Major General Philip Schuyler, June 17, 1776, Founders Online, National Archives, https://founders.archives.gov/documents/Washington/03-05-02-0016; originally published in *The Papers of George Washington*, Revolutionary War Series, vol. 5, *16 June 1776–12 August 1776*, ed. Philander D. Chase (Charlottesville: University Press of Virginia, 1993), 24–31.

13. George Washington to Jonathan Trumbull Sr. and Colonel Samuel Elmore, August 1, 1776, Founders Online, National Archives, https://founders.archives.gov/documents/Washington/03-05-02-0405; originally published in *The Papers of George Washington*, 5:540–41; George Washington to Colonel Samuel Elmore, August 7, 1776, Founders Online, National Archives, https://founders.archives.gov/documents/Washington/03-05-02-0449; originally published in *The Papers of George Washington*, 5:595–96.

14. Nathaniel H. Root PF S 18,573.

15. Austin Wells PF S 32,054.

16. Jabesh Gray PF S 43,643.

17. Nathaniel H. Root PF S 18,573.

18. Philip Schuyler, Saratoga, to John Hancock, November 19, 1776, Papers of the Continental Congress, Letters from General Schuyler, June 1775–December 1776, 2:497.

19. Email exchange, William Sawyer, Fort Stanwix, to William L. Kidder, November 3, 2022.

20. Heitman, *Historical Register*, 162; Robert Cochran, BLW 389–450-Lt-Col, issued August 4, 1791, Revolutionary War Pension and Bounty-Land Warrant Application Files, National Archives, NARA M804. While these may seem to be different men given the changes in geographic location, the accounts do not overlap, so it could be the same man.

21. The Vermont Historic Sites Commission erected a historical marker honoring Cochran in 1958 in Rupert, Vermont (Bennington County), on Vermont Route 153 at the Vermont–New York border. He is identified as Lieutenant Colonel Robert Cochran, the rank he attained after his service with the 3rd New York, a "Revolutionary Hero Settled Here, 1769." The inscription reads: "Condemned to death by the N.Y. Assembly, Col. Cochran fought the Yorkers for Vermont land grants. Joining the Green Mt. Boys, he was with Ethan Allen at Ticonderoga and Seth Warner at Crown Point. Later he commanded Continental forces in the Mohawk Valley campaigns and undertook dangerous espionage duties in Canada for the American cause."

22. Aaron Aorson was born in 1740 or 1741 in New York. He stood five feet, six inches tall and was a baker with a brown complexion. He married Altje Quakenbush, and by 1775 they had four children. The spelling of his name varies in documents (Aortis, Artoes, Austen), but he preferred Aorson. During the French and Indian War he served several years as a private in New York provincial troops beginning in 1759 at age eighteen. He was commissioned a first lieutenant in the first establishment 1st New York in June 1775 and took command of the company on December 31, 1775, after his captain was killed in the assault on Quebec City. Sypher, *New York State Society of the Cincinnati*, 8–9.

23. Gansevoort to Robert Cochran, December 1776, in Ranzan and Hollis, *Hero of Fort Schuyler*, 34. The date in December is not specified.

24. Revolutionary War Rolls, 1775–1783, 1776–1777, Elmore's Battalion, folder 206, NARA M246; Henry Curtis PF S 40,873. After the war he changed his name back to Curtis.

25. Jonathan Hunter PF S 39, 739.

26. James Warren PF S 45,452. In his pension application statement, Warren is off by a year in his dates.

27. This Captain Walker is not to be confused with the Captain Robert Walker whose company was part of Elmore's regiment. The Continental Congress authorized Colonel Lamb's Continental Artillery Regiment on January 1, 1777, for the third establishment army.

28. Watt and Morrison, *The British Campaign of 1777*, 108.

29. These included Abraham McKillip, Thomas Watkins, and William Williams, who served in Elmore's regiment until reenlisting in Savage's detachment in January 1777. See their Compiled Service Records, NARA M881. Ebenezer Temple had served in the Canadian campaign, joined Colonel Elmore's Regiment when it formed, and now reenlisted in the artillery (Ebenezer Temple PF S 14,658). Interestingly, a John Welch deserted from Elmore's regiment on June 15, 1776, and later a man with that name appears in the

artillery detachment. Were they the same man? Matross John Burroughs, who had been with Elmore since July 28, 1776, chose to reenlist on January 1 (John Burroughs PF S 22,667). Twenty-year-old Samuel Pangborn had enlisted in December 1776 at Saratoga Barracks (Samuel Pangborn PF S 43,778). Steven Hadlock from New Hampshire enlisted at Fort Stanwix after the detachment arrived there. He was twenty-nine years old and stood five feet, eight inches tall with brown hair, and gray eyes (Steven Hadlock NARA M881 Compiled Service Record). Ebenezer Temple later recalled that before his "time was out in the winter of 1777," he enlisted for the war in Captain Walker's company of artillery (Ebenezer Temple PF S 14,658). He had served in the Canadian campaign before enlisting in Elmore's regiment.

30. September 1, 1777, return of Fort Schuyler artillery stores signed by Savage, Horatio Gates Papers. A late June report noted only six "small" cannons and two fieldpieces, but by the end of August, a soldier noted in his journal that the fort had thirteen cannons. One description based on a variety of evidence states there were three cannons on the southwest bastion, four on the northwest bastion, three on the northeast, and four on the southeast. See Luzader, *Fort Stanwix*, 82, 36.

31. Graymont, *The Iroquois in the American Revolution*, 111–12; Taylor, *The Divided Ground*, 97.

32. Luzader, *Fort Stanwix*, 28–29.

33. Baldwin, *Revolutionary Journal*, 92, 94–95. Jeduthan Baldwin recorded in his journal on February 15 and 16 that "Capt. Marquize" and another French engineer were needed and had arrived at Albany, that on March 8, 1777, three French engineers came, and then on March 15 that the three French engineers left Ticonderoga. Who the three Frenchmen were is not known, but it is doubtful they included de Lamarquise.

34. Luzader, *Fort Stanwix*, 29–30.

35. Glatthaar and Martin, *Forgotten Allies*, 129.

36. Glatthaar and Martin, *Forgotten Allies*, 70, 89–90, 130–31, 144.

4. Creating a Third Establishment 3rd New York Regiment

1. Henry Tiebout was born in 1738 into a New York City Dutch family. He had married Margaret Hollock in the 1760s. In the spring of 1775, he joined a New York Sons of Liberty militia company, part of Colonel John Lasher's battalion. He had served in Lasher's battalion when it was upgraded to provincial regiment on January 29, 1776, then as second lieutenant, then first lieutenant on August 1, 1776, in the second establishment of the 1st New York Regiment. Sypher, *New York State Society of the Cincinnati*, 495–96.

2. *Journals of the Continental Congress*, 5:762–63. See also *Pennsylvania Gazette*, September 25, 1776. Congress used the term "battalions" rather than "regiments." The terms could be used interchangeably even though technically they could also refer to different types of units.

3. Several secondary sources say he participated at the siege of Havana in 1762 during the French and Indian War when he was only thirteen years old. This author has not seen any primary source reference to back that up, and

most biographical sketches do not mention it. If it is true, he quickly left military service for a dozen years until joining the Continentals in 1775.

4. Schuyler to Gansevoort, Fort George, June 9, 1776, in Ranzan and Hollis, *Hero of Fort Schuyler*, 17–18.

5. Horatio Gates to Gansevoort, Ticonderoga, July 17, 1776, in Ranzan and Hollis, *Hero of Fort Schuyler*, 24–25. This is just one of several letters relating to their struggle. See Ranzan and Hollis, *Hero of Fort Schuyler*, 25–31.

6. Luzader, *Saratoga*, xxiii; Corbett, *No Turning Point*, 210–11.

7. Gansevoort's brother Leonard, a prominent person in his own right, wrote the new colonel with advice on how to achieve success in his new position. Leonard Gansevoort to Peter Gansevoort, Albany, November 27, 1776, in Ranzan and Hollis, *Hero of Fort Schuyler*, 32.

8. For more detail on Gansevoort's career before assignment to Fort Stanwix, see Ranzan and Hollis, *Hero of Fort Schuyler*, 7–34.

9. See letters of Catherine Gansevoort Lansing in Baxter, *A Godchild of Washington*.

10. The most famous of his several taverns was the Province Arms at today's 115 Broadway, near Trinity Church.

11. Willett, *Willett Families of North America*, 111–13; Lowenthal, *Marinus Willett*, 10–11.

12. Lowenthal, *Marinus Willett*, 15; Berry and Morrison, *Marinus Willett*, 145,

13. Lowenthal, *Marinus Willett*, 15.

14. *New York Gazette, and Weekly Mercury*, October 19, 1772, 3. It appears that at this time he had a partner named Nixon.

15. *New York Gazette, and Weekly Mercury*, May 9, 1774, 3.

16. Berry and Morrison, *Marinus Willett*, 195.

17. Jones, *History of New York during the Revolutionary War*, 215. See also the biographical sketch of Willett at the website of the New York State Society of the Cincinnati, http://www.nycincinnati.org/Biographies.htm.

18. Bookstaver, *Willett Genealogy*, 36.

19. Lowenthal, *Marinus Willett*, 17; Willett, *Narrative*, 30.

20. This action was honored by the Sons of the American Revolution in 1892 when they placed a plaque at the site and in a 1907 painting by John Ward Dunmore. For more about it, see Willett, *Willett Families of North America*, 116–17; *New York Tribune*, November 26, 1892, 6.

21. Berry and Morrison, *Marinus Willett*, 36, 42. Like many families, the Willetts became divided in the growing dispute. Willett's father remained a steadfast Loyalist, returning to Jamaica on Long Island when the British occupied the area.

22. *Journals of the Provincial Congress*, 2:121.

23. *Calendar of Historical Manuscripts*, 2:16, 30, 33–34 (Mil. Commit. 25–845).

24. Heitman, *Historical Register*, 132; Sypher, *New York State Society of the Cincinnati*, 513. Van Bunschoten was born October 3, 1749, at Speckenkill, New York. He descended from a Dutch immigrant, Theunis Eliasen, who took the family name Van Bunschoten and first appears in records at Kingston, New York, in 1671. First lieutenant in Captain Lewis Du Bois's company,

commissioned June 28, 1775, he was promoted to captain November 25, 1775. Sypher, *New York State Society of the Cincinnati*, 513-14.

25. Gardner, "The New York Continental Line," 406.

26. "Officers Commissioned in the First Regiment in New York," in Force, *American Archives*, 4th ser., 3:708. This company had previously been known as the Bold Foresters. Alan C. Aimone and Eric I. Manders, "A Note on New York City's Independent Companies, 1775-1776," *New York History* 63, no. 1 (January 1982): 59-73; Schuyler, *Institution of the Society of the Cincinnati*, 311.

27. Leonard Bleeker was born on December 21, 1755, in New Rochelle, New York, descended from Dutch ancestors who came to New Amsterdam about 1658 and became prominent citizens owning farmland as well as land in town. His grandmother came from the powerful Schuyler family of Albany. The name is sometimes spelled Bleecker. He became second lieutenant on July 1, 1775, in Marinus Willett's company of the first establishment of the 1st New York Regiment. He became first lieutenant on May 14, 1776, in the second establishment of the 1st New York Regiment. Sypher, *New York State Society of the Cincinnati*, 32-34.

28. Cornelius Jansen was born in 1748 into a Dutch family settling early at Shawangunk, New York (Ulster County). On June 28, 1775, he became a first lieutenant in the first establishment of the 3rd New York Regiment and then a captain on June 26, 1776, in the second establishment of the 1st New York Regiment. Sypher, *New York State Society of the Cincinnati*, 237-38.

29. Gardner, "New York Continental Line," 405. See also Johnson, *The Campaign of 1776 Around New York and Brooklyn*, document 43, 139.

5. Recruiting and Training the 3rd New York Regiment

1. For a discussion of the types of men available for recruiting and the obstacles to enticing them to enlist, see Ruddiman, *Becoming Men of Some Consequence*, chap. 1, " 'The Eyes of All Our Countrymen Are Now Upon Us': Ambition, Coercion, and Choice in Joining the Army."

2. Sypher, *New York State Society of the Cincinnati*, 35.

3. Thomas De Witt was thirty-six, born in 1741 into an old, prominent Dutch family that came to New Amsterdam in the mid-seventeenth century. He was second lieutenant in June 1775 and then first lieutenant in the 1st Regiment of the Ulster County militia. He was first lieutenant in August 1775 in the first establishment and then the second establishment 3rd New York. He was promoted to captain June 26, 1776. Sypher, *New York State Society of the Cincinnati*, 128-29.

4. McClellan's NARA M881 Compiled Service Record gives him as enlisting in De Witt's company, but all other records show him in Tiebout's company for example, Christopher Hutton PF S 28,770.

5. February 28, 1777, letter from Lieutenant Colonel Marinus Willett acquainting the committee with the resignation of Major Goforth and recommending Ensign Hutton be placed high on the arrangement. *Calendar of Historical Manuscripts*, 2:10.

6. *Journals of the Provincial Congress*, 2:329. Willett wrote to Robert Harper, chairman of the Committee of Arrangements, on December 31, 1776, from Fishkill about Hutton. Schuyler, *Institution of the Society of the Cincinnati*, 235.

7. James Gregg was born at Little Britain, New York (Ulster County). His mother was connected to the important New York family that included Governor George Clinton and General James Clinton. He was not married. He had served as a second lieutenant, commissioned June 28, 1775, in the first establishment 3rd New York Regiment and then first lieutenant, commissioned June 26, 1776, in the second establishment Colonel Du Bois regiment. Sypher, *New York State Society of the Cincinnati*, 190–91.

8. Marinus Willett, Fishkill, to Peter Gansevoort, December 25, 1776, Calendar of the Military Papers of Peter Gansevoort, AO131, 103; hereafter Gansevoort Papers. Persee was sometimes spelled Pearcee or Pearcy. Willett had a partner in 1774 named Pearsey; see the *New York Gazette, and Weekly Mercury*, January 10, 1774, 4. For Captain Pearsee's military record, see his file in NARA M881, Compiled Service Records of Soldiers Who Served in the American Army during the Revolutionary War.

9. Peter Gansevoort to Marinus Willett, December 11, 1776, in Ranzan and Hollis, *Hero of Fort Schuyler*, 33.

10. Thomas Paine, *The American Crisis* (Philadelphia: Styner and Cist, December 19, 1776).

11. *Journals of the Continental Congress*, 5:762–63. See also *Pennsylvania Gazette*, September 25, 1776. Colonels qualified for 500 acres of land, a lieutenant colonel 450, a major 400, a captain 300, a lieutenant 200, and an ensign 150 acres.

12. Martin and Lender, "A Respectable Army," 96–97.

13. Martin and Lender, "A Respectable Army," 88–90.

14. Marinus Willett, Fishkill, to Peter Gansevoort, December 25, 1776, Gansevoort Papers, AO131, 103. George Fowler PF W 16,957 (Fowler was a sergeant in Gregg's company) confirms that Gregg's company was raised at Fishkill and fought at Peekskill and then Fort Stanwix. The officers given money were Captains Tiebout ($400), Van Bunschoten ($400), De Witt ($400), Jansen ($320), Swartwout ($280), and Gregg ($320), and Lieutenants Thomas Ostrander (Van Bunschoten's company, $200), Benjamin Bogardus (De Witt's, $240), Gilbert. B. Livingston (Swartwout's, $320), and James Du Bois (Jansen's, $160). Pounds and dollars often appear together because both types of currency were being used at the time.

15. Egly, *History of the First New York*, 39; *Journals of the Continental Congress*, November 12, 1776, 6:944–47.

16. Marinus Willett, Fishkill, to Peter Gansevoort, December 25, 1776, Gansevoort Papers AO131, 103–4.

17. James Kerr NARA M881 Compiled Service Record. Recruit John Peters had served in Captain John Cheeseman's company at the attempt on Quebec in 1775. Robert Glen and John/Joachim Frederick had served at Fort Ticonderoga in 1775. See their NARA M881 Compiled Service Records. Other men reenlisting from the 1st New York Regiment included Duncan Campbell, Jacob Harman, Jasper Stagg, Jacob Saylors/Sailor, twenty-six-year-old carpenter James Van Blarcum (who would later be promoted to sergeant), drummer George

Shell (who apparently did not continue as a musician in Tiebout's company), Henry Ash, Lewis Piper, and Ichabod Stoddard.

18. Ichabod Stoddard PF S 42,387. In his deposition, Tiebout states that the information on Stoddard comes from his size roll then in his possession in 1819. His Compiled Service Record references the Pay Roll for Captain Ledyard's company, March 1776.

19. Abraham Wright PF R 11,876. Wright recalled that he enlisted in November, but his service record shows December 3.

20. Each man is known through records in his NARA M881 Compiled Service Record.

21. Each man is known through records in his NARA M881 Compiled Service Record. See also Pay Roll for Captain Varick's company, February 24–March 31, 1776; Pay Roll of Captain David Lyon's company, March 31, 1776; Muster Roll of Captain Varick's company, October 6, 1775, at Ticonderoga; Muster Roll of Captain Quackenbos's company, September 20, 1775; Muster Roll of Captain Quackenbos's company, September 20, 1775; Pay Roll for Captain Ledyard's company, March 1776; Muster Roll of Captain Cheeseman's company, February 17, 1776; Muster Roll of Captain Ledyard's company, March 31, 1776.

22. Lockard Luce PF W 3,350. While recruiting had to be done only in New York, men native to other states could be enlisted if they were in New York at the time.

23. Willett, *Narrative*, 39.

24. The family name was originally Schryver, but during his life Peter apparently changed the spelling to Schriber. It is found in the records in several variations including Schriber, Scriber, Scriver, and Schryver.

25. *Calendar of Historical Manuscripts*, 1:71.

26. Information on the Schryver and Van Etten families is found in Burch, *Schryver Genealogy*.

27. Abraham Swartwout was born in 1743 in Poughkeepsie. He married Maria Polly North in 1764 at Poughkeepsie, and by 1776 they had four children. He had been a youthful lieutenant in the French and Indian War and then commissioned captain on April 27, 1776, in the second establishment 3rd New York Regiment. Sypher, *New York State Society of the Cincinnati*, 460-61.

28. Francis Chambers and Abraham Garrison NARA M881 Compiled Service Records.

29. Marinus Willett's Orderly Book, February 6, 1777.

30. Evert Lansing enlisted for three years on January 12. Jonathan Pinckney, an illiterate twenty-two-year-old laborer and veteran who, like several other recruits, had served in Captain Varick's company with Tiebout in 1776, enlisted for the war on January 23. That same day, illiterate thirty-three-year-old Kenneth Campbell, born in the Highlands of Scotland into a family that came to America in 1775, enlisted for the war. Evert Lansing NARA M881 Compiled Service Record; Jonathan Pinckney PF S43, 865; Kenneth Campbell PF S 44,726.

31. Croyle, "Future Manlius Postmaster." See also NARA M881 Compiled Service Record and Robert Wilson PF W 7,746.

32. Marinus Willett, Fishkill, to Peter Gansevoort, February 7, 1777, Gansevoort Papers, AO131, 105.
33. Willett, *Narrative*, 39.
34. Willett's Orderly Book, February 21, 1777.
35. Goring, *The Fishkill Supply Depot*, 20.
36. Marinus Willett, Fishkill, New York, to Peter Gansevoort, February 7, 1777, Gansevoort Papers, AO131, 105. Orders to captains to make such a return was repeated frequently, as on February 21, 1777. See Willett's Orderly Book, February 21, 1777.
37. William MacDougall, Peekskill, to ? (probably Schuyler), February 7, 1777, Philip Schuyler Papers.
38. Marinus Willett, Fishkill, to Philip Schuyler, February 18, 1777, Schuyler Papers.
39. Neagles, *Summer Soldiers*, 103, citing General Horatio Gates, Orderly Book, April 19–June 2, 1777.
40. Ward, *George Washington's Enforcers*, 40; Mayer, *Belonging to the Army*, 254–55.
41. The Tiebout company size roll was kept by Captain Tiebout, and he referred to it when he made his pension deposition for Ichabod Stoddard in 1819, when it was still in his possession.
42. Schuyler, *Institution of the Society of the Cincinnati*, 466.
43. Willett's Orderly Book, February 21, 1777.
44. *Journals of the Provincial Congress*, 1:831, 2:413.

6. Preparing to Relieve Elmore's Regiment

1. Philip Schuyler, Albany, to George Washington, March 25, 1777, Founders Online, National Archives, https://founders.archives.gov/documents/Washington/03-08-02-0685; originally published in *The Papers of George Washington*, Revolutionary War Series, vol. 8, *6 January 1777–27 March 1777*, ed. Frank E. Grizzard Jr. (Charlottesville: University Press of Virginia, 1998), 632–33.
2. This Fort Constitution at Peekskill should not be confused with the Fort Constitution at West Point.
3. Colonel Pierre Van Cortlandt, Fishkill, New York, to Colonel Peter Gansevoort, March 8, 1777, Gansevoort Papers, AO131, 107.
4. Four of those men came from the initial December 3 group, including 1st New York Regiment veterans Duncan Campbell, John or Joachim Frederick, and John Peters or Petris; also Lewis Piper, who had no known previous experience. There were in addition the two corporals who had joined the company on January 1, John Edgerley, a veteran of the old 1st New York Regiment, and Mark Karr, who had no known previous experience. Lastly, there was Peter Scriber. The long-term association experienced by these seven men and their captain was very unusual because not all the initial captains would serve through the full war, and the regiment would be restructured several times, transferring men from one unit to another. The third establishment Continental Army was not a consistent group of men. Both officers and men came and departed for a variety of official and unofficial reasons.

5. Peter Gansevoort, Albany, to Abraham Ten Broeck, Esquire, President of the Provincial Congress, March 17, 1777 (letter 1); circa March 17, 1777 (letter 2); and Peter Gansevoort, Albany, to Lieutenant Colonel Marinus Willett, circa March 17, 1777, Gansevoort Papers, AO131, 109, 110. While Willett and Gansevoort were forming their regiment on March 19, General Schuyler wrote to Colonel Samuel Elmore, who commanded the garrison at Fort Schuyler, seeking information about the officer who was in charge of remodeling the fort and making additional fortifications at that location. Schuyler had also been advised by Colonel Elmore to recommend to Colonel Gansevoort that he be friendly toward the Indians when he brought his regiment to the fort because "it is of consequence and helpful to the cause." General Schuyler to Colonel Samuel Elmore, March 19, Gansevoort Papers, AO131, 108.

6. Willett's Orderly Book; Willett, *Narrative*, 40.
7. Warren Roberts PF R 8,865.
8. Seth Rowley PF S 42,216 or W 24,777; Heitman, *Historical Register*, 530.
9. James Steward NARA M881 Compiled Service Record.
10. Henry Ritter PF S 19,449.
11. Jonathan Pinkney PF S 43,865.
12. Willett, *Narrative*, 41-42.
13. Nicholas Christman PF S 44,757; Barker, *Early Families of Herkimer County*.
14. See Lowenthal, *Days of Siege*, intro., 7-9, for information on this journal.
15. Peter Gansevoort, Albany, to Abraham Ten Broeck, Esq., March 31, 1777, Gansevoort Papers, AO131, 112; also *Journals of the Provincial Congress*, 2:432.
16. No muster rolls for this time period still exist. The numbers are figured from the evidence compiled and recorded in Broadhead, Fernow, and O'Callaghan, *Documents Relative to the Colonial History of New York*, vol. 15.

7. First Elements of the 3rd New York Regiment Arrive at Fort Stanwix

1. Samuel Benjamin PF S 31,546; Simeon Blin PF S 45,292.
2. Privates Jacob Harman and James Kerr of Tiebout's company, who had enlisted for the duration of the war on December 3 with the initial group of eighteen, deserted on April 7 and April 10, respectively, while new recruits Charles Jansen and Richard Welch enlisted for the war on April 26 and 27. NARA M881 Compiled Service Records. Captain Van Bunschoten encouragingly had six men enlist during April, but four of them deserted the day following their enlistment. Similarly, Captain De Witt gained four men and lost one, while Captain Jansen gained five, but two of them, along with another man, deserted before the end of the month. Captain Swartwout gained just two men, and Captain Bleeker added six. While those companies at least gained a small number of men, Captain Gregg recruited just one man but lost four to desertion for an overall negative change. Broadhead, Fernow, and O'Callaghan, *Documents Relative to the Colonial History of New York*, 15:197-209.
3. Jacob Saylor NARA M881 Compiled Service Record.
4. Willett's Orderly Book, April 22, 1777.

5. Marinus Willett, Fort Constitution, to the Convention of the State of New York, April 9, 1777, *Journals of the Provincial Congress*, 2:438.

6. Broadhead, Fernow, and O'Callaghan, *Documents Relative to the Colonial History of New York*, 15:138, 140; Sypher, *New York State Society of the Cincinnati*, 32–33; NARA M881, Compiled Service Records of Soldiers Who Served in the American Army During the Revolutionary War, shows a John Houston who served in the second establishment 2nd New York Regiment as a second lieutenant but nothing further. He either simply resigned or did defect to the British.

7. Sypher, *New York State Society of the Cincinnati*, 36–37.

8. Willett's Orderly Book, April 7, 1777.

9. Willett's Orderly Book, April 25, 1777.

10. Captain Bernard Lamarquisie, Schenectady, to Colonel G. Van Schaick commanding at Albany, April 9, 1777, Horatio Gates Papers. His name appears in various sources as de la Marquisie, de la Marquise, Lamarquise, Marquise, or Marquisie.

11. Austin Wells PF S 32,054; Samuel Benjamin PF S 31,546; Samuel Dickinson PF W 16,955; Simeon Blin PF S 45,292; Samuel Doty PF S 45, 326; Jabesh Gray PF S 43,643; Samuel Drew PF S 45,338.

12. Joseph Eldridge PF S 44,814.

13. Bernard De Lamarquisie, Fort Schuyler, to General Schuyler, April 30, 1777, Papers of the Continental Congress, [Miscellaneous] Letters Addressed to Congress, 1775–89, 15:181. This letter is written in French, and he signs himself B. De Lamarquisie. For his commission in the Continental Army, see *Journals of the Continental Congress*, August 29, 1776, 5:715.

14. James Elmore, Fort Schuyler, to General Schuyler, April 22, 1777, Papers of the Continental Congress, Letters from General Schuyler, January 1777–June 1785, 3:126.

15. Horatio Gates, Albany, to Peter Gansevoort, April 24 and 26, 1777, in Ranzan and Hollis, *Hero of Fort Schuyler*, 40.

16. Luzader, Torres, and Carroll, *Fort Stanwix*, 102.

17. Peter Gansevoort [Fort Schuyler] to Major General Philip Schuyler, June 15, 1777, Gansevoort Papers, A0131, 121. Delyrod occasionally appears as Degrau in some records.

18. Luzader, Torres, and Carroll, *Fort Stanwix*, 97.

19. Scott, *Fort Stanwix and Oriskany*, 99–100, citing Horatio Gates Papers.

8. Colonel Gansevoort Takes Command of Fort Stanwix

1. Peter Gansevoort, Fort Stanwix, to John G. Van Schaick, May 5, 1777, Gansevoort Papers, AO131, 112.

2. Ranzan and Hollis, *Hero of Fort Schuyler*, 40.

3. Willett's Orderly Book, April 24, 1777.

4. John Fink/Hans Finkanover PF R 3,549. He does not mention the stop at Fort Dayton and the several weeks De Witt's company stayed there.

5. William Fink PF S 23,218.

6. On May 6, twenty-four-year-old Michael Myers of German Flats, which lay on Willett's route, joined Tiebout's company as a sergeant. Those enlisting for the war in Tiebout's company included Philip Burch, Joseph Cornwell, Oliver Russel, Benjamin Van Eury/Every, and George Shall. NARA M881, Compiled Service Records. Tiebout also picked up several men for three years, including Corporals Abraham Van Dusen and William Haburn; Privates James Cowen, Stephen Sabine, twenty-two-year-old Luke Crandell (Luke Crandell W16931), eighteen-year-old 1st New York Regiment veteran Lawrence Schoolcraft (Compiled Service Record, PF S 4,226 or R 9,267), his son, and twenty-five-year-old Thomas Searles (NARA M881 Compiled Service Record).

7. Albert Acker PF R 15. In his pension file he mistakenly said he enlisted in 1776. Acker is a bit of a mystery, and it is hard to tell if he is truthful in his pension application deposition or if he deserted March 1, 1781, as his service record shows.

8. Broadhead, Fernow, and O'Callaghan, *Documents Relative to the Colonial History of New York*, vol. 15.

9. Joseph Hess/Han Jost Hess PF S 44,926. He was known by several similar names. His service record gives his name as John Uthest and has him wounded and in the hospital after the siege and, after several months, back on full duty.

10. Willett's Orderly Book, May 9–10, 1777.

11. Glatthaar and Martin, *Forgotten Allies*, 151.

12. Colonel Gansevoort garrison orders, Fort Stanwix, May 5, 1777, Gansevoort Papers, AO131, 113; Ranzan and Hollis, *Hero of Fort Schuyler*, 41.

13. Lowenthal, *Days of Siege*, 11.

14. Leonard Gansevoort, Albany, to Peter Gansevoort, May 17, 1777, in Ranzan and Hollis, *Hero of Fort Schuyler*, 42–43.

15. Willett's Orderly Book, May 12, 1777; Willett, *Narrative*, 42. In his *Narrative* he gives the departure date from Fort Constitution as May 18. Leonard Gansevoort, Albany, to Peter Gansevoort, May 17, 1777, in Ranzan and Hollis, *Hero of Fort Schuyler*, 43.

16. Willett's Orderly Book, May 12–20, 1777.

17. Joseph Purchase NARA M881 Compiled Service Record.

18. Willett's Orderly Book, May 20, 1777.

19. Henry Ritter PF S 19,449.

20. William Smith enlisted for the war on May 22 (William Smith NARA M881 Compiled Service Record). The next day, David Every, who had previously served for about three months in the first establishment 3rd New York in 1775 before deserting, enlisted in Tiebout's company for three years or the war (David Every NARA M881 Compiled Service Record). John Pearson enlisted for the war on May 24 (John Pearson NARA M881 Compiled Service Record Bounty Land Warrant 2486-120).

21. Conrad Friday (NARA M881 Compiled Service Record); deposed for Solomon Smith PF S 34,495 of Captain Scythe's company. PF S 43,564 does not appear to be the same man. John Lansing NARA M881 Compiled Service Record and PF W 16,627 is also not him.

22. Willett's Orderly Book, April 26, 1777.

23. Sypher, *New York State Society of the Cincinnati*, 473-74.

24. Details of this incident are drawn from Court of Inquiry order, Fort Dayton, May 25, 1777, Robert Cochran, Schuyler Papers.

25. Major Robert Cochran, Fort Dayton, to General Gates, May 26, 1777, Horatio Gates Papers.

26. Lender and Martin, *Citizen Soldier*, 13.

27. For more on Defendorff and references, see Philip D. Weaver, "Henry Defendorff: A Very Intelligent Man," *Journal of the American Revolution*, March 13, 2017, https://allthingsliberty.com/2017/03/henry-defendorff-intelligent-man/.

28. Christian Shell PF R 9,253.

29. Ranzan and Hollis, *Hero of Fort Schuyler*, 42.

30. *Journals of the Continental Congress*, 7:361, 8:375. Note that even this official document used the name Fort Stanwix instead of Schuyler.

31. Scott, *Fort Stanwix and Oriskany*, 99, citing Horatio Gates Papers.

32. Willett's Orderly Book, May 28, 1777; Willett, *Narrative*, 42. In his *Narrative*, Willett says he got to Stanwix on May 29. Lowenthal, *Days of Siege*, 12, gives the arrival date as May 28.

33. Watt and Morrison, *The British Campaign of 1777*, 116-17.

34. Patrick Mahan NARA M881 Compiled Service Record; BLW 7498-100-August 24, 1790, pvt. NY Line; NARA M853, Numbered Record Books, vol. 5, List of New York Troops, 1776-1783.

35. Henry Ritter PF S 19,449. See also his support statement for Christian Shell PF R 9,253.

36. Hanson and Hsu, *Casemates and Cannonballs*, 27; Luzader, Torres, and Carroll, *Fort Stanwix*, 94.

37. Willett, *Narrative*, 43.

38. Peter Gansevoort to Horatio Gates, ca. May 22, 1777, Gansevoort Papers, A0131, 114-15.

39. Willett, *Narrative*, 44.

40. Hanson and Hsu, *Casemates and Cannonballs*, 21-27.

41. Willett, *Narrative*, 44; Lowenthal, *Days of Siege*, 29.

42. Willett, *Narrative*, 45.

43. Glatthaar and Martin, *Forgotten Allies*, 151-52.

44. Luzader, Torres, and Carroll, *Fort Stanwix*, 79; Gansevoort to Gates, May 23, 1777, Gansevoort Papers, AO131, 114-15. See also Ranzan and Hollis, *Hero of Fort Schuyler*, 44.

45. Luzader, Torres, and Carroll, *Fort Stanwix*, 79; order signed by Col. P. Gansevoort, May 26, 1777, Miscellaneous American Revolution, New York State Library, Albany.

46. Scott, *Fort Stanwix and Oriskany*, 98, citing the Schuyler Papers.

47. Watt and Morrison, *The British Campaign of 1777*, 108.

48. Willett's Orderly Book, May 30, 1777.

49. Lowenthal, *Days of Siege*, 12-13.

50. Watt, *Rebellion in the Mohawk Valley*, 70-71; Luzader, *Saratoga*, 121, 124; Weddle, *The Compleat Victory*, 178-79.

51. Schnitzer and Troiani, *Campaign to Saratoga*, 22.

52. For more information on British officer ranks, see Don N. Hagist, "Untangling British Officer Ranks," *Journal of the American Revolution*, May 19, 2016, https://allthingsliberty.com/2016/05/untangling-british-army-ranks/. See also Schnitzer and Troiani, *Campaign to Saratoga*, 18, 90.

53. Taylor, *The Divided Ground*, 46-52, 88, and passim for much more on the life of Brant. See also Graymont, *The Iroquois in the American Revolution*, 52-53.

54. Glatthaar and Martin, *Forgotten Allies*, 117; Luzader, *Fort Stanwix*, 43.

55. Scott, *Fort Stanwix and Oriskany*, 240; Watt and Morrison, *The British Campaign of 1777*, 18.

56. Glatthaar and Martin, *Forgotten Allies*, 70, 89-90, 130, 144.

57. Peter Gansevoort to Mister Spencer at Oneida, May 22, 1777, Gansevoort Papers, AO131, 114.

58. Lowenthal, *Days of Siege*, 15.

59. Luzader, *Fort Stanwix*, 46, citing Gansevoort to Schuyler, July 4, 1777, Schuyler Papers.

60. Willett, *Narrative*, 46.

61. Willett's Orderly Book, May 30, 1777.

62. Glatthaar and Martin, *Forgotten Allies*, 104-5.

63. Glatthaar and Martin, *Forgotten Allies*, 125.

64. Lowenthal, *Days of Siege*, 12.

65. List of New York Troops, 1776-1783, NARA M853, Numbered Records Books Concerning Military Operations and Service, Pay and Settlement of Accounts, and Supplies in the War Department Collection of Revolutionary War Records, 5:52; NARA M881, Compiled Service Records of Soldiers Who Served in the American Army During the Revolutionary War.

9. Dealing with Too Many Needs and Dangers

1. Lowenthal, *Days of Siege*, 13-14, 16, citing Sir John Johnson's orderly book, June 6, 1777, Lachine. See also Luzader, *Saratoga*, 122.

2. Peter Gansevoort, Fort Schuyler, to John G. Van Schaick, June 1, 1777, in Ranzan and Hollis, *Hero of Fort Schuyler*, 46-47.

3. Peter Gansevoort, Fort Schuyler, to Catherine Van Schaick, June 5, 1777, in Ranzan and Hollis, *Hero of Fort Schuyler*, 47.

4. Peter Gansevoort, Fort Schuyler, to Major General Philip Schuyler, June 15, 1777, Gansevoort Papers, A0131, 121-22.

5. Peter Gansevoort, Fort Schuyler, to Major General Philip Schuyler, June 27, 1777, Gansevoort Papers, A0131, 127. For further details, see John Lansing Junior, Headquarters, Albany, to [Peter Gansevoort], March 10, 1777, Gansevoort Papers, A0131, 120; and General Philip Schuyler, Albany, to Peter Gansevoort, June 10, 1777, Gansevoort Papers, A0131, 120.

6. Peter Gansevoort, Fort Schuyler, to Major General Philip Schuyler, June 15, 1777, Gansevoort Papers, A0131, 121-22.

7. Willett's Orderly Book, June 16, 1777.

8. Major General Philip Schuyler, Albany, to Colonel Peter Gansevoort, June 9, 1777, Gansevoort Papers, A0131, 118.

9. Peter Gansevoort, Fort Schuyler, to Major General Philip Schuyler, June 15, 1777, Gansevoort Papers, A0131, 121.

10. Peter Gansevoort, Fort Schuyler, to Major General Philip Schuyler, June 15, 1777, Gansevoort Papers, A0131, 121.

11. Luzader, Torres, and Carroll, *Fort Stanwix*, 104–8; Hanson and Hsu, *Casemates and Cannonballs*, 21–27, 33–38.

12. Peter Gansevoort, Fort Schuyler, to Major General Philip Schuyler, June 15, 1777, Gansevoort Papers, A0131, 121.

13. Hanson and Hsu, *Casemates and Cannonballs*, 17–29.

14. Willett's Orderly Book, June 24, 1777.

15. Peter Gansevoort, Fort Schuyler, to Catherine Van Schaick, June 23, 1777, in Ranzan and Hollis, *Hero of Fort Schuyler*, 53.

16. Luzader, Torres, and Carroll, *Fort Stanwix*, 77, 79; Scott, *Fort Stanwix and Oriskany*, 131.

17. Philip Schuyler to —— Lewis, June 6, 1777, Schuyler Papers; Peter Gansevoort to Philip Schuyler, July 3, 1777, Gansevoort Papers, AO131, 134–35; Luzader, Torres, and Carroll, *Fort Stanwix*, 78–79; Philip Schuyler to Peter Gansevoort, June 9, 1777, Gansevoort Papers, A0131, 118.

18. Willett's Orderly Book, June 2, 1777.

19. Peter Gansevoort, Fort Schuyler, to Major General Philip Schuyler, June 15, 1777, Gansevoort Papers, A0131, 121

20. Willett's Orderly Book, June 13, 1777; Philip Schuyler, Albany, to Peter Gansevoort, June 9, 1777, Gansevoort Papers, A0131, 118.

21. Leonard Gansevoort, Albany, to Peter Gansevoort, June 13, 1777, in Ranzan and Hollis, *Hero of Fort Schuyler*, 50; Watt and Morrison, *The British Campaign of 1777,* 117.

22. Joseph Savage NARA M881 Compiled Service Record, citing a document of June 27, 1777, of items delivered to Savage from "Colo Lamb's Regimt Artillery to the Public Store of Cloathing at Albany Dr."

23. Philip Schuyler, Albany, to Peter Gansevoort, June 9, 1777, Gansevoort Papers, A0131, 118; Willett's Orderly Book, June 2, 1777.

24. On June 1, John Duncan Smith joined the company as a sergeant (John Duncan Smith NARA M881 Compiled Service Record), and during that week John Connelly, Benjamin Cummings, and Jeremiah Roobach enlisted for the war. Over the next two weeks, John Coventry and William McCormick enlisted for the war, and Steven Miller and John Smith enlisted for three years (NARA M881 Compiled Service Record).

25. Samuel Vader PF S 11,655. His NARA M881 Compiled Service Records use the name Samuel Veeder, and he sometimes appears as Veder. There is no evidence that he knew Peter Scriber, but it is certainly possible.

26. John Dop/Dops PF R 3,018.

27. Alexander Lemmon, PF S 4,1761.

28. John Connelly and Benjamin Cummings had enlisted early in the month but deserted on June 5 and 24, respectively. Connelly spent only one day on the roster. John Coventry, who had enlisted perhaps on June 11, also deserted the next day. William Smith had enlisted for the war on May 22 but deserted on June 10 (William Smith NARA M881 Compiled Service Record).

David Van Every, who had enlisted for three years or the duration of the war the day after William Smith, deserted the same day (David Van Every NARA M881 Compiled Service Record). Benjamin Van Eury, who had enlisted for the war in May, also deserted with him (Benjamin Van Eury NARA M881 Compiled Service Record).

29. Peter Genious NARA M881 Compiled Service Record; List of New York Troops, 1776–1783, NARA M853, Numbered Records Books Concerning Military Operations and Service, Pay and Settlement of Accounts, and Supplies in the War Department Collection of Revolutionary War Records, 5:52.

30. Timothy Scott NARA M881 Compiled Service Record.

31. Watt and Morrison, *The British Campaign of 1777*, 154, citing information researched by Lee Hansen, the first superintendent of the Fort Stanwix National Historic Site, published in the *Fort Stanwix Garrison Newsletter* 6, no. 3 (March 1982).

32. Willett's Orderly Book, June 15, 1777; Philip Schuyler, Albany, to Peter Gansevoort, June 9, 1777, Gansevoort Papers, A0131, 118.

33. Willett's Orderly Book, June 5, 1777.

34. Willett's Orderly Book, June 8, 1777. William Grimsby has not been found in the records.

35. Willett's Orderly Book, June 11, 1777.

36. Willett's Orderly Book, June 28, 1777.

37. Lender and Martin, *Citizen Soldier*, 90; Neimeyer, *America Goes to War*, 139; Luzader, Torres, and Carroll, *Fort Stanwix*, 96; Hanson and Hsu, *Casemates and Cannonballs*, 46; Ward, *George Washington's Enforcers*, 154, 162–63.

38. A Timeline History of the Oneida Carry, Fort Stanwix National Monument, https://www.nps.gov/articles/000/a-timeline-history-of-the-oneida-carry.htm.

39. The details of the Gregg incident have been told in various ways, and some information is contradictory. The sources for the Gregg story given here include Lowenthal, *Days of Siege*; Watt, *Rebellion in the Mohawk Valley*; and Luzader, *Saratoga*. See also Connie Myer, "Manlius War Hero Received British Flag," *Syracuse Post-Standard*, July 4, 1967; and Croyle, "A Future Postmaster." Young Robert Wilson continued to serve in the New York Line and played an interesting role at the Yorktown surrender of Lord Cornwallis. Two articles about that event also tell the story of this incident at Fort Stanwix based on records at the Onondaga Historical Association: Adam Happal PF R 4584, support statement of Captain Leonard Bleeker; and Timothy Dwight, "A Dog's Fidelity," in *A Library of American Literature, from the Earliest Settlement to the Present Time*, ed. Edmund Clarence Stedman and Ellen Mackay Hutchinson (New York: Charles L. Webster & Company, 1891), also at www.bartleby.com/poem/400, accessed April 17, 2023.

40. Willett, *Narrative*, 47. For the Gregg incident, see Thacher, *Military Journal*, 136–37; Lowenthal, *Days of Siege*, 16; Aaron Osborn PF W 4558. According to Aaron Osborn's wife, Gregg credited the button on his hat with preventing more serious damage to his head from the Indian tomahawk.

41. Sypher, *New York State Society of the Cincinnati*, 591.

42. Philip Conine Jr., Fort Stanwix, to Leonard Bronck, June 27, 1777, in Beecher, *Letters from a Revolution*, 18; Stone, *Life of Joseph Brant*, 226–28; Scott, *Fort Stanwix and Oriskany*, 132–33; Lowenthal, *Days of Siege*, 16.

43. *New York Gazette, and Weekly Mercury*, August 4, 1777, 2.

44. Samuel Mott PF S 40,178. See also his NARA M881 Compiled Service Record.

45. Glatthaar and Martin, *Forgotten Allies*, 48-49, 55-56; Taylor, *The Divided Ground*, 54; Graymont, *The Iroquois in the American Revolution*, 33.

46. Taylor, *The Divided Ground*, 67-68. Kirkland, like Mohawk leader Joseph Brant, had attended the Connecticut school of Reverend Eleazar Wheelock and then the College of New Jersey, now Princeton University, before becoming a missionary and taking up residence at Kanonwalohale. See Taylor, *The Divided Ground*, for extensive information about the work of Kirkland and Joseph Brant, who had been friends but split over allegiance to the king. See also Graymont, *The Iroquois in the American Revolution*, for more on the work of Kirkland.

47. Glatthaar and Martin, *Forgotten Allies*, 152; Scott, *Fort Stanwix and Oriskany*, 133-34.

48. Jones, *Annals and Recollections of Oneida County*, 331; Robertaccio, *Documents Relating*, 26. A receipt signed by John Butler indicates that the chief received ten dollars each for the two scalps.

49. Philip Schuyler, Albany, to Peter Gansevoort, June 30, 1777, Gansevoort Papers, AO131, 129.

10. Danger Builds for Soldiers and Civilians Alike

1. Peter Gansevoort, Fort Schuyler, to Philip Schuyler, July 4, 1777, in Ranzan and Hollis, *Hero of Fort Schuyler*, 58.

2. Peter Gansevoort, Fort Schuyler, to Philip Schuyler, July 3, 1777, Gansevoort Papers, AO131, 134-35; Ranzan and Hollis, *Hero of Fort Schuyler*, 57.

3. Philip Schuyler to Peter Gansevoort, July 10, 1777, Schuyler Papers; Luzader, Torres, and Carroll, *Fort Stanwix*, 78.

4. Peter Gansevoort, to Philip Schuyler, July 3, 1777, Gansevoort Papers, AO131, 134-35; Ranzan and Hollis, *Hero of Fort Schuyler*, 57; Scott, *Fort Stanwix and Oriskany*, 134-35.

5. Peter Gansevoort, Fort Schuyler, to Philip Schuyler, July 4, 1777, in Ranzan and Hollis, *Hero of Fort Schuyler*, 58.

6. Lowenthal, *Days of Siege*, 16; Peter Gansevoort, Fort Schuyler, to John G. Van Schaick, July 5, 1777, Gansevoort Papers, AO131, 138; Willett, *Narrative*, 48; Watt, *Rebellion in the Mohawk Valley*, 79, 86-88; Glatthaar and Martin, *Forgotten Allies*, 153; John Spoor PF W 25,065. Spoor was "detained about six months, and had his commission taken from him." Private Joel Ackley PF S 33,959 states that he was taken prisoner near the fort but gives no details or date other than that he was taken to Canada and held for over three years before being exchanged and rejoining his company, then in the 1st New York Regiment. Watt and Morrison, *The British Campaign of 1777*, 147.

7. Nicholas P. Bovee PF W 16,916.

8. John Jones NARA M881 Compiled Service Record; Conrad Frantz NARA M881 Compiled Service Record.

9. Watt and Morrison, *The British Campaign of 1777*, 149.

10. Conrad Frans/Frantz PF S 44,862 W 17,927, 38; Thomas Wilson NARA M881 Compiled Service Record.

11. Peter Gansevoort, Fort Schuyler, to Philip Schuyler, July 4, Gansevoort Papers, AO131, 136; Scott, *Fort Stanwix and Oriskany*, 136-37.

12. "Extract of a Letter from Fort Stanwix, Dated the 4th Instant," *Virginia Gazette* (Williamsburg), July 25, 1777. The publication of this letter in Virginia is an example of how people far from a situation or action could be aware of such incidents even on the frontier.

13. Peter Gansevoort, Fort Schuyler, to Catherine Van Schaick, July 5, 1777, in Ranzan and Hollis, *Hero of Fort Schuyler*, 59.

14. Luzader, *Fort Stanwix*, 44; Luzader, *Fort Stanwix*, 122-23; Scott, *Fort Stanwix and Oriskany*, 123; Watt, *Rebellion in the Mohawk Valley*, 86-88.

15. Leonard Gansevoort, Albany, to Peter Gansevoort, July 9, 1777, in Ranzan and Hollis, *Hero of Fort Schuyler*, 61.

16. Colonel Gansevoort, Fort Schuyler, to Catherine Van Schaick, July 12, 1777, in Ranzan and Hollis, *Hero of Fort Schuyler*, 62.

17. *Independent Chronicle and Universal Advertiser* (Boston), July 17, 1777, 1.

18. *Connecticut Gazette; and Universal Intelligencer* (New London), July 25, 1777, 2.

19. *Independent Chronicle and Universal Advertiser* (Boston), July 24, 1777, 1.

20. *Pennsylvania Gazette* (Philadelphia), Wednesday, July 30, 1777, 2.

21. Weddle, *The Compleat Victory*, 146.

22. Graymont, *The Iroquois in the American Revolution*, 117-18.

23. Daniel Claus, report to Secretary Knox, October 16, 1777, in Broadhead, Fernow, and O'Callaghan, *Documents Relative to the Colonial History of New York*, 8:719; Graymont, *The Iroquois in the American Revolution*, 125-26.

24. Watt and Morrison, *The British Campaign of 1777*, 65, 79, 150.

25. "Extract of a Letter from Fort Stanwix, Dated the 4th Instant," *Virginia Gazette* (Williamsburg), July 25, 1777.

26. Sypher, *New York State Society of the Cincinnati*, 302-3.

27. Philip Schuyler to John Hancock, July 5, 1777, in Papers of the Continental Congress, Transcripts of Letters from Maj. Gen. Philip Schuyler, 1776-1781, 2:195.

28. Peter Gansevoort, Fort Schuyler, to Philip Schuyler, July 4, 1777, in Ranzan and Hollis, *Hero of Fort Schuyler*, 58.

29. Watt and Morrison, *The British Campaign of 1777*, 1:117.

30. Lowenthal, *Days of Siege*, 17. This entry raises questions about the authorship of the diary.

31. Jeremiah Roobach, who had enlisted in Tiebout's company on June 4 for the duration of the war, deserted on July 1, and John Lansing, who enlisted for the war on May 25, deserted on July 3 (Jeremiah Roobach and John Lansing NARA M881 Compiled Service Records). Charles Jansen, who had enlisted for the war on April 26, deserted on July 25 (Charles Jansen NARA M881 Compiled Service Record).

32. Willett's Orderly Book, July 20, 1777.

33. Willett's Orderly Book, July 19, 1777.

34. Willett, *Narrative*, 49; Luzader, *Fort Stanwix*, 33, citing Philip Schuyler to Peter Gansevoort, July 10, 1777, Schuyler Papers.

35. Lowenthal, *Days of Siege*, 20.

36. *Mohawk Valley in the Revolution*, document 74, 121–24.

37. George Washington, Ramapo, to General Philip Schuyler, July 24, 1777, Founders Online, National Archives, https://founders.archives.gov/documents/Hamilton/01-01-02-0226, originally published in *The Papers of Alexander Hamilton*, vol. 1, *1768–1778*, ed. Harold C. Syrett (New York: Columbia University Press, 1961), 291.

38. Willett's Orderly Book, July 25, 1777.

39. Lowenthal, *Days of Siege*, 18.

40. Peter Gansevoort, Fort Schuyler, to Philip Schuyler, July 26, 1777, in Ranzan and Hollis, *Hero of Fort Schuyler*, 63.

41. Philip Conine Jr., Fort Stanwix, to Leonard Bronck, July 27, 1777, in Beecher, *Letters from a Revolution*, 18–19.

42. Lowenthal, *Days of Siege*, 19; Simms, *Frontiersmen of New York*, 2:28, 244; Watt, *Rebellion in the Mohawk Valley*, 136–37, citing Fort Stanwix Document Collection, document 14250, believed to have been written by Colonel Peter Gansevoort, possibly sent to the Tryon Committee about July 29 with the intent of arousing the population to oppose the British and Loyalists. John Steere's name often appears as Steene or Steeve.

43. Willett, *Narrative*, 48; Lowenthal, *Days of Siege*, 19 (Gansevoort's letter to Colonel Van Schaick); Scott, *Stanwix and Oriskany*, 162.

44. Lowenthal, *Days of Siege*, 20.

45. John Roof PF S 14,371. This is the pension file of John Roof, son of our John Roof, who joined the militia himself when he turned eighteen in 1778. Additional documented genealogical information on the Roof family is available at Ancestry.com. Another son, Nicholas, was born in 1762 but may have died young. Simms, *Frontiersmen of New York*, 2:91; Watt, *Rebellion in the Mohawk Valley*, 231.

46. Lowenthal, *Days of Siege*, 20; Willett's Orderly Book, July 29, 1777.

47. Nicholas Herkimer, Canajohary [sic], to Peter Gansevoort, July 29, 1777, in Ranzan and Hollis, *Hero of Fort Schuyler*, 66–67; Scott, *Stanwix and Oriskany*, 165; Gansevoort Papers, AO131, 152.

48. Lowenthal, *Days of Siege*, 20–21.

49. Henry Shell PF R 9,253; Lowenthal, *Days of Siege*, 20–21.

50. Lowenthal, *Days of Siege*, 20–21; Watt, *Rebellion in the Mohawk Valley*, 99–100. Scott, *Fort Stanwix and Oriskany*, appendix 4, points out that Wesson's regiment may well have included several Black soldiers, as was true of most Massachusetts regiments.

51. Lowenthal, *Days of Siege*, 21; Watt and Morrison, *The British Campaign of 1777*, 110.

52. Thomas Spencer, Oneida, to Peter Gansevoort, July 28, 1777, in Ranzan and Hollis, *Hero of Fort Schuyler*, 66.

53. Thomas Spencer, Oneida, to Peter Gansevoort, July 29, 1777, in Ranzan and Hollis, *Hero of Fort Schuyler*, 67.

11. St. Leger's Troops Begin Their Siege

1. Willett, *Narrative*, 49.
2. Willett's Orderly Book, August 1, 1777.
3. Willett's Orderly Book, August 1, 1777; Lowenthal, *Days of Siege*, 22.
4. Willett's Orderly Book, August 1, 1777; Lowenthal, *Days of Siege*, 22.
5. Luzader, Torres, and Carroll, *Fort Stanwix*, 78; Philip Schuyler to Congress, August 8, 1777, Schuyler Papers; Papers of the Continental Congress, Letters from General Schuyler, 3:236; Philip Schuyler to John Hancock, August 8, 1777, Papers of the Continental Congress, Transcripts of Letters from Maj. Gen. Philip Schuyler, 1776-1781, 2:212-19.
6. Luzader, Torres, and Carroll, *Fort Stanwix*, 78; Philip Schuyler to Congress, August 8, 1777, Schuyler Papers.
7. Luzader, Torres, and Carroll, *Fort Stanwix*, 78; Peter Gansevoort to Horatio Gates, December 12, 1777, Gansevoort Papers, AO131, 184.
8. Lowenthal, *Days of Siege*, 24.
9. This regiment had previously been the 9th Massachusetts Regiment, the 26th Continental in the second establishment, and then combined with the 21st Continental and known as Wesson's regiment for the third establishment on January 1, 1777.
10. Willett, *Narrative*, 50.
11. Watt, *Rebellion in the Mohawk Valley*, 126.
12. Glatthaar and Martin, *Forgotten Allies*, 157, citing testimony of Cornelius Doxtader, Draper MS, 11 U 202-204 (1980, R57), State Historical Society of Wisconsin, Madison.
13. Glatthaar and Martin, *Forgotten Allies*, 149-50.
14. Glatthaar and Martin, *Forgotten Allies*, 171-73.
15. Jacobson, "Battlefield Delineation," 39; Glatthaar and Martin, *Forgotten Allies*, 158-59.
16. Lowenthal, *Days of Siege*, 24; Schoolcraft, *Historical Considerations*, 7; Watt, *Rebellion in the Mohawk Valley*, 127.
17. Henry Ritter PF S 19,449.
18. Willett, *Narrative*, 49; Luzader, Torres, and Carroll, *Fort Stanwix*, 101.
19. Hanson and Hsu, *Casemates and Cannonballs*, 27-32; Luzader, Torres, and Carroll, *Fort Stanwix*, 100-102.
20. Willett, *Narrative*, 50.
21. Lowenthal, *Days of Siege*, 26; Luzader, Torres, and Carroll, *Fort Stanwix*, 99, 144.
22. Watt, *Rebellion in the Mohawk Valley*, 127.
23. For the diary of First Lieutenant Philipp Jakob Hildebrandt, see Retzer and Barker, "Hessen-Hanau Jägers," 36-37.
24. Watt, *Rebellion in the Mohawk Valley*, 127-28; Retzer and Barker, "Hessen-Hanau Jägers," 36; Jacobson, "Battlefield Delineation," 37.
25. Schoolcraft, *Historical Considerations*, 7.
26. Schoolcraft, *Historical Considerations*, 8-9.
27. Schnitzer and Troiani, *Campaign to Saratoga*, 93, 101.
28. Scott, *Fort Stanwix and Oriskany*, 235.

29. Lowenthal, *Days of Siege*, 15, 26.
30. Watt and Morrison, *The British Campaign of 1777*, 81; Berleth, *Bloody Mohawk*, 161.
31. Samuel Veeder PF S 11,655. Sometimes the name is spelled Vader.
32. Hanson and Hsu, *Casemates and Cannonballs*, 32–33.
33. Luzader, Torres, and Carroll, *Fort Stanwix*, 102–4; Hanson and Hsu, *Casemates and Cannonballs*, 41.
34. Lowenthal, *Days of Siege*, 26.
35. Watt, *Rebellion in the Mohawk Valley*, 128–30.
36. Hanson and Hsu, *Casemates and Cannonballs*, 46; Berleth, *Bloody Mohawk*, 47, 50.
37. Retzer and Barker, "Hessen-Hanau Jägers," 36–37.
38. Lowenthal, *Days of Siege*, 26.
39. Lowenthal, *Days of Siege*, 28.
40. Willett, *Narrative*, 50–51.
41. Retzer and Barker, "Hessen-Hanau Jägers," 36–37.
42. Retzer and Barker, "Hessen-Hanau Jägers," 37.
43. Jones, *Annals and Recollections of Oneida County*, 340.
44. Schoolcraft, *Historical Considerations*, 10–11.
45. He had enlisted on December 8, 1776, for the war. Thomas Owens NARA M881 Compiled Service Record.
46. Lowenthal, *Days of Siege*, 28; Hanson and Hsu, *Casemates and Cannonballs*, 39.
47. Jones, *Annals and Recollections of Oneida County*, 340; Watt, *Rebellion in the Mohawk Valley*, 133.
48. Lowenthal, *Days of Siege*, 29.
49. Lowenthal, *Days of Siege*, 29; Willett, *Narrative*, 44, 51; Greene, *History of the Mohawk Valley*, 1:856; Watt, *Rebellion in the Mohawk Valley*, 133–35.
50. Platt Sammons NARA M881 Compiled Service Record.

12. Willett's Sally and the Battle of Oriskany

1. Different accounts give different times for their arrival. Adam Helmer's account that he arrived at 1:00 p.m. is perhaps the most accurate one, although it may have been closer to noon. Adam Helmer statement, August 11, 1777, Papers of the Continental Congress, New York State Papers, 1775–1788, 2:69. For a discussion of the various times reported and what the actual situation may have been, see Sterling, *Defenders of Liberty*, 32; Glatthaar and Martin, *Forgotten Allies*, 161.
2. Willett, *Narrative*, 51.
3. Lowenthal, *Days of Siege*, 29.
4. Willett, *Narrative*, 53
5. Schoolcraft, *Historical Considerations*, 11. Coonrad France/Conrad Frans/Frantz (S 44,862 W 17,927) of Aorson's company likewise stated that he "was one of the volunteers that turned out of the Fort under Col. Willett for the relief of General Herkimer at the Battle of Oriskany."
6. John Burroughs S 22,667.

7. David Jones PF S 13,586.
8. Willett gives him as "Captain Allen," but he must have meant Lieutenant Samuel Allen of Wesson's regiment. See Samuel Allen NARA M881 Compiled Service Record.
9. Martin Langdon PF S 23, 759; Heitman, *Historical Register*, 80.
10. Marinus Willett to Jonathan Trumbull, August 11, 1777, in *The Remembrancer: or, Impartial Repository of Public Events. For the Year 1777*, 448-50.
11. John Ball PF W 5,767; Willett, *Narrative*, 53.
12. Luzader, *Fort Stanwix*, 53-54; Adam Helmer statement, August 11, 1777, 2:69.
13. Schoolcraft, *Historical Considerations*, 11.
14. Lowenthal, *Days of Siege*, 27; Watt and Morrison, *The British Campaign of 1777*, 47. Another Loyalist captured was Donald Grant Jr., who was exchanged in 1781.
15. Jacobson, *Battlefield Delineation*, 46; Watt and Morrison, *The British Campaign of 1777*, 46, 48, 53. Singleton was originally from Montreal. He was exchanged and returned to Canada. Another possible Loyalist captured was Donald Ross, whose wife later stated in a petition to recover losses that her husband contracted an illness at Fort Stanwix that led to his death. Loyalist Thomas Morgan is recorded both as a deserter and as dying in mid-August 1777 at Fort Stanwix.
16. Schoolcraft, *Historical Considerations*, 12. According to the journal attributed to Lieutenant William Colbrath, the Americans captured four flags (Lowenthal, *Days of Siege*, 31), while Willett (*Narrative*, 54-55) says five flags.
17. Willett's Orderly Book, August 6, 1777.
18. Willett to Trumbull, August 11, 1777, 448-50.
19. Adam Helmer statement, August 11, 1777, 2:69; Clinton, *Public Papers of George Clinton*, 2:212-13. Helmer mistakenly says it was Captain Lieutenant Savage who commanded the artillery piece.
20. Willett to Trumbull, August 11, 1777, 448-50.
21. Adam Helmer statement, August 11, 1777, 2:69.
22. John Ball PF W5767; Adam Helmer statement, August 11, 1777, 2:69; Lowenthal, *Days of Siege*, 31.
23. Adam Helmer statement, August 11, 1777, 2:69.
24. Lowenthal, *Days of Siege*, 31; Willett to Trumbull, August 11, 1777, 448-49. Just how significant those captured flags were is debated. It seems unlikely that they were regimental flags like those taken at Trenton and may have been less official.
25. Lowenthal, *Days of Siege*, 31.
26. Watt and Morrison, *The British Campaign of 1777*, 1:61, 175.
27. Henry Ritter PF S 19,449; *Mohawk Valley in the Revolution*, 312; Barker, *Early Families of Herkimer County*, 215.
28. William Fink PF S 23,218.
29. Glatthaar and Martin, *Forgotten Allies*, 166.
30. Watt and Morrison, *The British Campaign of 1777*, 1:172.
31. Moses Younglove W 4,410.

32. Graymont, *The Iroquois in the American Revolution*, 139–43. While books on the Saratoga campaign deal with the Battle of Oriskany in some depth, a good short overview and discussion is found in Graymont.

13. The Siege Settles In

1. Lowenthal, *Days of Siege*, 33; John Ball PF W 5,767.
2. Jones, *Annals and Recollections of Oneida County*, 339–41; Simms, *Frontiersmen of New York*, 2:107–8; Watt, *Rebellion in the Mohawk Valley*, 197–98. See also Jabez Spicer PF S 42,364.
3. Lowenthal, *Days of Siege*, 32.
4. Lowenthal, *Days of Siege*, 32.
5. Lowenthal, *Days of Siege*, 32; Thomas Cavin and Thomas Benson NARA M881 Compiled Service Records. They had enlisted in December, Cavin for the war and Benson for three years. Benson's record says he deserted August 8.
6. Lowenthal, *Days of Siege*, 33.
7. Broadhead, Fernow, and O'Callaghan, *Documents Relative to the Colonial History of New York*, 15:201. Jonathan Huggins's NARA M881 Compiled Service Record specifies a wound to the left shoulder and arm at Fort Stanwix. New York, US, Pension Claims by Disabled Revolutionary War Veterans, 1779–1789, Ancestry.com, online database. For the original data, see Certificates Submitted by Disabled Revolutionary War Veterans Claiming Pensions and Audited Accounts of Pensions, 1779–1789, microfilm, ser. A0174, 9 vols., New York State Archives, Albany.
8. Adam Helmer statement, August 11, 1777, 2:69.
9. Luzader, *Saratoga*, 133.
10. Willett, *Narrative*, 54–57; Watt and Morrison, *The British Campaign of 1777*, 35, 40.
11. Willett, *Narrative*, 57–58.
12. Lowenthal, *Days of Siege*, 34; Reid, *The Story of Old Fort Johnson*, 92–94.
13. Retzer and Barker, "The Hessen-Hanau Jägers," 38.
14. Leonard Gansevoort, Albany, to Peter Gansevoort, July 9, 1777, in Ranzan and Hollis, *Hero of Fort Schuyler*, 61.
15. Watt, *Rebellion in the Mohawk Valley*, 208–10.
16. Reid, *The Story of Old Fort Johnson*, 92–94; Campbell, *Annals of Tryon County*, 80; Retzer and Barker, "The Hessen-Hanau Jägers," 39; Lowenthal, *Days of Siege*, 37.
17. Retzer and Barker, "The Hessen-Hanau Jägers," 39.
18. Lowenthal, *Days of Siege*, 37; Reid, *The Story of Old Fort Johnson*, 92–94; Benjamin Price NARA M881 Compiled Service Record.
19. Henry Ritter PF S 19,449.
20. Daniel Still NARA M881 Compiled Service Record.
21. Retzer and Barker, "The Hessen-Hanau Jägers," 38.

14. The Siege Finally Ends

1. Lowenthal, *Days of Siege*, 38.
2. Philip Schuyler, Albany, to Peter Gansevoort, August 10, 1777, in Ranzan and Hollis, *Hero of Fort Schuyler*, 77.

3. Retzer and Barker, "The Hessen-Hanau Jägers," 44.

4. Retzer and Barker, "The Hessen-Hanau Jägers," 39. Jäger Lieutenant Hildebrandt had recommended to the artillery lieutenant to reduce the amount of gunpowder for each shot by a factor of 10 percent.

5. Lowenthal, *Days of Siege*, 38.

6. Retzer and Barker, "The Hessen-Hanau Jägers," 39.

7. Lowenthal, *Days of Siege*, 39; Luzader, Torres, and Carroll, *Fort Stanwix*, 96.

8. Watt and Morrison, *The British Campaign of 1777*, 1:123.

9. Lowenthal, *Days of Siege*, 39. Hildebrandt noted the detachment formed to divert the water supply to the fort on August 13; see Retzer and Barker, "The Hessen-Hanau Jägers," 39.

10. Lowenthal, *Days of Siege*, 39.

11. Ward, *George Washington's Enforcers*, 122–24.

12. Retzer and Barker, "The Hessen-Hanau Jägers," 39.

13. Lowenthal, *Days of Siege*, 40.

14. Lowenthal, *Days of Siege*, 40.

15. Willett's Orderly Book, August 14, 1777.

16. Lowenthal, *Days of Siege*, 41.

17. Lowenthal, *Days of Siege*, 43.

18. Willett's Order Book, August 15, 1777.

19 Lowenthal, *Days of Siege*, 43; Luzader, Torres, and Carroll, *Fort Stanwix*, 41.

20. John Roof PF S 14,371; Simms, *Frontiersmen of New York*, 2:91; Watt, *Rebellion in the Mohawk Valley*, 231.

21. George Washington to George Clinton, August 16, 1777, Founders Online, National Archives, https://founders.archives.gov/documents/Washington/03-10-02-0621; originally published in *The Papers of George Washington*, Revolutionary War Series, vol. 10, *11 June 1777–18 August 1777*, ed. Frank E. Grizzard Jr. (Charlottesville: University Press of Virginia, 2000), 634–37.

22. Lowenthal, *Days of Siege*, 43, 45.

23. Lowenthal, *Days of Siege*, 46.

24. Retzer and Barker, "The Hessen-Hanau Jägers," 39.

25. Lowenthal, *Days of Siege*, 46.

26. Willett's Orderly Book, August 18, 1777.

27. Barry St. Leger, Oswego, to John Burgoyne, August 27, 1777, in Burgoyne, *A State of the Expedition from Canada*, lxvii.

28. Retzer and Barker, "The Hessen-Hanau Jägers," 39.

29. Lowenthal, *Days of Siege*, 46.

30. Ebenezer Temple PF S 14,658.

31. Lowenthal, *Days of Siege*, 46; Watt and Morrison, *The British Campaign of 1777*, 113.

32. Muster roll at Fort Schuyler, "alias Fort Stanwix," for Captain Albert Chapman's company of Colonel Elmore's regiment, January 11, 1777, Revolutionary War Rolls, 1775–1783, NARA M246.

33. Gansevoort, Fort Schuyler, to —— Weston, August 19, 1777, Horatio Gates Papers.

34. Retzer and Barker, "The Hessen-Hanau Jägers," 39.

35. Leonard Maybus NARA M881 Compiled Service Record.
36. Willett's Orderly Book, August 21, 1777; Lowenthal, *Days of Siege*, 48.
37. Lowenthal, *Days of Siege*, 48.
38. Leonard Bleeker, support statement, in Adam Happal PF R 4,584. Bleeker notes that Happal correctly remembered this wound and the birth of their child the next day. While the name of Mrs. McCarty cannot be confirmed as Nancy, evidence gathered by the staff at Fort Stanwix National Monument makes a strong case for it.
39. Dennis McCartey/McCarty NARA M881 Compiled Service Record.
40. Han Jost Hess (Joseph Hess etc.) PF S 44,926. His service record gives his name as John Uthest. He commented that it was due to his being German and not speaking English well that so many variations in spelling developed.
41. Frederick Naugle (two spellings are given, Nagle and Naugle) and Thomas White NARA M881 Compiled Service Records; Watt and Morrison, *The British Campaign of 1777*, 236, 137.
42. Lowenthal, *Days of Siege*, 48; Cornelius Devan, George Smith, and John O'Neal NARA M881 Compiled Service Records; Watt and Morrison, *The British Campaign of 1777*, 150.
43. Lowenthal, *Days of Siege*, 49; Watt and Morrison, *The British Campaign of 1777*, 105, 106.
44. Thacher, *Military Journal*, 107–8.
45. Retzer and Barker, "The Hessen-Hanau Jägers," 41.
46. Lowenthal, *Days of Siege*, 49.
47. Graymont, *The Iroquois in the American Revolution*, 144.
48. Henry Ritter PF S 19,449.
49. Glatthaar and Martin, *Forgotten Allies*, 175–77.
50. Lowenthal, *Days of Siege*, 60, Lowenthal presents a photographic copy of the document that is located in the New York Public Library. A complete transcription is given in Ranzan and Hollis, *Hero of Fort Schuyler*, 83
51. Lowenthal, *Days of Siege*, 50.
52. Henry Ritter PF S 19,449.
53. John Dop/Dops PF R 3,018.
54. Lowenthal, *Days of Siege*, 51–52.
55. Graymont, *The Iroquois in the American Revolution*, 146.
56. Scudder, "Journal," 19.
57. Scott, *Fort Stanwix and Oriskany*, 290, citing the Horatio Gates Papers.
58. Willett's Orderly Book, August 23, 1777.
59. Willett's Orderly Book, August 26, 1777.
60. Benedict Arnold to General Horatio Gates, August 24, 1777, in Scott, *Stanwix and Oriskany*, 290-91.
61. Scudder, "Journal," 19.
62. Willett's Orderly Book, August 28, 1777.
63. *Pennsylvania Journal* (Philadelphia), September 3, 1777, 2.
64. Hugh Sommers NARA M881 Compiled Service Record.
65. Henry Witmozer NARA M881 Compiled Service Record.
66. Jones, *Annals and Recollections of Oneida County*, 142–43.
67. Glatthaar and Martin, *Forgotten Allies*, 176-78.

68. Luzader, *Fort Stanwix*, 35.
69. Luzader, Torres, and Carroll, *Fort Stanwix*, 99, 104.

15. Adjusting to Garrison Life after the Siege

1. John Adams to Abigail Adams, September 2, 1777, in *Letters of Delegates to the Continental Congress*, 7:589.
2. John Adams to Abigail Adams, August 19, 1777, in Adams, *Familiar Letters*, 292.
3. James Duane to Robert Livingston, September 3(?), 1777, in *Letters of Delegates to the Continental Congress*, 7:597–98. Livingston, though not then a delegate, had been a delegate previously and would be again.
4. Scott, *Stanwix and Oriskany*, 296.
5. Graymont, *The Iroquois in the American Revolution*, 128, 156, 177.
6. *Journals of the Continental Congress*, 9:771–72; John Hancock to Peter Gansevoort, October 5, 1777, and John Hancock to Marinus Willett, October 5, 1777, in *Letters of Delegates of the Continental Congress*, 8:53.
7. Scudder, "Journal," 19–20.
8. For more on this, see Luzader, *Saratoga*, 92, 185, 188, 195, 197, 199.
9. Third New York Regiment Officers, Fort Schuyler, to Peter Gansevoort, October 12, 1777, Gansevoort Papers, AO131, 178; Peter Gansevoort, Fort Schuyler, to the officers of the Third New York Regiment, October 12, 1777, Gansevoort Papers, AO131, 179.
10. Officers of the 3rd New York Regiment, Fort Schuyler, to Peter Gansevoort, October 12, 1777, Gansevoort Papers, AO131, 178. Officers signing the letter were Captains Aaron Aorson, Thomas De Witt, Cornelius T. Jansen, and Leonard Bleeker; Lieutenants Henry Defendorf, John Ball, Philip Conine, John Welch, Nanning Vanderheyden, George Syterz (Regimental Adjutant), Prentice Bowen, Gerrit Staats, Thomas Warner, Benjamin Boagardus, and Thomas Ostrander; Quarter Master Thomas Williams Junior; Ensigns William Colbrath, Christopher Hutton, Josiah Bagley, Samuel Lewis, and Ament Eldert; Pay Master Jeremiah Van Rensselaer; Surgeon Hunloke Woodruff; and Surgeon's Mate John Elliot.

Peter Gansevoort to the officers of the Third New York Regiment, October 12, 1777, Gansevoort Papers, AO131, 179.

11. John Henry Nemire, Michael Poulson, and Moret Grindel NARA M881 Compiled Service Records. Nemire's name is spelled several different ways in the records (PF S 43,062). Other enlistments included: Nicholas Hartman, October 15, three years, NARA M881 Compiled Service Record; Christopher Tice, October 15, three years, NARA M881 Compiled Service Record; Jason Varicker, October 15, three years, NARA M881 Compiled Service Record; John Henry Nemire, October 15, for the war, NARA M881 Compiled Service Record, PF S 43,062; Michael Poulson, October 15, for the war, NARA M881 Compiled Service Record; John Bearwart, November 6 at Albany, John Bearwart PF R 677; Christian Keanor, first muster December 7, for the war, NARA M881 Compiled Service Record; Henry Minac, first muster December 7, for the war, NARA M881 Compiled Service Record; Conrad Weeken, first muster December 7, for

the war, NARA M881 Compiled Service Record; John Cool, December 9, for the war, NARA M881 Compiled Service Record.

12. Peter Gansevoort, Fort Schuyler, to General Gates, October 1, 1777, Gansevoort Papers, AO131, 177; Horatio Gates Papers.

13. Willett's Orderly Book, October 16, 1777.

14. Marinus Willett, Fort Schuyler, to Horatio Gates, September 1, 1777 (misdated August 1, 1777), Horatio Gates Papers. The letter must be misdated as it describes conditions after the siege.

15. Willett's Orderly Book, September 21, 1777.

16. Willett's Orderly Book, September 2, 1777.

17. Willett's Orderly Book, September 10, 1777; Hanson and Hsu, *Casemates and Cannonballs*, 38.

18. Willett's Orderly Book, September 20, 1777.

19. Willett, Fort Schuyler, to Horatio Gates, September 11, 1777, Horatio Gates Papers.

20. Willett, Fort Schuyler, to Horatio Gates, September 2, 1777, Horatio Gates Papers.

21. Glatthaar and Martin, *Forgotten Allies*, 188, 191; Graymont, *The Iroquois in the American Revolution*, 164.

22. Lieutenant Colonel Marinus Willett, Albany, to Peter Gansevoort, September 30, 1777, Gansevoort Papers, AO131, 176; Glatthaar and Martin, *Forgotten Allies*, 183.

23. Willett's Orderly Book, December 11, 1777.

24. Willett's Orderly Book, October 22, 1777.

25. Willett's Orderly Book, October 29, 1777.

26. John Hill NARA M881 Compiled Service Record; Willett's Orderly Book, December 21, 1777; George Sytez and Christopher Hutton NARA M881 Compiled Service Records; Broadhead, Fernow, and O'Callaghan, *Documents Relative to the Colonial History of New York*, 15:197.

27 Christian Keanor, Henry Minac, Conrad Weeken, and John Cool NARA M881 Compiled Service Records.

28 Jeremiah Van Rensselaer, Albany, to Peter Gansevoort, December 16, 1777, Gansevoort Papers, AO131, 185. Jeremiah Van Rensselaer was born in 1738 into one of the most powerful Albany families. He was educated by tutors before attending the College of New Jersey, now Princeton University, from which he graduated in 1758. He returned to Albany and in 1764 was a vendor importing to supply the Indian trade. In 1766 he was a leader of the Albany Sons of Liberty. He served on the Albany Committee of Correspondence. He was elected to the city council in 1770. In 1771 he was a land agent and a surveyor. In 1774 he became proprietor of the "Van Rensselaer Patent" of more than 28,000 acres in today's Fulton County. At the outbreak of hostilities, then in his late thirties, he was commissioned an ensign in the 3rd New York and served as paymaster.

29. Watt and Morrison, *The British Campaign of 1777*, 126; Broadhead, Fernow, and O'Callaghan, *Documents Relative to the Colonial History of New York*, 15:200.

30. Watt and Morrison, *The British Campaign of 1777*, 148–49.

31. William Fink PF S 23,218.

32. Henry Ritter PF S 19,449 W 20,026; *Mohawk Valley in the Revolution*, document 83, 136. Ritter continued to actively serve in his local militia after his discharge. Cremer's service record indicates enlistment in mid-December 1777 and desertion December 29, 1778. Why the December enlistment date is not specified is unclear, unless it was backdated to cover Ritter's furlough absence. See Frederick Ritter's deposition in Henry Ritter's pension file and Frederick Ritter's's pension file W 20,026. See also John Witderstein PF W 18,341, deposition in Henry Ritter's pension file; Watt and Morrison, *The British Campaign of 1777*, 144.

33. Henry Ritter PF S 19,449.

34. Desertions included William McCormick, September 19, enlisted June 13 (NARA M881 Compiled Service Record; Watt and Morrison, *The British Campaign of 1777*, 144); Stephen Miller, September 22, enlisted June 15 (NARA M881 Compiled Service Record; Watt and Morrison, *The British Campaign of 1777*, 144); Moret Grindel, October 20, first muster in October (NARA M881 Compiled Service Record); Stephen Sabine, November 22, enlisted May 9 (NARA M881 Compiled Service Record); Nicholas Christman, mixed-race Oneida European, November 28, enlisted March 30 for three years, would later return and face court-martial (PF S 44,757).

35. Hugh Sommers NARA M881 Compiled Service Record.

36. Willett's Orderly Book, December 1, 1777.

37. Marinus Willett to Peter Gansevoort, September 30, 1777, Gansevoort Papers, AO131, 176; Ranzan and Hollis, *Hero of Fort Schuyler*, 86

38. Lieutenant Colonel Marinus Willett, Fishkill, New York, to Peter Gansevoort, October 6, 1777, Gansevoort Papers, AO131, 177.

39. Marinus Willett, Headquarters near Philadelphia, to Colonel Peter Gansevoort, November 16, 1777, Gansevoort Papers, AO131, 180.

40. *US and International Marriage Records, 1560–1900*, 2004, https://www.ancestry.com.

41. NARA M246, Revolutionary War Rolls, 1775–1783, folder 40, 2-3, 3rd New York Regiment, 1776–1780. Second Lieutenant Gilbert R. Livingston of Captain Swartwout's company was given furlough September 3, 1777, and was declared a deserter on October 12. He apparently did not return from furlough. See Gilbert R. Livingston NARA M881 Compiled Service Record.

42. Peter Gansevoort, Fort Schuyler, to General Philip Schuyler, December 12, 1777, Gansevoort Papers, AO131, 184.

43. Lourons/Lawrence Schoolcraft PF S 42260.

44. Willett's Orderly Book, December 23–24, 1777.

45. Willett's Orderly Book, September 8, 15, 20, 1777.

46. Willett's Orderly Book, November 2, 1777.

47. Aide-de-Camp Robert Troup, Headquarters, Albany, to Peter Gansevoort, November 21, 1777, Gansevoort Papers, AO131, 181; Seth Stow NARA M881 Compiled Service Record. Colonel Seth Warner commanded one of sixteen additional Continental regiments authorized in December 1776. This regiment contained mostly men from Vermont. Heitman, *Historical Register*, 569; Wright, *Continental Army*, 98–99.

48. Willett's Orderly Book, September 21, 1777.
49. Willett's Orderly Book, November 27, 1777.
50. Willett's Orderly Book, September 18, 1777.
51. Willett's Orderly Book, September 19, 1777.
52. Willett's Orderly Book, December 17, 1777.
53. Willett's Orderly Book, December 27, 1777.
54. Willett's Orderly Book, October 12, 1777.
55. Willett's Orderly Book, December 7, 1777.
56. Fort Schuyler, September 1, 1777, Return of Provisions at this Fort this day under the direction of John Hanson, A.D. Commissary, Horatio Gates Papers.
57. Marinus Willett, Fort Schuyler, to Horatio Gates, September 22, 1777, Horatio Gates Papers.
58. Willett's Orderly Book, September 28, 1777.
59. Willett's Orderly Book, October 30, 1777; Mayer, *Belonging to the Army*, 246.
60. Willett's Orderly Book, November 8, 1777.
61. Colonel Jacob Cuyler, Headquarters, Albany, to Peter Gansevoort, November 28, 1777, Gansevoort Papers, AO131, 182.
62. Peter Gansevoort, Fort Schuyler, to [?], December 12, 1777, Gansevoort Papers, AO131, 183.
63. Willett's Orderly Book, December 14, 1777.
64. Marinus Willett, Fort Schuyler, to Horatio Gates, September 1, 1777 (misdated August 1, 1777), Horatio Gates Papers. The letter must be misdated as it describes conditions after the siege.
65. A Return of Ammunition and Artillery Stores at Fort Schuyler, September 1, 1777, signed by Captain Lieutenant Joseph Savage, Horatio Gates Papers.
66. Marinus Willett, Fort Schuyler, to Horatio Gates, September 1, 1777 (misdated August 1, 1777), Horatio Gates Papers. The letter must be misdated as it describes conditions after the siege.
67. Jeremiah Van Rensselaer, Albany, to Peter Gansevoort, December 16, 1777, Gansevoort Papers, AO131, 185.
68. Glatthaar and Martin, *Forgotten Allies*, 186-87.
69. Willett's Orderly Book, December 25, 1777.
70. Willett's Orderly Book, December 28, 1777.
71. Willett's Orderly Book, December 31, 1777; James McCormick NARA M881 Compiled Service Record.
72. Sypher, *New York State Society of the Cincinnati*, 473-74. The Tapps named another son, born in 1789, after General Washington.

16. A Tiresome and Dangerous New Year

1. Officers of 3rd New York Regiment, Fort Schuyler, to Peter Gansevoort, February 26, 1778, Gansevoort Papers, AO131, 189. Those signing were Lieutenant Colonel Marinus Willett, Captain Aaron Aorson, Captain Thomas De Witt, Captain Cornelius T. Jansen, Captain Leonard Bleeker, Captain Henry Tiebout, Adjutant George Systez, Lieutenant Nanning Vander Heyden, Lieutenant Philip Conine, Lieutenant William Tapp, Lieutenant Gerrit Staats,

Lieutenant Thomas Warner, Lieutenant Benjamin Bogardus, Lieutenant Moses Yeomans, Lieutenant William Colbrath, Ensign Christ. Hutton, Ensign Peter Magee, Ensign Josiah Bagely, Ensign Samuel Lewis, Ensign George L. Deniston, Ensign Matthew Potan, Surgeon Hunloke Woodruff, and Surgeon's Mate John Elliot.

2. Peter Gansevoort, Fort Schuyler, to Henry Laurens, Albany, ca. January 26, 1778; Peter Gansevoort to Major General Horatio Gates, Albany, January 26, 1778, and Peter Gansevoort to William Duer and [Gouverneur?] Morris, January 26, 1778, Gansevoort Papers, AO131, 186, 187.

3. Ward, *George Washington's Enforcers*, 15.

4. The Marquis de Lafayette, Johnstown, New York, to Colonel Peter Gansevoort, March 5, 1778, Gansevoort Papers, AO131, 190. Corbett, *No Turning Point*, makes reference to Carleton.

5. Willett's Orderly Book, April 1, 1778.

6. Willett's Orderly Book, April 12, 1778.

7. Glatthaar and Martin, *Forgotten Allies*, 221.

8. Willett's Orderly Book, May 20, 1778.

9. Peter Gansevoort, Albany, to Marinus Willett, March 29, 1777 (should be 1778), Gansevoort Papers, AO131, 110–11.

10. Peter Gansevoort, Albany, to Horatio Gates, April 19, 1778, Gansevoort Papers, AO131, 198.

11. Willett's Orderly Book, May 9, 1778.

12. Willett's Orderly Book, May 15, 1778; Luzader, Torres, and Carroll, *Fort Stanwix*, 95.

13. Peter Gansevoort, Fort Schuyler, to Henry Laurens, January 26, 1778; Peter Gansevoort to Major General Horatio Gates, Albany, January 26, 1778; and Peter Gansevoort to William Duer and [Gouverneur?] Morris, January 26, 1778, Gansevoort Papers, AO131, 186, 187.

14. Peter Gansevoort to General Horatio Gates, ca. early April 1778, Gansevoort Papers, AO131, 202.

15. Peter Gansevoort, Albany, to [Horatio Gates?], April 19, 1778, Gansevoort Papers, AO131, 197.

16. Governor George Clinton, Poughkeepsie, to Peter Gansevoort, New York, May 17, 1778, Gansevoort Papers, AO131, 203.

17. Willett's Orderly Book, January 7, 1778.

18. Willett's Orderly Book, January 3, 1778.

19. Willett's Orderly Book, February 23, 1778.

20. Willett's Orderly Book, March 10, 1778.

21. Willett's Orderly Book, February 24, 1778.

22. Willett's Orderly Book, March 13, 1778.

23. Mayer. *Belonging to the Army*, 207, citing Willett's Orderly Book.

24. Willett's Orderly Book, April 17, 1778.

25. Willett's Orderly Book, May 19, 1778.

26. Willett's Orderly Book, February 8, 1778.

27. Willett's Orderly Book, April 21, 1778.

28. Willett's Orderly Book, May 2. For more on women with the army washing clothing, see Mayer, *Belonging to the Army*, 64, 140–42.

29. Willett's Orderly Book, March 15, 1778.
30. Heitman, *Historical Register*, 312, 530.
31. Willett's Orderly Book, April 15, 1778.
32. Peter Gansevoort, Albany, to Marinus Willett, March 29, 1777 (should be 1778), Gansevoort Papers, AO131, 110-11.
33. Lieutenant Colonel Marinus Willett, Fort Schuyler, to Peter Gansevoort, April 15, 1778, Gansevoort Papers, AO131, 196.
34. General Philip Schuyler, Caughnawaga, New York, by order of the Commissioners of Indian Affairs, to Peter Gansevoort, March 11, 1778, Gansevoort Papers, AO131, 193.
35. Peter Gansevoort, Albany, to Major General Gates, President of the Board of War, March 12, 1778, Gansevoort Papers, AO131, 193.
36. Willett's Orderly Book, April 23, 1778.
37. Glatthaar and Martin, *Forgotten Allies*, 196-99; Taylor, *The Divided Ground*, 206.
38. Glatthaar and Martin, *Forgotten Allies*, 202-3.
39. Peter Gansevoort, Albany, to Governor George Clinton, January 26, 1777 [should be 1778], Gansevoort Papers, AO131, 104.
40. Willett's Orderly Book, March 3, 1778.
41. Peter Gansevoort, Albany, to Captain Leonard Bleeker, March 12, 1778, Gansevoort Papers, AO131, 193. See also Ranzan and Hollis, *Hero of Fort Schuyler*, 95.
42. Peter Gansevoort, Albany, to Major General Horatio Gates, President of the Board of War, March 12, 1778, Gansevoort Papers, AO131, 193.
43. Willett's Orderly Book, March 20, 1778.
44. Clinton, *Public Papers of George Clinton*, 3:350-51.
45. Peter Gansevoort, Albany, to Governor George Clinton, ca. early April 1778, Gansevoort Papers, AO131, 201.
46. Lieutenant Colonel Marinus Willett, Fort Schuyler, to Peter Gansevoort, April 15, 1778, Gansevoort Papers, AO131, 196; Ranzan and Hollis, *Hero of Fort Schuyler*, 97.
47. Lieutenant Colonel Marinus Willett, Fort Schuyler, to Peter Gansevoort, April 15, 1778, Gansevoort Papers, AO131, 198; Ranzan and Hollis, *Hero of Fort Schuyler*, 98.
48. Willett's Orderly Book, April 21, 1778.
49. Lieutenant Colonel Marinus Willett, Fort Schuyler, to Peter Gansevoort, April 20, 1778, Gansevoort Papers, AO131, 198; Ranzan and Hollis, *Hero of Fort Schuyler*, 98.
50. Governor George Clinton, Poughkeepsie, to Peter Gansevoort, May 17, 1778, Gansevoort Papers, AO131, 203.
51. Robert Benson, Poughkeepsie, to Peter Gansevoort, May 17, 1778, Gansevoort Papers, AO131, 204.
52. Clinton, *Public Papers of George Clinton*, 3:350-51.
53. Willett's Orderly Book, March 17, 1778.
54. Willett's Orderly Book, May 21, 1778.
55. Hunloke Woodruff, Fort Schuyler, to Peter Gansevoort, April 2, 1778, Gansevoort Papers, AO131, 194.

56. Willett's Orderly Book, April 23, 1778.

57. Numbers derived from Broadhead, Fernow, and O'Callaghan, *Documents Relative to the Colonial History of New York*, 15:197–209.

58. Willett's Orderly Book, March 24, 1778.

59. *Muster and Pay Rolls of the War of the Revolution*, 430–31. For information on the itch, see Joseph Lee Boyle, "Starting from Scratch: Combating the Itch," *Journal of the American Revolution*, October 21, 2020, https://allthingsliberty.com/2020/10/starting-from-scratch-combating-the-itch/.

60. Private Zachariah Lowe appeared for the first time on the March muster of Tiebout's company but then deserted on March 16 (Zachariah Lowe NARA M881 Compiled Service Record). A sergeant from Captain De Witt's company deserted on March 26, and shortly after, on April 8, two privates of the company deserted. One of them was Zebulon Shippey, who had deserted previously and then returned. "Extract from A Journal by Ensign Christopher Hutton" (hereafter Hutton Journal), Gansevoort Papers, AO131, 248). Four men from Captain Aorson's company and one from Captain Swartout's company deserted on May 2, followed by a corporal and a private from Captain Tiebout's company on May 16 (Hutton Journal, Gansevoort Papers, AO131, 248).

61. Willett's Orderly Book, January 31, 1778; Nicholas Christman PF S 44,757.

62 Letters of granddaughter Catherine Gansevoort Lansing in Baxter, *A Godchild of Washington*.

63. Willett's Orderly Book, April 10, 1778.

64. Willett's Orderly Book, January 3, 1778.

65. Mayer, *Belonging to the Army*, 51.

66. Willett's Orderly Book, April 19, 1778. This was actually just after Sytez had been replaced as adjutant by Ensign Hutton, so Willett could have made a mistake in his orders and said Sytez.

67. Willett's Orderly Book, February 27, 1778.

68. Willett's Orderly Book, May 5, 21, 1778.

69. Willett's Orderly Book, April 13, 1778.

70. Willett's Orderly Book, January 17, 18 1778.

71. Willett's Orderly Book, January 23, 1778.

72. Willett's Orderly Book, April 8, 1778.

73. Willett's Orderly Book, April 26, 1778.

74. Willett's Orderly Book, September 23, 1777.

75. Willett's Orderly Book, May 1, 5, 1778.

76. Willett's Orderly Book, April 5, 1778.

77. Willett's Orderly Book, February 6, 1778.

78. Willett's Orderly Book, April 19, 1778.

79. Peter Gansevoort, Albany, to Major General Horatio Gates, president of the Board of War, April 4, 1778, Gansevoort Papers, AO131, 195.

80. Three men, William Barrett, Christian Brant (Christian Brant PF R1374, NARA M881 Compiled Service Record), and Frederick Brown enlisted in Tiebout's company and mustered for the first time in January, while John Toochman enlisted for the war on January 19. Surviving records show twelve

men enlisting or appearing on their first muster in January, including one in Captain De Witt's company, five in Captain Aorson's, four in Captain Tiebout's, and two in Captain Bleeker's. February was much slower, with only five men enlisting, one in Aorson's company and two each in Van Bunschoten's and Bleeker's companies. March saw nine men enlist, split between Swartwout's, Aorson's, Tiebout's and Bleeker's companies.

81. This arrangement was separate from the agreements with German rulers for complete German units to serve alongside the British regiments. Those men are better classified as auxiliaries, while the von Scheither recruits were mercenaries.

82. *Journals of the Continental Congress*, 10:203.

83. Godfrey Byerd PF S 44,721 NARA M881 Compiled Service Record. Enlisting British deserters may have been going on for several months, and was finally becoming official in March and April. After the war, Byerd made a good life for himself in the United States.

84. Numbers derived from Broadhead, Fernow, and O'Callaghan, *Documents Relative to the Colonial History of New York*, 15:197–209.

85. Lieutenant Colonel Marinus Willett, Fort Schuyler, to Peter Gansevoort, April 15, 1778, Gansevoort Papers, AO131, 198.

86. Captain Abraham Swartwout, Poughkeepsie, to Peter Gansevoort, Albany, May 4, 1778, Gansevoort Papers, AO131, 201.

87. Willett's Orderly Book, April 21, 1778.

88. Robert Cochran to Peter Gansevoort, February 21, 1778, Gansevoort Papers, AO131, 188.

89. Thomas Ostrander NARA M881 Compiled Service Record.

90. *Revolutionary War Rolls, 1775–1783*, folder 40, 5–6, 3rd New York Regiment, 1776–1780.

91. David Jones PF S13,586; and Thomas Jones PF S 39,794.

92. Peter Gansevoort, Albany, to Marinus Willett, March 29, 1777 (should be 1778), Gansevoort Papers, AO131, 110–11.

93. The Marquis de Lafayette, Johnstown, to Colonel Peter Gansevoort, March 5, 1778, Gansevoort Papers, AO131, 190.

94. Gouverneur Morris, Camp Valley Forge, to George Clinton, February 17, 1778, in *Letters of Delegates to Congress*, 9:117–18.

95. Governor Clinton, Poughkeepsie, to Colonel Peter Gansevoort, April 30, 1778, Gansevoort Papers, AO131, 199. See also Ranzan and Hollis, *Hero of Fort Schuyler*, 99. This structure was formally authorized for the Continental Army by the Continental Congress on May 27; *Journals of the Continental Congress*, 11:538–39. The lieutenant designated as captain lieutenant of the colonel's company received the same pay as regular lieutenants.

96. Peter Gansevoort, Albany, to Governor George Clinton, ca. early April 1778, Gansevoort Papers, AO131, 201.

97. For example, see Colonel Gansevoort, Fort Schuyler, to Levi Stockwell, May 30, 1778, in Ranzan and Hollis, *Hero of Fort Schuyler*, 99.

98. Colonel Peter Gansevoort, Fort Schuyler, to multiple officers, May 30, 1778, Gansevoort Papers, AO131, 205.

17. A British Plot Encourages Desertions

1. "Return of American Officers and other prisoners on parole on Long Island, undated, Traitor???" Lieutenant Colonel Marinus Willett, Schenectady, to Peter Gansevoort, June 3, 1778, Gansevoort Papers, AO131, 208; Richard Varick, Schenectady, to Peter Gansevoort, June 3, 1778, Gansevoort Papers, AO131, 208.

2. Colonel Peter Gansevoort, Fort Schuyler, to Governor George Clinton, June 1, 1778, Gansevoort Papers, AO131, 205.

3. Thacher, *Military Journal*, 137.

4. Aaron Osborn PF W 4558.

5. Leonard Gansevoort, Albany, to Peter Gansevoort, June 3, 1778, Gansevoort Papers, AO131, 207.

6. John Hanson, Albany, to Peter Gansevoort, June 15, 1778, Gansevoort Papers, AO131, 211.

7. Henry Glen, Schenectady, to Peter Gansevoort, June 6, 1778, Gansevoort Papers, AO131, 211; Richard Varick, Albany, to Peter Gansevoort, June 10, 1778, Gansevoort Papers, AO131, 212.

8. Colonel Jacob Cuyler, Albany, to Colonel Peter Gansevoort, June 29, 1778, Gansevoort Papers, AO131, 220.

9. General John Stark, Albany, to Peter Gansevoort, June 29, 1778, Gansevoort Papers, AO131, 221.

10. Marquis de Lafayette, Valley Forge Camp, to Colonel Peter Gansevoort, June 13, 1778, Gansevoort Papers, AO131, 213.

11. Glatthaar and Martin, *Forgotten Allies*, 216.

12. Deputy Commissary General of Purchases Jacob Cuyler, Albany, to Peter Gansevoort, New York, June 15, 1778, Gansevoort Papers, AO131, 213.

13. Richard Varick, Schenectady, to Peter Gansevoort, June 3, 1778, Gansevoort Papers, AO131, 208.

14. Lieutenant Colonel Marinus Willett, Fort Albany, to Peter Gansevoort, June 5, 1778, Gansevoort Papers, AO131, 210.

15. Lieutenant Colonel Marinus Willett, Schenectady, to Peter Gansevoort, June 3, 1778, Gansevoort Papers, AO131, 208.

16. Ruddiman, *Becoming Men of Some Consequence*, 126–27.

17. General Henry Clinton to Lord George Germain, New York, October 23, 1778, On-Line Institute for Advanced Loyalist Studies, http://www.royalprovincial.com/military/rhist/voi/voilet7.htm.

18. Report of the court-martial, Fort Schuyler, June 17, 1778, Gansevoort Papers, AO131, 215; Ranzan and Hollis, *Hero of Fort Schuyler*, 102–5.

19. For more information on the guardhouse, see Luzader, Torres, and Carroll, *Fort Stanwix*, 102.

20. Jeremiah Smith NARA M881 Compiled Service Record. Smith had enlisted on November 26, 1776, for three years in Captain Swartwout's company.

21. Extract from a letter from Fort Schuyler, June 11 1778, in a report from Fishkill, June 25, 1778, printed in the *Independent Ledger, and American Advertiser* (Boston), July 13, 1778, 2.

298   NOTES TO PAGES 229-234

22. James Deane, Oneida, to Colonel Peter Gansevoort, ca. June 27, 1778, Gansevoort Papers, AO131, 219.

23. Report of the court-martial, Fort Schuyler, June 17, 1778, Gansevoort Papers, AO131, 215; Ranzan and Hollis, *Hero of Fort Schuyler*, 102-5.

24. William Stephens enlisted for the war on November 24, 1776, and would desert on August 3, 1778 (NARA M881 Compiled Service Record). Stephens was also said to have taken one of the sentinels from Captain Jansen's company with him. See Hutton Journal, 248-49.

25. Hutton Journal, 248-49; John Howell NARA M881 Compiled Service Record.

26. General John Stark, Albany, to Peter Gansevoort, June 29, 1778, Gansevoort Papers, AO131, 221; Henry Glen, Schenectady, to Colonel Peter Gansevoort, June 31, 1778 [should be June 30], Gansevoort Papers, AO131, 221; John Pearson NARA M881 Compiled Service Record.

27. Peter Gansevoort, Fort Schuyler, to Jacob Cuyler, June 23, 1778, Gansevoort Papers, AO131, 218; Colonel Jacob Cuyler, Albany, to Colonel Peter Gansevoort, June 29, 1778, Gansevoort Papers, AO131, 220.

28. Henry Glen, Schenectady, to Colonel Peter Gansevoort, June 31, 1778 [should be June 30], Gansevoort Papers, AO131, 221.

18. Still More Desertions and Continuing Unease

1. Captain Abraham Swartwout, Poughkeepsie, to Peter Gansevoort by way of Jeremiah Van Rensselaer, August 29, 1778, Gansevoort Papers, AO131, 253. Henry Van Veghten was a resident of Albany who served on the Committee of Correspondence and served with the local militia and quartermaster. See exhibitions, New York State Museum, https://exhibitions.nysm.nysed.gov/albany/bios/vv/hevvechten2525.html.

2. *New York Gazette*, October 28, 1799, 2.

3. Sarah Culbertson, Schenectady, to Colonel Peter Gansevoort, July 1, 1778, Gansevoort Papers, AO131, 222.

4. Henry Starring, German Flats, to Peter Gansevoort, July 29, 1778, Gansevoort Papers, AO131, 235.

5. John Stark, Albany, to Peter Gansevoort, July 7, 1778, Gansevoort Papers, AO131, 224.

6. Leonard Gansevoort, Albany, to Peter Gansevoort, July 9, 1778, Gansevoort Papers, AO131, 224; General John Stark, Albany, to Peter Gansevoort, July 10, 1778, Gansevoort Papers, AO131, 226; Colonel Jacob Cuyler, Albany, to Peter Gansevoort, July 10, 1778, Gansevoort Papers, AO131, 226.

7. Lieutenant Colonel William Stacy, Caughnawaga, to Peter Gansevoort, July 12, 1778, Gansevoort Papers, AO131, 227.

8. Peter Gansevoort, Fort Schuyler, to General John Stark, July 10, 1778, Gansevoort Papers, AO131, 225; Graymont, *The Iroquois in the American Revolution*, 174.

9. Colonel Peter Bellinger, German Flats, to Peter Gansevoort, July 19, 1778, Gansevoort Papers, AO131, 228.

10. General Philip Schuyler, Albany, to Peter Gansevoort, July 19, 1778, Gansevoort Papers, AO131, 228.

11. Cal[eb] Stark, Major of Brigade, to Brigadier General John Stark, Albany, to Peter Gansevoort, July 19, 1778, Gansevoort Papers, AO131, 229.

12. Henry Glen, Schenectady, to Peter Gansevoort, July 24, 1778, Gansevoort Papers, AO131, 231. Captain Peterson is sometimes given as Peters. Watt and Morrison, *The British Campaign of 1777*, 184.

13. Major Robert Cochran, Fort Schuyler, to Colonel Peter Gansevoort, September 8, 1778, Gansevoort Papers, AO131, 256. See also incomplete letter in Ranzan and Hollis, *Hero of Fort Schuyler*, 112. Cochran mistakenly gives the soldier's name as Benjamin Acker. The NARA M881 Compiled Service Record for Benjamin Ackerson, however, gives death information that identifies him as this man.

14. Major Robert Cochran, Fort Schuyler, to Colonel Peter Gansevoort, September 18, 1778, Gansevoort Papers, AO131, 258; Ranzan and Hollis, *Hero of Fort Schuyler*, 113. See also Major Robert Cochran, Fort Schuyler, to Colonel Peter Gansevoort, September 28, 1778, in Ranzan and Hollis, *Hero of Fort Schuyler*, 114-15; Glatthaar and Martin, *Forgotten Allies*, 223-24.

15. Graymont, *The Iroquois in the American Revolution*, 59.

16. George Measam, Boston, to Peter Gansevoort, July 28, 1778, Gansevoort Papers, AO131, 233.

17. Jeremiah Van Rensselaer, Albany, to Peter Gansevoort, August 8, 1778, Gansevoort Papers, AO131, 236.

18. Colonel Jacob Cuyler, Albany, to Peter Gansevoort, July 10, 1778, Gansevoort Papers, AO131, 226.

19. Henry Glen, Schenectady, to Peter Gansevoort, August 10, 1778, Gansevoort Papers, AO131, 238.

20. Colonel Jacob Cuyler, Albany, to Colonel Peter Gansevoort, August 22, 1778, Gansevoort Papers, AO131, 248; John Stark, Albany, to Peter Gansevoort, August 22, 1778, Gansevoort Papers, AO131, 250.

21. Henry Glen, Schenectady, to Peter Gansevoort, August 23, 1778, Gansevoort Papers, AO131, 250.

22. George Clinton, Poughkeepsie, to General Washington, September 20, 1778, in Clinton, *Public Papers*, 4:59-60; Robert Cochran, Fort Schuyler, to Gansevoort, September 28, 1778, in Ranzan and Hollis, *Hero of Fort Schuyler*, 114-15; Bollen, *George Washington and the Mohawk Frontier*, 84; Graymont, *The Iroquois in the American Revolution*, 178.

23. George Clinton, Poughkeepsie, to General Washington, September 24, 1778, in Clinton, *Public Papers*, 4:78-79.

24. Jeremiah Van Rensselaer, Albany, to Peter Gansevoort, August 20, 1778, Gansevoort Papers, AO131, 244.

25. Lieutenant Colonel Marinus Willett, New Windsor, New York, to Peter Gansevoort, July 7, 1778, Gansevoort Papers, AO131, 223.

26. Jeremiah Van Rensselaer, Albany, to Peter Gansevoort, July 23, 1778, Gansevoort Papers, AO131, 230. He remained with the 3rd New York.

27. Twenty-nine-year-old artillery detachment Matross Stephen Hadlock, five feet, eight inches tall with gray eyes and whitish brown hair, from New

Hampshire, deserted in July (Stephen Hadlock NARA M881 Compiled Service Record). Gansevoort learned from General John Stark on August 13 that two additional men from Fort Stanwix's artillery detachment had been captured near Fort Edward and were being held at Albany. John Stark, Albany, to Peter Gansevoort, August 13, 1778, Gansevoort Papers, AO131, 240.

28. Officers of the 3rd New York Regiment, Fort Schuyler, to Colonel Peter Gansevoort, August 15, 1778, Gansevoort Papers, AO131, 243.

29. Peter Gansevoort, Fort Schuyler, to General George Washington, August 18, 1778, Gansevoort Papers, AO131, 240; Ranzan and Hollis, *Hero of Fort Schuyler*, 109–10.

30. John Fink (Hans Finkanover) PF R3,549; Watt and Morrison, *The British Campaign of 1777,* 1:153, are led astray in analyzing this incident by difficulties reading the name De Witt in Fink's pension file. They also erroneously suggest relating the deserters to the desertion of Lieutenant Livingston.

31. George Washington, Headquarters, White Plains, to Peter Gansevoort, August 18, 1778, Gansevoort Papers, AO131, 240.

32. Peter Gansevoort, Fort Schuyler, to General George Washington, August 18, 1778, Gansevoort Papers, AO131, 241; Hutton Journal, 249.

33. John Stark, Albany, to Peter Gansevoort, August 22, 1778, Gansevoort Papers, AO131, 250.

34. Leonard Gansevoort, Albany, to Peter Gansevoort, August 21, 1778, Gansevoort Papers, AO131, 245.

35. General George Washington, Headquarters, White Plains, to Peter Gansevoort, August 29, 1778, Gansevoort Papers, AO131, 254.

36. Gansevoort received an August 20 letter from Jeremiah Van Rensselaer stating that the bearers of his letter, Peter Buckstaf, Stephen Barns, and Abraham Williams, who faced military punishment for desertion, had thought it better to turn themselves in at Albany rather than abscond entirely. They had asked Van Rensselaer to request a pardon from Gansevoort. Rensselaer had forwarded their request to General Stark, who agreed to write to Gansevoort about their cases. Van Rensselaer told Gansevoort the deserters had promised, just like many other deserters, that if pardoned, they would never desert again. Jeremiah Van Rensselaer, Albany, to Peter Gansevoort, August 20, 1778, Gansevoort Papers, AO131, 244. On August 20, General Stark recommended they be pardoned. General John Stark, Albany, to Peter Gansevoort, August 20, 1778, Gansevoort Papers, AO131, 245.

37. Francis Cole PF S 43,351. Contains supporting statements from fellow 3rd New York privates Cornelius Blank and Baltus Ore.

38. Peter Gansevoort, Fort Schuyler, to Governor George Clinton, August 12, 1778, Gansevoort Papers, AO131, 238.

39. Marinus Willett, Danbury, Connecticut, to Peter Gansevoort, August 29, 1778, Gansevoort Papers, AO131, 255.

40. General George Washington, Headquarters, White Plains, to Peter Gansevoort, August 29, 1778, Gansevoort Papers, AO131, 254.

41. William Fink PF S 23,218. No record of Henry Belyer has been found.

19. The Exhausted 3rd Regiment Finally Departs Fort Stanwix

1. *Muster and Pay Rolls of the War of the Revolution*, 436–41, 446–50.

2. George Washington, Fredericksburg, New York, to George Clinton, October 17, 1778, Founders Online, National Archives, https://founders.archives.gov/documents/Washington/03-17-02-0438; originally published in *The Papers of George Washington*, Revolutionary War Series, vol. 17, *15 September–31 October 1778*, ed. Philander D. Chase (Charlottesville: University of Virginia Press, 2008), 418–19.

3. Alexander Hamilton, Aide-de-Camp to Washington, Fredericksburg, New York, to Colonel Goose Van Schaick, November 4, 1778, Founders Online, National Archives, https://founders.archives.gov/documents/Hamilton/01-01-02-0638; originally published in *The Papers of Alexander Hamilton*, vol. 1, *1768–1778*, ed. Harold C. Syrett (New York: Columbia University Press, 1961), 575.

4. Brigadier Generals James Clinton and Edward Hand, Albany, to General Washington, November 28, 1778, Founders Online, National Archives, https://founders.archives.gov/documents/Washington/03-18-02-0344; originally published in *The Papers of George Washington*, Revolutionary War Series, vol. 18, *1 November 1778–14 January 1779*, ed. Edward G. Lengel (Charlottesville: University of Virginia Press, 2008), 319–20.

5. Brigadier General James Clinton, Albany, to General Washington, December 18, 1778, Founders Online, National Archives, https://founders.archives.gov/documents/Washington/03-18-02-0509; originally published in *The Papers of George Washington*, 18: 446–47.

6. Glatthaar and Martin, *Forgotten Allies*, 227.

7. Corbett, *No Turning Point*, 257; Weddle, *The Compleat Victory*, 218.

8. Corbett, *No Turning Point*, 293, 297, 300. For more on this continuing civil war, see Greene, *History of the Mohawk Valley*, vol. 2.

9. Taylor, *The Divided Ground*, 98; Graymont, *The Iroquois in the American Revolution*, 219.

10. There are numerous publications concerning the Sullivan expedition. These include the good account of Joseph R. Fischer, *A Well-Executed Failure: The Sullivan Campaign against the Iroquois, July–September 1779* (Columbia: University of South Carolina Press, 1997). There are also collections of documents and individual narratives, including *The order book of Capt. Leonard Bleeker: major of brigade in the early part of the expedition under Gen. James Clinton, against the Indian settlements of western New York, in the campaign of 1779* (New York: J. Sabin, 1865); Cook, Frederick, ed., *Journals of the military expedition of Major General John Sullivan against the Six nations of Indians in 1779; with records of centennial celebrations* (Auburn, NY: Knapp, Peck & Thomson, 1887); and John L. Hardenbergh, William McKendry and William Elliott Griffis, *Narratives of Sullivan's Expedition, 1779: Against the Four Nations of the Iroquois & Loyalists by the Continental Army* (Driffield, UK: Leonaur, 2010).

11. Lowenthal, *Marinus Willett*, 65–66, 72–75; Graymont, *The Iroquois in the American Revolution*, 256–58.

12. Sypher, *New York State Society of the Cincinnati*, 473–75.

13. Sypher, *New York State Society of the Cincinnati*, 128–29.

14. Heitman, *Historical Register*, 162.

15. Taylor, *The Divided Ground*, 101; Graymont, *The Iroquois in the American Revolution*, 234.

16. Sypher, *New York State Society of the Cincinnati*, 8–9, 32–33, 190–91, 237–38, 495.

17. Sypher, *New York State Society of the Cincinnati*, 169–70, 591–92.

18. Graymont, *The Iroquois in the American Revolution*, 245.

19. For this account, see Robert Cochran, Fort Schuyler, to General James Clinton, May 13, 14, 1781; General Clinton, Albany, to Robert Cochran, May 16, 1781; and General James Clinton, Albany, to Governor Clinton, May 17, 1781, in Clinton, *Public Papers*, 6:877–82.

20. Governor George Clinton, Poughkeepsie, to General James Clinton, May 19, 1781; Governor George Clinton, Poughkeepsie, to Brigadier General Robert Van Rensselaer, May 19, 1781; and Governor George Clinton, Albany, to General James Clinton, May 2, 1781, in Clinton, *Public Papers*, 6:886–87, 892–93, 903–4; Taylor, *The Divided Ground*, 101.

21. Taylor, *The Divided Ground*, 93.

22. There are several accounts from Wilson's family about how he participated in the surrender at Yorktown, although there are some understandable inaccuracies in details. While the story is plausible, there are no official primary sources to support it. See Croyle, "Future Manlius Postmaster"; Robert Wilson PF W 7,746. The statement of his widow tells the story of Yorktown along with other information on his service. See also Lossing, *Pictorial Field-Book*, 2:318, 320. From information given by Wilson's family and a man who had served with him, Lossing writes:

> The delivery of the colors of the several regiments, twenty-eight in number, was next performed. For this purpose, twenty-eight British captains, each bearing a flag in a case, were drawn up in line. Opposite to them, at a distance of six paces, twenty-eight American sergeants were placed in line to receive the colors. Ensign Wilson of Clinton's brigade, the youngest commissioned officer in the army (being then only eighteen years of age), was appointed by Colonel Hamilton, the officer of the day, to conduct this interesting ceremony. When Wilson gave the order for the British captains to advance two paces, to deliver up their colors, and the American sergeants to advance two paces to receive them, the former hesitated, and gave as a reason that they were unwilling to surrender their flags to non-commissioned officers. Hamilton, who was at a distance, observed this hesitation, and rode up to inquire the cause. On being informed, he willingly spared the feelings of the British captains, and ordered Ensign Wilson to receive them himself, and hand them to the American sergeants.

See also "Sword Presented By Alexander Hamilton To Ensign Robert Wilson. Dress sword, 34 inches long, engraved on underside of guard, '*Presented to / Ensign Robert Wilson / From / Lieu't Col. Alexander Hamilton / Dec. 25th 1781.*'

Hilt originally wound with fine silver wire; the guard, pommel, bow and trimmings are all silver, and the scabbard is of black leather. The blade seems to be of Italian or Spanish workmanship, of the rapier pattern. The sword was presented by Hamilton to Ensign Wilson, the youngest commissioned officer in the American army, as a memento of the part he played in the surrender of Cornwallis' forces at Yorktown." Auction advertisement for Goldberg Coins & Collectibles, http://images.goldbergauctions.com/php/chap_auc.php?site=1&lang=1&sale=22&chapter=1&page=1, viewed March 23, 2023. The engraved information may have been placed by a later owner, weakening the provenance. See https://discoveringhamilton.com/alexander-hamilton-yorktown-to-albany-1781/, viewed March 23, 2023, for author Michael E. Newton's discussion of this story.

Epilogue

1. Sypher, *New York State Society of the Cincinnati*, 169–71; Heitman, *Historical Register*, 242; Corbett, *No Turning Point*, 316–17.

2. For his complete biography, see Lowenthal, *Marinus Willett*; Berry and Morrison, *Marinus Willett*.

3. Jacob G. Ullery, comp., *Men of Vermont: An Illustrated Biographical History of Vermonters and Sons of Vermont* (Brattleboro: Transcript Publishing Company, 1894), 52–53. This account contains several errors, including not mentioning Cochran's having been at Fort Stanwix at the time of the siege.

4. Sypher, *New York State Society of the Cincinnati*, 590–91.

5. See https://www.owlapps.net/owlapps_apps/articles?id=1421698&lang=en for a biography.

6. Sypher, *New York State Society of the Cincinnati*, 513–14; *Albany Register*, February 5, 1805, 3.

7. Sypher, *New York State Society of the Cincinnati*, 128–29; Thomas Grier Evans, *De Witt Family, Ulster County, New York* (New York, 1886), 12–13.

8. Sypher, *New York State Society of the Cincinnati*, 237–38.

9. Sypher, *New York State Society of the Cincinnati*, 459; *New York Gazette*, October 28, 1799, 2.

10. *Daily Advertiser* (New York), August 26, 1786, 1; Thomas E. V. Smith, *The City of New York in the Year of Washington's Inauguration, 1789* (New York, 1889), 121; Heitman, *Historical Register*, 72–73. Several different years appear in sources for his death, but none can be confirmed.

11. Sypher, *New York State Society of the Cincinnati*, 191; James Gregg PF W 17,025, statement of Captain Leonard Bleeker.

12. Robert Wilson PF W7,746; Connie Myer, "Manlius War Hero Received British Flag," *Post-Standard* (Manlius, NY), July 4, 1967; *The Columbian* (New York), June 20, 1811, 3.

13. *United States Gazette* (Philadelphia), November 5, 1806, 2.

14. Schuyler, *Institution of the Society of the Cincinnati*, 105; *Salem* (Massachusetts) *Gazette*, March 10, 1826, 3.

15. Ichabod Stoddard PF S42387.

16. *Trenton (New Jersey) Federalist*, November 5, 1810, 3.

17. Sypher, *New York State Society of the Cincinnati*, 495–96; *National Advocate* (New York), March 7, 1826, 2.

18. *New York Evening Post*, September 11, 1824, 2.

19. Sypher, *New York State Society of the Cincinnati*, 32–33.

20. Sypher, *New York State Society of the Cincinnati*, 474; *New York Weekly Museum*, March 14, 1795, 3.

21. The author, a direct descendant of Scriber, was graciously permitted to photograph the original painting in June 1995 at the home of another descendant, Ruth Jones Lindsay, near Catskill, New York.

22. Henry Ritter PF S 19,449.

23. Glatthaar and Martin, *Forgotten Allies*, 312.

24. Graymont, *The Iroquois in the American Revolution*, 240.

25. Taylor, *The Divided Ground*, 136–37, 145.

26. For more on the land issues and how the Indians suffered, see Taylor, *The Divided Ground*, chap. 5.

27. Graymont, *The Iroquois in the American Revolution*, 241; Taylor, *The Divided Ground*, 157–62, 179. Taylor gives a detailed explanation of the events that led to the takeover of vast amounts of Oneida and other Iroquois nations' lands.

28. Taylor, *The Divided Ground*, 210, 196.

29. For more on the development of Rome, New York, and the Fort Stanwix National Monument, see Christopher Zackey, "The Naming of Rome New York," http://www.jervislibrary.org/naming_of_rome.html; Foundation Document Overview—Fort Stanwix National Monument, https://www.nps.gov/fost/upload/FOST_Foundation-Doc.pdf; and Joan M. Zenzen, *Fort Stanwix National Monument: Reconstructing the Past and Partnering for the Future* (Albany: State University of New York Press, 2008).

Bibliography

Primary Sources—Unpublished

Calendar of the Military Papers of Peter Gansevoort [Senior], July 4, 1754, through December 31, 1780, New York State Archives Series AO131

Compiled Service Records of Soldiers Who Served in the American Army during the Revolutionary War, National Archives and Records Administration (NARA) M881

Founders Online, NARA, National Historical Publications and Records Commission (NHPRC). https://founders.archives.gov/

Horatio Gates Papers, New York Historical Society

Marinus Willett's Orderly Book, New-York Historical Society

Numbered Records Books Concerning Military Operations and Service, Pay, and Settlement of Accounts, and Supplies in the War Department Collection of Revolutionary War Records, NARA M853

Papers of the Continental Congress, NARA M247

Philip Schuyler Papers, New York Public Library

Revolutionary War Pension and Bounty Land Warrant Application Files, NARA M804

Revolutionary War Rolls, 1775-1783, 1776-1777, NARA M246

Primary Sources—Published

Adams, Charles Francis, ed. *Familiar Letters of John Adams and His Wife Abigail Adams, during the Revolution. With a memoir of Mrs. Adams.* New York: Hurd and Houghton, 1876.

Baldwin, Jeduthan. *The Revolutionary Journal of Col. Jeduthan Baldwin, 1775–1778.* Edited by Thomas Williams Baldwin. Bangor, 1906.

Beecher, Raymond, ed. *Letters from a Revolution, 1775–1783: A Selection from the Bronck Family Papers at the Greene County Historical Society.* Albany: New York State American Revolution Bicentennial Commission, 1973.

Broadhead, J. R., B. Fernow, and E. B. O'Callaghan. *Documents Relative to the Colonial History of the State of New York.* 15 vols. Albany: Weed, Parsons, 1853.

Burgoyne, John. *A State of the Expedition from Canada, as Laid before the House of Commons.* London: J. Almon, 1780.

Calendar of Historical Manuscripts, Relating to the War of the Revolution, In the Office of the Secretary of State, Albany, N.Y. Vols. 1-2. Albany: Weed, Parsons, and Co., 1868.

BIBLIOGRAPHY

Clinton, George. *Public Papers of George Clinton, First Governor of New York, 1777–1795–1801–1804*. 10 vols. New York and Albany: State of New York, 1900.

Elmer, Ebenezer. "Extracts from the Journal of Surgeon Ebenezer Elmer of the New Jersey Continental Line, September 11-19, 1777." *Pennsylvania Magazine of History and Biography* 35, no. 1 (1911): 103-7.

———. "Journal of an Expedition to Canada in 1776." *Proceedings of the New Jersey Historical Society* 2 (1847): 95-150.

Ewing, George. "Journal of George Ewing, a Revolutionary Soldier, of Greenwich, New Jersey." *American Monthly Magazine* 37 (July–December 1910): 471-73.

Force, Peter. *American Archives*, 4th ser., *Containing a Documentary History of the English Colonies in North America, From the King's Message to Parliament, of March 7, 1774, to the Declaration of Independence by the United States*. 6 vols. Washington, DC: M. St. Clair Clarke and P. Force, 1837-1846.

———. *American Archives*, 5th ser., *Containing a Documentary History of the United States of America, From the Declaration of Independence, July 4, 1776, to the Definitive Treaty of Peace with Great Britain, September 3, 1783*. 3 vols. Washington, DC: M. St. Clair Clarke and P. Force, 1848-1853.

Hamilton, Milton W., et al. eds. *The Papers of Sir William Johnson* 14 vols. Albany: University of the State of New York, 1921-1965.

Journals of the Continental Congress, 1774–1789. Edited by Worthington C. Ford et al. 34 vols. Washington, DC, 1904-1937.

Journals of the Provincial Congress, Provincial Convention, Committee of Safety and Council of Safety of the State of New York: 1775–1776–1777. 2 vols. Albany: Thurlow Weed, Printer to the State, 1842.

Lender, Mark Edward, and James Kirby Martin, eds. *Citizen Soldier: The Revolutionary War Journal of Joseph Bloomfield*. Yardley, PA: Westholme, 2018.

Letters of Delegates to Congress, 1774–1789. Edited by Paul H. Smith. 26 vols. Washington, DC: US Government Printing Office, 1976-2000.

Lowenthal, Larry, ed., *Days of Siege: A Journal of the Siege of Fort Stanwix in 1777*. [New York:] Eastern Acorn Press, 1983.

Mohawk Valley in the Revolution: Committee of Safety Papers and Genealogical Compendium. Franklin Park, NJ: Liberty Bell Associates, 1978.

Muster and Pay Rolls of the War of the Revolution, 1775–1783. Vol. 48. Collections of the New-York Historical Society for the Year 1915. New York: Printed for the Society, 1916.

New York Colonial Muster Rolls, 1664–1775. Vol. 1. Report of the State Historian of the State of New York. Madison: University of Wisconsin, 2000.

Proceedings of a General Court Martial, held at Major General Lincoln's quarters, near Quaker-Hill, in the State of New-York, by order of His Excellency General Washington, Commander in Chief of the army of the United States of America, for the trial of Major General Schuyler, October 1, 1778, Major General Lincoln, president. Philadelphia: Hall and Sellers, 1778.

Ranzan, David A., and Matthew J. Hollis, eds. *Hero of Fort Schuyler: Selected Revolutionary War Correspondence of Brigadier General Peter Gansevoort, Jr*. Jefferson, NC: McFarland & Co., 2014.

BIBLIOGRAPHY 307

The Remembrancer: or, Impartial Repository of Public Events. For the Year 1777. London, 1778.

Retzer, Henry J., and Thomas M. Barker. "The Hessen–Hanau Jägers, the Siege of Fort Stanwix and the Battle of Oriskany: The Diary of First Lieutenant Philipp Jakob Hildebrandt." *The Hessians: Journal of the Johannes Schwalm Historical Association* 15 (2012): 35-44.

Robertaccio, Joseph. *Documents Relating to the Battle of Oriskany and the Siege of Fort Stanwix*. 3rd edition. https://www.fort-plank.com/ORISKANY_Robertaccios_Notes_Updated.pdf.

Scudder, William, "The Journal of William Scudder, an officer in the late New-York line." Evan Early American Imprint Collection Text Creation Partnership. https://quod.lib.umich.edu/e/evans/N21073.0001.001/1:3?rgn=div1;view=fulltext.

Thacher, James. *A Military Journal during the American Revolutionary War, from 1775 to 1783*. Boston: Richardson & Lord, 1823.

Willett, William M. *A Narrative of the Military Actions of Colonel Marinus Willett, Taken Chiefly from his own Manuscript*. New York: G. & C. & H. Carvill, 1831.

Secondary Sources

Aimone, Alan C., and Eric I. Manders. "A Note on New York City's Independent Companies, 1775-1776." *New York History* 63, no. 1 (January 1982): 59-73.

Barker, William V. H. *Early Families of Herkimer County, New York*. Baltimore: Genealogy Publishing Co., 2001.

Baxter, Katharine Schuyler. *A Godchild of Washington: A Picture of the Past*. London: F. T. Neely, [c1897].

Berleth, Richard. *Bloody Mohawk: The French and Indian War and American Revolution on New York's Frontier*. New York: Black Dome, 2009.

Berry, A. J., and James F. Morrison. *Marinus Willett: Saviour of the Mohawk Valley*. CreateSpace Independent Publishing Platform, 2014.

Bollen, Norman J. *George Washington and the Mohawk Frontier*. Lulu Publishing Services, 2018.

Bookstaver, Jacob Edgar. *The Willett (Willetts–Willett–Willits) Genealogy: A Compilation of all the Branches in England and America*. Binghamton, NY: Twentieth Century, 1906.

Burch, Jeannette Scriver. *Schryver Genealogy*. Self-published, Cannon Falls, MN, 1988.

Campbell, William W. *Annals of Tryon County; or, the Border Warfare of New York, during the Revolution*. New York: J. & J. Harper, 1831.

Corbett, Theodore. *No Turning Point: The Saratoga Campaign in Perspective*. Norman: University of Oklahoma Press, 2012.

Croyle, Johnathan. "How a Future Manlius Postmaster Helped Accept the British Surrender at Yorktown in 1781." *Syracuse Post-Standard*, July 7, 2022.

Egly, T. W. *History of the First New York Regiment, 1775–1783*. Hampton, NH: P. E. Randall, 1981.

Gardner, Asa Bird. "The New York Continental Line of the Army of the Revolution." *Magazine of American History* 7 (December 1887): 401–19.

Glatthaar, Joseph T., and James Kirby Martin. *Forgotten Allies: The Oneida Indians and the American Revolution*. New York: Hill and Wang, 2006.

Goring, Rich. *The Fishkill Supply Depot and Encampment during the Years 1776–1778*. Waterford, NY: New York State Office of Parks and Recreation, 1975.

Graymont, Barbara. *The Iroquois in the American Revolution*. Syracuse: Syracuse University Press, 1972.

Greene, Nelson. *History of the Mohawk Valley, Gateway to the West, 1614–1925: Covering the Six Counties of Schenectady, Schoharie, Montgomery, Fulton, Herkimer, and Oneida*. 4 vols. Chicago: S. J. Clarke, 1925.

Hanson, Lee, and Dick Ping Hsu. *Casemates and Cannonballs: Archeological Investigations at Fort Stanwix, Rome, New York*. Publications in Archeology 14. Washington, DC: US Department of the Interior, National Park Service, 1975.

Heitman, Francis B. *Historical Register of Officers of the Continental Army during the War of the Revolution, April 1775 to December 1783*. Washington, DC: Rare Book Shop Publishing Company, 1914.

Jacobson, Michael. "Battlefield Delineation: Siege of Fort Stanwix and Battle of Oriskany." Battlefield KOCOA Assessment and Mapping Project, GA-2255-11-017. Rome, NY, 2013. http://npshistory.com/publications/fost/stanwix-oriskany-arpa.pdf.

Johnson, Henry P. *The Campaign of 1776 Around New York and Brooklyn*. Brooklyn, NY: Long Island Historical Society, 1878.

Jones, Pomroy. *Annals and Recollections of Oneida County*. Rome, NY: Published by the Author, 1851.

Jones, Thomas. *History of New York during the Revolutionary War*. Vol. 1. New York: New-York Historical Society, 1879.

Lothrop, Samuel K. *Life of Samuel Kirkland, Missionary to the Indians*. Boston: Little and Brown, 1848.

Lossing, Benson J. *The Pictorial Field-Book of the Revolution*. Vol. 2. New York: Harper & Brothers, 1852.

Lowenthal, Larry. *Marinus Willett: Defender of the Northern Frontier*. Fleischmanns, NY: Purple Mountain Press, 2000.

Luzader, John F. *Fort Stanwix: Construction and Military History*. Fort Washington, PA: Eastern National, 2001.

———. *Saratoga: A Military History of the Decisive Campaign of the American Revolution*. 2008. New York: Savas Beatie, 2010.

Luzader, John F., Louis Torres, and Orville W. Carroll. *Fort Stanwix: Construction and Military History, Historic Furnishing Study, and Historic Structure Report*. Washington, DC: Office of Park Historic Preservation, National Park Service, US Department of the Interior, 1976.

Martin, James Kirby, and Mark Edward Lender. *"A Respectable Army": The Military Origins of the Republic, 1763–1789*. 3rd edition. Chichester, UK: John Wiley & Sons, 2015.

Mayer, Holly A. *Belonging to the Army: Camp Followers and Community during the American Revolution.* Columbia: University of South Carolina Press, 1996.

Neagles, James C. *Summer Soldiers: A Survey and Index of Revolutionary War Courts-Martial.* Salt Lake City: Ancestry Incorporated, 1986.

Neimeyer, Charles Patrick. *America Goes to War: A Social History of the Continental Army.* New York: New York University Press, 1996.

Rees, John U. *"The uses and conveniences of different kinds of Water Craft": Continental Army Vessels on Inland Waterways, 1775–1782.* 2001. Academia.com. 2014.

Reid, W. Max. *The Story of Old Fort Johnson.* New York: Putnams, 1906.

Ruddiman, John A. *Becoming Men of Some Consequence: Youth and Military Service in the Revolutionary War.* Charlottesville: University of Virginia Press, 2014.

Schnitzer, Eric, and Don Troiani. *Don Troiani's Campaign to Saratoga—1777: The Turning Point of the Revolutionary War in Paintings, Artifacts, and Historical Narrative.* Guilford, CT: Stackpole Books, 2019.

Schoolcraft, Henry R. *Historical Considerations on the Siege and Defence of Fort Stanwix, in 1777.* New York: Press of the Historical Society, 1846.

Schuyler, John. *Institution of the Society of the Cincinnati: Formed by the Officers of the American Army of the Revolution, 1783, with Extracts, from the Proceedings of Its General Meetings and from the Transactions of the New York State Society.* New York: Society of the Cincinnati, 1886.

Scott, John Albert. *Fort Stanwix (Fort Schuyler) and Oriskany.* Sesquicentennial Edition. Rome, NY: Rome Sentinel, 1927.

Simms, Jeptha. *The Frontiersmen of New York: showing customs of the Indians, vicissitudes of the pioneer white settlers, and border strife in two wars.* 2 vols. Albany: G. C. Riggs, 1882.

Sterling, Alan E. *Defenders of Liberty: Fort Stanwix during the American War for Independence.* Whitesboro, NY: Mohawk Valley History Project, 2005.

Stone, William L. *Life of Joseph Brant—Thayendanegea.* New York: A. V. Blake, 1838.

Storbeck, Katherine M. *The Fort in the Wilderness.* Utica, NY: North Country Books, 1998.

Sypher, Francis J., Jr. *New York State Society of the Cincinnati: Biographies of Original Members and Other Continental Officers.* Fishkill, NY: New York State Society of the Cincinnati, 2004.

Taylor, Alan. *The Divided Ground: Indians, Settlers, and the Northern Borderland of the American Revolution.* New York: Alfred A. Knopf, 2006.

Ward, Harry M. *George Washington's Enforcers: Policing the Continental Army.* Carbondale: Southern Illinois University Press, 2006.

Watt, Gavin K. *Rebellion in the Mohawk Valley: The St. Leger Expedition of 1777.* Toronto: The Dundurn Group, 2002.

Watt, Gavin K., and James F. Morrison. *The British Campaign of 1777.* Vol. 1. *The St. Leger Expedition: The Forces of the Crown and Congress.* 2nd edition. Milton, Canada: Global Heritage Press, 2005.

Weaver, Philip D. *The 3rd New Jersey in New-York: Stories from "The Jersey Greys" of 1776.* Highland, NY: Continental Consulting, 2020.

Weddle, Kevin J. *The Compleat Victory: Saratoga and the American Revolution*. New York: Oxford University Press, 2021.

Willett, Albert James. *The Willett Families of North America*. Easley, SC: Southern Historical Press, 1985.

Wright, Robert K. *The Continental Army*. Washington, DC: Center of Military History, United States Army, 1983.

Index

The letter f or t following a page number denotes a figure or a table.

Albany, New York, 16–19
   3rd New York at, 38, 54, 62, 65–66, 75, 91, 244–46
   Elmore's regiment at, 36, 38, 54, 80
   Saratoga campaign, 1, 91, 104, 132, 149, 179, 181
Alden, Col. Ichabod, 233–34
Ament, Ens. Eldred, 144, 224, 239
Ancrum, Capt. William, 153–55
Aorson, Capt. Aaron, 185, 248, 253, 266n22
   at Fort Stanwix, 74, 78, 86, 129, 165
   recruiting, 40–41, 54, 165
Arnold, Gen. Benedict, 40, 116, 169–75, 181, 195
artillery at Fort Stanwix, 5, 26, 88, 201, 228, 267n30
   supplies for, 26, 109, 131, 183, 194, 225, 267n30
artillery, British, 92, 146–47, 150–52, 171
   inadequacy of, 111, 135, 166, 201–2
artillery detachment at Fort Stanwix, 41, 43, 73, 81, 90, 101, 144, 214, 227
   clothing problems, 90–91, 103, 192, 234, 278n22
artillery fire, 149, 159–60, 233
   as a signal, 143,
   cannon, 4, 27, 42, 88, 151, 127f, 267n30
   grapeshot, 133
   howitzers, 41, 163, 165
   mortars, 92
   on the British, 139, 146, 133
   on the fort, 151–52, 156–57, 162–67
attacks very near Fort Stanwix
   on civilians, 117–18, 229
   on soldiers, 96, 104–5, 110, 134, 229, 234–35
Aughneonh (Big Bear), 132, 169

Badlam, Maj. Ezra, 116, 120, 129, 144, 146
Bagley, Ens. Josiah, 83–84, 144, 229, 239
bakehouse at Fort Stanwix, 99, 133
bakers, 193
Baker, John, 103
Baldwin, Col. Jeduthan, 42, 267n33
Ball, John, 114, 144, 146, 220, 223
barns, 32, 97, 132–33, 139–40
barracks, 8, 25, 98, 203, 209, 228
   bunks, 76, 89–90, 98–99
   east barracks, 89, 99, 125f, 126f
   in casemates, 74–76, 90, 98
   inside Fort Stanwix, 87, 89–90, 99, 156, 183, 196, 233
   outside Fort Stanwix, 90, 97, 140
   west barracks, 89, 99, 124f, 126f
Bass (Curtis), Henry, 40–41
bastions, 5, 25–26, 88, 164, 201, 205
   artillery mounted on, 171, 267n30
   bombproofs, 99, 127f, 133, 156, 183, 205, 213
   defender's positions, 129, 171, 184–85
   northeast bastion, 124f, 140, 267n30
   northwest bastion, 126f, 133, 135, 139–40, 142, 151, 165–66
   southeast bastion, 99–100, 175
   southwest bastion, 124f, 125f, 126f, 127f, 131–34, 140, 156, 167
bateau
   description of, 20
   use by British forces, 116, 168, 170
   use by Fort Stanwix garrison, 86–89, 93, 98, 130–31, 230, 234, 236–38
bateau men, 81, 86, 134, 210, 231, 233–34, 236
Bateman, Adj. John, 83–85

311

INDEX

bayonets, 67, 145, 151, 160, 171
Bellinger, Col. Peter, 234
Bennington, Vermont, 40, 164, 174–75, 180
Bird, Lt. Henry, 131, 145
Bleeker, Capt. Leonard, 254, 269n27
   post-siege, 185, 192, 208, 212, 235, 239, 248
   pre-siege, 51, 72, 84, 103, 117
   siege, 129, 144
Bloomfield, Capt. Joseph, 17, 24–27, 30–32, 34, 36, 85, 86
Bogardus, Lt. Benjamin, 144, 193, 239
Bogart, Lt. Isaac, 54, 190, 213, 220, 223
bounty jumping, 61, 63, 72
Bowen, Lt. Prentice, 55, 72, 103, 114, 172, 239, 241
Brant, Joseph, 92, 131, 143, 200, 237, 247, 280n46
British army units with St. Leger
   8th Regiment of Foot, 32, 92, 135, 155
   34th Regiment of Foot, 92, 135, 153
   Butler's rangers, 93, 113, 118
   Hessen-Hanau Jägers, 92–93, 111, 136, 138, 171, 246
   King's Royal Regiment of New York (Royal Yorkers), 18, 92–93, 113, 135, 160, 167, 246
Burgoyne, Gen. John, 1–2, 43, 91–92, 180–81, 185, 199
Burns, John, 83–85
Butler, Lt. Col. John, 15, 28, 74, 92, 107, 152
Butler, Ens. Walter, 32
Byerd, Godfrey, 214–15, 296n83

camp color men, 94, 102, 163, 203
Canada
   Burgoyne campaign, 1, 96
   Canadian campaign, 16–17, 22, 25, 34, 47, 50
   Elmore's regiment, 36–38
   Loyalists, 18, 92
   St. Leger force, 31, 91, 93
Canajoharie, New York, 39, 79, 92, 97–98, 119, 159
Carleton, Christopher, 200, 246
Carleton, Sir Guy, 1, 28–29, 34, 200
Carry Place (Carrying Place, Oneida Carrying Place), 2, 19, 259n2
   colonial importance, 2–5, 8–10, 43, 60

Fort Stanwix location, 91, 96, 231, 245, 249
   Rome, New York, 257–58
   settlers at, 25–26, 39, 119
casemates, 26, 75, 89–90, 98–99
cattle, 29–30, 130, 192–93, 214, 230
   bringing to the fort, 174, 225, 230, 236–37, 239
   problems with, 201
   protection of, 119, 140
Caughnawaga, New York, 81, 89, 119, 246
Cayugas, 218
Cherry Valley, New York, 9–10, 224, 234
Clanis Kahiktoton (Cornelius), 132
Claus, Daniel, 109–11, 113, 115
cleanliness at Fort Stanwix, 94, 102, 130, 175, 190, 203
Clinton, George, 163, 218, 243, 252
Clinton, Gen. Henry, 224, 226
Clinton, Gen. James, 244, 246, 248
clothing for 3rd New York
   during training, 58, 62
   failure to supply, 53, 67, 87, 102, 136, 206
   for recruiting, 56–57
   soldiers selling, 73
   storage of, 98
   supplies of, 207t, 208–9, 236–37
   uniform, 88, 192
   washing, 163, 293n28
clothing for Elmore's regiment, 74
clothing for Oneida allies, 20, 245–46
clothing for Savage's detachment, 90, 101, 234
clothing for St. Leger's troops, 145
Cochran, Maj. Robert, 50, 252
   after the siege, 196, 217, 223, 230, 234–35, 238, 247–49
   before joining 3rd New York, 38–39, 40
   before the siege, 40, 65–66, 71, 73–74, 76, 82–85
   during the siege, 165, 168, 170
Cohoes Falls, 2
Colbrath, Lt. William, 68, 79, 114, 215, 238, 285n16
   diary, 165, 170, 175
Conine, Lt. Philip, 106, 117, 144, 238
construction of Fort Stanwix, 4–5
Continental Army
   first establishment, 16, 47, 50–51, 106, 198

INDEX   313

Northern Department, 27, 48, 75, 86–87, 103, 109, 113
  second establishment, 16, 36, 39, 46, 50–52, 56, 198
  third establishment, 39–41, 45–46, 50–52, 56–57, 219
Continental Army units
  3rd New Jersey, 16, 20, 24, 27, 31, 34, 85, 92–93
  3rd New York, 72, 219–20, 221t, 223
  Elmore's regiment, 31–34, 36–44, 54, 65, 73, 80
  Savage's artillery detachment, 73, 81, 90, 144, 190, 222
  Wesson's regiment, 120, 130, 143–44, 173, 282n50, 283n9
Continental Congress, 10, 21, 42, 46, 53, 180, 215
  Board of War, 202, 208
cooking, 90, 96, 99–100, 163, 202
Cornwallis, Gen. Charles, 56, 250, 279n39, 303n22
courts-martial cases, 63, 80, 104, 190, 213, 238
  abusing an officer, 103, 212
  allowing prisoner to escape, 172
  arguments, 212
  desertion, 63, 188, 229, 238–40
  disobeying orders, 103, 212–13
  drunk on duty, 103
  plundering, 72
  selling uniform, 19
  sleeping on duty, 103
  theft, 103, 190, 213
courts of inquiry, 33, 84–85, 191–92, 212
covered way exit, 25, 87–88, 124f, 184

Davis, Thomas, 28
Dayton, Col. Elias, 16–20, 22–23, 27–34, 92, 97, 100, 235
Deane, James, 235
Defendorff, Lt. Henry, 84–86, 114, 142, 144, 220, 223
Delyrod, Stephen, 39, 75, 205, 274n17
Deserontyon, John, 110
desertions, 28–29
  3rd New Jersey, 29
  British, 37, 49, 146, 167–70, 186, 215
desertions from 3rd New York regiment
  bounty jumping, 63
  during the siege, 166
  efforts to reduce, 72, 114, 184, 211

officers, 189
  post-siege, 174, 188, 197t, 211
  pre-siege, 59, 61, 66, 79, 81, 95, 102–4, 113–14
  reasons for, 211
  to the British, 113, 140, 152, 156–57, 160, 162, 167–69
DeWitt, Capt. Thomas, 247, 253, 269n3
  at Fort Dayton relief, 82, 84–88, 94
  building company, 270n14
  post-siege, 185
  siege, 119–20, 129
discipline issues, 57–58, 80, 82, 101, 103, 190, 199, 212
ditch around Fort Stanwix, 25, 76, 88, 124f, 140, 165, 196, 204
  as a shelter, 130, 140, 193
drill squads, 64, 216

Elmer, Lt. Ebenezer, 16, 18
Elmore, Col. Samuel, 33–44, 71, 73–75, 78–79, 100, 235, 273n5
embrasures, 5, 26, 88, 127f, 129, 133, 151
Ewing, George, 5, 17–18, 24–25, 28

fatigue parties, 32, 41, 88, 90, 186, 203–4
  artificers, 90
  fort cleanliness, 94
  fort restoration, 90, 97, 102, 108, 182–83, 191, 202
  road work, 97
  rum for, 104, 203–4
  sod collection, 90, 109, 143
  wagoners, 90
  wood collection, 90, 97, 160, 164, 166, 202, 204
Fink, William, 79, 147, 187, 241–42
Finkanover, Hans (John Fink), 79, 239, 274n4
firewood, 76, 98, 125f, 166, 196, 202–3
Fishkill, New York
  3rd New York organizes at, 54–55, 58–60, 62, 64–66, 83
  officers appointed at, 5
  recruiting at, 54, 59–60, 65, 270n14
  supplies at, 236–37
flags
  enemy, 147
  Fort Stanwix, 134–35, 156, 232
Fonda, Jelles, 39
food. *See* provisions at Fort Stanwix

INDEX

Fort Ann, 65
Fort Brewerton, 238
Fort Bull, 4, 228
Fort Constitution, 65–67, 71, 78, 80–81, 87, 272n2, 275n15
Fort Dayton
  3rd New Jersey at, 24
  3rd New York at, 82–86, 214
  Capt. DeWitt at, 119
  Col. Wesson at, 119, 139
  construction of, 31, 38
  Elmore's regiment at, 38–40
  Maj. Badlam at, 116, 120
  relief incident, 82–85
  road to Fort Stanwix, 90, 94, 108, 202, 233
  supply route, 130, 230–31, 233–34, 236–37
Fort Frontenac, 7, 48
Fort George, 46–47
Fort Newport, 4, 109, 131, 168
Fort Ontario, 7, 29
Fort Schuyler. *See various Fort Stanwix entries*
Fort Stanwix maintenance and repair
  3rd New Jersey, 27, 29, 31–32
  3rd New York, 74–75, 86, 89–90, 93, 97, 101, 107–9, 133
  after the siege, 182, 191, 202–3, 228
  Elmore's regiment, 42
Fort Stanwix structural elements. *See* bastions; covered way exit; ditch around Fort Stanwix; embrasures; glacis at Fort Stanwix; parapets; pickets; ramparts of Fort Stanwix
Fort Ticonderoga, 67, 86, 111–12, 115, 155, 179–80
Fort William Henry, 7, 47, 137
Frantz, Conrad, 110, 143–44, 284n5
French and Indian War (Seven Years' War), 1, 3, 11, 51
furloughs, 182–84, 187–90, 194–95, 197t, 201, 217–18, 230

Gansevoort, Col. Peter, 46–47
  actions during siege, 129–30, 132, 134, 142–143, 147, 149, 159
  after siege at Fort Stanwix, 160–66, 168–73, 179–83, 185–87
  appearance and personality, 48, 211
  as colonel commandant, 181–82, 199
  concern for food supplies, 205, 210, 225, 230–31, 236–37
  concern for fort cleanliness, 94, 102, 130, 175
  concern for fort supplies, 193–94, 200
  concern for Oneidas, 174, 194–95, 205, 225, 234
  concern for recruiting, 187
  concern for regiment strength, 214–15
  concern for soldier health, 190, 204
  concern for training, 216
  congratulated by his officers, 182
  dealing with fort women, 204
  disciplinarian, 212–13, 225–30, 237–41
  first weeks at Fort Stanwix, 43, 74–75, 78, 80–82, 86, 88–90, 93
  furlough after siege, 188, 195, 217
  life after Fort Stanwix, 243–46
  Oneida relationship, 81, 106–8, 120, 132, 169, 236
  organizing 3rd New York, 58, 61, 64–66, 68
  preparing for siege, 97–101, 105, 107–9, 114, 116–18, 120
  preventing local attacks, 200
  recruiting 3rd New York, 40, 54–55, 215
  refusal to surrender, 136–38, 150–56
  regimental clothing, 206, 208–9, 214, 237
  regimental restructure, 218–20, 224, 232–33
  restoration of the fort, 195, 201, 203
  retirement, 248–49, 251
  seeks heavier artillery, 201–2
  seeks transfer of regiment, 198, 218, 241
  sends out scouts, 200, 234
  Sullivan campaign, 246
  threats of post-siege attacks, 233–34
garden at Fort Stanwix, 99–100, 139, 201, 205
Gates, Maj. Gen. Horatio, 47–48, 75, 80, 82, 85–86, 113, 173–75, 185–86
Geake, Samuel, 215, 222, 225–30, 239–40
Germain, Lord George, 1, 180
German Flats, New York, 11, 15, 24–28, 31–34, 38, 169, 237
glacis at Fort Stanwix, 25, 88, 90, 97, 117–18, 126f, 160, 248
Glen, Henry, 86, 224, 230, 236–37
Good Peter (Oneida), 9, 234, 256

INDEX

Gouvion, Jean Baptiste, 201, 206, 225
Gregg, Capt. James, 61, 248, 253, 270n7
   scalping of, 104–8, 114, 189, 223, 229, 279n39, 279n40
guard duty, 97, 102–3, 165, 191, 228
   picket guard, 129, 184
guardhouse at Fort Stanwix, 75, 103, 201, 212–13, 228, 230, 239

Hamilton, Col. Alexander, 250, 254, 302n22
Hancock, John, 20–21, 29, 181
Hand, Gen. Edward, 244
Han Yerry Tewahangarahken or Han Yerry Doxtader, 132, 148, 185, 255
Hanyost T,hanaghghanegeaghu, 132
Hare, Lt. Henry, 118
Hare, Capt. John, 110
Haudenosaunee, 30, 94, 107–8, 246–47
   conferences with, 9, 11, 15, 93, 185, 256
   culture, 9, 30, 34
   divisions among, 10–11, 21–22, 94, 115, 149, 173, 180
   gifts to, 185
   help to British, 11, 172–74, 185, 246
   help to Patriots, 80, 172–74
   land, 3, 7, 246–47
   tendency to neutrality, 10, 94
   trade with at Fort Stanwix, 4, 20–21, 39, 91, 185, 196, 205–6, 245
   visits to Fort Stanwix, 74, 100, 108, 185
   See also Mohawks; Oneidas; Onondagas; Senecas; Tuscaroras
hay
   cattle food, 140
   collecting, 136, 139–40, 193, 196
   growing areas, 5, 205, 210
   harvesting, 119
   haystacks, 140, 158
   use for beds, 98, 136, 140, 158, 203, 210
Henry, John, 228–29
Herkimer, Gen. Nicholas, 39, 107, 119, 142–49, 163, 179
Hess, Han Jost/Joseph, 80, 167, 275n9, 288n40
Hildebrandt, Lt. Phillip, 134–36, 138–39, 155–56, 159, 287n4, 287n9
hospital at Fort Stanwix
   after the siege, 175
   location of, 76, 127f, 133, 156
   medicines and stores, 210
   patients, 118, 167–68, 210
   provisions for, 100, 213
   scalping victims, 110
   stewards, 39, 204
Houston, Capt. John, 55, 57, 72, 274n6
Hubbell, Maj. Nathaniel, 24, 27, 42–43, 115, 263n5
Hudson River (also North River), 1–3, 7, 38, 81, 114, 223, 257
Hutton, Ens. Christopher, 54, 269n5
   as adjutant, 191, 204–5, 213
   court martial duty, 84, 191

illnesses, 53, 103, 189–90
   death from, 59, 103, 210
   smallpox, 190, 204, 244
Iroquois. *See* Haudenosaunee

Jackson, Sgt. Francis, 227–29
Jansen, Capt. Cornelius, 129, 144, 146, 168, 248, 253, 269n28
   court martial duty, 213, 238
   recruiting duty, 270n14
Johnson, Col. Guy, 28
Johnson Hall, 11, 19–20
Johnson, Sir John, 11, 17–18, 92–93, 113, 145, 187, 246
Johnson, Sir William, 4, 8–10, 18, 39, 200
Johnstown, New York, 17–20, 34, 137, 206, 214, 246–47, 259n8
Jones, David, 144, 217
Jones, John, 59, 110, 113

Kanonwalohale, 107, 131, 185, 195, 206, 247, 280n46
Kay-ing-waur-to, 104, 107
Kertel, Sgt. John, 211, 227–29
Kirkland, Rev. Samuel, 10, 21, 42–43, 107, 217, 247, 255–56, 280n46

Lafayette, Marquis de, 200–201, 206, 225, 254
Lake Champlain, 7, 42–43, 47, 200, 246
Lake George, 7, 46
Lake Oneida, 2, 33, 117, 130, 238, 257
Lamarquise, Capt. Bernard de, 42, 73–78, 86–90, 97–98, 100, 103, 115
Lansing, Catharine Gansevoort, 48
Lemmon, Alexander, 102
Lewis, Abijah, 38
Lewis, Samuel, 144, 222, 226, 239
Livingston, Lt. Gilbert, 189
Livingston, Lt. Col. Richard, 82–85

INDEX

magazine at Fort Stanwix, 21, 212, 133, 163, 249
Magee, Ens. Peter, 144, 212, 238
Mason, Rev. John, 113, 116
Maxwell, Sgt. William, 80
Mayre (Mair), Thomas, 33, 97
McCarty, Dennis, 167, 233
McCarty, Nancy, 118, 167–68, 204, 288n38
McClellan, Lt. Thomas, 54, 101, 114, 144, 189, 208, 229, 233–34
McDougall, Col. Alexander, 50, 67, 72, 83
McMichael, Lt. Edward, 27–29
Mellon, Lt. Col. James, 130, 139, 153, 162–63, 166–67
Mississaugas, 33, 264n38
Mohawk River Valley, 10, 18–19, 39, 173, 245, 258
    military activity in, 7, 18, 92, 104, 140, 199, 231
    transportation route, 2–3, 104
    settler population, 3, 7–8, 60, 199
Mohawks, 30, 92–94, 115, 143, 200
Montgomery, Richard, 47, 51, 253
Montreal, Canada, 47, 68, 96, 285n15

National Park Service, ix, 257–58
necessary house at Fort Stanwix, 175, 190, 209, 246
New York City, 16, 22, 45, 48–51, 199, 251, 253–55
New York Convention, 46, 50–51, 62
New York Patriot military units
    associated exempts (militia), 252–53
    militia, 20, 31, 81, 86, 115–20, 147–50, 237
    New York independent companies, 4
    provincial troops, 4
    rangers, 4
    Tryon County militia, 25, 76, 112, 132, 142–43, 224
New York Provincial Congress, 64, 66, 68, 72
Niagara, 18–19, 28

Oneida Castle, 26, 107, 119, 130
Oneida River, 2
Oneidas, 3
    "castles" (villages), 8
    effects of Europeans on, 3, 7–9, 20–21, 30
    lifestyle, 3
    population maintenance, 3
    support for Fort Stanwix, 4, 11, 34, 42, 43, 93, 97, 107
    use of the Carry Place, 8
    white opinion of, 30–31, 80
Onondagas, 235
Oriska (Oriskany), 9, 21, 25, 32, 132, 174, 193–94
    Battle of, 142, 146–50, 163–64, 166
Osborn, Sarah, 223
Ostrander, Lt. Thomas, 114, 144, 192, 217, 220, 223, 289
Oswego, 3, 15, 19, 28–34, 43, 93, 113, 233–35
Oswego River, 2

Palatine Germans, 3, 18, 60, 67, 107
Palatine, New York, 187, 242
parapets, 5, 25, 76, 117, 124f, 126f, 129
Peekskill, New York, 65–67
Peters/Peterson, Capt. William, 231, 234, 236–37
pickets, 25, 88, 90, 96–97, 124f, 133, 196, 202
Pinckney, Jonathan, 67, 212, 250, 271n30
Poughkeepsie, New York, 79, 209, 215, 217, 227, 253, 271n27
Powless, Paul, 131–32, 171
provisions at Fort Stanwix, 20–21, 99–100, 116–17, 192–94, 228–30
    beef, 29–30, 130, 236
    flour, 29–30, 130, 192, 234, 236
    milk, 193, 213–14
    pork, 29–30, 192
    salt provisions, 29, 130, 183, 192, 236
    scarcity of, 100, 109, 116–17
    sources of, 225
    storage of, 75, 156, 205
    transportation to the fort, 120, 131, 234, 236
punishments at Fort Stanwix
    death, 63, 169, 229–30, 239
    drummed out of fort, 229
    execution, 118, 239–40
    firing squad, 238–39
    flogging, 63, 80, 103–4, 114–15, 188, 191, 211–13, 229–30
    hanging, 171, 187
    loss of cows, 213
    rum ration cut off, 213

Quebec, Canada, 16, 29, 37, 47, 60, 102, 253, 270n17

ramparts of Fort Stanwix, 5, 7, 25–26, 87–88, 124f, 125f, 133, 135, 140

INDEX

Rawdon, Lord Francis, 226–28
recruiting
  artillery detachment, 41, 91
  British desertion agents, 226–28
  competition for recruits, 39–41
  confusion, 79
  duty, 71, 114, 182, 189, 214
  Elmore's regiment, 36–38
  enemy deserters, 186, 215
  enlistment terms, 16, 57
  extending enlistment, 71
  motivations for enlisting, 37, 53, 55, 57, 64
  procedures, 38, 40, 46, 54–57, 59–60, 66, 72
Reed, Jacob, 235
Reyter, George, 7, 118
Ritter, Henry, 66, 68, 88, 133, 156, 169–70
  early discharge, 187–88, 255, 291n32
  father's death in battle, 147
Rome, New York, 257–58
Roof, John, 25, 80, 140, 235
  John Roof Jr., 163, 263n10, 282n45
  sends family to Canajoharie, 119
  servant girl, 118, 159
rum, 99
  discipline concern, 213
  for fatigue parties, 186, 192, 202–03
  gift to Indians, 42, 93, 185
  selling of, 33–34
  supply of, 234

Saratoga Campaign, 1–2, 136, 175–76, 180–81, 185, 199, 215, 245–46
Savage, Capt. Lt. Joseph
  building artillery detachment, 41, 73–74
  leadership issues, 91, 144, 214
  victim of assault, 103
Schenectady, New York, 2, 17–18, 38, 89, 181, 224, 234–36, 244
Schoolcraft, Lawrence, 135–37, 139, 143–45, 189–90, 215, 275n6
Schuyler, Catherine, 99, 111–12
Schuyler, Hanjost, 169, 171
Schuyler, Gen. Philip, 261n1
  concern for approaching siege, 107, 109
  Fort Schuyler named for him, viii–ix, 27
  Northern Department commander, 11, 48, 75, 86–87, 113, 172
  orders to Col. Dayton, 17, 19
  reconstructing Fort Stanwix, 73, 89, 115

reestablishing Fort Stanwix, 15, 20–22, 29, 33, 36, 42, 98
supplying Fort Stanwix, 100, 114
support for Oneidas, 15, 39, 42, 94, 245
scouting patrols, 4
  3rd New York regiment, 97, 108–9, 182, 184, 196
  Dayton's regiment, 27–29, 31–33
  Elmore's regiment, 42
Scriber, Peter, 60–61, 189, 204, 248, 250, 254–55
Scudder, William, 171, 173, 181
Senecas, 218, 224
sentry boxes at Fort Stanwix, 75, 201
Shell, Christian, 80, 86, 119, 187
Shonoghleoh (Anthony), 132
siege victory, reaction to, 173, 179
Singleton, Lt. George, 145–46, 285n15
Six Nations of the Iroquois. *See* Haudenosaunee
Skenandoah, 26, 206, 234, 263n11
Smith, Mary (Mrs. William Tapp), 83, 119, 196, 204, 254
Sons of Liberty, 49, 267n1, 290n28
Spencer, Thomas, 9–10, 26, 260n22
  death at Oriskany, 148
  helping Col. Dayton, 31–32
  helping Col. Elmore, 32, 43
  helping Col. Gansevoort, 93, 97, 115, 120–21, 155
Spoor, Ens. John
  attacked collecting timber, 228–29
  captured while collecting sod, 109–11, 114, 118, 280n6
Stanwix, Gen. John, 4
Stark, John, 174, 233–34, 240, 300n36
Steere/Steeve, Caty, 118
Steere/Steeve, John, 7, 118, 282n42
Stephane, Lenea, 118, 159
Steuben, Frederick von, 191, 218
Stockwell, Levi, 144, 155, 217, 220, 223
Stoddard, Ichabod, 58, 254, 271n18, 272n41
Stow, Seth, 190
structural evolution of Fort Stanwix
  in 1758, 4–5
  in 1763, 5
  in 1767, 7–8
  in 1776, 25–27, 30, 42
  in 1777–78, 78, 86, 88–90, 98–99
  in 1781, 248–50
  in 1976, 258
Sughagearat (White Skin), 34

318 INDEX

Sullivan, John, 16, 22, 246
Swartwout, Capt. Abraham, 129, 144, 209, 253, 271n27
   captured cloak, 67, 134
   derangement, 220, 223, 226, 232
   furlough, 217
   popularity, 212, 232
   recruiting duty, 215, 226
Sytez, Adj. George, 63, 98, 101–2, 145
   court of inquiry, 191
   from adjutant to captain, 191, 205

Tapp, Mary. *See* Smith, Mary
Tapp, Lt. William, 119, 196, 247, 254
   complaint against, 212
   court martial duty, 238
   engineer superintendent, 201, 203–4, 209
   Fort Dayton relief, 82–85
tattoo, 82, 84, 184, 228
Taylor, Thomas, 215, 228–30
Temple, Ebenezer, 165, 266–67n29
tents, 26, 32, 89, 98, 158, 168, 184, 233
Tice, Gilbert, 136–38
Tiebout, Henry, 51, 248, 253–54, 267n1
   after siege, 182, 185, 189, 217, 238
   before siege, 88, 101–3, 110
   commission, 45, 50, 54
   company formation, 58–61, 66–68, 79, 81, 270n14, 271n18
   during siege, 129, 162
tobacco, 99, 237
trading post at Fort Stanwix, 4, 16–17, 20–21, 42, 80, 245
Treaty of Fort Stanwix 1768, 8
Tryon County, New York, 18–19, 22, 214
   Committee of Safety, 11, 19, 33, 113, 115
   militia, 25, 79, 107, 119, 132, 142, 224
Tuscaroras, 10, 172, 206, 256
Tyonajanegen (Two Kettles Together), 132, 148, 185, 255

Valley Forge, Pennsylvania, 191, 206, 218, 224–25
Van Alstyne, Abraham, 224
Van Bunschoten, Capt. Elias, 50, 129–30, 144, 189, 220, 252, 268n24
   court martial duty, 84
Van Etten, Clara, 60, 189
Van Rensselaer, Henry, 224
Van Rensselaer, Ens. Jeremiah, 194, 217, 252, 290n28
   action with deserters, 300n36

   clothing help, 236–37
   paymaster, 186, 189, 232–33, 289n10
Van Schaick, Catherine, 111, 188, 195
Van Schaick, Goose, 37, 47, 63, 73, 85–86, 118, 243
Van Schaick, John G., 78
Varick, Richard, 222, 224–25

Wade, Barnard, 191
Walker, Capt. Robert, 37, 41, 266n27
Warner, Seth, 174, 190
Warner, Lt. Thomas, 84, 220, 223
Washington, George
   concerns for Fort Stanwix, 116, 163
   creating third establishment, 46, 50, 52, 65–66
   joined by Oneidas at Valley Forge, 206, 225, 230
   opinion of Elmore's regiment, 36–38, 40
   orders on deserters, 229–30, 239–41
   reestablishment of Fort Stanwix, 21–22, 29
   removal of 3rd New York from Stanwix, 241–44
water for Fort Stanwix, 5, 99, 134, 155, 160–61, 241
Wesson, Col. James, 119–20, 130, 143–44, 173
white settlers near Fort Stanwix, 7–11, 25–26, 33, 80, 97, 118–19, 159, 205, 235
Willett, Lt. Col. Marinus, 48–50
   after leaving Fort Stanwix, 246–47, 251–53
   after the siege, 172, 183–84, 216, 222–23, 226
   at Fishkill, 54–59, 61–64
   at Fort Constitution, 65–68, 71–72, 78, 80–81
   concern for fort's condition, 88–90, 129, 201
   during the siege, 134, 137, 143–49, 153–55, 165
   efforts to have regiment transferred, 198, 209, 241
   furlough, 188–89, 237, 241
   incidents before the siege, 117–28
   in command of Fort Stanwix, 188, 190–91, 194–95, 218
   interactions with Oneidas, 185
   recognition for siege success, 173–74, 179, 181

travel to Fort Stanwix, 81–82, 87
William Kayendalongwea, 206
Wilson, Robert, 61, 104–5, 250, 253, 279n39, 302n22
Witmozer, Henry, 174, 238, 240
Wood Creek, 2–4, 168, 172,
   obstructing passage on, 90, 93, 108, 116–17, 135, 151
   Oneida reservation, 257
   St. Leger's troops' use of, 135–36, 170
   upper landing, 131

Woodruff, Hunloke, 110, 134, 155, 167–68, 188, 189, 204
   Fort Dayton relief, 82
   medical supplies, 209–10
   on furlough, 217
   retirement, 248, 252
   treating Capt. Gregg, 105–6

Yorktown, Virginia, 248, 250, 279n39, 302–3n22
Younglove, Sgt. Maj. Isaiah, 29
Younglove, Moses, 148